Amos P. Catlin
The Whig Who Put
Sacramento On The Map

Amos P. Catlin

Published by Kevin Knauss

Edited by Bonnie Osborn

Author: Kevin Knauss

Library of Congress Control Number: 2021922480

ISBN: 978-0-9978188-88

Amos P. Catlin

Acknowledgements

This book could not have been written without the professional services and generous assistance from the following organizations and institutions.

The Bancroft Library, UC Berkeley

California Digital Newspaper Collection

California State Archives

California State Library

Center for Sacramento History

Chuck Spinks, P.E.

El Dorado County Recorder Clerk

El Dorado County Historical Museum

Folsom Historical Society & Museum

Historic Huguenot Street, New Paltz, NY

Old City Cemetery Committee Inc. of the Historic Sacramento Cemetery

Placer County Clerk Recorder

Sacramento County Clerk/Recorder

San Francisco Public Library

Wells Fargo Corporate Heritage, Wiltsee Collection

Amos P. Catlin

Contents

Amos P. Catlin

Introduction

Some people believe it was Sutter's Fort that put Sacramento on the map. Other people contend that Sacramento attained national prominence by being the gateway to the gold fields along the American rivers in 1849. However, it was Amos Parmalee Catlin who sponsored legislation in 1854 to move California's State Capitol from Benicia to Sacramento that has created the more enduring recognition for Sacramento City on the national map.

Without Sacramento being designated as California's state capital, the city at the confluence of the Sacramento and American rivers would have become just another Central Valley town with a notable historical background.

Some historians will argue that Sacramento cemented its national status by being the terminus for the Transcontinental Railroad. For a period of time, this was true. Sacramento was a natural for the terminus, as it had waterways that connected it to San Francisco. But as railroads developed and bridges were built over the various bodies of water hindering easy travel to the Bay Area, Sacramento's role as a conduit to "the city" diminished. Of course, Sacramento's status as the state's capital also helped sell it as the terminus of the transcontinental railroad.

By the middle of the 20th century, with the progress of rail, plane, and highway infrastructure projects, Sacramento was less of a necessary destination. What has prevented Sacramento from becoming just another dot on the state map is that it is the state capital. It is the center of legislative and executive power for a state that ranks in the top 10 economies of the world. This prestigious role could easily have remained in Benicia, San Jose, or Vallejo, all former sites of the state capital.

It was Amos P. Catlin, as a Senator from Sacramento and a member of the Whig Party, who pushed the legislation to move the capital to Sacramento through the California Senate. Catlin had his own self-interests for wanting Sacramento to be the state capital. He was engaged in water projects along the American River and was a director of the newly formed Sacramento Valley Railroad. But Catlin was not a man who pined to be a wealthy industrialist or necessarily had visions of grandeur. He was more moderate in his world view.

Amos Catlin is attached to some of the most important water projects in El Dorado, Placer and Sacramento counties. He initiated and helped manage the construction of the Natoma ditch on the South Fork of the American River and the North Fork Ditch on the North Fork of the American River. Amos traveled back to Washington, D. C., to argue before the U.S. Supreme Court for the original

Amos P. Catlin

map of the Leidesdorff land grant. His successful arguments prevented utter chaos in the land titles in the Folsom region.

Shortly after his arrival in California in 1849, Amos began practicing law in a territory that was not yet a state and had no official court system. Amos chose to remain in California and call it home. Specifically, he called Sacramento home. Amos did not take his gold back to New York, where he was born. He did not move to San Francisco, where the practice of law was more lucrative. He chose the Sacramento Valley to call home, get married, have children, pursue politics, and build his law practice.

His life's perspective might be summed up in a report he provided to the Sacramento Daily Union about gold prospects on the American River in 1851. He was reporting on the prospects for future gold production as miners shifted from panning for gold to damming the river to get access to the riverbed and employing steam engines to pump water for mining the dry diggings. He wrote, "The upturned bars, the piles of poor earth will be sluice-washed by the torrent, the gold lodged in crevices and pockets, and the sand again formed into bars and banks. Let industry increase, economy be practiced, skill be applied, and desires moderated, and the results will be the same."

Amos Catlin would apply his skill and practice economy in a number of areas of his life and activities in Folsom and Sacramento. He "moderated desires." Amos Catlin was an honest, ethical, and assiduous man who helped the Folsom and Sacramento communities develop. His life is an interesting study in the maturity of the Central Valley of California.

Amos P. Catlin

Chapter One: New York to Mormon Island, 1848 – 1851

1. Amos P. Catlin, 1852

Amos Catlin followed the events of the Mexican-American War from afar on the East Coast. The conflict began when the United States annexed Texas, which Mexico considered its territory, in 1845. When President Polk's diplomatic mission failed to negotiate a sale of the territory from Mexico, the conflict escalated, with the United States declaring war in 1846. While Amos was a young proud American, the Mexican conflict did not stir the patriotic passions like the American Revolution had for his grandfather 70 years earlier. The Mexican-American War was not about the lofty academic ideals of rights, liberty, governance or common law. It was about manifest destiny, extending the borders of the United States.

Born on January 25, 1823, in Red Hook, New York, Amos was working as a lawyer with his cousins George and Charles Catlin in New York at the time hostilities broke out with Mexico. When the United States finally achieved domination over the Mexican forces in 1848, the attitudes of young men like Amos contemplating travel to the West Coast would change. The 1848 announcement and verification of the discovery of gold in California, now firmly under the control of the United States, had many men looking westward. Reports began to filter into New York of men mining $500 and $1,000 in gold per day along the American River.

Amos P. Catlin

The prospect of easy riches, gold just strewn along the riverbanks, coupled with the adventure to the West Coast, was enough to make Amos dream of a life beyond New York and to make plans to travel to California. There were many perils in traveling to California. Some men would not survive the overland trek or ocean voyage on their way to the gold fields. Once in the wondrous land of California, men still had to deal with disease, hostile Native Americans, wild animals, and, just as frequently, their fellow man. Amos could have joined a mining company on the East Coast but opted against it.

A mining company of men provided strength in numbers. That Amos did not join in with a group of men was part of his personality. The trait of forging his own path, a form of independence, would be exhibited throughout his life. Amos chartered passage to California on the small brig of David Henshaw.[1] The small sailing ship held 15 passengers and a crew of 12 and left New York for California on January 7, 1849.[2] In addition to his personal belongings and some prospective mining equipment, Amos had $500 in his purse and two letters written by cousins George and Charles Catlin, with whom he had practiced law in New York.

The first, a letter of introduction written by Charles Catlin, was addressed to Walter Colton, who had been appointed Alcalde of Monterey. Colton was an old acquaintance of Charles Catlin.[3] The hope was that Colton could help Amos find work in government or make few connections in the legal community. By the time Amos finally arrived in San Francisco in the summer of 1849, Colton was concluding his duties as Alcalde, writing a book about his experience, and planning to return to the East Coast.

The second letter, written by George Catlin, came with explicit instructions not to be opened until Amos had been at sea for a week.[4] Composed on December 31, 1848, George wanted to impart some paternal wisdom to a young man whom he looked upon as a son. It was a letter that Amos' father, Pierce Catlin, could never have articulated on paper or in gentle counsel to his son.

"You are leaving home bound on a long and perhaps dangerous voyage to a distant port, on an enterprise full of promise for yourself and us – a boundless ocean is around you – an unknown land before you – that you will act with honour, zeal and ability, I have no doubt that our mutual hopes will be realized is more than probable, but should your success far exceed our brightest anticipation – should we once more have the pleasure of seeing your happiness – would that deprive death of its sting or grave of its victory [?]"

In short, California gold is not what makes a truly happy life. Gold and wealth are no comfort on a man's dying bed. George instructs Amos, "Look to history… Napoleon after all his conquest dies in grief in a distant island." It is a very philosophical letter on attaining happiness in life, primarily with a faith in God, and eschewing wealth and power as the centrality of a man's life. Over the seven-month voyage from New York to San Francisco, there is no doubt that Amos read George's heart-felt letter several times.

It was a little surprising to Amos' family that he chose to chase a golden dream in California. Aside from the daunting sea voyage, the physical demands of digging in the earth for gold was not part of his youth. Of Pierce Catlin's children, Amos had succeeded in graduating from the Kingston Academy and then continued his studies in law until he was admitted to the New York Bar. With his association with the law firm of George and Charles Catlin, Amos was assured a modest income to secure a happy home, if he chose.

It was never the intent of Amos to become a miner panning for gold in the American River. Nor was his vision to wield a pick and shovel on the banks of the river or in some hole in the ground. The plan was to do a little mining, scoop up some gold, practice law, and find investment opportunities. When Amos arrived in California, he was a young man stepping into a grand party that was in full swing, populated with men suddenly free of any social constraints imposed by polite society, church, parents, spouses, or even government.

Upon arriving in San Francisco on July 8th, Amos took a month-long rest and watched the chaotic legal machination churning in the vacuum of any state or federal authority. One of the first vigilance committees had been formed and demanded William Gwin and James Ward sit in judgement of alleged criminals with the duly elected Alcalde Thaddeus Leavenworth. This Revolutionary Court trio then convicted 12 men on various crimes.[5]

From the perspective of Amos, the justice of 1849, which would become known as pioneer law, was a mixture of Mexican law, English common law, and mob rule.[6] After taking in the spectacle of early California pioneer law, Amos loaded up his sizeable collection of mining equipment he brought west and headed up to the American River. Mormon Island, on the South Fork of the American River, just above the confluence with the North Fork, was the first gold field you would strike from Sacramento. There was gold below the confluence, but the combined flows of the north and south forks made it more difficult to get to the real pay dirt out in the middle of the American River.

Mormon Island had an emerging town structure, goods, services, and lodging on the bench above the river canyon. It was as good of place as any to start mining for gold.

Amos P. Catlin

The process of mining for gold was seriously hard work. Efficiency demanded more than one person when it came to washing and cleaning the dirt for gold. One man who worked with Amos was Abram Van Demark. Abram was born in Ulster County, New York, the same region where Amos went to school, and also traveled to California in 1849.[7] Amos and Abram mined through the autumn and then retreated up the hill to the emerging village of Natoma (to be christened Mormon Island later) to pass the winter.

By the time Amos arrived at Mormon Island, there was already considerable mining activity and organization. Sam Brannan was advertising a new ferry over the river at Mormon Island in April of 1849.[8] In that same month, the Mormon Island Mining Association was constructing two wing dams to divert the river into side canals. The de-watered river bed would then be mined for placer gold.[9] The American Mining Company, a mile above Mormon Island, was performing similar work of turning the South Fork of the American River out of its current water course.[10]

On July 4, 1849, miners from around the region convened at Mormon Island to celebrate Independence Day. James Queen, who was Secretary for the Mormon Island Mining Association, read a miner's declaration of sorts, in light of the lack of governance, to be published in the local papers. The miners recognized and regretted the inactivity of any sort of functioning federal, state, or local governance in the region. But they had faith, in the spirit of the 4th of July, that a just and fair government would be formed. However, to reinforce the pioneer passion of the day, they denounced slavery, hoping to stop its importation into the mining community. "Resolved, That believing slavery to be an evil inconsistent with the spirt of our free institutions and destructive of the best interests of any country where it exists, we will do everything in our power to prevent its extension to this country. W. C BIGELOW, President. James Queen, Secretary."[11]

The gold fields attracted a variety of different men from all over the world. Mostly, these men were strangers to one another with a common bond and experience of gold mining. The Mormon Island Mining Association reported in July of 1849 that three of their stockholders had been killed, purportedly by Native Americans. The association was opening up half of the shares of each dead man to be worked by other shareholders. The other half of the interest was to be held by the company and would be relinquished to verified heirs or administrators of the deceased. The problem was, beyond the names of the men, the mining association did not know where these men lived prior to coming to California or if they had spouses, children, or other family members.[12]

While Mormon Island was swelling in population from newcomers like Amos, other people were leaving. Sam Brannan placed an advertisement in the Placer

Amos P. Catlin

Times offering his store and land at Natoma (Mormon Island) for sale.[13] Brannan was focusing his attention on San Francisco and other pursuits like shipping between Hawaii and China. Other men were selling mining claims and stores at Mormon Island for cash to return home.[14]

At the time, "Natoma," reportedly a Native American term, was interpreted to mean clear water. With the advent of mining, the South Fork of the American River was anything but clear. Regardless, the region south of the river, encompassing Mormon Island, was being referred to as Natoma in 1849. By 1850, the population of Mormon Island had swelled to 1,500,[15] and the township was identified as a candidate for a Post Office.

When William Goggin of the United States Post Office visited Mormon Island, Amos was already a respected resident and businessman who owned the Natoma Mining Company. As Amos related the story decades later, Goggin inquired of him a descriptive name for the Post Office, and Amos replied, "Natoma," which just happened to be in the title of his mining company.[16] The name Natoma would eventually be extended to the township for the region in Sacramento County.

Trained as a lawyer, Amos got to practice his profession several times in the very gray legal structure of California before she became a state. While arguing for a jury trial before the local Alcalde, Amos sensed the Alcalde jurist favored the plaintiff. Amos adapted to the fluid legal structure and asked his client to summon as many friends as possible. When the room began to swell with the defendant's friends, the Alcalde relented and allowed Amos' request for a jury trial. The intimidation factor worked, and the jury returned a verdict of no cause of action.[17]

Amos would enter into similarly murky legal waters of California land by acquiring a piece of property from Joseph Vanderwood. The title to the land was more lease than title: For $1, Amos could use the land as he saw fit for one year, most likely for mining. Executed on March 18, 1850, there was no official county or state government to register the title or contract with. It was a mere gentleman's agreement. The description was in the metes and bounds boundary markers.

"…situated in the North eastern part of Natoma bounded and described as follows, commencing at a stump on the eastern line of said boundaries into the top of which is driven an iron wedge marked with the letter V and running thence first north northwest in a straight line to the bank of the river and secondly running from said stump south southeast in a straight line until said line strikes a gulch and thence following in a south westerly direction the course of said gulch to it juncture with a deep ravine which divides the wester from the eastern portion of the occupied part of the town of Natoma and thence following the centre of said ravine to its

Amos P. Catlin

termination on the river thence along the shape of the river up stream to the termination of the line first mentioned."[18]

John Currey Law Practice

To meet up with an old acquaintance from home was a valued and welcomed surprise among the California miners, but it was not out of the ordinary or improbable. Attorney John Currey from Westchester County, New York, arrived in San Francisco in August of 1849.[19] He made his way up to Mormon Island where he connected with Amos. Currey was not keen on mining. He and Amos decided to open a law practice in Sacramento in the spring of 1850. Amos would split his time between managing his mining claims, representing fellow miners before the Alcalde at Mormon Island, and working with Currey in Sacramento.

Sacramento had a burgeoning population with a demand for shelter. Currey and Amos saw an opportunity and, leveraging their connections on the East Coast, ordered prefabricated houses – probably closer to rudimentary cabins – to be shipped out to Sacramento. The duo's plan was to acquire some Sacramento lots, speculating that lot prices would increase, and sell the prefabricated homes. While putting the plan into action, Currey moved to San Francisco to practice law, while still maintaining a loose partnership with Amos. Sacramento soon would be convulsed by two events that would work to derail the plans of Amos and Currey.

Amos was in Sacramento in August of 1850 as tensions grew between settlers and landowners.[20] Much of Sacramento had been purchased by land speculators from John Sutter Jr., and the speculators were accusing the settlers of squatting on land they owned. California had not yet become a state, and there were little federal governance and few troops in the area. In addition, there were still questions about the validity of the Sutter land grant. The conflict between the settlers and the land speculators boiled over in the Squatter's Riots in mid-August.

A couple of months later, in October 1850, Sacramento would be enveloped by a cholera outbreak killing upwards of 10 percent of the population and driving thousands out of the city. While he avoided contracting cholera, Currey wrote to Amos from San Francisco in June to communicate he was ill with jaundice.[21] He was able to attend to some business delivering the gold dust of Gilbert & Foote for an assay. By July 1851, Currey had recovered from his illness but needed $100 from Amos for office rent and lodging. In his correspondence with Amos, Currey noted that Mr. Bigelow, with whom they were working to purchase and sell Sacramento lots, should be delivering $250 to Amos.[22]

Currey routinely wrote to Amos requesting, in addition to money, that Amos attend to various law matters, such as having the Sacramento Sheriff serve a summons, and updating Amos on client affairs. Unfortunately, Amos' sole focus was not on the law practice. He was still engaged in some mining investments that had him bouncing between Mormon Island and Sacramento. In early August 1850 he invested in the American River Damming Co., acquiring a 1/6 interest in the operation.[23]

Amos' lack of attention to the law practice did not go unnoticed by Currey. In late September, George Gilbert showed up at Currey's office in San Francisco to collect a claim he had against them. Currey was shocked that Amos had failed to notify him that Gilbert was calling to collect the debt. He scrambled around town and borrowed $150 to partially pay Gilbert. Currey wrote Amos, "I have quite enough to take care of since the downfall of the Sacramento City property."[24] Currey surmised that Bigelow had made a large sale of their lots back in July, but since that time had gone quiet, most probably with their money.[25]

In addition to the law practice, managing the Sacramento property and importing home-building kits, Currey was running for a district judgeship in San Francisco.[26] After Currey lost the election, his enthusiasm for California was starting to wane. He requested that Amos tabulate a settlement of all the different matters they were in partnership with. He gently prodded Amos by writing, "Don't let these things rest…so long that we should lose sight of things as they exist. Please let me hear from [you] without delay."[27]

Currey traveled to Sacramento, which he referred to as the city of "woes and misfortune," to settle up with Amos, who was not in town. Currey left a letter for Amos letting him know he was done with the business and was planning to return to New York. For Currey, the Golden State had been severely tarnished. He wrote to Amos, "The speculation has proved worse than an abortion—it has been a continuing curse to me ever since I embarked in it. It has cost me something like $3,200 besides a month of time since the first of March last."[28]

In the letter, Curry reports to Amos that Mr. Schoolcraft, from whom they had bought some of the Sacramento lots, had agreed to convey to them a certain portion of the lots in consideration for what they had already paid. However, the expense of the homes was still unresolved. "The house business is still unsettled. I know not what price you were to allow for the houses. Thoughts I have learned in respect to them that they have cost me about $600." Currey wants everything settled soon so he can leave the state.[29]

Unbeknownst to Currey at the time, Amos was ill and recuperating at Mormon Island. After recovering from the dysentery, Amos writes to Currey that his portion of the house sales is $150. Currey was baffled at the low dollar amount. "You speak of allowing me $150 for them. I do not understand how it is that every

Amos P. Catlin

remove of them reduces the value of the houses [?]" Curry then details his list of expenses from the original cost of the home kits of $170, freight from New York, and set up in Sacramento for a total of $680. There are other costs that Currey feels Amos has erroneously charged him for items such as office rent and furniture. Currey closes his letter, "I want to get the whole matter settled up and to know what I am to lose in this unfortunate house business. I have lost so much in this country that I feel really sick of beholding the sight."[30]

At Currey's urging, Amos did visit him in San Francisco. They settled their business as amicably as possible. Amos had a daguerreotype image taken of himself to send home with Currey. He also gave Currey $200 to be given to his father, Pierce Catlin.

At the time of these "woes and misfortunes," Currey and Amos were 36 and 27 years of age respectively. They were honorable men trying to capitalize on the emerging opportunities in the new territory of California. Political upheaval and natural calamity helped to undermine their plans.

In his December 19th letter to Amos, Currey philosophizes that the investment debacle had taught him valuable lessons, "...by this speculation that will be a beacon light the balance of my life."[31] Despite the financial losses Currey suffered, he later would return to California with his family. In 1853 Currey was residing in the then-state capital of Benicia, where Amos was serving as a state Senator from Mormon Island. In July of 1853, Currey sent Amos political intelligence on the past voting record of Governor John Bigler when he was an Assemblyman.[32]

In addition to the political dirt and a discussion of Whig politics, Currey wanted to borrow $400 in script in order to buy school warrants. He wanted to immediately secure some land in Vacaville to prevent squatters from taking over the land he wanted.[33] Currey would go on to establish a solid law practice in Benicia. In 1864 he was elected to the California Supreme Court, where he served until 1868, including two years as Chief Justice.

With John Currey's departure for New York in early 1851, Amos could have joined him. After all, he had told his family, his journey to California was intended to have been a short affair. However, it is doubtful that Amos entertained thoughts of leaving California at this juncture. He had just formed the Natoma Mining Company and posted notice on January 1, 1851, of the company's intention to mine on the South Fork of the American River.

"Mormon Island, Jany 1, 1851. To all whom it may concern, this is to certify that the Natoma Mining Company have taken up that portion of the South fork

Amos P. Catlin

between the lower end of Mormon Island and the upper end thereof which they intend to drain by means of a race on the southern side of the said Island."[34]

Amos and his assembled crew of miners acquired the claim from another company who were not successful in fully mining the riverbed. The plan was to build a dam and divert part of the river water into a "race" or ditch around that part of the river bed to be mined. A steam engine would be employed to pump water seeping into the river bed. Then, in the parlance of the day, the miners could turn the bed of the river and glean the placer gold.

Through 1850, Amos felt intense pressure, in letters from his family, to return home or at the very least to write a letter. Of the immediate Pierce Catlin family, Amos was the member with an advanced education. As an attorney, his counsel and guidance were respected. As son, sibling, and relative, his presence was genuinely missed. When a man left for California, it was often as if they had died, in the sense there were no communication, no letters, no word on their fate, for six months or more at a time. All the family back at home could do was write letters, hoping they would find their way to a living relative in California.

George Catlin captured that anxiety and longing in a letter to Amos shortly after he left for California on January 15, 1849.

"Dear Amos,

You have now been gone eight days and I feel confident [you] have made at least 113 miles a day since your departure and I trust that your passage will be safe and speedy and that your hopes will be realized."[35]

Amos would write home a couple times, but it was not with the frequency or intimacy that satisfied the family. George Catlin writes Amos in January of 1850 and gently scolds him for not writing more often. "It is now more than a year since you left us and at least four months since we last heard from you and we have been anxiously waiting for some time past to hear from you. The Cherokee arrived yesterday with the California mail of Dec. 1st and we expected a letter by her. You may imagine our disappointment in getting any."[36]

Jane Catlin, Amos' sister, wrote that some families receive letters from their boys in California, and others don't. The Catlin's being one of the latter. Amos' sister Emily had taken one of the letters he wrote home and framed it and "...hung up in her room and looks at it with as much reverence as it was yourself." Jane continued, "I expect you will be so rich when you get back. The folks here says you might rather stayed home and marry Harriet Naise. I wish someone would invite me to go to California, you would see me there soon, I can tell you."[37]

Amos P. Catlin

William Catlin, Amos' younger brother, wrote to him from Henderson, Kentucky, in May 1850. William wanted to know the cost of 10 acres of land in San Francisco and if any of it would make good pasture for a dairy. The daydream was to start a dairy and, when San Francisco grew, sell the land for a profit. He needed Amos to reply as soon as possible with a description of San Francisco and his opinion of it becoming a great city. Finally, the letter continued, William wanted Amos to write home more often.[38]

In August of 1850, word of one of Amos' bouts with dysentery reached his family in New York. George Catlin wrote that they were happy that Amos seemed to have recovered his health. However, they were crestfallen that they had not received money from Amos on their speculative mining investment. "I must confess I was a little disappointed," George writes, "and Charley more so, at the sudden overthrow of our castles in the air, but we agree that we have no reason to retract the confidence we had in you from the outset." He pointedly adds, "...I sincerely wish you had never gone and hope you will return soon. I have often wished you back again. Business (law practice) has greatly improved with me, and I think you have done better here than there."[39]

Pierce Catlin, Amos' father, wrote him in early September of 1850. Pierce had turned 61. He had plenty of work, but the profits were small. Of course, Pierce wrote, Amos being an attorney, he could make a comfortable living in New York. Pierce wanted both his sons, William and Amos, to come home. He closed his letter, "My dear son, I seldom lay my head on my pillow at night but think of you. O my, the blessing of almighty God...Put your trust in him and may he bring you safe home to your friends...the prayers of your affectionate father."[40]

The prospect of returning home also was a common refrain in Amos' letters to his family. A careful reading of Amos' letter to his father in January 1851 made it clear that a return trip was not coming soon.

"I am still located at Mormon Island yet where I still have hopes of making something of mining. I attempted to start in my profession at Sac City last summer but being much subject to diarrhea I was driven out by the cholera which killed 1/10 of the population."[41]

Amos instructs his father to use part of the $200 he sent with John Currey to pay off a few debts he forgot to settle before he left. "Beyond these I owe nothing at home. I wish I were able to send you enough to enable you to get rid of those mortgages, but my luck has been bad, but I keep hoping for the *good time that's coming*."[42] As if to keep hope alive for a return to New York, Amos adds that he is healthy, and, if all his plans stay on course, he could foresee coming home in another year.

Amos P. Catlin

During the tumultuous year of 1850 in Sacramento, Amos was working to establish himself within the legal community. Members of the Sacramento Bar had serious doubts about the legality of a session of the District Court set to convene in Sacramento. Amos, as a member of the Sacramento Bar, supported a committee to investigate the legitimacy of the vacancy of the current district court judgeship.[43] There was a swirl of uncertainty in Sacramento related to legal proceedings and land ownership, owing primarily to California not having yet been admitted as a state.

The Squatter's Riots of August 1850 highlighted the numerous questions concerning land titles in California. The rights to mining claims could also come into dispute. In the gold fields, any disputed boundaries to a mining claim were often adjudicated by men fighting over it, verbally, physically, or with weapons. Amos was neither an imposing nor intimidating man. When a couple of miners tried to encroach on one of Catlin's mining claims, Amos employed a much larger man to intervene as an arbitrator. William Higgins, who was mining nearby, offered a settlement from Catlin to the claim jumpers.[44] The terms were agreed to, and no blood was shed. William Higgins and Amos would meet again later, when both were involved with Republican politics.

Whig Politics

As if his mining business and practicing law were not enough to occupy his time, Amos jumped into politics by organizing a Mormon Island Whig meeting. The meeting was held at the Star of the West hotel in Mormon Island, and Amos was selected chairman.[45] He then traveled to Sacramento to attend the Whig County Convention in late November of 1850.[46] As would be his preferred role in future political conventions, Amos was selected for the committee to draft resolutions to outline the local Whig party platform.

The Whig Party developed in the 1830s and pulled positions from other political parties at the time, including the Republican, Democrat, and the defunct Federalist parties. Central to Amos' affinity for the Whig Party was his admiration for Henry Clay, who was the Whig Party Presidential candidate in 1844, losing to James Polk. Under President Polk, the United States would prosecute hostilities with Mexico, delivering California into the arms of the Union in 1848. Henry Clay espoused trade protectionist policies, with an emphasis on developing industry and manufacturing within the United States.

The exploitation of the country's natural resources - mining for gold - fell squarely within the realm of developing an industry. Mining operations on the river were being undertaken with little regard for any local, state, or federal laws. In reality, there were no specific laws or rules. Any disputes were settled first by the Alcalde, then later by the Justice of the Peace, whose office was brought into existence in April 1850. The order of the day was Common Law, which gave precedence to prior court cases – if there were any – and the established customs of the general populace. This contrasts to Civil Law, which refers to specific codes passed by a legislature for adjudicating disputes.

Similar to other parts of the American River, the South Fork was being completely diverted out of its bed by dams and canals. These water diversion projects were happening for miles along the river. It was estimated that by the autumn of 1851, the entire length of the North Fork of the American River, from the confluence with the middle fork down to the confluence with the South Fork, would be diverted out of its original channel.[47] Even though the boundaries of mining claims were generally respected, having an upstream mining company reroute the flow of the river onto another miner's claim could seriously impact the latter miner's ability to effectively work the ground.

Mormon Island.		
WHIG.	**DEMOCRATIC.**	
Reading 116	Bigler 169	
Baldwin 128	Purdy...........156	
Robinson 130	Heydenfeldt.......154	
Fair............132	Hastings 149	
Burt............123	Pierce 156	
Abell...........130	Roman............156	
Herron 130	Eddy 156	
Kewen..........132	McCorkle 157	
Moore 126	Marshall..........159	
Lisle 125	Ralston 138	
Cogswell 118	McComha.........114	
Berry 120	Tucker 144	
Catlin 158	Colby............150	
Blood...........118	Kipp 133	
Edwards 120	Aldrich 148	
McDowell 116	Patterson 151	
Queen 113	Long 154	
McKee..........109	Haines............158	
Chappell 121	Rowe 146	
Watson 121	Selkirk 147	
Harkness........121	May..............148	
Thompson.......122	Cantwell 148	
Sunderland......127	Carter 142	
Wallace.........125	Johnson..........144	

The vote for Justice of the Peace is as follows: F. S. Mumford 145; Wm. Miller 125; S. B. F. Clark 80; L. B. Dutton 68; Nickerson 60.
Constable—Wm. Maslin 155; C. E. Hamilton 110.

Sacramento Daily Union
September 5, 1851

2. 1851 Mormon Island Assembly seat election results.

When Amos wanted to delay, if not stop, the construction of a diversion dam above one of his claims, he was able to convince the local Justice of the Peace to issue an injunction to stop the other mining company from constructing the dam. The mining company owner who had just been enjoined from building his dam, S.W. Anderson, went to Placerville, in El Dorado County, to find a court to appeal the decision. The questionable legal maneuverings gave Amos enough time to complete his project, and then he withdrew his legal action with the Justice of the Peace.[48]

Amos P. Catlin

The Miners' Convention, as it was called, was convened in July 1851. Amos was asked to address the convention, held at Mormon Island, along with another local attorney, F.S. Mumford. The convention outlined some of the problems the miners were having in the absence of any rules or laws governing their mining process. Among the "innumerable evils" the miners faced were dam companies being forced to stop or abandon construction, claims with absentee owners not being worked, newcomers being driven off, and the expense of litigating disputes with the local Justice of the Peace.[49]

Amos would work with the loose-knit mining association to develop some high-level rules, most of which were not enforceable since there were no law enforcement officers. He also continued to represent miners, and his own company, in different disputes. As the massive deconstruction of the American River was taking place in order to find gold, Amos was selected to be a Whig Party candidate for State Assembly.[50] The September 1851 general election proved not to be fruitful for Amos, as he lost the race.[51]

Gold Prophecy

What did bear fruit was Amos' elevated presence at Mormon Island and in the mining community. The Sacramento Daily Union found Amos to be a reputable source of information. In October of 1851, the Union cited Amos as the knowledgeable informant stating that in the past mining season, nine steam engines had been employed for pumping water out of claims on the river. The Watson Company, he noted, had taken out $30,000 in gold in the last mining season.[52]

Later in October, Amos would compile a statistical chart of 20 mining companies operating from one mile above Mormon Island to 400 feet below the confluence of the north and south forks for the Sacramento Union. The report, titled South Fork Damming Companies, listed the length of the river claim in feet, name of the company, number of shares, and gross revenue since 1849. Amos' Natoma Mining Company had 150 feet of river under claim, 10 shareholders, and had mined $14,000 in gold. An asterisk next to the Natoma company indicated the claim had only been worked in the seasons of 1850 and 1851.[53]

Amos' report for the Sacramento Union was optimistic about the future. He assumed the freshets, or seasonal flooding events, would deposit more gold into the riverbed.

"The courses of the currents will be shifted in consequence of the great changes produced by digging, and by the erection of dams, and places; now known to be rich, will be swept by the waters and their golden deposits carried into the claim of some lucky company below. The upturned bars, the piles of poor earth will be sluice-washed by the torrent, the gold lodged in crevices and pockets, and the sand again formed into bars and banks. Let industry increase, economy be practiced, skill be applied, and desires moderated and the results will be the same. A. P. C. Mormon Island, Oct. 27th, 1851"

South Fork Damming Companies.			
Length of River.	Name of Co.	No. Shares.	Gross pro
600 ft	†Amer. Isl. Co.	10	$27,000 00
60 "	*Empire "	8	10,000 00
500 "	Placer "	10	10,000 00
300 "	*South Fork"	6	9 000 00
500 "	*Moffatt's "	5	18 000 00
600 "	Vermont "	17	11,000 00
800 "	*York "	12	24,000 00
100 "	British "	5	
100 "	Hancock "	5	
240 "	*Fairbank's"	8	13 000 00
600 "	Wisconsin "	8	4 000 00
850 "	Union "	16	15,800 00
150 "	*Natoma "	10	14 000 00
400 "	Watson "	9	55,000 00
600 "	Gibson "	16	30,000 00
200 "	*El Dorado "	32	
2000 "	*S. F. No. 1 "	30	42,000 00
250 "	†Fancy Dam"	9	17,000 00
225 "	*Pinkham "	10	25,000 00
200 "	Coffer Dam "	10	10,000 00

Companies marked thus (†) were worked during the summers of '49, '50 and 51. Those marked (*) were worked during the summers of '50 and '51.

Sacramento Daily Union
October 30, 1851

3. Gold Mining Companies on the South Fork of American River, 1851.

The optimism, so ebulliently invoked by Amos like a sermon for Easter Sunday, was shared by many other miners. But the forecasted wealth would never materialize in the size or grandeur predicted. Amos was an excellent writer and a good lawyer, but he was no geologist.

The magical appearance of volumes of placer gold brought down from raging floods of the American River, like God sprinkling mana across the fields, to replace the gold already scavenged, did not materialize. Miners who had vacuumed up all of the placer gold dust in their claims of the riverbed began to turn their attention to the canyon walls, river banks, and benches. They did find gold there, but not in the quantities originally scooped out of the river. Instead of $500 per day, the mining yields were considered good if a claim produced $10 or $20 per day.

There was an additional problem facing the miners: water. The focus of this new mining tactic was called "dry diggings," as operations were above the water line of the river. The task of hauling dirt down to the river to be washed and to separate out the tiny specs of placer gold was arduous. There had to be some way to put the river above the new mining activity. Of course, doing that would require a

Amos P. Catlin

dam to build up the water level to be diverted into a canal, and then let out down to the miners below. The concept was an enlarged and slightly altered design of what the damming companies had been doing for the previous three years.

Convinced that the river would continue to yield gold dust, Amos purchased the Red Bank mining claim in October 1851 on the South Fork of the American River. He paid $2,000 for 200 feet of river frontage, including rockers, pipes, and pumps for working the claim, to Elezer Rulison, Jerome Foster, and David Lewis.[54] Obviously charmed by the mining prospects of California, Amos also invested in the Empire Quartz Mine, purchasing 100 shares at $100 each.[55] This hard rock mine was located in Log Town, El Dorado County. Continuing to diversify away from placer gold mining, Amos acquired a claim to a quartz vein near Auburn, California.[56] The former owner was Luther Cutler, a member of the Amos' Natoma Mining Company.

As a small step toward putting down permanent roots in California, Amos bought a small lot south of the plaza at Mormon Island, often referred to as Natoma. He purchased the lot for $175 from John Hart and Dallas Kneass in April of 1851, next to a lot owned by Vanderwood. The 150 x 60-foot rectangular lot had a house where Amos could manage his mining and law businesses.[57] Perhaps best of all, the private shelter allowed Amos to indulge in one of his favorite pastimes, reading. A little more privacy allowed Amos to study legal decisions and write his thoughts.

Two of the legal contests Amos followed involved mining companies, some of which were fracturing and dissolving. In the first case, the Virginia Mining Company dissolved after having built a dam, ditch and flume to divert the American River around Negro Bar. One of the members, Hartford Anderson, purchased the lumber from the flume to use elsewhere. As one of the former Virginia Mining Company members, George Nutter, was working his claim, Anderson sought to take possession of his lumber by tearing down the flume, flooding Nutter's claim. Nutter sued Anderson for damages before Justice of the Peace S.B.F. Clark in Natoma Township. The court decreed Anderson was the rightful owner of the lumber, and any injury to Nutter caused by removing the flume was not Anderson's responsibility.[58]

In another dispute, members of the South Fork Mining and Damming Association were accused of excluding another association member from the company profits. Mr. Van Dyke, a one-thirtieth owner of the association, complained that he was ejected from the company in 1850. The company was mining a 150-yard claim at the confluence of the North and South Forks of the American River. Van Dyke was suing for $5,000 in damages from being denied a part of the gold taken from the claim.[59]

Amos P. Catlin

In lieu of a legal library, Amos would pay for copies of complaints filed with the court or create his own synopsis and transcription, as he did in the Negro Bar flume dispute. In an environment devoid of any government structure to act as a repository for legal decision reference, Amos had to create his own reference library. Current water and land disputes, settled by official judges, were creating precedents in California. Amos acquired the official decree of Judge Howell involving Yankee Jim's Union Water Co. vs. Ewing and Smith.[60]

Importantly, Judge Howell denied an injunction against Ewing and Smith from diverting water above the Yankee Jim's Union Water Co. dam. Ewing and Smith had constructed a dam on a creek on property they occupied and were mining. They diverted the water to their mining claim. The diversion decreased the water flowing into the stream the Yankee Jim's Union Water Co. had dammed and was subsequently selling to miners. Ewing and Smith, because they resided on the land next to the stream, had every right to divert the water.

Many entrepreneurial men with a background in business had already come to the gold fields, mined thousands of dollars' worth of gold, and left by 1852. With gold yields beginning to diminish, this would have been a prime opportunity for Amos to cash out, return to New York and resume his law career. He didn't do that. There were no wife or children waiting for him back in New York. There was enough of an income from mining and law clients, along with recognition as a leader in the local Whig Party, to induce Amos to stay in California.

Far from making plans to leave California, Amos accelerated his investments in the summer and autumn of 1851. He was developing a vision to address the water constraints faced by miners and their dry diggings. The notion of one large dam and big, long ditch was being formed and talked about amongst his mining company and other miners. The execution of the grand ditch plan would drive Amos almost into insolvency.

---

[1] Illustrated History of Sacramento County. By Hon. Winfield J. Davis, Chicago: The Lewis Publishing Company. 1890

[2] New York Daily Herald, New York, New York, April 19, 1849

[3] Bancroft Library, Charles Catlin to Walter Colton, December 31, 1848, BANC MSS C – B 626 Box 1

[4] Bancroft Library, George Catlin to Amos Catlin, December 31, 1848, BANC MSS C – B 626 Box 1

[5] History of the Bench and Bar of California. By Oscar Tully Shuck, Los Angeles, California, The Commercial Printing House, 1901.

[6] Sacramento Daily Union, Volume 83, Number 59, 29 April 1892

[7] Sacramento Bee, April 28, 1892

[8] Placer Times, Volume 1, Number 1, 28 April 1849

[9] Weekly Alta California, Volume I, Number 14, 5 April 1849

[10] Placer Times, Volume 1, Number 5, 26 May 1849

[11] Placer Times, Volume 1, Number 9, 30 June 1849

[12] Placer Times, Volume 1, Number 12, 21 July 1849

Amos P. Catlin

[13] Placer Times, Volume 1, Number 15, 18 August 1849

[14] Placer Times, Volume 1, Number 23, 13 October 1849

[15] Sacramento Transcript, Volume 1, Number 141, 14 October 1850

[16] Illustrated History of Sacramento County. By Hon. Winfield J. Davis, Chicago: The Lewis Publishing Company. 1890

[17] Sacramento Bee, May 19, 1887

[18] Title, Vanderwood to Catlin, March 18, 1850. California State Library, Catlin Collection Box 149

[19] San Diego Union and Daily Bee, 19 December 1912

[20] Illustrated History of Sacramento County. By Hon. Winfield J. Davis, Chicago: The Lewis Publishing Company. 1890

[21] Letter, Currey to Amos Catlin, June 25, 1850. California State Library, Catlin Collection Box 150

[22] Letter, Currey to Amos Catlin, July 11, 1850. California State Library, Catlin Collection Box 150

[23] Receipt Certificate, American River Damming Co., Sacramento, August 3, 1850. California State Library, Catlin Collection Box 149

[24] Letter, Currey to Amos Catlin, September 25, 1850. Bancroft Library, BANC MSS C – B 626 Box 1

[25] Letter, Currey to Amos Catlin, July 31, 1850. California State Library, Catlin Collection Box 150

[26] Letter, Currey to Amos Catlin, September 25, 1850. Bancroft Library, BANC MSS C – B 626 Box 1

[27] Letter, Currey to Amos Catlin, November 1, 1850. Bancroft Library, BANC MSS C – B Box 1

[28] Letter, Currey to Amos Catlin, December 19, 1850. California State Library, Catlin Collection Box 150

[29] Letter, Currey to Amos Catlin, December 19, 1850. California State Library, Catlin Collection Box 150

[30] Letter, Currey to Amos Catlin, December 31, 1850. Bancroft Library, BANC MSS C – B 626 Box 1

[31] Letter, Currey to Amos Catlin, December 19, 1850. California State Library, Catlin Collection Box 150

[32] Letter, Currey to Amos Catlin, July 15, 1853. California State Library, Catlin Collection, Box 150

[33] Letter, Currey to Amos Catlin, July 15, 1853. California State Library, Catlin Collection, Box 150

[34] Notice of Natoma Mining Company, California State Library, Catlin Collection Box 149

[35] Letter, George Catlin to Amos Catlin, January 15, 1849. Bancroft Library BANC MSS C – B 626 Box 1

[36] Letter, George Catlin to Amos Catlin, January 14, 1850. Bancroft Library, BANC MSS C – B 626 Box 1

[37] Letter, Sister Jane Catlin to Amos Catlin, Undated. California State Library, Catlin Collection Box 150

[38] Letter, William Catlin to Amos Catlin, May 14, 1850. Wells Fargo History, Wiltsee Collection.

[39] Letter, George Catlin to Amos Catlin, August 10, 1850. California State Library, Catlin Collection Box 150

[40] Letter, Pierce Catlin to Amos Catlin, September 7, 1850. California State Library, Catlin Collection Box 150

[41] Letter, Amos Catlin to Pierce Catlin, January 29, 1851. Historic Huguenot Street Archives, David and Pierce Catlin Family Papers.

[42] Letter, Amos Catlin to Pierce Catlin, January 29, 1851. Historic Huguenot Street Archives, David and Pierce Catlin Family Papers.

[43] 1850 Daily Alta California, Volume 1, Number 211, 30 August 1850

[44] Sacramento Daily Union, Volume 62, Number 1, 22 August 1889

[45] Sacramento Transcript, Volume 2, Number 27, 25 November 1850

[46] Sacramento Transcript, Volume 2, Number 27, 25 November 1850

[47] Sacramento Daily Union, Volume 1, Number 101, 15 July 1851

[48] Sacramento Bee, January 22, 1884

[49] Sacramento Daily Union, Volume 1, Number 108, 23 July 1851

[50] Sacramento Daily Union, Volume 1, Number 107, 22 July 1851

[51] Sacramento Daily Union, Volume 1, Number 145, 5 September 1851

[52] Sacramento Daily Union, Volume 11, Number 186, 23 October 1851

Amos P. Catlin

[53] Sacramento Daily Union, Volume 2, Number 192, 30 October 1851

[54] Deed Red Bank Mining Claim, October 4, 1851. California State Library, Catlin Collection Box 149

[55] Stock certificate and receipt, Empire Quartz Mine, December 1, 1851. California State Library, Catlin Collection Box 149

[56] Claim transfer receipt, Cutler to Catlin, December 10, 1851. California State Library, Catlin Collection Box 149

[57] Receipt – Deed for lot and house at Natoma. California State Library, Catlin Collection Box 149, Folder 4

[58] Legal synopsis of Amos Catlin, September, 1851. California State Library, Catlin Collection Box 149

[59] Van Dyke Plaintiff Complaint, November, 20, 1851. California State Library, Catlin Collection Box 149

[60] Yankee Jim's Union Water Co. v Ewing and Smith. California State Library, Catlin Collection Box 149

Amos P. Catlin

Chapter Two: Natoma Ditch & Sawmill to Senator, 1851 – 1852

John Veatch was mining on the South Fork of the American River at McDowellville. His mining claim was about three miles upstream of Mormon Island where Amos' Natoma Mining Company was working its claim. In the summer of 1851, Veatch would buy four other mining claims along the river in the vicinity of McDowellville, at times referred to as McDowell Hill. Many of the receipts or titles used similar language to describe the claims and read like formal legal documents. It was as if a lawyer had written the title transfer document. Veatch would purchase all of the mining claims for $342.

On December 11, 1851, Veatch transferred ownership of all the claims he purchased to Amos.[1] Additionally, Veatch sold his mining claim, with partner George Hill, to Amos for $300. On December 19, 1851, a formal notice of intent to build a dam on the South Fork of the American River and divert water into the ditch was drafted, posted, and sent to local newspapers. The notice was signed by John Veatch, Secretary of the Natoma Water Company.

The notice was as simple as it was audacious.

"Notice is hereby given that a Company under the name of the Natoma Water Company has been formed for the purpose of taking water by means of a canal from the South Fork of the American River at or near the rapids known as Salmon Falls and carrying it thence on the southerly side of said south fork down to the place in the vicinity of Mormon Island and from then in lateral canals to the places in the vicinity of Mormon Tavern, Rhodes Diggings, Willow Springs, Alder Springs, Negro Bar, Texas Hill, Mississippi Bar, and such other known and unknown places as may be within the reach of said lateral canals or any of them. The Company intend to commence said work forthwith and to have the same completed as soon as practicable. They intend to lease their water for the purpose of place washing, quartz mining, irrigation of tillable lands, and for such other useful purposes as the same may be desired. They intend to take as much water from the south fork as may be necessary at all times to fill a canal eight feet wide and four feet deep with a current running ten miles per hour."

Amos wrote the notice with enough legal structure to give it authority as the jurisdictional organizations, California counties, were beginning to organize. The damming of a river with the intent of constructing a several miles-long water ditch did not necessarily seem out of the ordinary. Mining companies had been partially or fully damming rivers and diverting the water into ditches and flumes for the past couple of years. A dam and ditch on the scale Amos proposed was a logical step in the development of the mining regions that had been operating with little

Old Natomas Head Dam and Ditch

4. Original dam and water ditch of the Natoma Water and Mining Co. on the South Fork of the American River. California State Archives

government oversight.

The significant differences between the Natoma Water Company's proposal and local damming associations were the plan to run the ditch across a county line, cross over established mining claims, and sell the water flow to miners and others. There seemed to be no serious opposition to the Natoma ditch. On the contrary, it would spur other men to start the planning process to potentially crush the Natoma ditch before it even got started.

The initially proposed Natoma ditch was a solid concept, even if the legal foundation was as murky as the river waters were from all of the gold mining. There were a few other improbabilities listed within the intent notice. The first was the construction of a ditch with a water flow of ten miles per hour. The Natoma ditch was to be all gravity flow, mainly within earthen sides. Such a high flow rate would rip through the earth and rock the retaining walls. The force of

Amos P. Catlin

water traveling at ten miles an hour, with a depth of four feet, could easily destroy a wooden flume with a slight imperfection.

The second problem was locating the dam site at Salmon Falls. The waterfalls below the town of Salmon Falls was an ideal site for a dam. The river made a horseshoe bend at this location with the waterfalls at the apex of the bend. On the south was the Higgins Point, with its steep slope down to the river. On the north side was a near vertical wall of the river canyon. At this point, the water pushed through a narrow canyon that required a relatively small dam.

The problem with the Salmon Falls location was its elevation of 350 feet above sea level. With a modest slope of less than 1 percent to keep the water flowing, when the ditch reached Mormon Island it would be at an elevation of approximately 320 feet. The ditch's exit out of the river canyon, in order to deliver water south to Willow Springs and Rhodes Diggings over four miles to the south, would have to be above the canyon rim of approximately 375 feet.

Consequently, the dam site would have to be moved upriver, above the town of Salmon Falls, to a location known as Rocky Bar. This site on the South Fork of the American River was wide, several hundred feet in width between canyon walls and low hills. The elevation was approximately 450 feet and, with a modest dam height, would put the water flowing into a ditch at about 455 feet. The gentle slope of the ditch (3 to 4 feet per mile) downriver would put the ditch at 390 to 395 feet of elevation in the Red Bank district and necessarily high enough to flow out of the river canyon south.

The original ownership structure for the Natoma Water Company was based on the mining companies along the river. The company would be owned and operated by the miners participating in the association. In the summer of 1851, Amos was already approaching the miners to inquire if they wanted to participate. The Golden Damming Mining Company declined to become involved but informed Amos they could buy their claim for $3,000.[2]

George Catlin posed a question to Amos in one of his letters that was of interest to many people wanting to invest in California. "I have felt some interest and curiosity in relation to the laws of California whether they are Spanish or American. What are the titles to land, how divided and how proved?", George inquired. "If you have a leisure moment I would like to hear something on the subject." It would take more than an idle moment for Amos to describe the chaotic legal structure men were laboring under in California.

Did Amos and his band of merry miners have any legal basis for declaring, much less prosecuting, their intention to dam a major river in California? With the exclusion of Spanish and Mexican land grants, everyone assumed the new

California land was owned by the federal government. Except for personal property and mining claims, the issue of land ownership was quietly ignored. Amos had not abandoned his law practice. He was representing numerous clients in various transactions and complaints. There was a question as to whether Amos had the legal power to sell a ferry across the South Fork of the American River.[3]

Amos' family still did not have a grasp of what he was doing in California. Their vision of him was of the grizzled miner sloshing around in the water with a pan, rocker, or long tom, mining for gold. They had heard of the troubles in Sacramento and the cholera outbreak. They had also received news that other men who had gone to California had died in that foreign land. Pierce Catlin wrote to Amos, "I beg of you not to stay much longer. I know you can make a good living here, and what is the use of your spending your time in that unhealthy part of the world[?]"[4]

A common theme within the family letters to Amos was that there was no shame in returning home to New York without a fortune in gold. They would rather have him home and poor, they wrote, than to have him die rich in California. Plus, George Catlin had plenty of law business for him to attend to. Amos' brother, William, wrote letters that addressed him as an adult. William wanted to know how he was doing, was he getting ahead in business, and was he married?

William expressed some confidence in Amos, "I suppose you do not intend to come back until you make a fortune," he wrote "If it was to be had in California and I were there, I would have it. If you do not seriously impair your health, I have no doubt you will succeed, but if you should make money and at the same time lose your health, you will be worse off than with good health and no money."[5] William also reported that he had no luck in getting a judgment released from their father's assets. The judgment was granted to a relative who had loaned money to Pierce Catlin, who was unable to repay the loan.[6]

Amos wrote his father a letter in June 1851 with scant information. Amos was more focused on why he had not heard from his father, specifically in regards to the $200 he sent him. In the tone of a petulant child, Amos writes, "Dr. Father, I have written you mail two letters since the last of January and one by Mr. Curry formerly of Kingston who left here for home 1st Feb. As yet I have rec.'d no answer, and as my letters related to some money which I sent you by Mr. Curry I am much annoyed at receiving no intelligence of it after a period of five months."[7]

Amos had read the pleas of his family to return home and their grave concerns about his health. Yet, he begins his letter excoriating his father over the lack of news regarding money. For his comfort and reading pleasure, Amos instructs his father to pay the editor of the Ulster Republican to continue mailing copies of the newspapers. As John Shaw was now the Post Master of the new post office, he should continue to direct correspondence to Mormon Island.[8]

Amos P. Catlin

At a nominal attempt to inform his father of his welfare, he writes that the weather is warm and thus far he had escaped any bouts of diarrhea. As a small token about his financial situation he writes, "I can't tell you how I am doing as I don't know myself. I have about $3,000 worth of mining claims which ought to bring me $10,000 next winter, but uncertainty governs everything here." To emphasize the focus of his letter, Amos resorts to a little emotional blackmail, informing his father he will write no more letters until he receives information about the $200 he sent him. And by the way, he wanted Pierce to persuade his mother and sisters to write more often.[9]

Part of the uncertainty Amos referenced in his letter to his father was river flow. If the river was high and flowing too fast, no river bed mining could be undertaken. In late fall and early winter, the river flow may be too little to properly wash claims on the river bank. Hence, the prospect of a water ditch above the river would greatly extend the mining season. As the mining season of 1851 was winding down, Amos decided to sell some of the assets of the Natoma Mining Company.

Shingle Springs Sawmill

Amos listed his company's steam engine for sale in November 1851. He described the 10-horse locomotive engine as a, "...superior rotary force pump with 20 feet of six-inch copper pipe – all in good running order."[10] With no immediate buyers, Amos was persuaded to haul the steam engine up to a location, west of Placerville, where they were splitting timber for shingles. There also happened to be a water spring nearby, and the place was being referred to as Shingle Springs.[11]

STEAM ENGINE.—For sale, at Mormon Island, one 10-horse Locomotive Engine.
Also, one superior Rotary Force Pump, with 20 feet of six inch copper pipe—all in good running order. Inquire of [o27 tf] A. P. CATLIN, Mormon Island.

Sacramento Daily Union, November 3, 1851

5. Amos lists his Natoma Mining Company steam engine for sale, 1851.

The steam engine configured to pump water was ill suited to any serious sawmill purpose. However, the prospect of a lumber mill plucked Amos' imagination. The proposed Natoma ditch would need lumber for flumes that crossed over creeks and ravines. Milled lumber was in demand for houses, buildings, fences, and a variety of other projects. While Amos could not run the lumber mill, he could sell the lumber.

A real lumber mill would need a larger steam engine to drive the saw into the wet wood. Such an engine was being sold at a Sheriff's Sale right up the river.[12] Amos was the high bidder of $1,000 for the steam engine.[13] Compared to running a sawmill and lumber business, gold mining was relatively easy. Even planning to dam a river and opening a 10-mile-plus ditch in the earth was more straightforward than the lumber business. Amos committed to the lumber business and pushed forward.

Before Amos could get the lumber mill sawing, he would learn that other men had their sights on his water ditch proposition. Darius Mills wrote to Amos on December 25, 1851, warning him of a competing group of men. Mills informed Amos that a Mr. Laird was preparing a similar water ditch company to compete with his. Amos, John Veatch, and Edgar Mills should immediately occupy locations along the route of the ditch from the dam to critical junctures along the path. Since there was no means of buying the land, all Amos could do was station men at the various points to intimidate any interlopers.[14]

D. O. Mills, being in the banking business in Sacramento, came across the confidential information about the competing ditch company. The act of breaking confidentiality regarding a business plan could have serious repercussions for D. O. Mills' own business. "As we fully understand the importance of this advise [sic] to you, we know such a special messenger and as soon as you comprehend the contents of this letter please destroy it as the sound of this information would at once be understood by Mr. L if he should in any way learn of it."[15]

Winters on the river could be kind of dull. The weather was cold and wet. Many men retreated to Sacramento to spend their gold dust on drink and gambling. Amos indulged in neither of those activities to pass his time. In addition to putting together a sawmill, he was still practicing law. Perhaps a better description would be that he was called upon to be a detective, debt collector, and real estate agent. John Gray wrote Amos from Marysville requesting he find his horse and take legal steps to acquire it from a Mr. Anderson.[16]

Other men who had left the mining region would grant Amos Power of Attorney to sell their claims or other property. Charles Faulkner contacted Amos and wanted him to procure a deed to his property and have Amos sell it for $1,500.[17] Andrew Ransom wrote to Amos from New York and wanted to know if he had collected any money from his loan to Faulkner since Ransom had left Mormon Island.[18]

Many men had left California without a fortune in gold. In February of 1852, Ransom found himself in the cold winter of New York with no work and no money. He was desperate for Amos to collect some money for him and send it back to him.

Amos P. Catlin

Ransom wrote, "Please write and give me some information in respect to the matter if you can and likewise how the miners are doing. The winter has been cold and stormy and I wish I had funds enough to go to California. I should not wish to live here. No money is to be had. I cannot get any at all and all business seems dead. I would advise any man not to come home unless he has got enough to live on and pay no attention to what may be said of the wants of California."[19]

Amos was most likely ambivalent on the nature of a man's prospects in California. One of the most insightful comments Amos wrote to his family was, "Uncertainty governs everything." He was experiencing the uncertainty of gold mining, attempting to build a water ditch, getting a sawmill operational, and staying healthy. Amos was in agreement with Ransom that it was better to be broke in California than in snowy New York.

In the spring of 1852, Amos entered into a contract with William Messinger and Charles Knowlton to build and operate a sawmill at Shingle Springs. The steam engine Amos bought at McDowell Hill would be hauled over to Shingle Springs as the power plant for the sawmill. In addition to the engine and some cash to fund the construction of the mill, Amos' primary responsibility would be as the sales agent. There was to be an equal split of any profits, with Amos as half owner receiving half and Messinger and Knowlton dividing the remainder.[20]

Messinger and Knowlton got the mill built and immediately ran into problems. The steam engine bought by Amos was not set up to power a sawmill. It just was not working efficiently to cut the logs that were brought in to be milled. Amos was in contact with Charles Hill, who was involved in the first steam engine Amos bought at McDowell Hill. Hill wrote Amos from San Francisco that he could get him a steam engine expressly set up for a sawmill for $3,000, delivered to Shingle Springs. The steam engine would have a boiler 26 feet long with a 3-foot diameter. with three flues, a 12-inch cylinder and a 3-foot stroke, it was designed to cut 1,000 feet per hour.[21]

Eager for the sale and potential mill business, Hill wrote Amos, "If we could get the contract for all the lumber [for the Natoma water ditch] at a fair price say $80 [price per thousand feet] at the mill, I would make a rush at it, always understanding that you were equally interested. I think I can manage matters so that we can make a big pile out of it and then sell the saw mill if we want to do so for a good advance on the first cost. Please write me immediately by Adams & Co. Express and tell what you think about it. I want to throw sixes if possible."[22]

The gambling metaphor of "throwing sixes" to win a pot of money was not unfamiliar to Amos. Implicit in Hill's letter is structuring a business deal for short-term gain. What was becoming apparent was that many men were looking to ride on Amos' plans and investments. Shortly after the correspondence with Charles

Amos P. Catlin

Hill, Amos received a letter from John Bensley in Sacramento. Bensley informed Amos that another company had designs for a water canal on the South Fork of the American River and had supposedly contracted for 300,000 feet of lumber to be delivered at $70 per thousand feet.[23]

Similarly, to the D. O. Mills letter, Bensley advised Amos to station men at Rocky Bar to secure the location of the dam and head waters of the canal. Plus, Amos should formally record the business plan with El Dorado County in Coloma and Sacramento County. Bensley's intelligence indicated that local men, being Grove, Craig, Berry, French, and Kens, were putting the competing canal proposal together.[24] Amos knew most of these men from mining and other business transactions.

Curiously, Bensley added about the men, "…and that they were in hopes that you would join them."[25] Bensley then informed Amos that he had delayed publishing that the Natoma Water Company would be selling shares and requesting bids for construction. He cited the recent floods in Sacramento as the reason for the delay, saying he thought it best to wait five days for business to get back to normal.[26] The delay also telegraphed to Amos that he had time to scrap the Natoma Water Company and join the competition.

With the help of his neighbor, Vanderwood, Amos had acquired a horse and saddle and became a reluctant horseman.[27] On the eve of announcing the formation of the Natoma Water Company, Amos' March 1852 letter home to his father took on a different tone than the previous letters. He greets his father with the happiness he feels knowing his father's health is good and that he has received his father's letter. There is also a sadness in his letter. Amos is holding back information. He tells his father that he wishes he were at home, but his financial situation still isn't where he needs it to be.

"I wish I was at home but it will [never] answer for me to come home now unless I have enough to live upon. And although I do not say that I am farther from being ready to go home now than at any time since being here. Yet I do say that my affairs are so situated that I could not wind up as well now as I could have done at many times heretofore."[28]

Amos uses his numerous business enterprises as a reason why he can't leave California without losing money on his investments. He also attempts to explain the complicated nature of his life and business.

"It would be useless for me to attempt to explain to you the nature of operations in which I am engaged. They are quite different from affairs at home. I am interested to some extent in quartz veins, damming companies, and water companies. But the thing from which I expect to realize the most during the

Amos P. Catlin

ensuing season is the steam saw mill. I am one half of the proceeds the engine belongs to me a beautiful 12 horse locomotive which cost me $3,000. Two men [one] are engineers the other a lawyer build the mill and employ their time as ever against me. I am to look for contracts and sale of lumber. The other expenses are paid half by me & half by them."[29]

The Catlin family lived near the Hudson River in New York. The Hudson could be as much as a mile wide in some spots. How does one properly explain that the current undertaking in California is to dam a river and build a water ditch? Unless you had been to California, the scale of what is known as a river, along with drought conditions for six months of the year, was hard to grasp. It is not immediately clear that Amos' lumber mill ties into the dam and water ditch enterprises via the construction of wooden flumes. Perhaps it was easier to write of the prospects of a lumber company than to explain the plan to permanently dam a river and then run a water canal above the river for more than 10 miles.

While he can't explain his business enterprises in his letters home, Amos can complain about country life. He tells his father that expenses are heavy; he has to own a horse and pay to feed it, about $2 per day. Amos also relays that he lost about $1,500 in mining equipment in the last flooding event on the river. As with every letter, he bemoans the fact that his family is not writing him enough. There is even a tinge of self-pity or depression. He writes, "I shall consider that they have forgotten me unless they write me sometimes and tell all the current news among the young people. They do not understand how interesting old remembrances are to a person far from home and among strangers."[30]

One of the more insightful passages of Amos' March 1852 letter home is over his father's latest business adventure.

"Every time I hear of your making a trade of your property I imagine that you are the loser. But of course, I can't tell any thing about it here. But I was very much surprised to hear from you that you had traded your farm for the grist mill at Rhinebach. You did not tell me whether you intended to move over there or not. In your next, let me know more particulars about it."[31]

Amos had to wonder if part of the money he sent home funded the trade of the farm for the grist mill. There is a sense of resignation in the letter. Amos went from being indignant that he had not heard from his father and the $200 he sent, to acceptance that he can change nothing back in New York. Absent in this letter is any hint of Amos' political involvement or aspirations.

While Amos wrote his father about the $3,000 steam engine that was going to propel his prospects to great heights, he hadn't actually signed the contract for the engine. He was still making payments on the steam engine he had bought at

Amos P. Catlin

McDowell Hill; the engine was working, but not necessarily profitable. Charles Hill wrote Amos from San Francisco in May confirming that the new steam engine he had found was ready for sale. The asking price was $3,000, plus another $1,000 for alterations.[32]

Hill also confirmed that news of the proposed Natoma ditch was floating through Northern California. Hill mentions that he had not heard from John Bensley, who wrote Amos about the competing ditch company, but he was ready to take up with those investors. Hill seems to be under the impression that Amos may also join the competing group. He writes, "I have not heard from Bensley as yet, but if they want me to take hold of the canal, I am ready to do so for a consideration."[33] It must have been a surprise to Amos that rumors were circulating that he was going to abdicate his plans to build the Natoma ditch. However, since his primary occupation was as an attorney, and he was focusing most of his energies on the sawmill, his competitors may have made the natural assumption that the water canal was not his first priority.

Up at Shingle Springs, Messinger and Knowlton were using the existing steam engine to mill some lumber for sale. Messinger wrote to Amos to inform him that another sawmill was being constructed in the area, and the mill owners had plans to bid on the Natoma ditch lumber.[34] Amos had been in negotiations with Lucien Brooks and Francis Clark to bid on part of the construction of the ditch. Brooks wrote that men cutting timber up at Shingle Springs were part of their crew, but they had also heard of plans for another sawmill.[35]

By late May, Messinger and Knowlton were tired of wrestling with an under-powered steam engine. They gave Amos an ultimatum that he either purchase the new steam engine he spoke of, or they would go purchase it themselves and dissolve their partnership with Amos.

"...as Mr. Knowlton says that you promised to make other arrangements by Sunday. As you have failed to do so we are in doubt w[h]ether you have been prevented by unforeseen circumstances or wither [sic] you decline any change at all. When we take everything into consideration we could not expect to go on to the end of this season as we are and make anything clear more than Laborers on Machanic's [sic] wages. Therefore, we consider it necessary for our advantage that we have another engine or run this [on] different terms. We have both of us been to see another engine which will suit us. The owner call it 20 horse power! It is new and one of the most highly finished engines I have seen in California. I expect it can be bought for $3,000 or there abouts. There is another party ready to join us in the business on len[d] us some assistance if you decline the proposed change. We wait to hear from you early tomorrow."[36]

Amos P. Catlin

Just as John Currey had to push Amos to attend to their business, Amos was forced to reckon with his promises on the sawmill. He finally contracted with George Gordon & Stein Company and the Vulcan Iron Foundry in San Francisco. The engine was larger than the one Amos was offered by Charles Hill. The steam engine had a boiler 12.5 feet in length, 42 inches in diameter, with 25 tubes, each 2.25 inches in diameter. The steam engine had a 16-inch stroke. The crank wheel for the saw was 3.5 inches in diameter, 5 feet long. This was a similar configuration to the power plant Brooks and Clark used at their mill.[37]

The purchase price of $3,050 did not include freight. Gordon and Stein did offer Amos a payment plan, at 3 percent interest, with sufficient collateral.[38] The June 3, 1852, purchase stated a 10-day turnaround time to construct engine and boiler. That date got pushed out by George Gordon, and the package would not be delivered until July. The boiler for the steam engine, weighing in at 3,354 pounds,[39] arrived in Sacramento July 7th on board the steamboat Confidence.[40]

The Sacramento River was the highway for goods and people to travel from San Francisco to Sacramento. Once the people disembarked and goods were offloaded from the steamer, the roads to transport them to their destinations were rough and not always maintained. There was a general lack of infrastructure outside of Sacramento, be it roads, water systems, or bridges. Mormon Island resident Dallas Kneass was hoping to build a toll bridge across the South Fork of the American River. His bridge site was in El Dorado County, just a couple miles east from Mormon Island, and he had retained Thomas Williams, of Coloma, to represent his application to El Dorado County.

In April of 1852, Thomas Williams wrote to Kneass to update on the progress of bridge application and highlight the embryonic nature of government in California. "I will say to you that the Justice of the Peace of this town [Coloma] will in all probability sit as an associate at the hearing…He also rooms with our presiding Judge." Williams refers Kneass to Amos for a consultation since there were issues with a competing toll bridge proposal. Because all of the laws and regulations were still being written and interpreted, Williams notes he had also written to Amos on the topic.[41]

Procrastination was not a trait of Amos. At the age of 29, Amos was juggling multiple endeavors of water canal construction, sawmill operations, and maintaining his law practice. Thomas Williams wrote Amos in late April inquiring about the condition of the bridge application.

"About one week since I wrote to you by express enclosing a form for a petition for your bridge and as I have not heard from you I apprehend danger that you have not received it. You know that our application must be filed ten days before court and court meets on the 10th of May."[42]

Amos P. Catlin

There was no decision on the bridge application in May. A lack of organized and responsive government authority led many men to just build what they wanted, as in the case of a water canal. The chaotic and confusing state of local government was outlined in Thomas Williams' letter to Amos in August 1852.

NATOMA WATER COMPANY.

A COMPANY being formed to construct a flume to convey water from ROCKY BAR, on the South Fork of the American River.

TO MORMON ISLAND,

Negro Bar, Texas Hill, Rhodes' Diggings, Mississippi Bar, and other adjacent places, for the purpose of supplying Miners with water for mining purposes, under the name and title of the "Natoma Water Company," the following officers were duly elected:

President.
A. P. CATLIN, Esq.
Vice President,
J. H. BERRY, Esq.
Secretary,
EDGAR MILLS, Esq.
Treasurer,
D. O. MILLS. Esq.

Directors.
John Bensley, Sac. City.
E. J. Townsend, do.
Dr. John A. Yeach,
Mormon Island.
John Craig, Esq. do.
Amos P. Laird, Nevada.
B. M. Coates, do.

Books of subscription of stock in the above company are open at the following places:
At D. O. MILLS & CO., Sacramento.
At WILLIAMSON & CO., Nevada.
At A. P. CATLIN'S, Mormon Island.
SEALED PROPOSALS for the construction of the above canal may be left at the above named places. until the 1st of May, where also specifications of said work may be examined. [ap13 tf] EDGAR MILLS, Sec'y.

THE STOCKHOLDERS of the Natoma Water Company are requested to meet at the Willow Spring House, near Mormon Island, on Saturday, May 15th, at 5 o'clock P.M., at which time the books of subscription to the capital stock will be closed. All the stockholders are particularly requested to attend, as business of importance will be transacted.
ap15   A. P. CATLIN, President.

Sacramento Daily Union
May 1, 1852

6. Announcement of Natoma Water Company elected officers and solicitation of bids for ditch construction, 1852.

"We have yet no Board of Supervisors [El Dorado County], but the Court of Sessions informs me that they intend to resume their jurisdiction in regard to bridges, ferries, etc. They have a call Session on the second Monday in September for that purpose. My opinion is that they have not proper jurisdiction in the matters. But as there is no other power to apply to, I intend risking it in several cases that I have. If you feel willing to risk it, send me proof of your notices of the necessity of your bridge, your bonds, etc. and I will put your case through."[43]

A toll bridge across a river needed county approval, but a dam across a river, miles of canal and wooden flumes spanning two counties with the intent to sell the water was a proposition that needed no government approval. This was the juxtaposition that was manifest in front of Amos. By April of 1852, Amos, who had convinced some men conspiring against his Natoma Water Company to join his efforts, advertised the formation of the company.

With Amos obviously elected as President, the other officers and directors on the list were seen as solid businessmen. James H. Berry was Vice President. Edgar

Amos P. Catlin

Mills and D.O. Mills were Secretary and Treasurer, respectively. John Bensley, who operated steamers on the Sacramento River, including the steamboat Confidence, was a director, along with E.J. Townsend, Dr. John Veatch, John Craig, Amos Laird, and B.M. Coates.[44] Edgar Mills wrote Amos at the end of April apologizing for the delay in getting the notice into the Sacramento Union.[45] In addition to a stockholder's meeting to be held May 15th at the Willow Springs House, there was an announcement that the company was accepting proposals for the construction of a water project.[46]

The Willow Springs ranch and hotel would become the default corporate meeting place for the Natoma Water Company. The Willow Springs ranch was described as being on the eastern boundary of the Leidesdorff land grant on the road to Coloma, 24 miles from Sacramento. The 160-acre ranch contained a two-story hotel originally named the Ohio House.[47] Amos facilitated the sale from Samuel Stewart to James Berry and John Craig in October 1851.[48]

Perhaps inspired by Berry and Craig, Amos purchased a half interest in the Exchange Hotel in June 1852 from John Shaw. The investment in the hotel cost Amos $2,500 and included stables, outbuildings and, most importantly, a saloon.[49] As the name implied, goods were also exchanged at the hotel. In addition to his other business interests, Amos would become a bookkeeper for the hotel invoicing guests for room, board, horse feed, clothes, and mining equipment. A typical statement to the local mining company Hart and Kneass included a pair of boots $8, pants $6, slate and pencil $1.25, drawers $1.50, two gallons lamp oil $6, 100 pounds potatoes $15, 95 pounds flour $11.40, 24 pounds butter $21.60, 20 pounds beans $2.50, 2 yards muslin $0.40, 18 pounds candles $10.50, and 5 gallons whiskey $7.50.[50]

Between Natoma Water Company Board meetings, Exchange Hotel bookkeeping, and a little bit of law work, Amos was galloping on his horse over the dry dusty hills around the American River trying to sell lumber. In July, he made a small lumber sale to the Hope Steam Mining Company working a claim at Big Gulch, which was a creek that emptied into the American River right across from Negro Bar.[51] Amos would make a nice lumber sale to Dallas Kneass' Pioneer Mining Company later in July. The 4,000 feet of lumber for flumes, that included 30 square timbers 8" x 8" x 20 feet in length, was to be delivered on the south side of the river within 10 days of the order.[52]

Amos sold lumber for a structure on Negro Hill across the river from Mormon Island. Thomas Burns bought $123 in lumber for his building.[53] Amos filed a Mechanics Lien in August on the sale of the lumber that was to be used for the business called Our House.[54] As energetic as Amos was, a young man high on the adrenaline of California pioneer business, politics, and speculation, he could not

Amos P. Catlin

handle the lumber business all by himself. One of the Natoma Mining Company members, Luther Cutler, agreed to manage the lumber yard at French Hollow, down the road from Shingle Springs.

Luther Cutler, born in Maine in 1818, had no pretense about him. He frequently wrote to Amos about the difficulties at the lumber yard with due respect to Amos' position. However, his correspondence with Amos was candid with jocularity and familiarity that few men could claim with Amos. Cutler had no problems giving Amos financial advice or scolding him when he thought Amos had stumbled. Above all, Cutler was extremely loyal, and Amos would return the allegiance. While there existed no formal business partnership between Amos and Luther, they worked so closely together that vendors and customers would refer to them as Cutler and Catlin Co.

While up in French Hollow setting up the lumber yard, Luther heard that Amos was thinking of sending up men to cut logs for the mill. Cutler advised against it as they needed to sell the inventory they already had in stock. Cutler wrote, "I think you had better get a lot of reservations [lumber orders] and send them up with your team if you can buy them on short time in the city, you had better, for every dollar we can save is as good as earned." Luther then continued to give Amos a list of necessities he needed that included flour, potatoes, dried apples, pepper, mustard, syrup, sugar, coffee, tea, pickles, cheese, butter, tea kettle, coffee boiler, plates, knives, forks, butcher knife, and three or four mattresses to sleep on.[55]

Cutler finished up his letter explaining that while it seemed like he was asking for a large lot of housekeeping articles, he was almost broke.[56] Without hesitation and delay, Amos purchased Cutler's list in Sacramento and had it shipped up to him.[57] Amos could almost claim the same financial situation as Cutler. Money was getting tight for him, too, beginning with his delinquent assessment on his Natoma Water Company shares.

James Meredith wrote to Amos earlier in 1852 from his cabin at Negro Bar, where he was working on one of the flumes, that they needed his stock assessment in order to purchase lumber for flume construction.[58] Amos tried selling the remaining pumps and pipes from the Natoma Mining Company, but there were no buyers.[59] Amos, with 12 shares of the Natoma Water Company, was the largest shareholder, but that just meant the shares were in his name, not that he had paid in the $4,800. The Natoma Water Company was struggling for money to order supplies and pay its bills.

Lucien Brooks of Brooks and Clark Co. wrote to Amos in August demanding a $400 progress payment for their lumber and work on the Natoma ditch. "If you can let us have four or five hundred dollars then we should like it. The 20 ft. sticks

Amos P. Catlin

we will have ready tomorrow. We have let two sections of the canal and shall probably close with a company for three miles more tomorrow. We have four men at work at the Sa[lmon] Falls and a gang getting out timber here."[60]

Cash Flow Crunch

Beyond business obligations, Amos also owed money to men who had worked for him. William Willis sent Amos a desperate letter in August begging for $50 on the balance that Amos owed him. Willis was stuck in Coloma and could not get any work. He was coming down to Mormon Island and wanted to collect the money. Willis pleaded, "Please don't fail."[61]

Amos could have structured the Natoma Water Company to feed money into his own pockets. He could have made sure all the lumber for the flumes came from his sawmill and controlled the contractor digging the ditches and constructing the wooden flumes. But he had too much integrity to engage in such unethical business practices. He also was not a good enough sales person or nefarious backroom negotiator to build an enterprise to enrich himself and his friends at the expense of investors.

Unfortunately, integrity and honesty do not pay the bills. Amos needed money to continue funding the construction process. George Gordon of Vulcan Iron Works in San Francisco offered an infusion of cash into the company in October 1852. The cost to Amos was losing control of the Natoma Water Company and his valued relationships with other shareholders and contractors.

George Gordon had been informed there were 60 to 85 shares of the Natoma Water Company still outstanding.

"I have had some talk with my friends down here about your Natoma Canal. Myself and 4 or 5 friends are willing to take up these 60 shares provided my own personal inspection of the work proves satisfactory and the company are willing to give us 2 places on the direction.

"I need not tell you that our coming into this thing will immediately improve the market value of the whole property. That is the shares we wish [to] take every share out of the market. If we buy so large an interest as 60 shares it is fair that we should have two voices in the direction, for which two of the present directors will have to resign. About this, I presume there would be no trouble.

"Please see the officers and directors at once and by return write me making me an official offer of the whole of the 60 shares or 85 of the 25 [that] were not taken up. The offer to become binding for one week from my receiving it to allow me time to examine the work and if I am satisfied I will on the spot arrange to pay up the installments that are past on the shares taken."

Amos P. Catlin

Gordon appended the hostile takeover letter with an appraisal of the state of the project.

"That junction canal will cost more than $45,000. It needs 140,000 feet of sawed lumber and an equal of round flatted timbers. I doubt [it] can be done under $60,000. If you will disband the old company and form a new one, I will take hold."

It is true that Amos had no background in engineering and managing a large construction project such as the Natoma ditch. He did have Augustus T. Arrowsmith, a civil engineer, as a shareholder and laborer on the project. Otherwise, the Natoma ditch could be characterized as a California pioneer project, being built by pioneers whose primary experience was damming and diverting rivers to mine for gold.

If experience is the best teacher, then Amos received confirmation that he was on the correct path with the canal from a fellow canal builder. James Edwards, who was a builder and investor of the Bear River ditch,[62] was glad to hear that Amos had already made a good start on the canal. "I am satisfied you are right in adopting excavation instead of fluming," he wrote. Edwards made a couple of suggestions. The first being, "The outer embankments can be made of dirt from the hillsides this is an important thing to attend to in its construction."[63]

Edwards advised Amos to begin the ditch below Rocky Bar. "So as to avoid that long line of exposure to high water. Let the ditch be wide, consequently shallow… until you get out of the way of the floods." Unfortunately, the ditch had to begin at Rocky Bar for the elevation it provided. Edwards was correct about river floods, as the Natoma ditch and flumes close to the river were routinely washed out by high flow events. From his experience, Edwards noted that rivers flow with a slope as small as 3 feet to the mile. He wrote having a slight slope of 4 feet to the mile would be sufficient to convey enough water to the miners.[64]

In the summer of 1852, while riding the countryside selling lumber, Amos also apprised miners and others of the opportunity to invest in the Natoma Water Company. One mining company on the river originally consented to participate and help build the water canal. In a later reply, the miners Atkinson, Hollister, and Hannibal stated that they had been advised not to participate.[65]

James Edwards was convinced of the value of the Natoma Water Company and told Amos to subscribe him to seven shares. The only caveat to the purchase offer was that the company was not embroiled in any lawsuits. Aside from that condition, Edwards completely trusted Amos and wrote, "You said nothing about paying in a percentage on subscribing. If such is your demand write me and the money will be immediately sent."[66]

Amos P. Catlin

Amos had the confidence of his fellow Natoma Water Company shareholders and a confirmation that the ditch would deliver the water sales promised. George Gordon backed down from his overtures of a hostile takeover of the company. Gordon wrote to Amos that, in addition to the boiler parts being sent for the steam engine sawmill, "As to the matter of the canal stock, we will take our chance of purchasing when the [water] comes."[67]

While Amos had maneuvered out of an unpleasant reorganization of the Natoma Water Company, he still had to contend with the sawmill. Sawmill partner Messinger wrote Amos to update him on their thin inventory in September 1852. The first challenge was just getting logs; there seemed to be a shortage of men willing to haul the logs in from the forest. Next, the mill had also been plagued with mechanical failures, reducing its production down to just 500 feet of lumber milled the previous day.[68]

Messinger felt ashamed that he had to inform a McDowellville customer that they could not complete his order. "The great trouble has been with the chain," Messinger reported. "We have now put the large rope onto the side that gigs back and use the chain to feed up with only. It has worked first rate so far. No sooner was this fixed than the pitman gave out." Messinger reckoned with the current fix he could commence on the last lumber order Amos placed for a customer.[69] Messinger requested a personal favor of Amos: "P. S. If you come up in your buggy or can send up without its [sic] getting damaged, I should like a [stack] or two of letter paper as I am quite destitute."

Amos had traded in his saddle for a buggy pulled by a horse, not necessarily the image of a pioneering gold miner. With the writing paper delivered, Messinger wrote to Amos on October 1 about more sawmill management issues. The mill was down to two or three days of wood to fire the boiler. The cords of wood looked small, and Messinger encouraged Amos to inspect the cord size before accepting any more loads. Mr. Birdsall, one of the mill employees, had been mending the rope repeatedly, and a new chain for the drive was sorely needed. Birdsall was also in need of the money Amos owed him.[70]

Sawmill Management

The Shingle Springs sawmill was Amos' biggest investment outside of the Natoma ditch. As Messinger would detail in his numerous letters to Amos, steam engine-sawmill management was far more demanding than digging a ditch. By November, Messinger reported that the mill was running very well, the problem was demand. The winter rains had come, building construction was down, and roads were a muddy mess, making deliveries difficult. The rain added moisture content to the logs brought in to be sawed, slowing down the mill.

Amos P. Catlin

Messinger wrote Amos, "You will perceive the truth of the statement made to you when you were up. That the Mill is doing very little and unless some improvement can be made will not be very profitable. Birdsall is no doubt partly if not wholly right in ascribing it to the wood – but that is a fault which cannot be remedied as the wood is as good as can be got now. Birdsall is at work making a blower. He commenced on it Sunday while I was away and has Lyman Roe at work in his place. I have never had experience enough in those machines to judge the probable benefit from one. Where the draught is as strong is we have it from the exhaust steam. But I hope the best from it."[71]

Another problem, specific to the boiler, was the time it took to heat the water and develop the head of steam necessary to drive the saw blades through the wet wood. The down time waiting for steam was reducing the amount of lumber they could cut.

"There is another cause which I mentioned to you before which is no trifle and which was not formally [*sic*] the case – The great length of time the mill stands still unnecessarily. For instance, an hour at every meal with up to an hour to get up steam afterwards makes from 4 to six hours per day generally. Not so long at Noon but at midnight always. This time if improved would pay all the expenses of running the mill."[72]

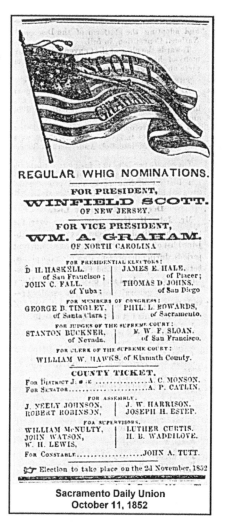

REGULAR WHIG NOMINATIONS.

FOR PRESIDENT,
WINFIELD SCOTT.
OF NEW JERSEY.

FOR VICE PRESIDENT,
WM. A. GRAHAM.
OF NORTH CAROLINA

FOR PRESIDENTIAL ELECTORS:
D. H. HASKELL, of San Francisco; JAMES E. HALE, of Placer;
JOHN C. FALL, of Yuba; THOMAS D. JOHNS, of San Diego

FOR MEMBERS OF CONGRESS:
GEORGE B. TINGLEY, of Santa Clara; PHIL. L. EDWARDS, of Sacramento.

FOR JUDGES OF THE SUPREME COURT:
STANTON BUCKNER, of Nevada. W. W. F. SLOAN, of San Francisco.

FOR CLERK OF THE SUPREME COURT:
WILLIAM W. HAWKS. of Klamath County.

COUNTY TICKET.
For District J...E ....A. C. MONSON.
For Senator...............A. P. CATLIN.

FOR ASSEMBLY.
J. NEELY JOHNSON, J. W. HARRISON.
ROBERT ROBINSON, JOSEPH H. ESTEP.

FOR SUPERVISORS.
WILLIAM McNULTY, LUTHER CURTIS.
JOHN WATSON, H. B. WADDILOVE.
W. H. LEWIS,
For Constable...............JOHN A. TUTT.

☞ Election to take place on the 2d November, 1852

Sacramento Daily Union
October 11, 1852

7. Amos Catlin candidate for California Senate with the Whig party, 1852.

When Messinger and Knowlton put the steam engine into operation, it was summer, with high daily temperatures and low humidity. By November, the ambient air temperature was much lower and the humidity higher. The lower temperatures and higher humidity were retarding the boiler efficiency, leading to

Amos P. Catlin

longer time to reach critical steam pressure. As Messinger was needed to work the steam engine, he had to rely on Amos for errands to pick up parts and management decisions.

One issue that had developed was a scale or deposit in the boiler tubes. Scale is usually a result of hard water or the minerals (calcium, magnesium carbonate, sulfates) precipitating out of the water as it expands to steam. Messinger had Amos pick up some acid to dissolve the scale. Messinger report to Amos, "I reminded you of the acid and mentioned the expediency of first sending me a vial full before purchasing sufficient for the desired object. It arrived here Saturday and I immediately tested the incrustation deposited by this water and find that neither in solution or pure will it produce any more effect than if it were glass. What this substance is I don't know. I only know that it is neither of the two most common things deposited by water when evaporated."[73]

Messinger goes on to complain about some of the employees. He heard the head sawyer over at Brooks and Clark, Mr. Culven, wanted to move over to their sawmill. Even though sales had been anemic at best, Messinger still wanted to haul in more logs to build up a supply. Perhaps even more scarce than sales were men, in Messinger's opinion, who could do the work.[74] Amos did not volunteer to work as a fireman on the boiler, cut down trees, or saw the logs. His job was to generate sales. Unfortunately for the sawmill, politics had been consuming much of his attention.

In 1852, the Mormon Island Whig Party delegated Amos to attend the county convention.[75] He was then nominated to represent the Whig Party as a candidate for State Senator.[76] Amos, along with other Whig Party members, went on a speaking tour around the region.[77] After the votes were counted on November 4th, Amos P. Catlin was elected a State Senator from Mormon Island, in Sacramento County.[78] News of Amos' election probably reached his family in New York before his letters did. On receiving the news, they immediately knew Amos was never coming home. California was now his home.

---

[1] Veatch mining claim transfers, December 11, 1851. California State Library, Catlin Collection Box 149

[2] Letter, Golden Damming Mining Co. to Amos, June 3, 1851. California State Library, Catlin Collection Box 150

[3] Letter, Woodford to Amos Catlin, January 29, 1851. California State Library, Catlin Collection Box 150

[4] Letter, Pierce Catlin to Amos Catlin, April 26, 1851. Bancroft Library, BANC MSS C – B 626 Box 1

[5] Letter, William Catlin to Amos Catlin, May 20, 1851. Bancroft Library BANC MSS C – B 626 Box 1

[6] Letter, William Catlin to Amos Catlin, May 20, 1851. Bancroft Library BANC MSS C – B 626 Box 1

[7] David and Pierce Catlin Family Papers, Historic Huguenot Street, New Paltz, NY. Correspondence to Pierce Catlin from Amos Catlin, 1851 - 1852

Amos P. Catlin

[8] David and Pierce Catlin Family Papers, Historic Huguenot Street, New Paltz, NY. Correspondence to Pierce Catlin from Amos Catlin, 1851 - 1852

[9] David and Pierce Catlin Family Papers, Historic Huguenot Street, New Paltz, NY. Correspondence to Pierce Catlin from Amos Catlin, 1851 - 1852

[10] Sacramento Daily Union, Volume 2, Number 195, 3 November 1851

[11] Sacramento Bee, April 2, 1888

[12] Receipt, Sheriff's sale of steam engine. California State Library, Catlin Collection Box 149

[13] Receipt, steam engine for $1,000 from Charles Hill to John Wood, debt settlement. California State Library, Catlin Collection Box 149

[14] Letter, Mills and Brown to Catlin, Veatch, Mill, December 25, 1851. Bancroft Library, BANC MSS C – B Box 1

[15] Letter, Mills and Brown to Catlin, Veatch, Mill, December 25, 1851. Bancroft Library, BANC MSS C – B Box 1

[16] Letter, John Gray to Amos Catlin, January 27, 1852. Bancroft Library BANC MSS C – B 626 Box 1

[17] Letter, Charles Faulkner to Amos Catlin, April 12, 1851. California State Library, Catlin Collection Box 150

[18] Letter, Andrew Ransom to Amos Catlin, February 8, 1852. Bancroft Library, BANC MSS C – B 626 Box 1

[19] Letter, Andrew Ransom to Amos Catlin, February 8, 1852. Bancroft Library, BANC MSS C – B 626 Box 1

[20] Contract, Messinger, Knowlton, Catlin, March 1852. California State Library, Catlin Collection Box 149

[21] Letter, Charles Hill to Amos Catlin, March 20, 1852. Bancroft Library, BANC MSS C – B 626 Box 1

[22] Letter, Charles Hill to Amos Catlin, March 20, 1852. Bancroft Library, BANC MSS C – B 626 Box 1

[23] Letter, John Bensley to Amos Catlin, March 15, 1852. Bancroft Library BANC MSS C – B 626 Box 1

[24] Letter, John Bensley to Amos Catlin, March 15, 1852. Bancroft Library BANC MSS C – B 626 Box 1

[25] Letter, John Bensley to Amos Catlin, March 15, 1852. Bancroft Library BANC MSS C – B 626 Box 1

[26] Letter, John Bensley to Amos Catlin, March 15, 1852. Bancroft Library BANC MSS C – B 626 Box 1

[27] Letter, Vanderwood to Amos Catlin, May 7, 1850. Bancroft Library BANC MSS C – B 626 Box 1

[28] David and Pierce Catlin Family Papers, Historic Huguenot Street, New Paltz, NY. Correspondence to Pierce Catlin from Amos Catlin, 1851 - 1852

[29] David and Pierce Catlin Family Papers, Historic Huguenot Street, New Paltz, NY. Correspondence to Pierce Catlin from Amos Catlin, 1851 - 1852

[30] David and Pierce Catlin Family Papers, Historic Huguenot Street, New Paltz, NY. Correspondence to Pierce Catlin from Amos Catlin, 1851 - 1852

[31] David and Pierce Catlin Family Papers, Historic Huguenot Street, New Paltz, NY. Correspondence to Pierce Catlin from Amos Catlin, 1851 - 1852

[32] Letter, Charles Hill to Amos Catlin, May 25, 1852. Bancroft Library, BANC MSS C – B 626 Box 1

[33] Letter, Charles Hill to Amos Catlin, May 25, 1852. Bancroft Library, BANC MSS C – B 626 Box 1

[34] Letter, William Messinger to Amos Catlin, May 12, 1852. Bancroft Library, BANC MSS C – B 626 Box 1

[35] Letter, Brooks & Clark to Amos Catlin, May 19, 1852. California State Library, Catlin Collection Box 150

[36] Letter, Knowlton & Messinger to Amos Catlin, May 25, 1852. California State Library, Catlin Collection Box 150

[37] Purchase contract, Gordon & Stein, June 3, 1852. Bancroft Library, BANC MSS C – B 626 Box 1

[38] Purchase contract, Gordon & Stein, June 3, 1852. Bancroft Library, BANC MSS C – B 626 Box 1

[39] Scales ticket, Eleventh and M Street Hay Scales, July 9, 1852. California State Library, Catlin Collection Box 149

[40] Freight receipt, Steamboat Confidence, July 7, 1852. California State Library, Catlin Collection Box 149

Amos P. Catlin

[41] Letter, Thomas Williams to Dallas Kneass, April 18, 1852. Bancroft Library, BANC MSS C – B 626 Box 1

[42] Letter, Thomas Williams to Amos Catlin, April 25, 1852. Bancroft Library BANC MSS C – B 626 Box 1

[43] Letter, Thomas Williams to Amos Catlin, August 14, 1852. Bancroft Library BANC MSS C – B 626 Box 1

[44] Sacramento Daily Union, Volume 3, Number 347, May 1, 1852

[45] Letter, Edgar Mills to Amos Catlin, April 30, 1852. California State Library, Catlin Collection Box 150

[46] Sacramento Daily Union, Volume 3, Number 347, May 1, 1852

[47] Property deed, Willow Springs Ranch, George Stewart to Samuel Stewart, February 18, 1851. California State Library, Catlin Collection Box 149

[48] Sales contract, Willow Springs Ranch, October 1851. California State Library, Catlin Collection Box 149

[49] Title transfer, John Shaw to Amos Catlin, June 1, 1852. California State Library, Catlin Collection Box 149

[50] Exchange Hotel Statement, Hart & Kneass, October 1852. California State Library, Catlin Collection Box 149

[51] Lumber order, Hope Steam Mining Co., July 18, 1852. California State Library, Catlin Collection Box 149

[52] Lumber Sale Contract, Pioneer Mining Co., July 21, 1852. California State Library, Catlin Collection Box 149

[53] Lumber Sale, Thomas Burns, August 7, 1852. California State Library, Catlin Collection Box 149

[54] Lien notice, Our House, Negro Hill, August 14, 1852. California State Library Box 149

[55] Letter, Luther Cutler to Amos Catlin, July 12, 1852. California State Library, Catlin Collection Box 150

[56] Letter, Luther Cutler to Amos Catlin, July 12, 1852. California State Library, Catlin Collection Box 150

[57] Cutler & Co. item list, July 11, 1852. California State Library, Catlin Collection Box 149

[58] Letter James Meredith to Amos Catlin, January 22, 1852. Bancroft Library BANC MSS C – B 626 Box 1

[59] Letter Van Dyke to Amos Catlin, March 1, 1852. California State Library, Catlin Collection Box 149

[60] Letter, Lucian Brooks to Amos Catlin, August 3, 1852. California State Library, Catlin Collection Box 150

[61] Letter, William Willis to Amos Catlin, August 25, 1852. Bancroft Library, BANC MSS C – B 626 Box 1

[62] Sacramento Daily Union, Volume 4, Number 477, 2 October 1852

[63] Letter, James Edwards to Amos Catlin, July 7, 1852. Bancroft Library, BANC MSS C – B 626 Box 1

[64] Letter, James Edwards to Amos Catlin, July 7, 1852. Bancroft Library, BANC MSS C – B 626 Box 1

[65] Letter, Atkinson, Hollister, Hannibal to Amos Catlin, July 1852. California State Library, Catlin Collection Box 150

[66] Letter, James Edwards to Amos Catlin, July 7, 1852. Bancroft Library, BANC MSS C – B 626 Box 1

[67] Letter, George Gordon to Amos Catlin, October 22, 1852. Bancroft Library BANC C – B 626 Box 1

[68] Letter, William Messinger to Amos Catlin, September 14, 1852. California State Library, Catlin Collection Box 150

[69] Letter, William Messinger to Amos Catlin, September 14, 1852. California State Library, Catlin Collection Box 150

[70] Letter, William Messinger to Amos Catlin, October 1, 1852. Bancroft Library, BANC C – B 626 Box 1

[71] Letter, William Messinger to Amos Catlin, November 15, 1852. California State Library, Catlin Collection Box 150

[72] Letter, William Messinger to Amos Catlin, November 15, 1852. California State Library, Catlin Collection Box 150

Amos P. Catlin

[73] Letter, William Messinger to Amos Catlin, November 23, 1852. Bancroft Library BANC MSS C – B 626 Box 1

[74] Letter, William Messinger to Amos Catlin, November 23, 1852. Bancroft Library BANC MSS C – B 626 Box 1

[75] Sacramento Daily Union, Volume 3, Number 366, 24 May 1852

[76] Sacramento Daily Union, Volume 4, Number 482, 8 October 1852

[77] Sacramento Daily Union, Number 503, 2 November 1852

[78] Sacramento Daily Union, Number 505, 5 November 1852

Amos P. Catlin

Chapter Three: Senator Catlin, California Capitol, 1853 - 1854

In a little over three years since his arrival in California, Amos had successfully mined for gold, started a sawmill, launched a water canal project, and been elected a state senator.

If Amos had ever seriously entertained any thoughts of returning home to New York, they were vanquished with his election to the California State Senate. Not only was he an elected official from Mormon Island, the Natoma Water and Mining Company was beginning to take shape. As a senator, Amos was engaged in changing the state of California. As a businessman, he was changing the face of the state's landscape with mining and water projects.

The fourth session of the California Senate opened in Vallejo. The Senate was composed of 27 members, with the majority being Democrats. Amos was one of the seven Whig members in the minority.[1] It was not too long after the Senate had convened that it voted to move the Capital over to Benicia. Amos was assigned to the Commerce and Navigation,[2] and Mining and Claims committees.[3] Later in the session, Amos would be selected to be on a special committee investigating the extension of the San Francisco waterfront.[4]

Like any elected representative, Amos was lobbied by people on behalf of pet projects and associates. Augustus Arrowsmith wrote a letter to Amos in January 1853 requesting assistance with the appointment of Dr. White as Visiting Physician to the proposed U.S. Marine Hospital at Point Rincon in San Francisco.[5] All Amos could possibly do was to make the suggestion to Governor Bigler, who made the appointments and was also a Democrat. Arrowsmith was a civil engineer from New York working on the construction of the Natoma ditch. He was the default engineer and would become a company executive by 1855.[6]

Amos, now 30 years old, was not a spectator in the Senate. He introduced a bill relating to corporations and another to allow Sacramento to sell bonds to build a hospital. As a means to show popular support for some of his causes, Amos introduced several petitions signed by Sacramento County citizens. George Williams of Sacramento wrote to Amos concerned about a recently Democrat-proposed law concerning state appropriations to hospitals and the organization of county Supervisors.

Williams wrote to Amos in Benicia, "I appeal to you as a Whig and as a friend to defeat, if possible, this Democratic operation. If you can possibly have the

Supervisor system established do so. If no and you find you cannot have any appropriation made for this county so the Supervisors can have the management of it. I sincerely hope and trust you will support the bill to abolish the present system, and let each county take care of its own sick...”[7]

At that time, even though counties had elected officials such as Sheriff, Treasurer, and District Attorney, many of the financial decisions were made by judges in the Court of Sessions relative to state laws. Williams felt the current system was tilting toward developing a Democratic political machine. It would take a California Supreme Court decision that interpreted the state's constitution to allow counties to be managed by an elected board of supervisors. California government was very much a top-down management system. Part of the reason for this was because so much of California was vast open land with few or no inhabitants. At least, inhabitants that the new California state determined worthy of participating in government; Native Americans were ignored.

If California could be compared to the formation of a solar system, the state's constitution was the gravity pulling all of the material together. The members of the legislature were trying to create a habitable planet. California was a huge and diverse landscape. There was even legislation introduced to break California into smaller states. Amos voted for this amendment to the constitution to break California apart.[8] Part of the impetus for fracturing California was to allow some of the newly created states to incorporate the institution of slavery within their borders.

California, with all of its faults, seismic and otherwise, remained whole. Governor Bigler's message to the Legislature in 1853 painted the picture of reality. California was a state that had gone from a population of 50,000 people to 300,000 in a matter of three years. Governor Bigler plainly stated, “In the present embarrassed condition of our State finances, it becomes us to search out every avenue to economy which does not entrench on principle or justice.”[9]

California had a debt of $2.2 million, annual expenses of $1.1 million, and an estimated revenue of $434,150.[10] The Governor placed much of the blame for the state's fiscal problems on its constitution. Governor Bigler proposed amending the constitution to make the legislature biennial, rather than annual, consolidating or eliminating some elected state elected officials, eliminating a constitutional provision mandating the printing of certain legislative bills, acts, and amendments, and finally, reducing legislative salaries and per diems.[11] And like all legislatures before and since, this one ignored the Governor's fiscal suggestions.

Amos P. Catlin

Land Grants

One issue that could not be ignored was the disposition of land ownership. For the most part, when California was flooded with gold seekers, the question of who held title to a particular swath of land was ignored. There were varying opinions on whether California, excluding Mexican and Spanish land grants, was owned by the federal or state government. There was never a consideration given to the right of Native Americans to any parcel of land. Even John Sutter's New Helvetia land grant, encompassing the emerging city of Sacramento, was called into question. The concerns over the legitimacy of the New Helvetia land grant led to the settlers' riots of 1850, where squatters contended the land was within the federal purview.

The numerous Mexican land grants were delineated most often in descriptive terms accompanied by crude maps. Outside of a well-defined river or stream, the foundation of land grant boundaries may have been a large oak tree, rock formations, or the beginning of low hills. One example of a topographical description is that of Leidesdorff land grant Rancho Rio de los Americanos.

"Beginning at an oak tree on the bank of the American River, marked as a boundary to the lands granted to John A. Sutter, and running thence south with the line of said Sutter two leagues; thence easterly, by lines parallel with the general direction of the said American River..."[12]

Land grant boundary lines were further complicated by the fact that the land grants were written in Spanish and some of the translations of the descriptive terms were open to interpretation. In the case of the Leidesdorff land grant, one of the descriptors was the Spanish term *lomeria*. Some people interpreted lomeria as low hills, range of hills, or foothills. Where the lomeria began was the eastern boundary of the grant. The final boundaries of the Mexican land grants were of intense interest to settlers who had already laid claim to a piece of property. The ultimate title to the land would be greatly impacted by whether the land was part of a land grant or under federal or state control. The Treaty of Guadalupe Hidalgo of 1848 between the U.S. and Mexico stipulated that the land grants would be honored.

In April of 1853, Amos presented three petitions to the Senate, signed by approximately 500 men from Sacramento, requesting a law releasing the state of California from any interest in potential land within the City of Sacramento.[13] The assumption was that the lands belonged to the state. By removing any potential claim to land within a Mexican or Spanish land grant, there would be one less party for the settlers to negotiate with in order to obtain clear titles to their land. Later in the legislative session, Amos introduced another petition from

Sacramento residents requesting an act to cede unoccupied lands over to the City of Sacramento.[14]

Prison Contract Stance Ethics

Amos was a genial and cordial man. He was not given to grandstanding or pontification for political benefit. What did trigger his ire was sanctioned government waste, bordering on corruption. California had been struggling with getting a state prison built. A bill before the Senate in late April sought to nullify an existing prison contract and replace it with a new contract. Amos took issue with the first prison contract and railed against the proposed iteration as laden with contractor gifts.

Speaking of the contractors who wanted a new contract and more money on the Senate floor in Benicia...

"Two years ago when we supposed we could not afford to build a prison, (and I apprehend we are in no better condition now) we gave away [prisoner] labor for ten years; and what was the price of this valuable gift, which has well been disposed of for $200,000? All we asked was that they should feed, clothe and keep them in security, and this they agreed to do; and entered into bonds to that effect in the sum of $100,000. No body doubts their ability to keep them in security – why not hold them to the bond? They have a good bargain and should not ask us to give $135,000 for their benefit – yes, for their benefit and not for the State – a prison will be of service to the State after the expiration of the lease and not before."[15]

Speaking of the new contract, Amos offered:

"This money will go like the $10,000 appropriated by the act of last winter for the purchase of a site for the prison, into the pockets of individuals instead of to the benefit of the State. They don't pretend that twenty acres of barren land was worth $500 per acre. I could have bought it for $10. They say the grantor of the land agreed to build a wharf upon it worth $5,000. What does the State want of a wharf at Court street? Why, sir, the wharf is for the benefit of the brickmakers in that vicinity. But they say there is a valuable quarry upon it worth $5,000. Who gets the marble from the quarry? Not the State. Why, sir, it is taken to San Francisco by individuals and sold by the parties interested in the labors of State prisoners. I would like to vote for the repeal of the State prison law of last year, incorporated in this bill, but in doing so I must vote for making another contract nearly as odious as that."[16]

Amos was not the only legislator to point out the embedded windfall benefits to the prison contractor at the expense of California. His speech on the deficiencies

Amos P. Catlin

of the prison contract spoke to his integrity and ethical standards. Amos could be brutally honest, much to the detriment of his own political capital. He would learn that he could not change politics or its actors. All he could do was to forcefully state the facts and use the element of logic to attempt to sway fellow legislators, or voters, to his opinion.

The legislators were meeting, working, and going absent in Benicia. The tiny community offered a locale bereft of distractions that would allow elected officials to focus on their duties. Benicia was a little too spartan for many of the men, who took the short steamer ride to San Francisco for long nights and days in the city. At this point, Sacramento still had some muscle as a destination supported by numerous hotels, meeting spaces, and saloons. Amos introduced legislation to move the State Capitol to Sacramento late in the 1853 session. In May, the Senate voted down Amos' bill and agreed to continue with Benicia as the capital.[17]

The Senate was controlled by the Democrats, and having the state capital closer to the Democratic stronghold of San Francisco seemed more reasonable. Amos was also a Whig, a minority in the Senate, and, as a freshman Senator, did not command as much respect as more senior Democratic legislators. There was no denying the growth and importance of Sacramento as a population hub and center of industrial activity. Amos introduced a bill to increase Sacramento County's representation to three Senators and six members of the Assembly. This bill, like the State Capital legislation, was never approved.[18]

For all of Amos' work in the legislature of 1853 on behalf of Sacramento County, he was awarded kindly platitudes by the Sacramento Union newspaper, which viewed Amos and his fellow Sacramento legislators in a favorable light. "They have also watched with sleepless vigilance the interests of the State of California as well as of the county of Sacramento, and whenever necessary have advocated those interests upon the floor of the Senate and Assembly, with an ability, ardent zeal, and high degree of patriotism unsurpassed by the Representatives of any other county in the State."[19]

Congratulatory newspaper ink aside, while Amos was fighting for a balanced state budget, his own balance sheet was deteriorating. William Willis, who had found his way back to Mormon Island, was demanding $150 Amos owed him.[20] In early February, W.T. Reilly informed Amos that a property arrangement had gone sour. Henry Tuttle had transferred title of the property to his sister and had no money. Tuttle offered to make weekly installments to repay Amos.[21]

Jerome Dutton, now managing the Exchange Hotel and other properties for Amos, reported that all of the boarders at the hotel, most of whom were miners, were gone. The water in the river was too high to carry out any mining operations. Should they close up the hotel, Dutton asked. On the bright side, Van Horn wanted

Amos P. Catlin

to pay some money he owed on a note to Amos, and another gentleman wanted to rent Amos' room.[22] Dutton's next letter posed a dilemma for Amos. A family wanted to rent his Mormon Island house for $100 per month.[23] Of course, since there were few boarders at the Exchange Hotel, Amos could find a room at his own boarding house.

Contractor Loan

The money Amos owed to individuals, along with the diminishing revenue from the Exchange Hotel and sawmill, were dwarfed by his monetary obligations to the Natoma Water Company. Late in paying his assessments for his designated Natoma Water Company shares, Amos was at real risk of losing his investment because the company needed the money to pay contractors Brooks and Clark. Charles Nichols outlined the dire situation to Amos in a letter on March 10, 1853.[24]

"I give you a brief acct of this day's proceedings. As soon as I saw Mr. Brooks I presented your matter to him whereon he very politely refused to comply leaving him to deliberate upon your proposition. I called a meeting of the board to take into consideration the selling of what few shares remained unpaid. Blakeley and your own being a majority of those in arrears. I therefore suggested to the board to extend the time of sale until the 19th inst. At which time I have ordered a general meeting of the stockholders at Willow Springs when I presume, we shall enter into a contract perhaps with B.C. & Co. [Brooks & Clark Co.] for the extension of the canal into the Rhodes Diggings.

"I would like very much if you could be here at the time as matters of considerable importance will be transacted. After the close of our meeting Brooks submitted the following proposition to me for your acceptance. Viz – that you now owe them in notes and interest $1,475 and that you pay upon your shares the six hundred dolls. That I am to be in receipt of, leaving a balance due on stock of $360, which added to the $1,475 will make $1,835…"[25]

The loan from Brooks provided for Amos to repay the note within 60 days at 3 percent interest.

Suddenly, it seemed, all these miners who had swept up thousands of dollars in placer gold from the river did not have a dime to their names. Nichols informed Amos that Mumford wanted to rent Amos' house, but Mumford did not have any rent money.[26] Amos contacted Harvey A. Thompson for a loan, but Thompson was short on cash also. Thompson did relay that water should be flowing in the Natoma ditch by the end of April. In addition, Messinger from the sawmill told Thompson that lumber prices had dropped to $50 per thousand feet and he couldn't keep the mill operating at those prices.[27]

Amos P. Catlin

Amos was able to make arrangements to hold onto his Natoma Water Company shares, but it was apparent that spending most of his time in Benicia as a Senator was complicating his business enterprises. There were many decisions that were being delayed, costing Amos money. Nichols wrote Amos that he could have rented his house to a family with money in hand, had he been able to communicate with Amos a week earlier.[28] Now the house sat empty because Mumford had no gold to pay rent. Mumford and Amos were eventually able to strike a deal, and Amos leased the Exchange Hotel saloon to Mumford for $100 a month.[29]

No one could give Amos a reality check like Luther Cutler, who dispensed with pleasantries in favor of raw reality. Cutler was also operating the first steam engine to mill small orders of lumber. Cutler informed Amos, "We have wore the Mill all most out and have got no money on it yet or I have not. I have something to eat and drink but no cloths to wear and I am ragged, so I dare not go out to the road for fear I should see some woman barefoot and sour. Miller from our Mill goes like hel thrasting [sic] rat."[30]

Cutler told Amos that everyone else in the sawmill business was doing better than they were. He had sold one load into Sacramento, but the roads were still muddy from spring rains. The mill had one regular customer at Mormon Island. Dallas Kneass ordered some lumber against an outstanding debt Amos owed to Kneass. Cutler would not release it without Amos' consent. Cutler had grown frustrated with the lack of communication regarding the mill business, not to mention the shares in the Natoma Water Company Amos had promised him.

"Please tell me if you have done anything about my shares in the matter so this is all that I can think of that is bad." Cutler finished up the letter with a friendly jab at his friend, "Write to me soon for G_d sake and let us know if you are in California. Come up soon if you don't I shall come down after you with a sharp stick."[31]

Dallas Kneass wrote to Amos that he lost a 2,600-foot order because Cutler would not release the lumber.[32] Cutler had written to Kneass to apologize for the delay in processing his lumber order. Cutler had to wait for Amos' approval. As there were no hauling teams around, the order would be further delayed.[33]

The apology from Cutler did not extinguish the anger Kneass felt toward Cutler. Kneass wrote to Cutler, "From the tone of your note you cannot know how affairs stand between us and as I never asked you to credit me or deliver me lumber on Mr. Catlin's acct. I only demanded that which is due me and I thought Mr. Catlin had the same interest in the lumber as you had."[34]

Kneass went on to outline a debt of $97.02 from October 1852 for flour, potatoes, butter, and beans. Amos also had a balance of another $507 from Kneass for other

Amos P. Catlin

supplies. "This amt. against Mr. C[atlin] has been running since March '52, over one year, so you see I did not ask for lumber before the amount has [been] due me."[35] Only Amos knew how much debt he owed to people scattered across the region.

Once the water from the Natoma ditch starting flowing down to Mormon Island it had immediate effects, but not necessarily of a positive nature. Dallas Kneass wrote to Amos in May of 1853 about errant sluicing for gold. Gold miners were directing water from the water ditch onto the riverbank to erode the soil into a sluice box. The heavier gold settled in grooves of the sluice box, while the bulk of the soil washed out to the river.

As Kneass explained, the miners were sluicing the riverbank and eroding land next to his garden. Plus, the miners were also sluicing close to the Mormon Island Cemetery. As a constituent of Senator Catlin's, Kneass wrote, "If you can have a bill passed to protect a man's property also for the protection of grave yards, as there is a number of [miners] washing down the grave yard hill and they have sluiced about 20 ft of the back part of my garden. At least a man's grave should be respected and protected by the law."[36]

Few California pioneers recognized the havoc they heaped up the land originally populated by Native Americans. Now that some of the immigrant miners had decided to permanently squat upon the federal land after they were through mining, they were suddenly concerned about the effects of their previous occupation. Like Amos, Kneass did not have any formal recognition of the ownership of the land he sat upon. It would not be until the federal government's public land surveys mapped out the Townships and Ranges that the squatters could officially file for a preemption and purchase the land from the federal government.

The deeds filed with the county, in most cases, transferred a right-of-use between individuals and created a historical record for legal disputes. The official recognition of a water canal, a legal issue that concerned Amos, was not confirmed until 1866. In that year the Thirty-Ninth Congress passed an act on July 26 that formally acknowledged and confirmed the rights of water canals.[37]

Kneass and all of the land holders who saw their property eroded or swamped with debris from hydraulic mining would have to wait until the Sawyer decision of 1884 that halted such mining operations. With the assumption that the Mormon Island town would not be sluiced down the American River, Kneass requested that Senator Catlin help him get the contract for the Post Office at Mormon Island.[38] Regardless of their business challenges or the money owed to Kneass, Amos was a State Senator who had some influence when it came to local, state, or federal decisions.

Amos P. Catlin

By the end of May 1853, Luther Cutler was feeling abandoned, as Amos focused on issues other than the lumber business. Cutler wrote Amos, "I would be pleased if you would come up hear [sic] and see this place once more. I want to know whare [sic] we are going to put this lumber and what it is best to do about a number of things. I have ben [sic] wanting to see you far [sic] the last three weeks. Please call up and see me, no one shall hurt you. Yours in hast[e] Luther Cutler"[39]

In reality, Amos was in no danger of being accosted. Cutler's comment about "no one shall hurt you" was a little joke. There was tension around the sawmill, lack of sales, and one sale was in dispute. On June 1st, Messinger notified Amos that he and Knowlton were leaving the sawmill partnership they had with Amos. They had found two men to take their place. One man, Mr. Taylor, owned the Shingle Springs House, and the second gentleman, Mr. Mallery, was a millwright. Messinger wanted to close up the partnership. Messinger wrote Amos that he could take what was owed to him in lumber, or they could set up a payment schedule for Amos to pay him for Messinger's expenses.[40]

Amos was involved in a lawsuit over lumber that was delivered and for which he had not been paid. W. S. Lorry, representing Amos in the lawsuit, informed Amos that Mr. Wells answered their complaint in court. Wells stated he paid $4,000 for lumber he never received. The lawsuit was set to be heard in the June term of the Court of Sessions in Sacramento.[41] The whole sawmill enterprise, between the steam engine, lumber sales, lumber yard, and operators of the mill, was a giant headache for Amos. What was once a promising investment became a constant tug on Amos' time, with very little return on the investment.

Since the close of the 1853 Senate session, Amos' attention was focused on reorganizing the Natoma Water Company. With changes to state law regarding corporations, Amos knew the company would have to formally incorporate. He sat down and drafted some corporate by-laws. One notable change was that the name would change to the Natoma Water and Mining Company. Amos drafted Article 8, "No share in arears for assessments due shall be entitled to vote on any question until such arears are paid in full.[42]

The water company held a shareholder meeting on June 1st at Willow Springs, where 193 of the 200 shares were represented. Amos, along with Thomas Williams, J. A. Perry, Lucien Brooks of Coloma, D.N. Hamilton of Mormon Island, Stroud of Placerville, and J. W. Colby of Sacramento, were elected to the Board of Directors.[43] Amos was the largest registered stockholder with 10 shares. The share price was $380.[44]

The corporation was notarized and submitted to the State of California on June 25, 1853. The incorporation papers noted a capital stock of $200,000 divided into 200 equal shares of $1,000 each. The paperwork was then officially submitted to

El Dorado and Sacramento counties, complete with a description of the purpose of the water canal and places in the respective counties where it would deliver water. Absent was any notification to the federal government over whose land the water ditch was traversing.

The Natoma Water Company was not the only organization building a water canal. John Harmon, an attorney in Coloma, sought advice from Amos regarding a water ditch he was representing. In the absence of any specific laws governing water ditches across federal property, attorneys were arguing their legal disputes on the fundamentals of common law, possession, and compliance with the local process of recording deeds.

"This whole question is [beset] with difficulties and our District Judge is rather of opinion that compliance with the [California] Act of 1852 as to recording the claim is essential to the maintenance of the possessory actions. Indeed, he yesterday, dissolved an injunction on this very ground in a case where the [plaintiff] had occupied the land since 1851 and [defendant] had recorded his claim some 5 weeks ago. The question, however, if the action on common law principles did not avail [plaintiff] because his land was not enclosed. This difficulty about these unrecorded claims must find its solution in the final decision of our courts as to whether they will, or will not, take judicial notice that the lands in California are public lands."[45]

Harmon thought that because the state was painted with Spanish and Mexican land grants, whose boundaries were not always easily definable by settlers, that proof of possession should take primacy when determining legal disputes until something better was devised by law.[46]

In October of 1853, a meeting of incorporated water companies was held. The object of the meeting was not to compare construction methods, but to discuss how to solidify land titles, easements, and protection of their dams and canals. These companies did not seek permission to build dams or cut canals into the sides of hills. They just started construction. The gamble was that the momentum and popular support for the mining industry would allow future laws to be retroactive to protecting their investments. For the most part, they were correct: they received favorable legislation and courtroom decisions.

The Natoma ditch was one of the larger water companies represented at the meeting. By comparison, the Bear River and Auburn Water and Mining Company, which would run a water ditch to Rattlesnake Bar, was capitalized at $650,000.[47] A smaller water canal venture on the opposite side of the South Fork of the American River from Amos' ditch, the Salmon Falls and Negro Hill Canal Company, had an investment of $25,000.[48] All of these water companies, and several others, gathered in Sacramento in October for a water ditch convention.[49]

Amos P. Catlin

Amos attended the convention representing the Natoma Water and Mining Company, along with Augustus Arrowsmith. Amos was appointed to a committee to draft a position paper outlining the perceived difficulties of constructing water projects and suggested legislation to grant certain rights to the water companies. As a California State Senator, who better to tackle proposed legislation than Amos?[50] The issues of water, water projects, and the role of water companies would eventually dominate California politics and economy. Water-related litigation would also play a significant role in Amos' future life as an attorney.

Before Amos could practice his preferred profession of attorney full-time, he had to attend to his water and lumber businesses first. On June 20th, the Natoma Water and Mining Company would vote to assess each stockholder an additional $20 per share for construction costs. Amos' assessment was $200, money that was not readily available to him at that time. He would make installment payments toward meeting the assessment on July 1st of $60, August 6th for $80, and finally a December 16th payment of $60.[51]

Even though there was a board to attend to the corporation, it fell to the President, Amos, to manage the stumbles that took place with the ditch construction. Augustus Arrowsmith wrote to Amos in July about lumber issues for the flume. The order of lumber was of the wrong type and delivered to the wrong place. Arrowsmith updated Amos that both the Negro Bar and Alder Creek flumes would be finished that week if he receives the ordered lumber. He concluded, "…but my hands are tied and I can do nothing. If the lumber is to come, send it along as soon as teams can haul it, if you cannot furnish it in time, let me know, as I am placed in a devilish unpleasant position with the miners."[52]

Amos Gets Sued

Amos was in an unpleasant situation himself. William Messinger commenced a complaint against him for the $774 owed from the dissolution of the sawmill partnership.[53] Among the expenses not reimbursed, Messinger claimed the cost of travel from Mormon Island to Coloma to pay Amos' taxes.[54] The court awarded a judgment to Messinger. Messinger's representative J.H. Gass wrote Amos in September about payment in the matter, "I have done nothing with the matter since the Judgement was entered up. If you will pay the judgement in that our order as Sale, it will save a considerable amount of cost. Let me hear from you in relation to the matter."[55]

Luther Cutler was also hounding Amos to go out and collect money on the sales he had shipped. The money was needed as Cutler informed Amos the boiler he was using to operate the small steam engine and cut lumber was beginning to fail. Cutler needed Amos to send up a repair man to patch it.[56] In order to meet his financial obligations, Amos arranged for a loan from A.A. Van Guildes for $1,000 with 5 percent interest. He secured the loan with three of his shares of the Natoma Water and Mining Company.[57]

Amos took a break from business to attend a candidates' forum at Mormon Island. He wrote a review each candidate's performance with an obvious bias for men of his political party. Amos praised Lauren Upson, who would become an editor at the Sacramento Union, for his clear explanation of the financial history of California. Sarcasm and ridicule were heaped upon one of the candidates who constantly interrupted the other speakers. Of the last speaker's address, Amos wrote, "He was repeatedly interrupted by Mr. Colby in anything but a courteous manner and that gentleman forced himself upon the stand which Mr. Johnson was speaking to contradict him by reading from a manuscript which he called a 'dockyment.' But he received payment with interest for his interference from the speaker's ready manner and superior knowledge of the subject."[58]

Sacramento Valley Railroad

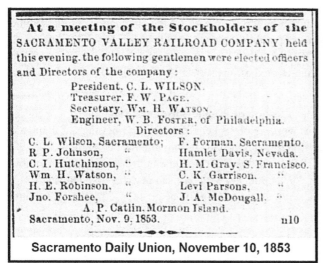

At a meeting of the Stockholders of the SACRAMENTO VALLEY RAILROAD COMPANY held this evening, the following gentlemen were elected officers and Directors of the company:

President, C. L. WILSON.
Treasurer, F. W. PAGE.
Secretary, WM. H. WATSON.
Engineer, W. B. FOSTER, of Philadelphia.

Directors:

C. L. Wilson, Sacramento;   F. Forman, Sacramento.
R. P. Johnson,   "   Hamlet Davis, Nevada.
C. I. Hutchinson, "   H. M. Gray, S. Francisco.
Wm. H. Watson, "   C. K. Garrison,   "
H. E. Robinson,   "   Levi Parsons,   "
Jno. Forshee,   "   J. A. McDougall,   "
        A. P. Catlin, Mormon Island.
Sacramento, Nov. 9, 1853.   n10

Sacramento Daily Union, November 10, 1853

8. Amos Catlin listed as a Director for the Sacramento Valley Railroad, 1853.

While Amos was undertaking to build a dam across the South Fork of the American River and the miles of water canals, the only way to get from Mormon Island to Sacramento was by foot, horseback, buggy or stagecoach. The proposition of a railroad line from Sacramento to the gold fields, beginning at Negro Bar, just below Mormon Island, was universally encouraged. The construction of a railroad faced similar problems to that of building a water ditch. Aside from raising the capital, there were issues with engineering and easements across land of which ownership (federal, state, land grant, or individual) had not been wholly determined.

Amos P. Catlin

Nonetheless, Amos subscribed to twenty shares of the Sacrament Valley Railroad[59] and was then appointed to the Board of Directors.[60] This was the third attempt at organizing and capitalizing a railroad that would become the first on the West Coast. The short-line railroad, 22 miles from Sacramento to Folsom, would face other challenges with management and funding. Amos would form a life-long friendship with the current president of the Sacramento Valley Railroad, Charles Lincoln Wilson, and forge a relationship with Lester L. Robinson. He would also become well acquainted with Theodore Judah and maintain close ties with Anna Judah after Theodore's death. Of course, it was politically advantageous to have an elected state senator as a shareholder and on the Board of Directors for the fledgling railroad.

Negro Bar Meeting

Just as water projects and railroad construction moved forward, so did politics. Amos attended the Whig convention in Sacramento and nominated Henry Eno, formerly of New York, now residing in Calaveras County, for Lieutenant Governor.[61] Eno's nomination was supported by the convention. In the summer of 1853, Amos was part of a political debate held at Negro Bar, attended mainly by the local miners. Estimates put the meeting attendance at 150 men, who gathered to listen to local elected officials discuss regional and state affairs.[62]

Amos approached the debate as if he were arguing a court case; he had the facts and worked to direct the attention of the audience toward the logical conclusion that the Whig party was working on its behalf. He began pointing out that under Democratic Governor Bigler, the State was falling into debt at a rate of $700,000 per year.[63] Some $218,000 of this deficit spending was attributed to public printing expenses that were contracted with partisan newspapers.[64] In an effort to close the spending gap, a new tax on mining had been proposed and was attributed to the Whig Party.

In reality, as Amos pointed out, the mining claim tax was introduced by Democrat Senator Hubbs,[65] and only an amendment had been proposed by a Whig Party member. The author of the bill or amendment was of little consequence to Amos. The central focus of the convention was on the great question of the day that hobbled California on many different fronts: Who owned the land? Amos went to great lengths to show that mining claims were not considered taxable property because they were on land owned by the United States. However, if the Supreme Court decision was correct, and the mines belonged to the state of California, then the state could consider a mining claim tax as a source of revenue.[66]

Amos P. Catlin

Stand Against Land Grab

Amos had spent so much time detailing the jurisdictional aspects of land ownership, he was not able to finish his attack on Gov. Bigler's proposed extension of the San Francisco waterfront.[67] The hour-long dissertation on state budgets, property ownership, and Supreme Court decisions, recited extemporaneously, without notes, cemented the image of Amos as a man in command of the facts. There could be little room to question Amos' legal acumen. Nor could Amos' ethical standards be called into question. He resumed his forceful denunciation of the San Francisco waterfront extension, routinely appended with the term "swindle" in local papers, at a Whig meeting later in the month. Similar to the sweetened prison contract, Amos showed how the originators of the waterfront extension would profit from the provision and new land.[68]

Amos was one of the speakers at a Sacramento meeting on reforming a government that was increasingly seen as corrupt.[69] There were numerous government acts, laws, and proposed legislation with hidden measures to enrich politicians, contractors, and businesses friendly with the Bigler administration. This bothered Amos, and many other men, as they saw this new state of California crumbling before it got off the ground.

Whether Amos liked it or not, his attendance was requested at a Social Ball held at Smith's Exchange in the Natoma Valley, not far from Mormon Island.[70] Amos was not a particularly gregarious individual or a man given to ingratiating chatter with strangers and voters. But there was no escaping the reality that Amos was now the president of a developing water company, a State Senator, and on the board of the Sacramento Valley Railroad. He would attend social events when necessary and, later in life, avoided all those he thought were superfluous.

1854 Senate Session

A new year dawned in California. Senator Amos Catlin, representing Sacramento County, was dutifully present at the opening of the Fifth Senate session in Benicia in January 1854.[71] The second largest state in the Union, California's 163,696 square miles of land had never been accurately mapped. Everyone knew that California's topography was diverse, with soaring mountain ranges, huge deserts, long ocean coastline, and fertile Central Valley waiting for irrigation, but state legislators did not have anything resembling an accurate map of the state.

One of the first pieces of business for Amos in the new session was to propose a resolution requesting the Secretary of State to provide the legislature with any information he may have had regarding the publication of an official state map.[72] The resolution was adopted. Amos was assigned to the Claims, Commerce and

Navigation, and Judiciary committees. The assignment to the Judiciary Committee was a new one for Amos, a tacit acknowledgement of his legal knowledge.

In what would turn out to be a stunning understatement, the Sacramento Daily Union reported on the activities of the Legislature in Benicia by reporting, "Nothing of particular interest transpired in either branch of the Legislature, yesterday. Mr. Catlin, in the Senate, gave notice of intention at an early day to introduce a bill for the permanent location of the seat of Government."[73] From the perspective of some of the Senators, Amos introducing a bill to move the State Capitol was just a rerun of his failed 1853 attempt and not particularly noteworthy. However, 1854 was a new year, and Amos had a better understanding of how the political game was played.

Most of the men elected to the 1854 California Senate were not originally from California. At best, they were only residents in the past five years, having migrated to California in 1849 during the Gold Rush. While some men had put down roots in one location early on, the new residents in California were mobile, moving between different mining claims, from tent to cabin to wood frame house, and were constantly displaced by floods and fire.

Consequently, having a state capital that had moved from San Jose, to Vallejo, then to Benicia, was inconvenient, but also in accordance with the experience of most California newcomers. The state was just a toddler compared to its established counterparts on the Eastern Seaboard with rich colonial histories. California was a petri dish of different organisms growing on the substrate of mining, agriculture, and transportation. Small communities were forming all over the state, and only time would determine if they would be viable.

Sacramento was one of those communities that exploded. It was the gateway to the mining districts along the forks of the American River. The Sacramento River offered the watercourse to deliver men and supplies from San Francisco. Sutter's Fort was seen as a modest symbol that, in addition to providing some shelter, demonstrated that the interior of California was suitable for habitation.

Land speculators quickly secured title to the land from John Sutter's son and began mapping and selling lots. Sacramento had its problems. There were questions over Sutter's land title that led to a settler's riot. There were a cholera outbreak and the flood of 1850 that surprised many of the new inhabitants. But Sacramento had many advantages, including two rivers, flat topography, arable soil for agriculture, and wide-open expanses for ranching.

Communities live and die by their associated business interests. There must be wealth generators in order for the community to create a sustainable circulation of goods, services, and money. Sacramento had the base business to sustain itself. Not only was Sacramento importing mining supplies, building materials, and people, it was also exporting gold and a growing list of agricultural products. This meant that Sacramento was less dependent on one industry and slightly more insulated from macro-economic downturns.

As a testament to Sacramento's industrial spirit and desire to grow, the Sacramento Valley Railroad was forging ahead in the midst of uncertain expenses and management. Even with the challenges the railroad company faced, few other communities could boast of serious railroad plans. The Natoma Water and Mining Company, led by Amos himself, was pushing forward with a water works project that would ultimately deliver water into Sacramento County.

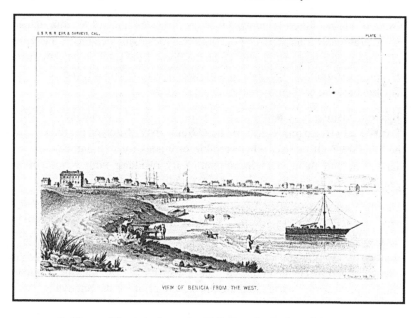

VIEW OF BENICIA FROM THE WEST.

9. View of Benicia from the U.S. Pacific Railroad Survey.

While Benicia did not have the economic engine that Sacramento was developing, it was quiet and easy to get to, as it was situated on the Carquinez Strait, where steamers from San Francisco up to Sacramento passed on a daily basis. Benicia also lacked any serious discussion or attempt by its representatives to keep the State Capitol with proposals to build additional buildings for the government. Other communities seemed more eager to host California's Capital by putting forth proposals to house the various branches of government.

Amos P. Catlin

One argument in Benicia's favor was the Pacific Railroad Surveys. Authorized by Congress in 1852, the Pacific Railroad Surveys were designed to determine the most practical rail route from east out to the Pacific Ocean. Benicia, on the north side of the Carquinez Strait, had a relatively wide and flat topography extending into water. This landscape made Benicia a good candidate for the terminus of a rail line where goods and people could then be transferred to ships for the final leg to San Francisco.

Push to Move Capitol to Sacramento

Fellow senators opposed to moving the Capital from Benicia to Sacramento presented some of their objections in a minority report on the introduced legislation. Many of their arguments were as flimsy as some of the mining cabins they had previously inhabited. Opponents noted the quaint lock on the Sacramento Court House safe, the partitions by which the floors were subdivided, and a nearby house of prostitution,[74] the location of which was no doubt known to many legislators because of their own previous patronage.

Legislators wishing to remain in Benicia also countered that Sacramento offered no great benefit based on its location. In addition, they estimated the removal costs to be $46,000.[75] Of course, other credible estimates for moving expenses were much lower, and there were Sacramento City residents who were willing to indemnify the State for the amount of $30,000 for the cost of removal.[76]

In less than seven days after Amos had introduced his Capital removal bill, the Senate voted it down, 14 to 19.[77] Shortly after the vote, Senator Hall from Livermore[78] announced his intention to convene a joint resolution with the Assembly on the removal of the Capital from Benicia.[79] While the Sacramento newspapers had been favorable to the prospect of moving the Capital to Sacramento, they now started making the case in print for the removal.

In 1854, California had an official population of 264,000 residents.[80] Given that a majority of the citizens resided in Northern California at the time, the Sacramento Daily Union determined that three-quarters or 176,000 residents, could communicate with their representative in Sacramento within 24 hours.[81]

The Union went on to illustrate how Sacramento was the hub of communication for most of the state. Sacramento had fourteen stage lines that left the city daily, plus two to four steamboats that traveled to San Francisco on a daily basis and made runs up to Marysville and Colusa. In addition, Sacramento had numerous telegraph lines radiating from the city, and their reach to various parts of the state was growing steadily. As a matter of pride, Sacramento was on track, within a

Amos P. Catlin

couple of years, to have one of the first fully functioning railroad lines to major gold mining regions.[82]

After laying out its arguments for Sacramento as being a communication hub in California, and thereby a perfect place for the State Capitol, the Sacramento Union concluded, "If these considerations are insufficient to overcome the opposition of Senators, we conclude that nothing would, unless they give way under direct instructions from their constituents."[83]

The Grass Valley Telegraph published a letter drafted by local residents, and signed by over 500 additional men, stating the unanimous opinion, regardless of political affiliation, that Sacramento should be the Capital of California. The letter argued, "...Sacramento in every light in which she may be considered is the great interior central city of the State, commanding all advantages of a frequent, rapid and varied communication with every part of California, thus affording with readiness all the means and facilities of general intelligence and knowledge, which are eminently necessary to the enactment of wise and useful laws. The easy accessibility of the Capital of a State to the constituency of the Legislature is a matter of important moment among the interests of a Commonwealth."[84]

By the end of January, numerous legislators had introduced petitions from their districts requesting that the capital be moved from Benicia.[85] The citizens of Sutter Creek, in their resolution, made perhaps one of the more elegant appeals for making Sacramento the State Capital.

"Whereas, in the opinion of this meeting, Sacramento city is more acceptable to a majority of the citizens of California than any other point proposed for the permanent capital of the State; and whereas, her citizens have evinced a spirit of energy, perseverance and liberality unsurpassed in the history of this, or perhaps any other state; and whereas, in the opinion of this meeting, it would be greatly to the interest of this county, as well as of the State at large, to locate the State capital permanently in that city; therefore, Resolved, That we respectfully request the Calaveras delegation now in the Legislature of this State, to use their utmost exertions to locate the capital permanently at Sacramento city."[86]

With the exception of the Alta California newspaper, which wanted the State Capitol in San Francisco, most newspapers were calling for the removal of the capital to Sacramento.[87]

As public opinion was growing in support of Sacramento as the State Capital, the deficiencies of Benicia were being felt. Numerous bills were held up due to a lack of meeting rooms where legislative committees could review and report back to the respective chambers.[88] The legislature was also struggling with absentee members: It seems the short steam boat ride from Benicia to San Francisco helped

Amos P. Catlin

create four-day weekends for the legislators. Often falling short of a quorum before and after the long weekends, the legislature's work week effectively was reduced to three days.[89]

The San Francisco Chronicle called for the Capital to be located anywhere but Benicia. In short, the editors opined, there were too many distractions in San Francisco, pulling the legislators away from their work like a magnet. Sacramento, with fewer temptations for extended relaxation, was a better location to sequester the legislators while they were in session, leading to higher productivity.

Amos introduced another bill in the Senate in early February to permanently move the Capital to Sacramento.[90] Other bills were also introduced to either move the capital to another city, send the question to the voters, or delay the relocation until after the current legislative session.[91] Amos' bill, "To provide for the permanent location of the seat of government at Sacramento," had its first reading on February 15th and was referred to the Finance Committee. The Finance Committee reported the bill back to the full Senate without any recommendation on February 16th.[92]

With the relocation bill back before the full Senate, Amos laid out some of the logistics of the facilities and move to Sacramento. He presented an order of the Court of Sessions of Sacramento County tendering the use of the Court House and rooms for the state officers as long as the legislature might require them. In addition, Amos outlined the bonds offered by Mayor Hardenburgh of Sacramento and Ferris & Smith in the amount of $30,000 for the transportation of the archives, members of the legislature, and State officers to permanently move from Benicia to Sacramento.[93]

One legislator questioned the legality of Sacramento city offering bonds as potentially beyond the scope of the city charter.[94] Upon the final reading of the bill, it was passed 15 to 12 in the Senate. The one caveat noted was that Senator Crabb voted for the bill and the inference was made that Crabb would likely call for a reconsideration of the vote.[95] Two days later, the bill was called up for reconsideration, along with all manner of parliamentary procedures to delay or kill the bill altogether.[96]

Even after the passage, the senatorial assault on the bill continued. Senator Colby moved to strike from the title of the bill the words "permanent location at Sacramento" and insert "capital of the State." Senator Smith offered an amendment to change the title to the "Seat of Government to San Jose."[97] Amos, who had been most diplomatic through the political charade of trying to kill his legislation, called the men to order. He deftly noted that no amendment could be offered to a bill that destroyed or changed the meaning of its subject. Senator

Amos P. Catlin

Tuttle argued that a title change was not an essential feature to its full force and effect.[98]

After what seemed like an endless barrage of maneuvers and tactics to scuttle the removal bill, the Senate swatted down the attempts to derail the legislation. Amos offered a resolution that the Secretary of the Senate be instructed to report the bill to the Assembly immediately.[99] On February 23rd, the Assembly received the Senate bill and referred it to the Public Buildings and Grounds committee for ascertaining the cost of removal.[100]

Additional Assembly amendments were offered in an effort to bind up the legislation. There was the amendment to delay the removal by 40 days, change the capital to Marysville, and another to discontinue the legislative per diems while the move was in progress.[101] None of the amendments passed.

When the different amendments had been offered and voted down, Assemblyman Hunter from Los Angeles resorted to bribery allegations. Hunter said he had heard from a good authority that the Capital had not been moved to Sacramento earlier because Mayor Hardenburgh would not buy Judge McGowan a house for $3,000. This exploded the Assembly into a flurry of disbelief and recriminations. Assemblyman Conness, born in Ireland and later selected as a U.S. Senator in 1863, objected to the insinuation without evidence.[102]

Assemblyman Hunter continued that the constant interruptions of a certain gentleman reminded him of the Irishman's fly that was in everybody's dish. Hunter was chastised for his bigoted remarks pertaining to a person's nationality. The San Francisco representatives were particularly irked. Assemblyman Bradford surmised that any man who left his native country of his own accord and adopted the laws and customs of the United States was more to be honored than one born on this soil, and was thus an American citizen by accident.[103]

On February 25, 1854, Governor Bigler signed legislation to permanently move California's Capital to Sacramento.[104] The Senate and Assembly then passed a concurrent resolution that when they adjourned on the 25th, they would convene in Sacramento the next week.[105] The furniture from Benicia arrived by March 1st, but the first substantive session of the legislature did not occur until March 3rd in Sacramento.[106]

Amos P. Catlin

Sacramento, often referred to as the "Queen City of the Plains," was now the State's Capital.[107] It took quite a battle in a short period of time for Amos to get his legislation approved. As the State's Capital, Sacramento would become the center of political activity, hosting numerous conventions throughout the 19th century. At the time, the city of Sacramento had only

10. California State Capitol, Sacramento, 1879.

been in existence for six years, not really enough time to fully anticipate the natural hazards of its location at the intersection of two major waterways: the Sacramento and American rivers.

Even though Sacramento had been addressing the known flooding issues by constructing some modest berms that passed for levees at the time, no one was prepared for the flood of 1862. The epic rainfall, beginning in winter of 1861, would create a massive flood in Sacramento that forced newly elected Governor Leland Stanford to travel by rowboat to his Sacramento inauguration. However, by 1862, California's government was tightly tucked into Sacramento as the State Capitol building was being built. There was little chance of the designation of Capital being removed from Sacramento.

Amos may have raised a glass of wine with fellow supporters at his accomplishment at moving the Capital to Sacramento, but no large party was held. That was not Amos' style. There was also little mention that Amos Catlin was a Whig, a minority party in the legislature. He was able to persuade his fellow party members and many Democrats, the majority party, that Sacramento was, at the time, the right place for the State's Capital. He was the Whig who put Sacramento on the map for years to come.

Hospital Tax and Other Bills

Amos was not a one-issue wonder. Other state and local issues occupied his energies in the Senate. Elected officials who did not like the new Sacramento location sought to wiggle out of conducting business at the new Capital. Amos authored a bill to require the Supreme Court to hold its sessions at Sacramento.[108] He would also introduce legislation to fix the offices of the Governor, Secretary of State, Comptroller, Treasurer, and Surveyor General in Sacramento.[109] The actions of Senator Amos Catlin were meant to organize and centrally locate California's growing executive bureaucracy within the city limits of Sacramento.

The disconnected State departments and operations were highlighted when the State of California missed its bond interest payment to creditors in New York in January of 1854. The banking house Duncan, Sherman & Co. stepped forward and fulfilled the payment while the California Treasurer sorted out what happened.[110] This embarrassing blunder of incompetence spurred Amos to introduce a resolution requesting the Treasurer furnish the Senate a complete statement of public monies deposited with Palmer, Cook & Co., the banking house responsible for paying the state's bond interest.[111] In order to keep the finances closer to Sacramento, Amos introduced a bill that would require the Treasurer to deposit funds with a local Sacramento banking house.[112] Amos would revisit the transparency of the banking operations of the Treasurer in a few more years, as an Assembly member investigating a different Treasurer for embezzlement.

Sacramento was under pressure to deliver services to its growing population. As a matter of financing public infrastructure, the city had issued bonds in excess of its forecasted property tax revenues. The charters issued to cities by the state were very narrow in scope with limited authority to tax residents. Amos introduced a bill to allow Sacramento to levy a tax of one percent on property to retire the city's indebtedness.[113]

A more specific tax levy was aimed at retiring the debt Sacramento had incurred by treating hundreds of people stricken with cholera at the local hospital from 1850.[114] Amos followed up with additional hospital tax legislation in 1854 to increase the tax levy to fund the County Hospital to care for indigent residents.[115] Sacramento, because of its location in the Central Valley, was the focal point for people throughout Northern California residing in communities with very few community support services such as hospitals. This burden of community service, from hospital care to law enforcement, would only increase after the construction of Folsom Prison.

Slavery Questions

The California constitution banned slavery within the state's border, but the stench of the institution continued to pervade the Capital. As most of California's elected representatives were Democrats and sympathetic to the institution of slavery, in 1852 they passed a California fugitive slave act. It allowed slave owners who brought their enslaved individuals to California before it became a state, to confiscate the slaves and return them to the owner's slave state. This act was set to expire on April 15, 1854.[116]

In March 1854, the Assembly passed a bill granting a one-year extension for slave owners to hunt down individuals they owned. Most of the rancorous debate happened in the Assembly before the bill was passed and sent to the Senate. The extension raised serious constitutional questions by allowing recaptured slaves no bail, no attorney for legal defense, and no appeal before being forcefully taken by the slave owner on little more than an affidavit presented to a local Justice of the Peace.[117]

Amos voted in favor of the extension under the fugitive slave act.[118] After the vote, a furious physical fight broke out between Senator Colby, who voted against the bill, and proponent Senator Leake. Leake struck Colby with his walking stick as Colby sat writing at his desk. Colby rose and tackled Leake, and the confrontation continued on the floor until they were separated.[119]

Amos was not from a slave state, and he never owned slaves. However, there were many men who thought the institution of slavery to be an anathema but were willing to tolerate it based on the principle of federalism, or states' rights. At the national level, the Kansas-Nebraska Act was being considered in Congress. This act would repeal the Missouri compromise and allow new states and territories to decide if they wanted the institution of slavery within their borders. The Nebraska Act was an extension of the Compromise of 1850, which admitted California as a free state and left the question of slavery in newly acquired territories after the Mexican-American war up to residents in those regions.

In April of 1854, a resolution endorsing the Nebraska Act was introduced into the California Senate. An alternate endorsement also was introduced, with different language but the same states' rights theme. The resolution specifically stated, "…That all questions involving personal freedom and title to slaves, shall be decided by the local tribunals of the States and Territories, with right of appeal to the Supreme Court of the United States."[120]

Many California legislators did not want to be tethered to the term "abolitionist" even if they were against slavery. A move toward the abolition of the institution of slavery would most certainly result in a civil war. California's constitution banned slavery, thus conveying a certain degree of absolution from the question of slavery in the rest of the country. There was a fear that if the Nebraska Act proposed by Senator Douglas prevailed, California could be surrounded by slave-holding states in the future. The concern was not so much for the welfare of the slaves, but for the potential loss of manufacturing jobs in the state due to cheap labor provided by slaves just across state lines. Regardless of the realities, many

Amos P. Catlin

of California's elected officials wanted to endorse the Nebraska Act, if for no other reason than to support the sovereignty of states to make their own decisions, free from interference from the federal government. There was also recognition that California statehood was a product of a compromise in 1850, which in large measure superseded the 1820 compromise.

The Senate resolution supporting the Nebraska Act was passed on April 20th, with Amos voting in favor with the majority of other Senators.[121] Conjecture by some elected officials and newspapers was that the Nebraska Act put the United States one step closer to being torn apart over the issue of slavery. One of the defining issues for legislators voting for the resolution was the position that California should not attempt to dictate how another state handles its business.

Of course, in just six short years, the nation would be embroiled in a civil war. Most of the politicians who vociferously supported the Fugitive Slave Act and the Nebraska Act would suddenly become rock-solid Union men. Their memories of having supported slavery would be only foggy recollections, and they would support the full intervention of the federal government in states that wanted to secede and had waged war against the United States.

While Amos did not have the booming oratory of the politician he admired, Henry Clay, he rarely shrank away from standing on any platform to espouse his political convictions. On the issues of the fugitive slave act and the Nebraska Act resolution, he was notably quiet. Politics was a queer and dirty business. The Whig Party back East favored the abolition of slavery if not a containment. The Whigs in California were more closely aligned with the Democrats. There was even a movement within the California Whig Party to support splitting California into multiple states so some could ratify slavery into their constitutions.

Amos was not friendly to the latter idea, nor was he interested in a cozy relationship with Democrats. On these counts, as well as his New York roots, Amos was asked to stand aside as a congressional Whig candidate at the party's state convention.[122] It would not be the last time Amos would feel like an outsider in his own political party. Until the Whig Party imploded at the next election cycle, he defended the Whig Party and its principles.

A reporter for the Alta California attended the July Whig State Party convention in Sacramento and noted that Amos, to the great regret of many in the state, would not run again for the Senate nor would he be a candidate for Congress.[123] The reporter's correspondence continued, "The heat in this place is perfectly unbearable. San Francisco, with all thy winds, I love thee. It [Sacramento heat] is of a most peculiar description, oppressing every muscle and sinew in the human frame, and from 10 o'clock A. M. until 6 P. M. rendering a man, as far as activity is concerned, perfectly helpless. Why they hold conventions, which naturally

Amos P. Catlin

engender heat, in such a hot place as this? I cannot conceive, unless it is that perspiration may have its effect. – B."[124]

Common Law Settler's Rights

The heat would continue, as is typical in Sacramento through the summer months, and was present during a Settlers' Committee meeting in late August. From the early days of the Gold Rush, an active Settlers' Committee routinely gathered in Sacramento to discuss issues pertinent to settlers and endorse political candidates. The Whig Party was generally seen as more friendly to settlers' rights than Democrats.

The genesis of the Settlers' Committee was rooted in the early disputes over Sacramento land. Land speculators, aligned with John Sutter Jr., had acquired most of the lots within the boundaries of the city and were forcing settlers, many of whom had come to work in the gold mines, off of the land in Sacramento. California had not yet become a state, the Sutter land grant was in question, and it seemed absurd to many immigrants that they had to move their canvas tents and wooden shanties off of lots owned by a few individuals speculating on land prices. Amos and John Currey being among the land speculators.

The land speculators called the Gold Rush immigrants "squatters"; the immigrants called themselves "settlers." The ongoing confrontation between immigrants and landowners convulsed into a riot in August of 1850, in which several men on both sides were killed. After the conflagration, physical hostilities faded, Sacramento continued on its course of subdivision, and the settlers continued to advocate for their perceived land rights.

The notion or definition of a "settler," who had some entitlement to public land newly acquired in the United States, seemed to morph depending on the perspective and experience of the individual. The popular perception was that a settler was an immigrant to California and, by virtue of being a United States citizen, had a right to public land to settle on for the purposes of farming, ranching, mining, or industrial enterprises. By this definition, virtually all of the immigrants were settlers in California.

The conflict arose between those settlers who just wanted a little piece of public land to call home and those settlers who acquired large tracts of land and lots, preventing an agrarian settlement. Large swaths of land were already tied up in Mexican and Spanish land grants. Sutter's land grant encompassed Sacramento City. The Alexander Leidesdorff land grant, by 1854 controlled by Captain Joseph Libbey Folsom, spanned 30,000 acres south of the American River up to Negro Bar. North of the American River were the Rancho Del Paso and San Juan land grants.

Amos P. Catlin

Layered on top of the land grants were the developments of the planned Sacramento Valley Railroad from Sacramento up to Negro Bar and new water canals being constructed along the North and South Forks of the American River. There was added confusion with respect to land ownership: California had just created a land grant commission to perfect the boundaries of those tracts of land, and the federal Public Land Survey System had only just begun to create a systematic map grid of the state. Consequently, California was constantly grappling with balancing the interests of large landowners with the demands of settlers.

Amid the dynamically changing landscape that was California in 1854, the Settlers' Committee hosted a public meeting where Democrat and Whig party candidates could discuss their positions relative to the settlers' interests. Mr. Turner, a Democrat from Mormon Island and candidate for Assembly, spoke first. The Whig Party candidate, Mr. Meredith, was not in attendance, but Amos was at the meeting. In the absence of any Whig candidate, the audience called for Amos to speak, and he obliged. As he noted before his comments, Amos had come to hear the discussion about protecting settlers' rights, not the comparative merits of Whiggery or Democracy.[125]

On that hot August evening, Amos stood before the assembled crowd not as a candidate for political office. His identity as a settler may have been a point of consternation for some people, as he was an investor in a railroad, was developing a water system, and was neither a farmer nor a rancher. He took the opportunity to address the fundamental problems encountered by settlers when it came to political promises from either side. The issue, as Amos saw it, was peculiar to California because of the nature of the state's birth.

As gold-seeking immigrants were streaming into California in 1848 and 1849, the region was governed by Common Law. Disputes, crime, and land boundaries were adjudicated by the inherited Mexican Alcalde system, along with local rules and rights established by mining regions. A large component of Common Law was local customs and precedents. It wasn't until California became a state, adopted a constitution, and began passing legislation that statutory law became the rule of the land.

Amos' comments were captured by a reporter for the Sacramento Daily Union and paraphrased in a story about the Settlers' Committee meeting. As the law related to settlers' rights, Amos lectured:

"The principle was a just one, and was recognized by the Common Law, though not to the extent demanded by the peculiar situation of the people of California, which had no precedent in the history of the settlement of any State. The Common Law which was in force in this State, in the strictness of its reasoning could not

Amos P. Catlin

separate the improvements from the soil itself. When a principle of the Common Law, the offspring of by-gone feudal ages, becomes unsuited to the condition of the people, and oppressive in its operation, it should be, and often has been relaxed, modified and annulled. For this purpose are statutes enacted to extend or curtail, its principles as circumstances may require. Such a change as will secure to the settler his portion of what constitutes the value of the land, and to the owner of the soil that which in equity belongs to him, is what is demanded, and should be granted. If the settlers asked anything more than that he was not aware of it."[126]

In an effort to bolster the credentials of Whig candidates, Amos pointed out that it was Henry Clay, a Whig, who helped devise the Pre-Emption Act of 1841 that helped settlers purchase public land at reasonable prices.

It was this sort of honest, historical, and pedagogical oratory that endeared Amos to so many people. The speech also provides a glimpse of the real Amos Catlin. He was a man smitten with the law. He loved reading about the law, discussing it, and practicing it. He mined for gold, built water dams and canals, and was at times happy to be an elected official, all for the sake of paying his bills. But his true passion, the thing he lived for, was the law.

---

[1] Daily Alta California, Volume 3, Number 321, 20 November 1852

[2] Daily Alta California, Volume 4, Number 26, 7 January 1853

[3] Sacramento Daily Union, Volume 4, Number 560, 8 January 1853

[4] Daily Alta California, Volume 4, Number 39, 9 February 1853

[5] A.T. Arrowsmith letter to Amos Catlin, Vallejo, January 1853. San Francisco History Center of the San Francisco Public Library.

[6] Sacramento Daily Union, Volume 8, Number 1224, 24 February 1855

[7] Letter, George Williams to Senator Catlin, March 9, 1853. Bancroft Library, BANC C – B 626 Box 1

[8] Sacramento Daily Union, Volume 4, Number 603, 28 February 1853

[9] Journal of the Senate of the State of California, Fourth Session, 1853. San Francisco, George Kerr, State Printer.

[10] Journal of the Senate of the State of California, Fourth Session, 1853. San Francisco, George Kerr, State Printer.

[11] Journal of the Senate of the State of California, Fourth Session, 1853. San Francisco, George Kerr, State Printer.

[12] United States v. Halleck et al., U.S. Supreme Court, December 1863.

[13] Sacramento Daily Union, Volume 5, Number 646, 19 April 1853

[14] Sacramento Daily Union, Volume 5, Number 661, 6 May 1853

[15] Sacramento Daily Union, Volume 5, Number 654, 28 April 1853

[16] Sacramento Daily Union, Volume 5, Number 654, 28 April 1853

[17] Sacramento Daily Union, Volume 5, Number 669, 16 May 1853

[18] Sacramento Daily Union, Volume 5, Number 662, 7 May 1853

[19] Sacramento Daily Union, Volume 5, Number 670, 17 May 1853

[20] Letter, William Willis to Amos Catlin, January 21, 1853. Bancroft Library, BANC MSS C – B 626 Box 1

[21] Letter, W.T. Reilly to Amos Catlin, February 4, 1853. California State Library, Catlin Collection Box 150

Amos P. Catlin

[22] Letter, Jerome Dutton to Amos Catlin, February 14, 1853. California State Library, Catlin Collection Box 150

[23] Letter, Jerome Dutton to Amos Catlin, March 5, 1853. Bancroft Library, BANC MSS C – B 626 Box 1

[24] Letter, Charles Nichols to Amos Catlin, March 10, 1853. Wells Fargo History, Wiltsee Collection

[25] Letter, Charles Nichols to Amos Catlin, March 10, 1853. Wells Fargo History, Wiltsee Collection

[26] Letter, Charles Nichols to Amos Catlin, March 10, 1853. Wells Fargo History, Wiltsee Collection

[27] Letter, H.A. Thompson to Amos Catlin, April 22, 1853, Folsom Historical Museum Archives

[28] Letter, Charles Nichols to Amos Catlin, March 10, 1853. Wells Fargo History, Wiltsee Collection

[29] Lease agreement, Mumford and Amos Catlin, March 20, 1853. California State Library, Catlin Collection Box 149

[30] Letter, Luther Cutler to Amos Catlin, April 23, 1853. California State Library, Catlin Collection Box 150

[31] Letter, Luther Cutler to Amos Catlin, April 23, 1853. California State Library, Catlin Collection Box 150

[32] Letter, Dallas Kneass to Amos Catlin, April 23, 1853. California State Library, Catlin Collection Box 150

[33] Letter, Luther Cutler to Dallas Kneass, April 26, 1853. California State Library, Catlin Collection Box 150

[34] Letter, Dallas Kneass to Luther Cutler, April 26, 1853. California State Library, Catlin Collection Box 150

[35] Letter, Dallas Kneass to Luther Cutler, April 26, 1853. California State Library, Catlin Collection Box 150

[36] Letter, Dallas Kneass to Amos Catlin, April 23, 1853. California State Library, Catlin Collection Box 150

[37] Water & Mining Co. v. Bugbey, U.S. Supreme Court decision, October 1877.

[38] Letter, Dallas Kneass to Amos Catlin, May 4, 1853. California State Library, Catlin Collection Box 150

[39] Letter, Luther Cutler to Amos Catlin, May 31, 1853. California State Library, Catlin Collection Box 150

[40] Letter, William Messinger to Amos Catlin, June 1, 1853. California State Library, Catlin Collection Box 150

[41] Letter W.S. Lorry to Amos Catlin, June 2, 1853. California State Library, Catlin Collection Box 150

[42] Draft by-laws, Natoma Water and Mining Company. California State Library, Catlin Collection Box 149

[43] Sacramento Daily Union, Volume 5, Number 702, 23 June 1853

[44] Stockholders Journal, entry June 1, 1853. Folsom History Museum Archives

[45] Letter, John Harmon to Amos Catlin, June 7, 1853. California State Library, Catlin Collection Box 150

[46] Letter, John Harmon to Amos Catlin, June 7, 1853. California State Library, Catlin Collection Box 150

[47] Sacramento Daily Union, Volume 6, Number 789, 4 October 1853

[48] Sacramento Daily Union, Volume 6, Number 789, 4 October 1853

[49] Sacramento Daily Union, Volume 6, Number 789, 4 October 1853

[50] Sacramento Daily Union, Volume 6, Number 789, 4 October 1853

[51] NWMC Journal, Folsom History Museum Archives.

[52] Letter, A.T. Arrowsmith to Amos Catlin, July 15, 1853. California State Library, Catlin Collection Box 150

[53] Messinger v A.P. Catlin, July 15, 1853. California State Library, Catlin Collection Box 149

[54] Messinger v A.P. Catlin, July 15, 1853. California State Library, Catlin Collection Box 149

[55] Letter, J.H. Gass to Amos Catlin, September 19, 1853. California State Library, Catlin Collection Box 150

[56] Letter, Luther Cutler to Amos Catlin, July 15, 1853. Bancroft Library, BANC C – B 626 Box 1

Amos P. Catlin

[57] Promissory Note, Amos Catlin to Van Guildes, August 18, 1853. California State Library, Catlin Collection Box 149

[58] Draft letter to the Editor, Amos Catlin, September 1, 1853. California State Library, Catlin Collection Box 150

[59] California Farmer and Journal of Useful Sciences, Volume 46, Number 3, 1 February 1877

[60] Sacramento Daily Union, Volume 6, Number 821, 10 November 1853

[61] Sacramento Daily Union, Volume 5, Number 714, 8 July 1853

[62] Sacramento Daily Union, Volume 5, Number 749, 18 August 1853

[63] Sacramento Daily Union, Volume 5, Number 749, 18 August 1853

[64] Daily Alta California, Volume 4, Number 129, 10 May 1853

[65] Sacramento Daily Union, Volume 5, Number 749, 18 August 1853

[66] Sacramento Daily Union, Volume 5, Number 749, 18 August 1853

[67] Sacramento Daily Union, Volume 5, Number 749, 18 August 1853

[68] Sacramento Daily Union, Volume 5, Number 752, 22 August 1853

[69] Sacramento Daily Union, Volume 5, Number 763, 3 September 1853

[70] Sacramento Daily Union, Volume 6, Number 826, 16 November 1853

[71] Sacramento Daily Union, Volume 6, Number 868, 3 January 1854

[72] Daily Alta California, Volume #, Number 6, 6 January 1854

[73] Sacramento Daily Union, Volume 6, Number 877, 13 January 1854

[74] Sacramento Daily Union, Volume 6, Number 878, 14 January 1854

[75] Sacramento Daily Union, Volume 6, Number 878, 14 January 1854

[76] Sacramento Daily Union, Volume 6, Number 879, 16 January 1854

[77] Sacramento Daily Union, Volume 6, Number 882, 19 January 1854

[78] Sacramento Daily Union, Volume 6, Number 883, 20 January 1854

[79] Daily Alta California, Volume 5, Number 19, 19 January 1854

[80] Sacramento Daily Union, Volume 6, Number 883, 20 January 1854

[81] Sacramento Daily Union, Volume 6, Number 883, 20 January 1854

[82] Sacramento Daily Union, Volume 6, Number 883, 20 January 1854

[83] Sacramento Daily Union, Volume 6, Number 883, 20 January 1854

[84] Sacramento Daily Union, Volume 6, Number 886, 24 January 1854

[85] Sacramento Daily Union, Volume 6, Number 887, 25 January 1854, Sacramento Daily Union, Volume 6, Number 888, 26 January 1854

[86] Sacramento Daily Union, Volume 6, Number 897, 6 February 1854

[87] Sacramento Daily Union, Volume 6, Number 891, 30 January 1854

[88] Sacramento Daily Union, Volume 6, Number 890, 28 January 1854

[89] Sacramento Daily Union, Volume 6, Number 903, 13 February 1854

[90] Sacramento Daily Union, Volume 6, Number 902, 11 February 1854

[91] Sacramento Daily Union, Volume 6, Number 905, 15 February 1854

[92] Sacramento Daily Union, Volume 6, Number 907, 17 February 1854

[93] Daily Alta California, Volume 5, Number 48, 18 February 1854

[94] Daily Alta California, Volume 5, Number 48, 18 February 1854

[95] Sacramento Daily Union, Volume 6, Number 908, 18 February 1854

[96] Sacramento Daily Union, Volume 6, Number 909, 20 February 1854

[97] Sacramento Daily Union, Volume 6, Number 910, 21 February 1854

[98] Sacramento Daily Union, Volume 6, Number 910, 21 February 1854

[99] Sacramento Daily Union, Volume 6, Number 910, 21 February 1854

[100] Sacramento Daily Union, Volume 6, Number 913, 24 February 1854

[101] Daily Alta California, Volume 5, Number 55, 25 February 1854

[102] Daily Alta California, Volume 5, Number 55, 25 February 1854

[103] Daily Alta California, Volume 5, Number 55, 25 February 1854

[104] Sacramento Daily Union, Volume 6, Number 915, 27 February 1854

[105] Daily Alta California, Volume 5, Number 56, 26 February 1854

Amos P. Catlin

106 Sacramento Daily Union, Volume 6, Number 919, 4 March 1854
107 Sacramento Daily Union, Volume 6, Number 915, 27 February 1854
108 Sacramento Daily Union, Volume 7, Number 941, 30 March 1854
109 Sacramento Daily Union, Volume 7, Number 965, 27 April 1854
110 Sacramento Daily Union, Volume 6, Number 929, 16 March 1854
111 Daily Alta California, Volume 5, Number 74, 16 March 1854
112 Sacramento Daily Union, Volume 7, Number 932, 20 March 1854
113 Sacramento Daily Union, Volume 7, Number 959, 20 April 1854
114 San Joaquin Republican, Volume 3, Number 36, 4 May 1853
115 Daily Alta California, Volume 5, Number 35, 4 February 1854
116 Daily Alta California, Volume 5, Number 88, 30 March 1854
117 Daily Alta California, Volume 5, Number 90, 1 April 1854
118 Sacramento Daily Union, Volume 7, Number 953, 13 April 1854
119 Daily Alta California, Volume 5, Number 102, 13 April 1854
120 Placer Herald, Volume 2, Number 31, 15 April 1854
121 Sacramento Daily Union, Volume 7, Number 960, 21 April 1854
122 Empire County Argus, Volume 1, Number 37, 29 July 1854
123 Daily Alta California, Volume 5, Number 205, 26 July 1854
124 Daily Alta California, Volume 5, Number 205, 26 July 1854
125 Sacramento Daily Union, Volume 7, Number 1070, 28 August 1854
126 Sacramento Daily Union, Volume 7, Number 1070, 28 August 1854

Amos P. Catlin

Chapter Four: North Fork Ditch, 1854 – 1856

11. Amos P. Catlin, California State Senator and Assemblymember, California State Library

Before Amos left the Senate in 1854, he introduced legislation related to the protection and advancement of water canals, an enterprise in which he was deeply involved. The water ditch bill defined the rights of water ditch companies specifically as it pertained to the right to direct water out of its natural course, provided the diversion did not injure any upstream or downstream consumers. The bill also provided right-of-way protection when the water ditch traveled over open prairie land, with proper compensation to any property owner whose land was traversed by the ditch or flume, similar to the railroad right-of-way laws already in place.[1]

The Natoma Water and Mining Company would battle with many landowners over the course and improvements of the Natoma Canal. Some of these disputes, with monetary awards against the Natoma Company, would not be settled until Congress passed an act in 1866 granting land to established water ditch companies. Over time, some people would come to see Amos not so much as a settler, but rather as just another land speculator and capitalist, unduly penalizing honest settlers with lawsuits over property disputes.

The forks of the American River around Mormon Island, Beal's Bar and Negro Bar had grown relatively quiet by the autumn of 1853. The major riverbed damming and mining projects had largely concluded. The focus was now on the riverbanks and other gold-bearing soils. Men, like Amos, who found a pleasant

Amos P. Catlin

place to call home, were directing their energies into other endeavors, such as ranching, farming, and mercantile businesses.

Amos was part of the emerging fabric of the community. His lumber business had stabilized, and he was shipping lumber on a regular basis, generating much needed money for he and Cutler. As a result of the improved revenue streams, Amos was repaying the loans he had taken out and also advancing cash to other men. Like any good neighbor, Amos was hiring local men to do repair and painting work on his house and the Exchange Hotel.[2]

In May, the rolling hills around Mormon Island were green with native grasses, and bright orange and gold poppies were blooming. The mornings were cool and the sunshine comfortably warm. With his Senate duties concluded, Amos could sit back and reflect on his time thus far in the new State of California and consider future opportunities. It was also a time to catch up on the correspondence he had received.

Philosophy of Law Practice

Amos received a letter from one of his former legal associates from Kingston, New York, Theodoric Westbrook. Amos had written earlier in the year to Westbrook to congratulate him on his election to congress as representative from New York and to advocate on the behalf of a Mr. Whitman to a government post he desired. Westbrook was equally elated at Amos' election to the State Senate, as he wrote, "…and permit me to assure you, that the news which reaches me, that you have made your mark in the Golden State, and occupied a position in the Senate, afforded me equal pleasure."[3]

At 31 years of age, Amos had certainly left his mark on the Golden State. Some of Amos' relatives were in California trying to find their fortunes. His cousin Seymour wrote to him from Mormon Bar near Mariposa. Seymour reported his health was improving after a very challenging winter of illness and that he was looking to get back to mining on his claim.[4] Amos received another letter from a relative that gave him pause to reflect on the future prospects in California.

Daniel Roberts, cousin of Amos and fellow attorney practicing in Vermont, wrote to Amos that he had been offered a position at the law firm Billings, Peachy & Park of San Francisco. While the position paid $10,000 per year, Roberts was concerned that he was 43 years old, with a wife and four children. His options for making a better than modest income were limited in Manchester, Vermont, and he was getting weary of the small legal affairs he was handling.[5] Roberts wanted Amos' counsel on coming out to California with the potential of practicing law in Sacramento.

Amos P. Catlin

Amos quickly dispatched an ebullient reply, with the opening, "I am at once convinced of the propriety and safety of my advising you to come to Cal. And in saying this I feel as if it were almost impossible in the ordinary course of events for anything to befall your enterprise which would cause me to regret giving the advice."[6] Amos wrote that he was personally acquainted with the San Francisco law firm but cautioned that a $10,000 salary was not an extravagant amount for that city.

Beyond encouraging Roberts to relocate to California, Amos outlined the qualities he felt enabled an attorney to be successful and the specific area of practice that was allowing lucrative legal incomes. "There are a great many lawyers here who are able and brilliant men, but...whose habits are irregular and their practice careless," Amos noted. "They are absent from their families..." Whether it was the natural or moral atmosphere, Amos wrote, for some men, there was something corrosive to the character in California. Attorneys who succumbed to this moral erosion generally monopolized the criminal defense business, in Amos' opinion.[7]

From experience, Amos knew that criminal defense work could pay the bills but was not very remunerative. Civil litigation paid better, but the clients were more discerning of their representation. "The client who has heavy civil business usually prefers the man whose personal quality and whose moral deportment belong more to the solid order," Amos wrote. "I have noticed that among the wealthy men of S. F. great confidence is manifested for N. Y. and Eastern lawyers. The plain and solid acquaint of the sober reliable careful industrious well read lawyer are prized by those whose favor is most valuable much more than the showy and superficial...half lawyer, half politician, and part speculator."[8]

A quick glance at Amos from afar may have yielded the impression that he sought to avoid: half lawyer, half politician, and part speculator. A brief interaction with Amos or hearing him speak in public would reveal a sober and conservative man, not given to hasty decisions. He was the East Coast lawyer that could do very well in San Francisco. Instead of seeking wealth in San Francisco, Amos opted to stay in Mormon Island and tend to his own business and legal garden of income.

In terms of Roberts' setting up a law practice in Sacramento, the opportunities were far better in San Francisco, Amos opined, specifically, the area of land title litigation, which was the specialty of the Halleck, Peachy, Billings & Park law firm. Amos briefly outlined the historical events that made not only San Francisco, but a good portion of California, subject to questionable land titles. There were the Spanish and Mexican land grants and those made by Alcaldes, Justices of the Peace, and Town Councils. In short, Amos wrote, "The title to all real estate in the city is uncertain. Millions are held by the frailest of tenancy."[9]

Amos P. Catlin

Amos commented that the Halleck law firm was "deep in the gravel of this rich mine" of land litigation.[10]

If Amos yearned for any of the rich gravel mine of land litigation, he was not pursuing it in 1854. He was more concerned about the legal entanglements of the Natoma ditch crossing over mining claims and land grants. Amos was very aware that the Natoma ditch had crossed onto the Leidesdorff land grant, with branches down to Negro Bar and Alder Creek. It remained to be seen how the owner of the Leidesdorff land grant, Captain Joseph Folsom, would respond to the trespass.

Editorial Job Offer

The past four years had been a huge learning experience for Amos. Possibly the most valuable lesson he had learned was the ability to say "no." James Crane wrote to Amos in July of 1854 offering him the position of editor for a new publication launching in San Francisco.[11] The journal would have a political bent toward the Whig perspective. Such a position would have dramatically elevated Amos' political identity on a statewide level.

As enticing and flattering as the offer was, Amos had to respond, "All my means and hopes in a pecuniary way are actively employed in mining enterprises in this vicinity (mostly in canals) and my success depends entirely upon my personal attendance and execution. The acceptance of the proposal which you and your friends have so generously honored me with would involve such a change in the economy of my affairs as I would willingly make, were it possible."[12]

Bear River Ditch

The construction of canals to deliver water to mining districts was the growth industry of the 1850s. Miners were clamoring for water to wash their dry diggings far from the rivers that they had already prospected. Amos read with interest the reports of the progress of the Bear River and Auburn Canal Company beginning in 1851. By the spring of 1852, the Bear River ditch was delivering water to Dry Creek and Spanish Flat, and the company was working on a 2,000-foot tunnel to get the water to the town of Auburn.[13]

After many delays, in June the tunnel under the ridge was opened, and the water flowed over to Auburn. From there, it was downhill to cut the ditch down to Rattlesnake Bar. The ditch wound its way toward the North Fork of the American and was delivering to Rattlesnake Bar by the middle of July 1853. It must have seemed odd to some people that water from the Bear River had to be diverted and supplied to the mining districts adjacent to the North Fork of the American River, which carried a much greater flow of water.

Amos P. Catlin

The Bear River ditch into the Rattlesnake Bar region highlighted the challenging nature of damming and ditching next to the North Fork. The river canyon above Rattlesnake Bar could be steep and of pure rock. It would be a serious engineering and construction task to build a water canal along the North Fork. However, the Bear River could only deliver so much water into the region, and the demand for water south of Rattlesnake Bar down to Beal's Bar was great.

A small group of men, informally called the North Fork Ditch Company, began surveying a potential water canal next to the river in the summer of 1853. W.A. Eliason of Placer County was doing the preliminary survey and engineering work. Even though the Natoma ditch had a turbulent construction process, Amos was viewed as a good project and corporate manager. The North Fork Ditch would have its origins in Placer County, with a dam at Tamaroo Bar below Auburn, on the North Fork of the American River. In 1854, Amos got down to business setting up a corporation for the dam and ditch.

American River Water & Mining Company

To keep the North Fork Ditch separate from the Natoma ditch, Amos created the American River Water and Mining Company.[14] This company was formed to manage the construction of the North Fork Ditch on the North Fork of the American River from Auburn down to Beal's Bar, along with soliciting investors and handling the water sales. With the two water companies, Amos controlled miles of canals on the major forks of the American River, delivering water to miners, farmers, and ranchers.

NOTICE—American River Water and Mining Co.—The Stockholders of this Company will meet at Gridley's Hall, at Doton's Bar, on the 26th day of March, next, at 2 o'clock P. M., for the purpose of electing seven Trustees to manage the concerns of said Company for the ensuing year; also, for the purpose of considering and determining the propriety of increasing the capital stock to the sum of $300,000.

A. P. CATLIN,
L. B. BROOKS,
A. G. KINSEY,
J. S. CRAIG,   } Trustees.
E. RULISON,
S. PALMER,
fe24-tm26   A. T. ARROWSMITH,

Sacramento Daily Union, February 24, 1855

12. American River Water and Mining Co. notice of Trustee meeting for the North Fork Ditch on the North Fork of American River, 1855.

By 1855, Amos was presiding over and managing both the American River WMC (North Fork Canal Company) and Natoma WMC enterprises fulltime. The American River WMC elected Amos as President and C.T.H. Palmer as Secretary at their March stockholders meeting. The Directors comprised

Amos P. Catlin

W.A. Eliason, A.T. Arrowsmith, A.G. Kinsey, John L. Craig, L.B. Brooks, along with Catlin and Palmer.[15]

Between the Natoma and North Fork Ditch projects, Amos was extremely busy. He did find time to travel to Sacramento and keep his fingers in the political pot. Lauren Upson wrote to Amos in August 1854 regarding efforts to keep the rapidly dissolving Whig Party intact. Upson sensed the growing Know Nothing political movement was spreading and that it might be the unfortunate home of former Whig supporters.[16]

Granite Cornerstone

Amos was not a Puritan, but he did feel a calling to have Christian worship as part of his life. He did not hold strictly to one denomination and would attend Sunday services at different churches. While in the Senate, Amos introduced a petition signed by 175 residents of the Natoma Township requesting a law for the better preservation of the Sabbath.[17] In 1854, Amos donated the cornerstone for the Congregational Church in Sacramento. Joseph Benton of the church would write to Amos with a note of thanks, "We hope that this corner-stone will remain in place and endure long after we shall have passed from the stage of action...."[18] Amos was in attendance in 1899 at the church's golden jubilee and was once again thanked for donating the granite block quarried at Mormon Island.[19]

The Natoma canal was not made out of granite. The tall flumes that carried the water over deep ravines resembled nothing like the Roman aqueducts built of stone. The Natoma flumes were built of wood, with the goal of quick assembly with acceptable water loss from leaks. As prophesied by fellow ditch builder James Edwards, who warned that wooden flumes can be destroyed by high river flows, the large wooden flume over New York Creek was undermined by a swollen South Fork of the American River.[20] Amos had to have 40,000 feet of lumber hauled from his mill to New York ravine in the autumn of 1854 to rebuild the compromised tall flume structure.[21]

Amos P. Catlin

13. Flume over New York ravine. "A Historical Journey Through The American River - New York Ravine Area, 1840s - 1900s." by Alfred Roxburgh

By the end of 1854, the worst of Amos' cash flow problems had been resolved. The Natoma ditch was producing revenue through water sales, and miners were back patronizing the Exchange Hotel. In December of 1854, the Natoma Water and Mining Company split the stock resulting in a new stock price of $100 per share. At the close of business in 1854, Amos - still the largest shareholder - owned 180 shares of stock.[22] Amos was not some corporate executive project manager. He was also the primary bookkeeper handling the billing and writing receipts.

Doton's Bar

While he mostly handled Natoma ditch water sales from Mormon Island, in order to be more convenient for North Fork Ditch customers, he purchased a building at Doton's Bar in 1855. Amos paid $70 for a custom frame structure from J.A. Leibert of Negro Hill. The building was moved to be next to the North Fork Ditch reservoir at Doton's[23] Bar.[24] From this little structure, Amos would handle the affairs of the North Fork Ditch, selling water, usually one miner's inch, for $1 per day.[25]

Amos was fortunate to have men around him who were resourceful. Luther Cutler up at the mill was working on a thin budget for maintenance but found ways to keep the operation going as long as Amos got the repair parts ordered and shipped to him.[26] When the North Fork Ditch at Tamaroo Bar broke apart in June 1855, dam manager Waldo Taylor wrote Amos that there was no reason for Amos to travel up to the dam site. Taylor informed Amos that Mr. Waterhouse would commence filling the break with trees and brush. They were confident that, in a couple of days, the repairs would allow the water to rise in the ditch by 12 to 18 inches.[27]

Business was good for the Natoma Water and Mining Company, which declared a dividend of 3 percent as of April 2nd. Stockholders could collect their dividend

Amos P. Catlin

from President A. P. Catlin at the company office at Mormon Island.[28] The declared dividend, on $300,000 of capital stock, was before the Natoma canal system had been completely built out. The company would go on to pay two more dividends of 2 percent each before 1855 had ended.[29][30]

By the spring of 1855, the North Fork Ditch had been completed to above Beal's Bar. The bulk of the construction work was undertaken by Brooks and Clark, who also worked on the Natoma ditch.[31] The first dam for the North Fork Ditch was at Tamaroo Bar. Later, a larger dam would be constructed downstream. By 1856, the North Fork Ditch had built an earthen dam in a small ravine for storage of water to be delivered down to Mississippi Bar.[32] The dam was 17 feet tall, 72 feet at the base, and several hundred feet in width. The surface area of the reservoir was close to 100 acres. Amos proudly displayed the dam and reservoir to the Sacramento Daily Union in May of 1856.[33] In later years, the structure would be known as Baldwin Dam.

The North Fork Ditch was 8 feet wide at the top of the canal, 4 feet at the bottom, with a depth of 4 to 5 feet, carrying a depth of water approximately 3 feet. Except where the canal was cut through solid granite or flumed in wood, it was an earth-lined canal. In many places, hand-constructed rock retaining walls supported the river side of the ditch. By 1855, there were 10 reservoirs along the ditch line for mud settling and flow control.

As the North Fork Ditch was put into operation delivering water to the stagnant mining operations, the towns along its path grew in population. The relatively easy placer gold laying on the bedrock of the riverbed had been scooped up in previous years. The miners built diversion dams and flumes to direct the river water away from a claim so they could excavate down to the river bed for the free placer gold. Then, like Amos, they used steam engines to pump the water out to get at the gold on top of the bedrock. While some miners continued to pan and use long toms along the river's edge, the next sites to exploit for gold were the river's bank and benches.

Doton's Bar, south of Rattlesnake Bar, blossomed with the advent of the North Fork Ditch. In addition to Amos' office, the town of Doton's Bar would include a two-story hotel, candy shop, bakery, blacksmith shop, numerous saloons, a Wells, Fargo & Co., and Pacific Express offices. The population was estimated to be several hundred residents.[34]

Many of the mining locations, like Doton's Bar, were 75 to 150 feet above the river. The North Fork Ditch rose 50 to 100 feet above the towns or mining camps. This provided enough pressure from the elevated ditch water traveling through large riveted cast iron pipes for either sluicing or hydraulic operations. Some of the mining claims were paying $25 a day for use of the North Fork Ditch water.[35]

Amos P. Catlin

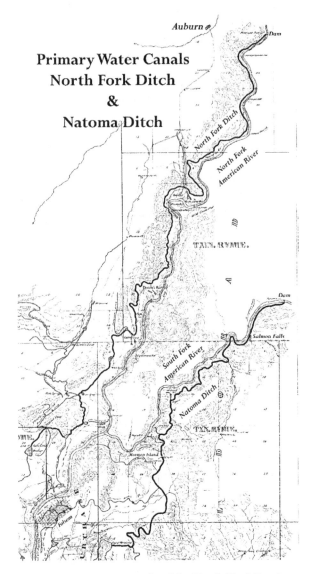

14. Primary water canals of the North Fork Ditch
and the Natoma ditch.

Both the Natoma canal and the North Fork Ditch extended the life of placer mining along the forks of the American River. They also increased the debris flowing into the river. The debris flow, caused in part by the water canals, would result in legal action in which Amos would take part as a lawyer 20 years in the

Amos P. Catlin

future. But in 1855, the water canals were selling all of the water they could deliver to mining operations.[36]

The canals and their water delivery would last for another 100 years, until the construction of Folsom Dam and Reservoir made them obsolete. However, the allotted water flow did not vanish. The appropriated water of the Natoma Canal, approximately 32,000 acre-feet per year, now resides with the City of Folsom. The water rights to the flow in the North Fork Ditch resides with the successor of the North Fork Ditch Company, the San Juan Water District. In 1954, the San Juan Water District entered into a contract with the United States to receive 33,000 acre-feet of water annually from Folsom reservoir.[37]

The Sacramento Valley Railroad was fast approaching its terminus above Negro Bar. Mormon Island was only a short ride from Folsom, but not always a smooth excursion. Amos and George Corey petitioned the County of Sacramento Supervisors to approve a public road from the railroad depot out to Mormon Island.[38] The Board approved the road and set the survey in motion.[39]

1856 Railroad Town Folsom

A shining city on a hill. That's how many men, including Amos, envisioned the temporary terminus of the Sacramento Valley Railroad at Negro Bar. A town, laid out by Theodore Judah, would sweep away the mining camp of Negro Bar and be christened Granite City. This new town, with streets named after prominent historical figures, situated on the bluffs overlooking the American River, would be far above the flood waters that plagued Sacramento.

With the death of Captain Libby Folsom in 1855, the town poised to spring from the dusty foothills would be renamed Folsom in his honor. The grid layout of the town was comprised of 98 blocks, each of which contained 16 lots, with the exception of those blocks where the Sacramento Valley Railroad bisected or truncated the block. The railroad entered the town on the southeast and cut northwards on its proposed route over the American River.

The original design for the Sacramento Valley Railroad was to run east to Folsom from Sacramento, then turn north and run along the base of the foothills up to Marysville near the confluence of the Yuba and Feather Rivers. The concept was to connect all of the mountain mining camps to Sacramento via a railroad. There was even speculation that branch lines would run up to towns such as Auburn. Folsom was just the first stop on a proposed rail line connecting mining and agriculture to Sacramento.

Most men in the Folsom region had witnessed the rapid development of Sacramento City, complete with all of the new buildings, floods, riots, and cholera outbreak. It was easy to speculate that Folsom would have all of the benefits of Sacramento without all of the unpleasantries. Amos was in a unique position to survey all of Folsom's benefits and future prospects, as his Natoma Water and Mining Company was supplying water in and around the Folsom region. While placer mining had seriously dwindled by the mid-1850s, hard rock mining was just getting underway in the foothills above Folsom.

Even though the Sacramento Valley Railroad struggled financially to complete the line to Folsom, the town's future looked bright. The optimism over Folsom was imbued with the pioneer spirit of manifest destiny. The rapid economic development of California, flush with so many opportunities yet to be exploited, added to the enthusiasm of the moment. Some men who had come to California to mine for gold, now turned their attention to agricultural pursuits along the American River. Other men, such as Amos, were focusing on regional development.

Folsom Lot Investment

In preparation for the launch of Folsom and his new venture as land speculator, Amos sold his interest in the Exchange Hotel at Mormon Island in 1855.[40] At the initial offering of the Folsom lots, handled by the executors of the Captain Joseph Libby Folsom estate, Halleck, Peachy, & Van Winkle, Amos purchased 163 lots across 12 blocks.[41] He paid $321 for the properties in February 1856, with an average cost of $2 per lot. Amos was also in a buying mood for Natoma Water and Mining Company stock. From late 1855 through 1856, Amos would purchase 340 shares of Natoma stock from other stockholders.

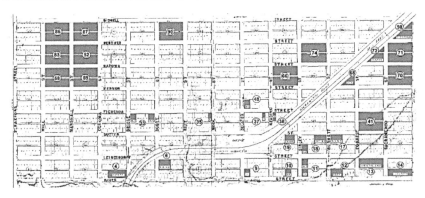

15. Original blocks and individual lots Amos Catlin purchased in the town of Folsom between 1856 and 1857.

Amos P. Catlin

Amos would add to his Folsom portfolio by purchasing another 122 lots across 19 different blocks from the Folsom Estate in November 1857.[42] The total purchase price for the additional lots was $1,340, or approximately $11 per lot. At one point, Amos owned 13 complete blocks in the town of Folsom. He would also be a co-owner in another 69 lots throughout the town. In partnership with Horatio Gates Livermore, the two owned all of the lots in blocks 59, 82 and 87.[43]

Of course, the whole region around Folsom seemed to be in motion, as the first railroad west of the Mississippi was about to make its inaugural trip from Sacramento to Folsom in February 1856. Amos, along with a long list of dignitaries, including Governor Johnson and former Governor Bigler, were part of a large railroad celebration at Meredith's Hotel in Folsom on February 22.[44] Later that year, Amos would again become a hotel owner, with the purchase of the Mansion House on the corner of Figueroa and Sibley streets in Folsom for $2,000.[45]

Folsom did not experience the same frenzy to buy lots and build homes as had happened in Sacramento six years earlier. With the exception of commercial development along Sutter Street and lots near the railroad, home construction was slow. Several of the lots sold were then used for entrances to drift mines, tunneling under the new town. Over the next 20 years, Amos would sell his Folsom lots to a variety of people for homes and mining. With his investment in Folsom, Amos was embedded in the new community. He established his law practice in the McCamley Building at 803 Sutter Street.[46]

American Party

The Whigs had given Amos the cold shoulder, so he looked elsewhere for a political home. Amos would attend various political forums, which also passed for entertainment in 1855, around his region. In early September, he was in attendance at a candidates' forum for the American Party at Negro Hill, directly across the river from his home at Mormon Island.[47] One of Amos' Whig Party compatriots, J. Neely Johnson, had migrated to the American Party and was running for governor. When Johnson won the election, securing the legitimacy of the American Party and squashing the remnants of the California Whig Party, Amos could see himself aligned with the American Party. Amos was also being associated with a loose group of politicians that circled around Governor Johnson, known as the Sacramento Regency.[48]

The American Party was the official and public political apparatus of the Know Nothing movement. Begun as somewhat of a secret society, when asked about the political platform of the movement, the respondent would reply, "I know nothing." Know Nothing filled the political void after the Whig Party collapse as opposition to the Democratic Party. Know Nothing members tended to be populist, nationalistic, xenophobic, and suspicious of the Roman Catholic church. The Know Nothing movement and subsequent American Party would not have been the first horse Amos chose to ride into town on. On the other hand, he did not see many options, and a leap to the Democratic Party was a ravine too deep and wide to cross with any philosophical flume.

With Governor Johnson a member of the American Party, and because Amos still wanted to have at least one foot in politics while the other foot ran the water companies, he acceded to the invitation to lead the American Party in Folsom. The presidential election was in full swing by the summer of 1856, and Amos organized a large Folsom gathering to celebrate the nominations of Fillmore and Donelson. Amos arranged a special train from Sacramento to Folsom for the big festivities. As the Sacramento Valley RR train arrived, with eight passenger cars loaded with men, rockets were shot into the sky, and artillery rounds were fired. In addition to the hundreds of men brought up by the railroad, another 500 or more gathered to hear the political speeches.[49]

A large railroad platform car, festooned in patriotic bunting and political banners, acted as the speaker's platform. Amos climbed on the platform car and welcomed the crowd to the political theater. Excited at the prospect that Millard Fillmore would be elected President of the United States, Amos threw glancing criticism at the other nominated presidential candidates, Buchanan, the Democrat, and Fremont, the Republican. As a skilled political speaker, Amos ignored the tepid support thus far for Fillmore by noting how the gathered assembly reflected the growing excitement for the Fillmore and Donelson ticket.[50]

The debate over the Nebraska Act, which could potentially expand slavery into new states and territories, combined with its passage, had torn the Whig Party apart. The American "Know Nothing" Party filled the resulting political gap and created a home for men who either endorsed slavery or were indifferent to its expansion, but could not cross the line and become Democrats. Some of the men gathered to hear a Fillmore promotion still identified as Whigs, including Col. George. W. Bowie, who spoke in favor of Fillmore. While some speakers shied away from the slavery topic that evening, others did not.

Col. Balie Peyton, working as a prosecuting attorney in San Francisco, faulted Buchanan for supporting resolutions against admitting Missouri or any slave state into the Union.[51] After Peyton's extended remarks in support of Fillmore, the Sacramento Glee Club performed a tune written expressly for the Fillmore-Donelson ticket. One of the stanzas read:

"The Loco Focos[52] cower before us,
The Black Repubs.[53] fly far and fast,

Amos P. Catlin

The "Stars and Stripes" are floating over us,
That flag we'll stand by to the last."

Henry Crabb, who held the distinction of introducing the Fugitive Slave Act in California in 1852,[54] spoke next. Crabb was also suspected of writing a secret Whig Party circular calling for California to be divided into three states, with two or more of the three legalizing slavery.[55] The remarks of David. T. Bagley, who was running for the position of Clerk of California Supreme Court,[56] were paraphrased by the Sacramento Daily Union on the first page, capturing the mood and sentiment of the assembled Fillmore clan.

"Mr. Bagley said that before coming upon the ground he could not realize the fact that such a goodly array could be produced. Lies had been told about Americans where he had come from. They said there were not friends enough to make mile stones between Sacramento and Folsom, but on looking around him he found there were enough and to spare tombstones for every Democrat and nigger worshipper in Sacramento county. [Shouts]"[57]

Assembly nomination and election 1856

Amos' work on behalf of the fledgling American Party was not taken for granted. At the American Party county convention, he was nominated to run for an Assembly seat.[58] With the bulk of the construction completed on both the North Fork Ditch and the Natoma Canal, Amos could afford to spend some of his waking hours campaigning and, if elected, legislating as an Assemblyman.

The battle in Sacramento County was very fiercely contested. The Know Nothings made more noise, expended more money, and worked harder than in any previous contest. Indeed, they made the most extraordinary exertions to secure a victory. The result is that Buchanan has a majority of only some fifty votes. Our candidate for State Senator, Mr. Johnson, and one of our Assymblymen, Mr. McKune, are elected; and the K. N's have elected Messrs. Ferris, Catlin, and Clark. It is astounding to us that, under the circumstances, without money and without "strikers," we succeeded even thus far.—*State Journal, Nov. 6th.*

Placer Herald, November 8, 1856

16. Placer Herald editorial noting Amos Catlin's election associated with the Know Nothing political party, 1856

In the spring of 1856, the San Francisco Vigilance Committee was reawakened from its typical slumber through generally acknowledged lawlessness in the city.

Amos P. Catlin

Notably, the members of the Vigilance Committee took the law into their own hands by hanging two men for murder. In the press, the Vigilance Committee was credited with bringing some safety and sanity back to San Francisco. In terms of the law, their actions could be construed as murder, as neither man hanged was tried, convicted, or sentenced in a court of law. Approval or disapproval of the extra-judicial killings of the men by the Vigilance Committee was used as a litmus test for candidates for political office. The Sacramento Daily Union queried candidates with three questions about their support for the San Francisco Vigilance Committee. Specifically, the Union wanted to know if candidates for the legislature would vote for amnesty for men involved in the Vigilance Committee.[59]

Amos responded, "In reply to your first and second questions, I say that I did favor, generally, the acts of the San Francisco Vigilance Committee. I regarded the extraordinary circumstances which called that body into existence as being sufficient to excuse them."[60]

Because of Amos' position of amnesty for the San Francisco vigilantes and other reasons, the Sacramento Daily Union endorsed him for Assembly.

"Of the nominees for the Assembly, Mr. Catlin has represented the county two sessions in the Senate, with a devotion, faithfulness, integrity and marked ability never exceeded, if ever equaled, by any Senator elected by the people of Sacramento county. The interests of the county and State were his polar stars as a legislator, and so steady and consistent was he, that no Senator stood fairer among his peers, and no Senator ever left that body with a purer legislative record or reputation."[61]

With the endorsement and his generally good reputation in Sacramento County, Amos was elected to the Assembly in November of 1856.[62] He would enter an Assembly that was composed of 60 Democrats, 11 Republicans, and eight representatives from the American Party.[63]

---

[1] Sacramento Daily Union, Volume 7, Number 959, 20 April 1854

[2] Invoice, receipts, December 30, 1853 and February 28, 1854. California State Library, Catlin Collection Box 149

[3] Theodoric R. Westbrook letter to Amos Parmalee Catlin, 30 May 1854. Bancroft Library, BANC MSS 2018/89

[4] Letter, D. Seymour to Amos Catlin, May 6, 1854. Bancroft Library, BANC MSS C – B 626 Box 1

[5] Letter, Daniel Roberts to Amos Catlin, May 15, 1854. California State Library, Catlin Collection Box 150

[6] Draft Letter, Amos Catlin to Daniel Roberts, June 18, 1854. California State Library, Catlin Collection Box 150

[7] Draft Letter, Amos Catlin to Daniel Roberts, June 18, 1854. California State Library, Catlin Collection Box 150

Amos P. Catlin

[8] Draft Letter, Amos Catlin to Daniel Roberts, June 18, 1854. California State Library, Catlin Collection Box 150

[9] Draft Letter, Amos Catlin to Daniel Roberts, June 18, 1854. California State Library, Catlin Collection Box 150

[10] Draft Letter, Amos Catlin to Daniel Roberts, June 18, 1854. California State Library, Catlin Collection Box 150

[11] Letter, James Crane to Amos Catlin, July 6, 1854. Bancroft Library, BANC MSS C – B 626 Box 1

[12] Letter, Amos Catlin to James Crane, July 9, 1854. Bancroft Library, BANC MSS C – B 626 Box 1

[13] Sacramento Daily Union, Volume 3, Number 312, 22 March 1852

[14] Sacramento Daily Union, Volume 8, Number 1121, 26 October 1854

[15] Sacramento Daily Union, Volume 9, Number 1251, 28 March 1855

[16] Letters, Lauren Upson to Amos Catlin, August 27, 1854. Bancroft Library, BANC C – B 626 Box 1

[17] Sacramento Daily Union, Volume 5, Number 643, 15 April 1853

[18] Letter, Joseph A. Benton to Amos Catlin, September 21, 1854. Bancroft Library, BANC C – B 626 Box 1

[19] Sacramento Daily Union, Volume 98, Number 63, 23 October 1899

[20] *A Historical Journey Through The American River South Fork – New York Ravine Area, 1840s – 1900s*, Alfred Roxburgh, 2005.

[21] Hauling receipts, September and October 1854. California State Library, Catlin Collection Box 148

[22] Natoma Water and Mining Company shareholder journal. Folsom Historical Museum Archives

[23] There are various spellings including Dotan, Doten, and Doton.

[24] Purchase receipt, J.A. Leibert to Amos Catliln, 1855. California State Library, Catlin Collection Box 149

[25] Peter Kingsinger water receipt, $90 for three months. Bancroft Library, BANC C – B 626 Box 1

[26] Letter, Luther Cutler to Amos, October 23, 1855. Bancroft Library, BANC C – B 626 Box 1

[27] Letter, Waldo Taylor to Amos Catlin, June 20, 1855. Bancroft Library, BANC C – B 626 Box 1

[28] Sacramento Daily Union, Volume 9, Number 1252, 29 March 1855

[29] Sacramento Daily Union, Volume 10, Number 1411, 3 October 1855

[30] Sacramento Daily Union, Volume 10, Number 1465, 5 December 1855

[31] Sacramento Daily Union, Volume 9, Number 1262, 10 April 1855

[32] Sacramento Daily Union, Volume 11, Number 1599, 10 May 1856

[33] Sacramento Daily Union, Volume 11, Number 1599, 10 May 1856

[34] Sacramento Daily Union, Volume 9, Number 1268, 17 April 1855

[35] Sacramento Daily Union, Volume 9, Number 1268, 17 April 1855

[36] Sacramento Daily Union, Volume 9, Number 1350, 24 July 1855

[37] *Historical Development Of Water Use From American River In The Reach Affected By Construction Of Folsom Dam And Reservoir*, US Bureau of Reclamation, 1958

[38] Sacramento Daily Union, Volume 10, Number 1489, 3 January 1856

[39] Sacramento Daily Union, Volume 10, Number 1492, 7 January 1856

[40] Sacramento County Deed book 18560129, page 536

[41] Sacramento County Deed book 18560325, page 13

[42] Sacramento County Deed book 18571127, page 71

[43] Sacramento County Assessor Map Folsom, 1861

[44] Sacramento Daily Union, Volume 10, Number 1523, 12 February 1856

[45] Sacramento County Deed book 18560816, page 568

[46] Folsom Telegraph, July 16, 1864

[47] Georgetown News, Volume 1, Number 46, 5 September 1855

[48] Empire County Argus, Volume 2, Number 51, 17 November 1855

[49] Sacramento Daily Union, Volume 11, Number 1683, 18 August 1856

[50] Sacramento Daily Union, Volume 11, Number 1683, 18 August 1856

[51] Sacramento Daily Union, Volume 11, Number 1683, 18 August 1856

[52] Derogatory term for Democrats

Amos P. Catlin

[53] Racist term for Republicans who supported the abolition of slavery
[54] Negro Rights Activities in Gold Rush California, Rudolph M. Lapp, http://www.sfmuseum.org/hist6/blackrights.html
[55] Empire County Argus, Volume 1, Number 37, 29 July 1854
[56] Sacramento Daily Union, Volume 11, Number 1696, 2 September 1856
[57] Empire County Argus, Volume 1, Number 37, 29 July 1854
[58] Sacramento Daily Union, Volume 11, Number 1709, 17 September 1856
[59] Sacramento Daily Union, Volume 12, Number 1742, 25 October 1856
[60] Sacramento Daily Union, Volume 12, Number 1742, 25 October 1856
[61] Sacramento Daily Union, Volume 12, Number 1749, 3 November 1856
[62] Sacramento Daily Union, Volume 12, Number 1755, 10 November 1856
[63] Sacramento Daily Union, Volume 12, Number 1755, 10 November 1856

Amos P. Catlin

Chapter Five: Assemblyman Catlin, Treasurer Impeachment, 1857

The legislative session opened with the Assembly and Senate still in temporary chambers at Sacramento, as the State Capitol had not yet been built. Amos found himself in an Assembly with more members he had to deal with, as opposed to the smaller Senate. Amos was appointed to the Judiciary, Ways and Means, and Prison committees.[1] The item sucking most of the political energy at the beginning of 1857 was the selection of U.S. Senator.

Former State Senator and Lieutenant Governor David Broderick from San Francisco was in the hunt for the U.S. Senate seat. Broderick, a Democrat, controlled San Francisco politics and was a less-than-ethical political operative who was not above asking for or paying bribes to get the results he wanted. Amos voted against Broderick for the U.S. Senate, but as the American Party was a small minority of the Assembly, no one was paying attention to his vote.[2]

After the vote, numerous rumors of back room deals and bribes surfaced involving Broderick's quest for the Senate seat. Many of the Assembly members feigned ignorance about Broderick's corrupt practices. In an effort to introduce a little humor into the absurd situation, Amos rose and spoke:

"I confess that I am a member of the American Party. I voted in the late Senatorial contest for James W. Coffroth and Henry A. Crabb. If any gentleman believes that I had any sinister motive in acting as I did, I will lay my hand upon my heart and assure him he is mistaken. Messrs. Coffroth and Crabb never promised me any office. Indeed, I was not ambitious to occupy any distinguished position. The only position I could have hoped to occupy was upon the Gadsden Purchase[3], and I never even applied for that."[4]

The levity Amos' remarks brought to the situation was appreciated, and the sarcasm did not go unnoticed. The Sacramento Daily Union opined that Amos' little speech was "…a well-timed and scathing rebuke, as well as a rich burlesque upon the ridiculous farce played by certain members who had risen in their places, and, as a matter of personal privilege, disclaimed all knowledge of any bargain — between Gwin and Broderick on the Senatorial question — and that they had not been influenced in their votes by any promise of office or hope of other reward."[5]

While Amos' levity about Broderick's corruption was good-natured, it was also meant as a signal that he was an ethical individual. He wasn't so subtle when the California Steam Navigation Company offered free passage to members of the legislature to San Francisco for the big send-off for Senators Broderick's and

Gwin's return to Washington, D. C. He advised members of the Assembly against accepting any free transportation because he was certain the company had an ulterior motive in making the gift.

Amos outlined his reasoning against accepting the trip on the Assembly floor. "If the proprietors of any stage route, railroad or steamboat company wish to give members of the Legislature a free pass, or excursion ticket, there is a mode of doing it in much better taste than the mode adopted by the Company in San Francisco. I don't think our journals ought to be incumbered with invitations to sailing and dancing parties. If they want to invite us, let them send their invitations in the ordinary way, enclosed in an envelope and laid on our desks."[6]

Printing Bills

The lack of a printed invitation for a free boat ride was representative of a larger printing issue in the Assembly, in Amos' mind. Amos felt that entirely too much business was being pushed through the Assembly based on the initial reading of a proposed bill, with no printed text being made available for review. Assemblyman Curtis introduced a bill to allow a toll bridge to be built from Sacramento City over to Yolo County, with the toll fixed by Sacramento County. Amos did not have an issue with the proposed bridge, but he wanted the bill printed so he could study the proposal.[7]

Amos then took the opportunity to make the point that he thought far too many bills were being introduced and assigned to committees without the members knowing the contents of the bills. The Clerk informed the Assembly that about 30 bills had already been introduced. Amos replied:

"Well, sir, we have already had thirty or forty before this house. Now, I have endeavored, through the newspapers, to keep up some sort of acquaintance with our proceedings. Often times, when I am asked for information relative to our doings, I find myself totally unable to give any answer. And the reason is the bills are not printed."[8]

Amos went on to give an example of a bill that included a fatal flaw with respect to a procedure for issuing duplicate land warrants.

"Now, this bill was passed without any such provision. I venture to say that not three men in the House knew what its provisions were. If that bill had been printed, twenty members would have observed the omission. I hope the legislature hereafter will see the necessity of having most if not all of their bills printed."[9]

One method to defeat a bill was to complain about its costs. Many members, preferring some of their legislation to continue to be shrouded from public view, argued that the extravagance of printing proposed legislation was a waste of taxpayer money. Amos stood and addressed the Assembly, "I am one of those gentlemen whose conduct has been criticized for advocating the printing of bill[s].... I give notice I shall vote hereafter against all bill[s] of whose character and provisions I am ignorant."[10]

It was a rather ridiculous amount of effort on the part of Amos to attempt to push the California Legislature into a more professional state. However, from his perspective, printing proposed legislation was a basic necessity. Failure to do so was sloppy record keeping that led to mistakes. It was also the absence of printed records that led to crime and corruption. By this time in his tenure as an Assemblyman, Amos was gaining a reputation as a man who was a stickler for the details, if not a little impatient and pugnacious over his points of order. It was his intense curiosity and the search for the facts that would thrust Amos into a scandal that demanded an accurate account.

Treasurer Bates

Dr. Henry Bates was a young physician when he traveled from Massachusetts to California during the Gold Rush. He found himself practicing medicine at Sutter's Mill in Coloma in May of 1849.[11] Dr. Bates made his way up to Shasta in Northern California, where he went into practice with Dr. E. B. McLaughlin.[12] While living in Shasta, Dr. Bates made the acquaintance of Edwin Rowe, who bought gold dust in Weaverville and expressed it to Shasta on behalf of Adams and Company.[13]

In addition to medicine, and perhaps dabbling in gold futures, Dr. Bates was also interested in politics. He ran for the Assembly in 1854 as a member of the American Party, which was the official political organ of the Know Nothing party. Dr. Bates was elected, and in 1855 he was appointed to a Joint Special Committee to investigate potential corruption of the State Marine Hospital. Under Dr. Bates' leadership, the committee uncovered rampant corruption by the doctors, who inflated invoices to pocket the difference and ordered numerous personal items – cigars, champagne, housewares – paid for with hospital funds.[14]

It was evident that Dr. Bates understood bookkeeping and accounting practices if he was able to uncover such government corruption. Based on his notoriety for saving public money and his M.D. credentials, Dr. Bates was nominated by the American Party in 1855 for the position of State Treasurer. He won the election and became California's Treasurer in January 1856, at the age of 32.

In March of 1856, there was a little hiccup with the bookkeeping in the Treasurer's office. The County of San Francisco said they deposited money with Palmer, Cook & Co. to be forwarded to the State Treasury for taxes collected. For some reason, the San Francisco funds were not accounted for at the Treasurer's office.[15]

Dr. Bates said he was amenable to have anyone inspect the books of the Treasurer's office, and he was confident everything would be in place.[16]

The little irregularity with Palmer, Cook & Co. would foreshadow an even larger headache for the physician turned Treasurer. News broke in late July that California had missed the interest payment on its bonds due to bondholders in New York on July 1st.[17] Once again, the blame was placed on Palmer, Cook & Co. for not forwarding $82,558 in State interest and $19,600 interest due from the City of San Francisco.[18]

While the credit rating of California was dropping like a rock in a muddy pond, Dr. Bates was not in Sacramento. Edwin Rowe, now a cashier in the State Treasurer's office, released a statement to the newspapers on August 2nd that the interest due on the bonds should have been paid by the 20th, and if not, the Treasurer's office would forward money on August 5th. Rowe emphasized that a bond was taken from Palmer, Cook & Co. as security for the payment, so there was no cause for concern.

For their part in the debacle, Palmer, Cook & Co. blamed one of their principles in New York. The firm's representatives told newspaper reporters that Mr. Wright in New York said he had sufficient funds to cover the bond payments, and there was no need to forward the gold coin to the East Coast.[19] Mr. Wright claimed he never had the funds, Palmer, Cook & Co. had no credit in New York, and it looked like the firm could not make good on the bond they put up as security for the interest payment.

It quickly became apparent that Palmer, Cook & Co. did not have the gold coin in their possession in California. Instead of suing Palmer, Cook & Co., Treasurer Bates began a mad rush around California to bandage up what looked like a self-inflicted wound, not only to himself, but to California as well. The Marysville Herald reported on August 22nd that Treasurer Bates was in town to raise money to pay the state debt. He was only able to secure $27,000. He trekked back to Sacramento and then to San Francisco. He was able to get Wells, Fargo & Co. to lend him $50,000. This still left Treasurer Bates $6,000 shy of the balance owing.[20] He was able to pull the rest of the money from an advance from Palmer, Cook & Co.[21]

Also, in the autumn of 1856, Edwin Rowe left his position as Cashier at the Treasurer's office and assumed the presidency of the Pacific Express Company.[22] The Pacific Express Company was not a bank, but a company that delivered items of value, like gold coins to banks.

Treasurer Bates let it be known that he would no longer be working with Palmer, Cook & Co. Wells, Fargo & Co. would handle interest remittances to New York

Amos P. Catlin

in the future. Even though Treasurer Bates made the agreement with Wells, Fargo & Co. in April, he met with Louis McLane, an agent for Wells, Fargo & Co. on December 31st, with Edwin Rowe also in attendance. Rowe proposed that his Pacific Express Company give Wells, Fargo & Company a bond for the delivery of the July 1, 1857, interest payment. The implied plan was that Pacific Express would take control of the gold coin interest payment and, at some date in the future, transfer the money to Wells, Fargo & Co. McLane declined the offer.[23]

The proposed transfer from Pacific Express to Wells, Fargo & Co. was not the only odd event to transpire under the supervision of Treasurer Bates. Mr. Bunker, one of the clerks in the Treasurer's office, recounted how Treasurer Bates instructed him to leave Sacramento between December 27th and January 4th. Bunker thought it had something to do with a Grand Jury investigation into the Treasurer accepting warrants from counties as payment for their tax receipts.[24] Regardless, this left only one clerk in the office at the beginning of January 1857.

On January 3, 1857, Treasurer Bates authorized the payment of $124,000 to Edwin Rowe of the Pacific Express Company for interest due in New York on July 1st.[25] In sworn testimony, Treasurer Bates confessed there was no Controller's warrant for the disbursement.[26] Bates left the Treasurer's office at 1:30 p.m., while Rowe took charge of the gold coin. Treasurer Bates told the clerk to drop the key to the safe at his hotel room later that evening. The clerk, Mr. Bunker, left the office at 3:30 p.m., while Rowe was still in the office counting the money.[27]

Treasurer Bates testified in an action brought by the Attorney General to force Bates to increase his bond from $100,000 filed with the Governor in 1855. But one of the witnesses in the court action against Bates was missing. Edwin Rowe was nowhere to be found in early February. He finally showed up at Judge Monson's Sacramento Courtroom to describe the transfer of gold coin into his possession. Unfortunately, he declined to state who helped him move $124,000 in gold coins from the Treasurer's safe, whom he deposited it with, or where the money might be located currently.[28]

Similar to California's credit rating, Dr. Bate's credibility as an honest, ethical, and competent Treasurer was rapidly deflating. Word of the extremely early payment of bond interest to Edwin Rowe caught the attention of the State Legislature in mid-January. Some legislators contended that State Treasurer Dr. Bates was an honest man and that Pacific Express would eventually transfer the money to Wells, Fargo & Company by June 5th to be shipped to New York by July 1st.

In the Assembly, a resolution was offered to appoint a committee to investigate the transfer of money to Pacific Express. Amos was incredulous at the weak

Amos P. Catlin

resolution. He wanted a full investigation, including information as to why Palmer, Cook & Co. had never returned the missing interest payment from 1856. In an address to his fellow Assembly members, Amos said:

"Also, why it was that the Treasurer of the State did not institute a suit against this company, or in some other mode attempt the recovery of the money; for I have been creditably informed that no action whatever — except, perhaps, such as lay in the persuasive powers of the Treasurer himself, had been taken until a very few days before the assembling of this Legislature. Now, this fact seems very strange to me. After what I have been made cognizant of, it seems very strange to me that this House will placidly sit and listen to eulogies upon the personal character of the Treasurer. We are told that he is very polite, a gentleman of the utmost integrity, and members sit here and take this and say no more about the whole matter."[29]

Amos was rather shocked at how sanguine so many legislators seemed to be over the situation. He was puzzled that so few Assembly members were as alarmed as he was over the missing money. Amos tried to rally the senses of his fellow Assembly members:

"Gentlemen, you may draw your own inferences. These bonds [provided by Pacific Express and Palmer, Cook & Co.] may be perfectly good; but I say that it is contrary to law and policy to establish this mode of doing business. It is a simple operation, by means of which we are to pay so much for taking care of the funds. For five months they will have this money, which will bring them $20,000. I can bring a man forward who will pay that amount in hard cash for its use. But these bankers enjoy it for nothing. Nay, the Treasurer gives them 3 per cent, for the privilege of taking charge of it! There was some purpose in sending out this money so long before it was necessary, some purpose not manifested."[30]

For all of Amos' passion on the topic, he was appointed as the committee chairman to investigate the Treasurer. The committee report was released by Amos on February 10th and characterized by the Sacramento Bee as "one of the most able, thorough and scathing reports ever read in that house."[31] The committee interviewed both Treasurer Bates and Edwin Rowe about the $124,000 transfer and other short-term loans from Wells, Fargo & Co. that they were involved with. The report stated, "The attempts of Mr. Rowe and the Treasurer to explain these facts are exceedingly lame. Their efforts to extricate themselves from the unfortunate dilemma in which the proofs place them, excite emotions of pity, so strong as to overcome any feelings of indignation which the fraudulent nature of the transactions are calculated to produce."[32]

As he did in the court case involving increasing Treasurer Bates' bond, Edwin Rowe refused to answer specific questions from the special Assembly committee about how he disposed of the $124,000 from the Treasurer's office. Amos and the other committee members surmised that a large portion of the money went to speculation with Palmer, Cook & Co. and the failed Adams & Co. of California business.[33] The committee concluded that Dr. Bates was guilty of malfeasance in the office of California Treasurer. They also determined that he was guilty of a felony for allowing Edwin Rowe, in the form of short-term loans from state coffers, to be used for his personal use.

The Assembly quickly resolved to impeach Treasurer Bates. Amos was appointed with several other members to draft the articles of impeachment and then present them to the Senate in a trial.[34] On the day of the impeachment vote, Dr. Bates sent a letter to the Assembly offering to answer all their questions with his attorney present. This led some Assembly members to ask for a delay in the impeachment vote. After having put in so much work writing the committee report, with indisputable evidence of Bates' malfeasance, a delay in the impeachment process triggered Amos to take to the floor of the Assembly.

"I am opposed to this motion mainly upon the ground that a further delay in our proceedings is wholly unnecessary. The counsel for the Treasurer, who probably drew up this letter that we have just heard read, seems to have supposed that the Treasurer was to be tried by this Assembly. That trial will take place before another tribunal [Senate.] The House tendered to the Treasurer a usual act of courtesy, allowing him, if he saw fit, to make any exculpating statement here to-day. He has chosen to make the statement which we have just heard. I suppose we are to take that as his statement made to this body by virtue of the privilege granted to him. He asks to be tried before this Assembly — for that is what his communication amounts to — and states that urgent business requires his immediate attendance in the city of San Francisco.

"I offered his attorney, before sundown yesterday, a printed copy of the evidence in the case, which he declined accepting. His [Dr. Bates] object in going to San Francisco is a matter of public notoriety, so I suppose I may have no hesitation in referring to it. It is for the purpose of procuring additional official bonds in the sum of $200,000, as demanded by the Judge of the District Court for this district. His absence will continue, in all probability, during the entire period of ten days. It matters not whether he is here personally or by attorney — that matter is quite immaterial. We certainly ought not to be delayed in such an important matter as this, by any excuses of this kind."[35]

All the sound and fury of protestation against the Treasurer and for impeachment were for naught. Dr. Bates resigned as California's State Treasurer the next day. While Bates had been impeached, he had not been convicted in the Senate. Until

Amos P. Catlin

he was found guilty in the Senate, he could conceivably run for public office again. Amos led the prosecution of Dr. Henry Bates before the Senate.[36]

One of the reasons Amos was tapped to lead the special Assembly committee investigation and the prosecution of Treasurer Bates was that both were members of the American Party. The American Party was a minority party in the legislature. Amos was also seen by his peers as having a higher allegiance to the law than to politics. As the Senate trial commenced, they received a letter from Dr. Bates' attorney stating he would not enter a plea of guilty or not guilty, arguing that Dr. Bates had resigned his elected position and was therefore a private citizen. In addition, the letter stated, Dr. Bates was being tried in a criminal court for the same offenses as outlined in the articles of impeachment.

The argument in defense of Dr. Bates stopped Amos in his tracks. While he was sure Bates was guilty, the refusal to plead in relation to current statutes and the larger realm of common law put Amos into a reflective mode. He then urged the Senate to pause and consider the implications of the situation. His thoughts before the Senate were paraphrased in the Sacramento Daily Union.

"The rule in common law pleading is, that if the party refuse to answer, it is equivalent to a plea of not guilty, but here the statute seems to direct that it is equivalent to a plea of guilty. But there is such a thing as it being possible that the provision of the statute may not be in conformity to the true intent and meaning of the Constitution. And if it be so it is our duty to disregard it. I think — indeed I have no doubt— myself now at this very moment of the correctness of the position that the refusal to answer is equivalent to a plea of guilty. Yet, I would suggest, as it is now no great object, that a temporary adjournment take place, in order to enable the managers to have a consultation among themselves, so that they may be unanimous upon what course they may take. I would suggest that an adjournment to this evening take place, leaving the proceeding to stand where it is now."[37]

But the elected members of the Senate did not have Amos' propensity to ponder over constitutional questions. They convicted Dr. Bates of the charges brought forth by the Assembly, which disqualified Dr. Henry Bates from holding office ever again in California.[38] If Amos' fellow legislators had not previously discerned his fascination with contemplating different aspects of the law, it was now in plain sight. Amos was willing to suspend the satisfaction of a quick guilty verdict in order to thoroughly review the legal questions and implications.

Ex-Treasurer Bates would be tried twice on multiple offenses in Sacramento. The first trial concluded on May 29th with a hung jury.[39] His second trial commenced in mid-November and was the subject of scorn in a Sacramento Bee editorial. The Bee felt the Sacramento County Sheriff had intentionally selected a jury pool

Amos P. Catlin

biased in favor of Dr. Bates.[40] The motion for a new trial venue was granted, and Dr. Bates was moved to Placer County for trial in 1858.[41] The result was the same. Dr. Bates was acquitted by a jury in Auburn, but more charges against him still remained.[42]

There were other attempts by California to recover some of the nearly $200,000 lost by Treasurer Bates. The State did sue the sureties of Treasurer Bates' 1855 bond and won a judgment.[43] Most of the men who had pledged assets for the bond were either broke or had nothing of value. However, one man, Samuel Norris, was forced to sell his property. The Norris Ranch was sold to Lloyd Tevis, and the proceeds went to the State.[44]

Before the scandal with Edwin Rowe broke, Dr. Bates married Miss Tilden in a fashionable wedding in San Francisco in early December 1856.[45] After all of the trials, Dr. Bates and his wife made their home in San Francisco. His wife would die three years later, and Dr. Bates would succumb to tuberculosis on November 18th, 1862, at the age of 38.[46]

Attorney-at-Law

Even though politics and politicians were exasperating to Amos, he did enjoy practicing law. In 1857, he started taking small steps to build a law practice. By the spring he had seven lawsuits on the calendar of the Sixth Judicial Court in Sacramento.[47] Amos' knowledge and wisdom was in demand. He had two successful water canal companies, he had sat on the Board of the Sacramento Valley Railroad, and he had been elected to the Senate and Assembly.

In May of 1857, Amos was elected as a delegate to the Wagon Road Convention.[48] The object of the convention was to explore ways to fund and build a wagon road over the Sierra Nevada range, based on a route surveyed by Sherman Day.[49] Later in the year, Amos attended a Ditch Owners Convention representing the Natoma Water and Mining Company.[50] The purpose of the water ditch owners convention was to get the California legislature to cajole Congress into granting rights and protections for the numerous water ditches and dams constructed on public property.[51] Amos was elected to the committee to lead the lobbying effort directed at the California legislature.[52]

With his Assembly duties now over, Amos focused his political ambitions on the American Party. If the American Party hoped to squeeze out the Republican Party and become the majority-minority party in California, it needed a reorganization and identity check. Amos was appointed to the statewide Constitution and By-Laws committee for the American Party.[53] That was followed up by being elected to the Executive Committee,[54] where he quickly became the chairman.[55]

Amos P. Catlin

American County Nominating Conven-
TION.—The several Ward and Precinct Clubs of Sacramento county will assemble in their respective districts
on SATURDAY, THE EIGHTEENTH OF JULY, and pro-
ceed to elect delegates to a County Nominating Convention. Said Convention will assemble in Sacramento on
MONDAY, THE TWENTIETH OF JULY, instant, at two
o'clock P. M., for the purpose of making county nominations and electing delegates to a State Nominating Convention.
The following is the ratio of representation, as determined by the Central Committee, to-wit:

	Delegates.		Delegates.
Sacramento—1st Ward	15	Iowa House	2
" 2d Ward	10	Michigan Bar	4
" 3d Ward	18	Live Oak	2
Patterson's	1	Daylor's Ranch	2
Magnolia	1	Southerland Ranch	1
Alder Creek	2	Buckner's House	2
Folsom	5	Hicks' Ranch	1
Prairie City	2	Fugitt's Ranch	1
White Rock Spring	1	Sidwell's Ranch	1
Walls' Diggings	1	Sharp's Ranch	2
Mormon Island	2	Bunyan's Ranch	1
Big Gulch	1	Williams' Ranch	1
Mississippi Bar	1	Twelve Mile House	2
Wilson's	2	Tivoli	1
Star House	1	American Union Hotel	2

All proxies shall be residents of the respective districts
which they claim to represent.
By order of the American Executive Committee.
A. P. CATLIN, Chairman.

Sacramento Daily Union, July 7, 1857

*17. Amos Catlin, Chairman of the American party
county nominating convention, 1857.*

Amos helped write an introduction of principles of the American Party that was run as an advertisement in newspapers. In short, all the ills that California were experiencing was the fault of the Democrats.[56] Of course, conveniently omitted was the fact that one of the biggest swindles ever to hit California was perpetrated by former State Treasurer Bates of the American Party.

At the American Party State Convention, there was noticeable tension with the San Francisco contingent of delegates, whom Amos denounced as a petty faction of doubtful politics.[57] The resolutions passed at the convention, and read into the minutes by Amos, were weak proclamations declaring patriotism, settlers' rights, and the Democrats were to blame for anything they had not done.[58] Colonel George Washington Bowie was selected to be the American Party candidate for governor.[59] Thomas B. McFarland, an attorney from Nevada City, was nominated for the office of Attorney General.[60]

A party platform with no distinguishing qualities along with internal squabbling ended the run of the American Party in California after the 1857 election cycle. While many of the men running for office under the American Party banner were well liked and respected, there was very little difference between Democrats and the American Party in the eyes of voters. Amos tried his best to keep the American Party afloat, but it sank.

Amos P. Catlin

[1] Daily Alta California, Volume 9, Number 10, 11 January 1857

[2] Daily Alta California, Volume 9, Number 11, 12 January 1857

[3] The Gadsden Purchase, or Treaty, was an agreement between the United States and Mexico, finalized in 1854, in which the United States agreed to pay Mexico $10 million for a 29,670 square mile portion of Mexico that later became part of Arizona and New Mexico. Gadsden's Purchase provided the land necessary for a southern transcontinental railroad and attempted to resolve conflicts that lingered after the Mexican-American War. https://history.state.gov/milestones/1830-1860/gadsden-purchase

[4] Sacramento Daily Union, Volume 12, Number 1820, 26 January 1857

[5] Sacramento Daily Union, Volume 12, Number 1820, 26 January 1857

[6] Sacramento Daily Union, Volume 12, Number 1814, 19 January 1857

[7] Sacramento Daily Union, Volume 12, Number 1816, 21 January 1857

[8] Sacramento Daily Union, Volume 12, Number 1816, 21 January 1857

[9] Sacramento Daily Union, Volume 12, Number 1816, 21 January 1857

[10] Sacramento Daily Union, Volume 12, Number 1824, 30 January 1857

[11] Sacramento Daily Union, Volume 10, Number 1510, 28 January 1856

[12] Shasta Courier, Volume 4, Number 4, 7 April 1855

[13] Sacramento Bee, 1857 February 7

[14] Shasta Courier, Volume 4, Number 4, 7 April 1855

[15] Sacramento Daily Union, Volume 10, Number 1543, 6 March 1856

[16] Sacramento Daily Union, Volume 10, Number 1546, 10 March 1856

[17] Sacramento Daily Union, Volume 11, Number 1668, 31 July 1856

[18] Sacramento Daily Union, Volume 11, Number 1669, 1 August 1856

[19] Wide West, Volume 3, Number 21, 3 August 1856

[20] Marysville Daily Herald, Volume VII, Number 15, 22 August 1856

[21] Sacramento Daily Union, Volume 11, Number 1687, 22 August 1856

[22] Sacramento Bee, 1857 February 10

[23] Sacramento Bee, 1857 February 6

[24] Sacramento Bee, 1857 February 8

[25] Sacramento Bee, 1857 February 6

[26] Sacramento Bee, 1857 February 6

[27] Sacramento Bee, 1857 February 6

[28] Sacramento Bee, 1857 February 10

[29] Sacramento Daily Union, Volume 12, Number 1812, 17 January 1857

[30] Sacramento Daily Union, Volume 12, Number 1812, 17 January 1857

[31] Sacramento Bee, 1857 February 10

[32] Sacramento Daily Union, Volume 12, Number 1833, 10 February 1857

[33] Sacramento Daily Union, Volume 12, Number 1833, 10 February 1857

[34] Sacramento Daily Union, Volume 12, Number 1834, 11 February 1857

[35] Sacramento Daily Union, Volume 12, Number 1834, 11 February 1857

[36] Sacramento Daily Union, Volume 12, Number 1858, 11 March 1857

[37] Sacramento Daily Union, Volume 12, Number 1860, 13 March 1857

[38] Sacramento Daily Union, Volume 12, Number 1860, 13 March 1857

[39] Sacramento Daily Union, Volume 13, Number 1927, 30 May 1857

[40] Sacramento Bee, November 23, 1857

[41] Sacramento Daily Union, Volume 14, Number 2132, 26 January 1858

[42] Sacramento Daily Union, Volume 14, Number 2155, 22 February 1858

[43] Sacramento Daily Union, Volume 14, Number 2033, 1 October 1857

[44] Sacramento Daily Union, Volume 14, Number 2050, 21 October 1857

[45] Daily Alta California, Number 334, 10 December 1856

[46] Daily Alta California, Volume XIV, Number 4654, 19 November 1862

Amos P. Catlin

[47] Sacramento Bee, 1857 April 6
[48] Sacramento Daily Union, Volume 13, Number 1908, 8 May 1857
[49] Sacramento Daily Union, Volume 13, Number 1911, 12 May 1857
[50] Sacramento Daily Union, Volume 13, Number 2005, 29 August 1857
[51] Sacramento Daily Union, Volume 14, Number 2064, 6 November 1857
[52] Sacramento Daily Union, Volume 14, Number 2064, 6 November 1857
[53] Sacramento Daily Union, Volume 13, Number 1951, 27 June 1857
[54] Sacramento Daily Union, Volume 13, Number 1952, 29 June 1857
[55] Sacramento Daily Union, Volume 13, Number 1959, 7 July 1857
[56] Sacramento Daily Union, Volume 13, Number 1962, 10 July 1857
[57] Sacramento Bee, 1857 July 29
[58] Sacramento Daily Union, Volume 13, Number 1979, 30 July 1857
[59] Sacramento Bee, 1857 July 29
[60] Sacramento Daily Union, Volume 13, Number 2004, 28 August 1857

Amos P. Catlin

Chapter Six: Folsom Home, Railroads, Marriage, 1858 - 1860

As a cold January 25th dawned in 1858, Amos celebrated his 35th birthday. He was an eligible bachelor who had spent most of his time apportioned to the water canal business, to politics, or to building his law practice. The community of Mormon Island was nice, but Folsom, with the arrival of the Sacramento Valley Railroad, had become the social and business center for eastern Sacramento County.

18. The Wide West illustration of Folsom, 1856

While Amos pined for home, with his family, friends, and all the memories of youth spent at the Kingston Academy and his grandfather, he knew he would never return to New York. While the climate of the California foothills was radically different from the Hudson Valley where Amos grew up, Folsom, with its grid street layout and gently rolling hills could aspire to be like one of those quaint East Coast villages. All Folsom needed were men with a vision to build a sustainable community, with thriving businesses, homes, churches, and institutions of higher learning.

Amos' vision of community had been formed in Kingston, a small New York village steeped in colonial and revolutionary history. Originally founded by Dutch settlers in the 17th century, Kingston was designated as New York's capital in 1777. British troops, moving up from New York City, came across Kingston and burned it down. David Catlin, Amos' grandfather, served in the Connecticut Militia fighting the British and participated in the battle of Danbury.[1]

Later in life, David Catlin moved to Kingston. The Kingston Academy was constructed in 1774, with a curriculum focused on the humanities, mathematics,

Amos P. Catlin

and science. Upon admission to the Kingston Academy, since his family did not live in the immediate area, Amos moved in with his grandfather David Catlin, living with him during the school year for six years until David's death in 1839.[2] Amos graduated from the Kingston Academy in 1840 and then began to study law at a local Kingston law office.[3]

After three and half years of study, Amos was admitted to the bar of the Supreme Court of New York at Albany in 1844.[4] For four years, Amos practiced law in Ulster County, where he met fellow attorneys John Currey and Theodoric Westbrook. In 1848, Amos entered a law partnership with his cousin George Catlin in New York.[5] Of course, when the gold discovery in California was announced and confirmed, Amos, after years of relatively sedate law practice and study, could not contain his youthful exuberance for adventure.

In 1856, Amos stood on a bluff overlooking the American River at the foot of Leidesdorff Street in Folsom, wondering if this new village could be the Kingston of his youth. While California development was still very fluid with emerging industries and economic sectors, Amos gravitated toward Folsom, calling it his home for the foreseeable future.

In the summer of 1856, John Bowker sold Amos the Mansion House hotel at Figueroa and Sibley streets for $2,000.[6] In 1857, Amos would purchase another 122 lots in Folsom for $1,340 from the Folsom Estate.[7] The purchase included the entire blocks of 41, 66, 74, and 90. Each block contained 16 lots. Some of the lot purchases were made jointly with other men such as H. A. Thompson and Horatio Livermore, but most were held completely by Amos.

Folsom Literary Institute

Even though Amos wasn't married and had no children, he knew the foundation of any strong and sustainable community was a solid school system. In addition, in order to cultivate and attract a community that valued scholarly pursuits, an institution of higher learning was necessary. Amos and other men who identified Folsom as their new home came together to propose the Folsom Literary Institute. The vision was to have the academy focus on rhetoric, Latin, Greek, French, penmanship, mathematics, drawing, and music. The Folsom Literary Institute was part of the grand vision to make the town of Folsom into a genteel and respected community.

A corporation was formed, with Amos as a member of the Board of Trustees along with Dr. Alexander Donaldson, C.T.H. Palmer, Francis Clark, A.G. Kinsey, Dr. Levi Bradley, E. D. Hoskins and S.V. Blakeslee. The trustees approached Horatio G. Livermore, who had purchased several blocks in Folsom, with the proposition for using the lots for the small literary institute. In 1857, Livermore deeded four

Amos P. Catlin

and a half blocks to the institute. The grant came with certain conditions. First, the property was only to be used for the school. Second, the trustees were to incorporate. Third, the Board of Trustees had to be independent. Finally, the school could never be under ecclesiastical or church control.[8] Residents of Folsom were excited about this new addition to the community and contributed $3,200 for the construction.[9]

Initially a frame building was constructed as the school. Increased enrollment and fundraisers financed the construction of a brick building in the heart of Folsom. One of the driving forces for the Folsom Literary Institute was S.V. Blakeslee, who was also an ordained minister. The school added students and teachers, but maintaining its operation was a continual struggle. When Blakeslee died in 1869, the heart that kept the school beating stopped.[10] The school closed, and the building fell into disrepair.

Water, Land, & Chinese

19. Wire rope suspension bridge over the American River at Folsom, 1866. Library of Congress

In addition to schools, the town of Folsom was constructing infrastructure to support the region's growth. A.G. Kinsey and Harvey A. Thompson, business associates of Amos, had constructed a wire rope suspension bridge over the American River a few years earlier.[11] This allowed wagon teams and stagecoaches to depart Folsom for Auburn and other mining communities. In addition to the pedestrian and wagon bridge, a new railroad bridge was being designed that would extend the reach of the railroad up to Marysville.

Part of the industrial expansion happening around Folsom was the extension of the Natoma Canal into mining and farming land on the south side of the American River. Whereas most of the Natoma Canal had been on federally controlled public land, the town of Folsom and points west were within the William Alexander

Amos P. Catlin

Leidesdorff Mexican land grant, Rancho Rio de los Americanos. Captain Joseph Libby Folsom had acquired the immense land grant after Leidesdorff's death in 1848. Folsom himself died in 1855, which precipitated the planned terminus of the Sacramento Valley Railroad to be changed from Granite City to Folsom.

The boundaries of the Leidesdorff land grant, while not exactly marked, were known to residents in the region. Regardless, Amos and the Natoma Water and Mining Company, in the exuberance of the Gold Rush days, constructed parts of the water canal, dams, and holding ponds on property now in the possession of Joseph L. Folsom. From the perspective of Amos and other ditch owners, the construction of a water canal only enhanced the property value of the land. However, Joseph L. Folsom did not necessarily subscribe to the notion that any increase in land value compensated him for property lost to a water canal. Folsom had his attorneys initiate proceedings to recover back damages, with a demand for more than a third of the gross receipts from water sales as rents. [12]

20. Amos Catlin's purchase of the northeast portion of the Leidesdorff land grant.

In order to stop any future disputes, Amos decided he needed to formally purchase the land traversed by the Natoma Water and Mining Company water ditches. Somewhat conveniently, most of the land that Amos needed was owned by one man, Charles Nystrom. In March 1858, Amos closed on the sale of 9,643 acres from Nystrom for $36,800. [13] The purchase excluded the town of Folsom and the Sacramento Valley Railroad right-of-way, leaving 9,226 acres in the control of Amos.

The boundaries of the property were described in the metes and bounds system, using landmarks and topographical characteristics to outline the land. The deed description begins with, "Commencing at the north eastern corner of the Rancho Rio de los Americanos at a tree marked L (Leidesdorff). Thence south four hundred and twenty and seventy-five one hundredths chains." The part of the deed that would become very important to Amos was, "…reference being hereby made to the maps of the official survey of said Rancho…approved by John G. Hayes, U.S. Surveyor General for California." [14]

Amos P. Catlin

This huge piece of property that surrounded the town of Folsom and several miles of the railroad was in the name of Amos P. Catlin. In a testament to Amos' honesty and integrity, he filed with the Sacramento County Recorder a Declaration of Trust. Amos declared that Charles Nystrom of San Francisco had sold him the property and from that day forward he would hold it in trust for the use and benefit of the stockholders of the Natoma Water and Mining Company.[15]

Most of the property outside of Folsom was wide open prairie and rolling hills down to the American River. There was still a fair amount of mining being prosecuted, with miners squatting on land next to their mining claims. Most of the miners had received permission from landowners such as Amos to sluice the ground for gold. Sprinkled amongst the operations of white miners were Chinese immigrants, also trying to coax out a little bit of gold dust from the earth. Inevitably, the competition led to assaults by subsistence white miners against their Chinese counterparts.

The boundaries of the Leidesdorff land grant were in dispute. Even though the Folsom Estate was selling parts of the land grant to companies like the Natoma Water and Mining Company, not all of the residents agreed that those sales were proper. Rumors swirled that Joseph L. Folsom's dying wish was to dispose of the land first to settlers at reasonable prices. In a letter to the Sacramento Bee, an anonymous letter writer outlined the speculative land dealings of Amos to acquire property for the Natoma Canal and himself.[16]

The letter, full of inaccuracies, misrepresentations, and speculation, contended that the current boundary of the Leidesdorff land grant was too far to the east. The proper eastern boundary should be located at Alder Creek.[17] This more westerly alignment of the land grant would exclude the town of Folsom from the land grant as well as much of the land purchased by Amos and controlled by the Natoma Water and Mining Company. The author, pen-named Justice, accuses the "Ditch Company" of unlawful trespassing actions against settlers.[18]

Amos did have to initiate lawsuits against men squatting on the Natoma property and cutting wood. In one instance, he sought an injunction to restrain men from cutting trees on the Natoma property and carrying off the wood. Amos represented the Natoma Water and Mining Company and Edwin B. Crocker represented the defendants.[19] Shortly after the letter was published in February, a mob of white men attacked Chinese miners in the Folsom vicinity.

In early March, Hartford Anderson and Michael Wallace inflamed the passions of white men at Alder Creek against Chinese immigrant miners in the area. As soaked with racism as they were with whiskey, approximately 150 men marched to the locations of Chinese miners, destroying their mining equipment, burning their homes, physically assaulting the Chinese, and stealing their money.[20]

Amos P. Catlin

Hartford Anderson denied any culpability with the crimes and accused the Sacramento Daily Union, who reported the incident, of being biased in favor of Amos.[21]

From the very beginnings of Chinese immigration to California, there was prevailing sentiment that the Chinese, because they were willing to work for less pay, took jobs away from white men. A new version of this logic applied to the Natoma Water and Mining Company. Because the Natoma Canal sold water to Chinese miners, many believed the company was guilty of depriving white men of an income from mining. Therefore, not only were the Chinese evil, so was the water company, for supplying them water to sluice the ground in search of gold.

The Sacramento Daily Union pointed out that the state and county had levied a monthly foreign miner tax on the Chinese, contributing over $15,000 to the state and county treasuries each year.[22] An attack on the Chinese only served to reduce tax revenues for public services. Instead of Folsom aspiring to be a shining city on a hill, the violence was making the area look like "bloody Kansas."

Between the smears on his reputation, attacks on his Natoma Water and Mining Company, and the violence that was smashing the tranquility of Folsom, Amos felt he needed to address the situation. In a letter to the Sacramento Daily Union, Amos explained that the Natoma Canal had to purchase the property of the Leidesdorff land grant. The Folsom Estate was suing for damages and rents. Amos stated that it was the express wishes of the miners receiving water from the Natoma Canal that the company acquire the property to keep the water flowing.[23]

With respect to his company's attempts to restrain some men from cutting down the trees, "The timber upon the land is sparse and scattered, and is required for the domestic and mining uses of the people resident upon it, and for necessary repairs in and about the ditches and canals of the Company." The Natoma Company had to stop the continued slaughter of the timber in a malicious manner, wrote Amos.[24]

Then Amos addressed the rumor that the Natoma Company intended to supplant the white miners and introduce Chinese, "…by a gradual system of preferring the latter to the former in the distribution and sale of water."[25] He then traced the origin of the ludicrous Chinese conspiracy to a misunderstanding about how water was distributed. Near Alder Creek, a group of Chinese men had purchased a claim from two white men. The mining claim, and the outlet on the water ditch that supplied it, lay on higher ground, above other claims owned by white men. If the Chinese were using their full allotment of water, mining claims below them might not receive as much water, Amos explained. However, he went on to add that the Chinese men were using some 20 miner's inches less water than the previous white miners.[26]

Amos P. Catlin

In Amos' opinion, it was only a few men who had instigated the attack on the Chinese, primarily over the restraining order preventing them from cutting down the trees in the area. "The few malicious and evil disposed persons who have fanned into a flame a feeling of ill-will, which often prevails against the Chinese, until it culminated to the bursting point at Alder Creek, will be disappointed. It will not avail them anything in the injunction suit."[27]

The water ditch companies were often compared to the railroads in terms of monopolizing resources and land. When Amos arrived in California in 1849, he was like most every other man who wanted to do some gold mining and then go back home with a full purse. It was never in Amos' imagination that he would become the public face of a large corporation hated by some settlers.

Amos closed his letter in defense of his company:

"The Ditch Company, which has always pursued an undeviating course of impartiality to all its customers, has been denounced as a 'monopoly,' a 'soulless corporation,' and sundry other hard names, by insane scribblers and idle Ishmaelites, the pests of every neighborhood. Nothing short of a sense of duty to those whose private interests are in some measure in my keeping, as President of the Natoma Company, could have induced me to notice in a public manner these efforts to injure the stockholders of said Company. A. P. Catlin"[28]

Amos seems to have been wounded more by the attacks on his integrity and intentions by fellow pioneers and miners than by those made by his political opponents. At his core, he identified as a pioneer, gold miner, and instigator of industrial progress in California. He had always put the interests of settlers above that of large corporations or government. Now, in addressing the rumors and racism of the day, he had to defend the Natoma Company, both as a corporation and as an extension of who he was.

Amos P. Catlin

California Central Railroad

21. California Central Railroad bridge over the American River at Folsom, ca. 1860. Center for Sacramento History, 1968-129-01

The grand plan for the Sacramento Valley Railroad, as initially envisioned by Charles Lincoln Wilson, was to create a road that would connect Sacramento to the mining communities. Wilson organized the Sacramento Valley Railroad, became the first president, and went back East to recruit Theodore Judah to engineer and map the railroad. Judah's plan was to run the line from Sacramento up to Negro Bar on the south side of the American River. The road would cross the American River at Negro Bar to Big Gulch on the northside and wind its way up to Marysville.

As a stockholder and director on the Sacramento Valley Railroad, Amos became personally acquainted with both Wilson and Judah. The trio would become life-long friends. The railroad, like the Natoma ditch, had money problems. Whereas the water ditch could start generating revenue fairly quickly before the entire project was completed, that was not the case with the railroad. Management and

Amos P. Catlin

money issues resulted in Charles Wilson getting pushed out of the Sacramento Valley Railroad. Joseph L. Folsom would take over control of the railroad in 1855.

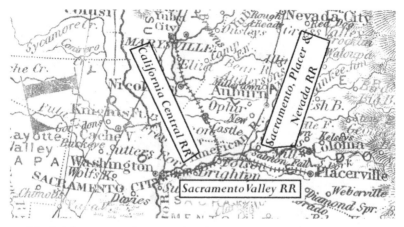

22. California map depicting the Sacramento Valley RR, California Central RR, and proposed Sacramento, Placer & Nevada RR, 1862

With the completion of the first leg of the railroad to Folsom in 1856, the Sacramento Valley Railroad stalled future expansion up to Marysville until the line could generate revenue and become profitable. Theodore Judah was a civil engineer and project manager. With the cessation of construction of the first railroad west of Mississippi completed to Folsom, Judah moved on to other projects. However, Wilson had not given up on his vision for a rail line to Marysville and created the California Central Railroad to complete the road that Judah had laid out.

In support of Wilson's railroad vision, Amos purchased 10 shares of California Central Railroad (CCRR) stock at $100 each in May 1858.[29] Amos was elected by the shareholders to serve on the Board of Directors of the CCRR. An exodus of men up to new gold regions on the Frazier in Canada led the CCRR to become one of the first railroads to employ Chinese labor. The CCRR was estimated to have 50 Chinese men employed at building the road in June of 1858.[30]

Similar to the design of Folsom, Charles Lincoln Wilson acquired the property along the proposed rail line and established the town of Lincoln in Placer County.

Amos P. Catlin

Amos showed his support for Wilson and the little burg by purchasing seven lots in November of 1859 for $340.[31]

23. Amos Catlin stock certificate for 10 shares of the California Central Railroad Co., 1859. California State Library

In January of 1859, Amos bought another 60 shares of the CCRR. He loaned 10 of the shares to Judah later in the summer.[32] The stock loan was in addition to Amos' $1,600 loan to Judah the month before for Judah's American River Railroad.[33] After Judah completed his work on the Sacramento Valley RR, he organized the American River Railroad. Amos, along with A.G. Kinsey and H. A. Thompson, invested in the railroad venture. Judah with fellow civil engineer Leet, made surveys for a rail route from Sacramento northwest toward Auburn.[34]

By 1859, as work on the CCRR was winding down, Judah was becoming fixated on finding a route over the Sierras for a Pacific Railroad. Judah's survey work and passionate belief that a rail route of the Sierra Nevada range could be found attracted the attention of men who would go on to form the Central Pacific Railroad and contract with Judah for Chief Engineer.

As the California Central Railroad completed the wooden bridge over the American River, the small town of Auburn put in motion the construction of a railroad from Folsom. The proposed Sacramento, Placer & Nevada Railroad would connect with the California Central Railroad on the north side of the American River at the Ashland depot. Suddenly, from most parts of Folsom, residents like Amos could see three different railroads operating or under construction by 1860.

Amos P. Catlin

Privately financing the construction of a railroad was a daunting task, as the struggles of the Sacramento Valley Railroad illustrated. By 1860, Charles Wilson was running into cash flow problems. He sold Amos and Benjamin F. Hastings 450 acres of land that surrounded the town of Lincoln for $10,000.[35] Eight months later in 1861, Amos and Hastings would sell the land to Harry Rood for the same amount of money.[36]

24. *"Aug. 29, 1859, Borrowed this day of A. P. Catlin a certificate of 10 shares of stock of Cal Central RR to be returned on demand. Theo. Judah." California State Library*

In a previously agreed upon exchange, Amos would then buy nine complete blocks and another 10 individual lots in Lincoln from Rood for $2,000.[37] In February 1862, Amos would deed block 63 in the town of Lincoln to Rood to be held in trust for Sarah E. Wilson, wife of Charles Wilson. With President Lincoln's signature on the Pacific Railroad Act in the summer of 1862, the three operating railroads (Sacramento Valley, California Central, and the Sacramento, Placer & Nevada) would begin to be strangled. The Central Pacific Railroad, beginning in Sacramento and heading up to Auburn, would take most of the railroad traffic in that direction.

Amos had never wanted to have a significant presence in the town of Lincoln, for his growing legal practice was in Folsom and Sacramento. He was able to shed most of the property he owned in Placer County by 1865. Unlike his Folsom lot sales, which generally netted a profit for Amos, he lost several hundred dollars disposing of the Lincoln lots.

Independent Party

Notwithstanding some misplaced grievances by local miners, Amos was an admired and respected resident of Folsom. He was in the central vortex of numerous academic and industrial initiatives that were driving the Folsom region. It was no surprise when his name started to be floated around for County Supervisor or another run for the Assembly. The only problem was that he was politically homeless. Amos was of the mind that, if you had a product you wanted to get to market, but you had no mode of transport, you built yourself a wagon.

Along with other men who were similarly dissatisfied with the candidates nominated in the two main political parties, Amos and his cohorts called a meeting for the establishment of an Independent Party in the summer of 1858. In Sacramento, at the National Theater on K Street, the August meeting was called to order for the formation of an independent ticket of candidates. Amos was chosen as President and chair of the meeting. Amos in his opening remarks tipped his hand and showed his political weakness. He announced his intention to act with impartiality.[38] He was trying to operate more like a courtroom judge than a political partisan.

One of Amos' great political faults was assuming that men could act like rational adults. He never developed, nor was he inclined towards, political tactics and strategies to silence and render impotent his political opponents. The mass people's party meeting devolved into an absurd comedy. Out of Amos' control were the crowds of men from the other political parties in attendance for the sole purpose of sowing discord. They succeeded. When hisses, boos, and derisive laughter broke out over one of his procedural decisions as chair of the meeting, Amos responded, "Cries and hisses fall harmless on me. I shall do my duty, regardless of all attempts at intimidation."[39]

The Independent Party was successful at nominating a slate of candidates for local and legislative offices. Amos himself was nominated for Assembly.[40] The reviews of Amos' efforts at corralling politically independent men to counter the established political machines were mixed. The Sacramento Bee said there was no better man than Amos to lead an independent movement focused on electing men of merit and capacity.[41] Other observers complained that it wasn't an independent ticket, it was the ticket of Amos Catlin.[42]

As the derision poured in over the nominating process of the Independent Party and Amos' motives, candidates started declining the nominations. Leland Stanford declined the nomination for State Senator, and Dr. Harkness dropped out of the nomination for Supervisor.[43] Other men nominated would step away from the endorsement of the Independent Party. Amos' popularity in Sacramento County was not enough to get him elected. He was defeated in his bid for an Assembly seat. The political experience of 1858 illustrated how most men were blindly loyal to their chosen political party.

Law Practice & Marriage

The bulk of Amos' legal work revolved around corporate law concerning water ditches and railroads. In 1860, he was appointed to a committee to review and propose amendments to a Sacramento County consolidation bill before the legislature.[44] The bill sought to consolidate the municipal government of Sacramento City with the county government. His fellow committee members were A.C. Monson, Mark Hopkins, L.A. Booth, W.C. Hopping, and Robert Robinson. Outside of the city, the consolidation bill was viewed as a vehicle to help the City of Sacramento, as it was under considerable debt from public works projects such as flood control levees and water and sewer projects.

As political demands on his time grew, Amos was beginning to pull back from his duties at the water canals. A. T. Arrowsmith took over as President of the American River Water and Mining Company that was managing the North Fork Ditch.[45] Amos began to focus more of his energies on his law practice. Land disputes were becoming more frequent as the Commission on Land Grants and the federal Government Land Office surveys were completing their work in the region. Amos and Edwin. B. Crocker represented Oliver. C. Lewis in District Court in an action by Wesley Myers disputing the boundaries of the town of Folsom.[46]

While working to establish the Folsom Literary Institute, Amos became close friends with Dr. Alexander Crawford Donaldson and his family. Dr. Donaldson had come to California in 1852 and settled in Folsom in 1855.[47] In Folsom, Dr. Donaldson opened an office and drug store on the corner of Wool and Sutter streets.[48] He was also involved in Trinity Episcopal Church in Folsom.[49] Dr. Donaldson also had a daughter, Ruth Anne.

Ruth Anne Donaldson and Amos grew acquainted with each other and were married on May 1, 1860, in Folsom.[50] Amos was 37 years old and Ruth 20 at the time of their nuptials. Amos moved in with the Donaldson family in Folsom until he could build a proper home for his new bride. A short walk from Dr. Donaldson's drug store, Amos would open his law practice in the McCamley Building.[51] Folsom was an ideal location for Amos, as he could hop on the train for the short trip into Sacramento for meetings and court appearances.

After Joseph L. Folsom took control of the Leidesdorff land grant, he served notice that, except for some taverns and hotels, all others would be considered trespassers.[52] The stern notice was legally necessary if Folsom needed to exercise any evictions. However, some ranches and mining claims were allowed to operate. When Amos and the Natoma Water and Mining Company purchased the part of the original Leidesdorff land grant, they too allowed for some existing operations.

Dr. Alexander Donaldson, Amos' future father-in-law, sold Amos his Sulky Flat mining claim in 1860 for $350.[53] Sulky Flat, situated just north of where Willow Creek entered the American River, one and one-half miles south of Folsom, was

Amos P. Catlin

on the Natoma Water and Mining Company property. That same year, Amos would buy 160 acres, directly south of Folsom, from Jules Vaillant for $1,500.[54]

While Folsom held Amos' heart, he flirted with being a ranch owner, acquiring a piece of property that would bear his name. The Natoma Water and Mining Company sold Amos 240 acres next to the Vaillant in 1862 for $750.[55] However, after a couple years, Amos determined that being a ranch owner wasn't in his blood. He would sell the Catlin Ranch back to the Natoma Water and Mining Company in 1865.[56]

Amos would invest in a variety of different mining claims and land in northeast Sacramento County. In 1857, he bought a 20 percent interest in the Rancho de San Juan land grant on the north side of the American River from John Semple for $5,000.[57] Two years later, in 1859, he would sell the same interest in the San Juan land grant to John Currey for $2,000.[58] Amos would also invest in the Rhodes Northerly Extension Gold Mining Company with several other men in 1863.[59] Rhodes Diggings, southeast of Prairie City, was receiving water from Rhodes water ditch supplied by the Natoma Water and Mining Company.

Bell and Everett Constitutional Party

The United States in 1860 was bitterly divided over the question of slavery. As a great admirer of Henry Clay, who engineered many congressional compromises to keep the Union from disintegrating, Amos also prioritized keeping the Union together over seriously addressing the issue of slavery. The Constitution was the singular principle that was binding the states together in the Union. It was only natural that Amos would move to support the emerging Constitutional Union Party on behalf of the candidacy of John Bell of Tennessee for president and Edward Everett of Massachusetts for vice president.

In late July, Amos chaired the first organizational meeting for the new Constitutional Party and was selected for the Sacramento County Central Committee. The real order of business was to organize a state convention and nominate Bell and Everett so that California could send Electoral College electors back to Washington, D. C. At the September State Convention, Amos and George W. Bowie were appointed to draft resolutions for final endorsement. Similar to Amos' resolutions from the Independent Party platform, the resolutions were all patriotic pronouncements and nothing about the question of slavery.[60]

For all of Amos' hard work, John Bell did not even come close to carrying California. Lincoln won California and would go on to be elected President. As the nation braced for the coming secession crisis that would lead to Civil War, Amos stepped back from politics. For the next several years, until after the civil war had concluded, he would hibernate from any party politics. Instead, he focused on management of the Natoma Water and Mining Company, expanding his law practice, and real estate investments.

[1] Application for Membership, The California Society of the Sons of the American Revolution, Amos Catlin, May 26, 1896

[2] Application for Membership, The California Society of the Sons of the American Revolution, Amos Catlin, May 26, 1896

[3] The National Cyclopedia of American Biography, Volume 8, 1898, page 87

[4] History of the Bench and Bar of California, by Oscar Tully Shuck. 1901

[5] History of the Bench and Bar of California, by Oscar Tully Shuck. 1901

[6] Sacramento County Deed book 18560816, page 568

[7] Sacramento County Deed book 18571127, page 71

[8] Sacramento County Deed book 18571209, page 118

[9] Sacramento Daily Union, Volume 15, Number 2299, 10 August 1858

[10] Lone Pine Breeze, Folsom Telegraph, December 5th, 1941. Folsom History Museum archives

[11] Sacramento Daily Union, Volume 9, Number 1350, 24 July 1855

[12] Sacramento Daily Union, Volume 14, Number 2169, 10 March 1858

[13] Sacramento County Deed book 18580417, page 46

[14] Sacramento County Deed book 18580417, page 46

[15] Sacramento County Deed book 18580621, page 267

[16] Sacramento Bee, 1858 February 23

[17] Sacramento Bee, 1858 February 23

[18] Sacramento Bee, 1858 February 23

[19] Sacramento Daily Union, Volume 16, Number 2428, 7 January 1859

[20] Sacramento Daily Union, Volume 14, Number 2166, 6 March 1858

[21] Sacramento Bee, 1858 March 9

[22] Sacramento Daily Union, Volume 14, Number 2166, 6 March 1858

[23] Sacramento Daily Union, Volume 14, Number 2169, 10 March 1858

[24] Sacramento Daily Union, Volume 14, Number 2169, 10 March 1858

[25] Sacramento Daily Union, Volume 14, Number 2169, 10 March 1858

[26] Sacramento Daily Union, Volume 14, Number 2169, 10 March 1858

[27] Sacramento Daily Union, Volume 14, Number 2169, 10 March 1858

[28] Sacramento Daily Union, Volume 14, Number 2169, 10 March 1858

[29] California Central RR stock certificate. California State Library, Catlin Collection Box 500

[30] Sacramento Daily Union, Volume 15, Number 2252, 15 June 1858

[31] Placer County Deed book E, page 558

[32] Promissory note, Judah to Amos Catlin, August 29, 1859. California State Library, Catlin Collection Box 500

[33] Promissory note, Judah to Amos Catlin, July 19, 1859. California State Library, Catlin Collection Box 500

[34] Themis, Sacramento, August 31, 1889, Vol. 1, No. 28

[35] Placer County Deed book F, page 579

[36] Placer County Deed book G, page 398

[37] Placer County Deed book G, page 400

[38] Sacramento Daily Union, Volume 15, Number 2300, 11 August 1858

[39] Sacramento Daily Union, Volume 15, Number 2300, 11 August 1858

[40] Sacramento Daily Union, Volume 15, Number 2300, 11 August 1858

[41] Sacramento Bee, 1858 August 11

[42] Sacramento Bee, 1858 August 12

[43] Daily Alta California, Volume 10, Number 222, 14 August 1858

[44] Sacramento Daily Union, Volume 18, Number 2774, 16 February 1860

Amos P. Catlin

[45] 1860 Sacramento Daily Union, Volume 18, Number 2799, 16 March 1860
[46] Sacramento Bee, 1860 March 13
[47] Sacramento Daily Union, Volume 47, Number 7165, 23 March 1874
[48] The Folsom Telegraph, 1865 August 12
[49] Sacramento Bee, 1861 April 8
[50] Sacramento Daily Union, Volume 19, Number 2840, 3 May 1860
[51] The Folsom Telegraph, 1865 May 20
[52] Daily Alta California, Volume 1, Number 95, 19 April 1850
[53] Sacramento County Deed book 18600216, page 295
[54] Sacramento County Deed book 18601113, page 538
[55] Sacramento County Deed book 18640822, page 217
[56] Sacramento County Deed book 18650410, page 788.
[57] Sacramento County Deed book 18571222, page 164
[58] Sacramento County Deed book 18590415, page 616
[59] Sacramento County Deed book 18630331, page 117
[60] Sacramento Daily Union, Volume 19, Number 2947, 6 September 1860

Amos P. Catlin

Chapter Seven: U.S. Supreme Court - Leidesdorff Land Grant

Abraham Lincoln was elected U.S. President and sworn into office in 1861. Shortly thereafter, the grand experiment in democracy fractured into Civil War, and the Union was torn apart. Even though California had voted for Lincoln by a narrow margin in the election, the state was predominantly controlled by the Democratic Party. The question then became, would California side with the states' rights argument, as they had done with the Kansas-Nebraska Resolution, or place the cohesion and stability of the Union as the priority in the conflict?

California politicians went for supporting the Union. Party politics were pushed to the side, and almost overnight, like some odd dream, the overwhelming majority of residents became Lincoln enthusiasts. There were still ardent secessionists living in California, some of whom plotted violence in California to support the Confederacy. To meet this security challenge, local militias were formed in many communities across California.

Amos, while not a young man at 37 years old, did not volunteer for any local militia groups or enlist in the regular army. He was a patriotic man. His grandfather, David Catlin, with whom Amos had lived for six years, fought in the Revolutionary War. Publicly, Amos did not state his thoughts on the Civil War, other than to support the Union. Just the mere hint that a man supported the Confederacy was enough to get him labeled as a Copperhead and blackballed from political circles.

Instead of involving himself with the politics of the times, Amos focused on his law practice, representing clients in civil actions[1] and probate work[2]. He also became more involved in the Sacramento Pioneer Association. One of his fellow pioneers was James Anthony, publisher of the Sacramento Daily Union.[3] In 1862, Amos and B. C. Quigley donated a lot in Folsom as the site for the new Trinity Episcopal Church.[4] Amos and his wife Ruth attended a grand 4th of July celebration in Folsom organized by Mr. Sibley. Amos was in the parade with his cream-colored mules, and Ruth played the melodeon at the picnic.[5]

As the Civil War raged in the East, a smaller land conflict continued in the West. The boundaries of the Leidesdorff land grant were still in dispute. A number of men, not recognizing the map of the land grant as confirmed by the California Board of Land Commissioners, continued to squat on the property and cut down trees. Amos was hired to be the lead attorney for the Folsom Estate and eject the

Amos P. Catlin

men from the Leidesdorff land grant.[6] Eventually, Amos would travel back to Washington, D.C., to defend the Folsom Estate.

Leidesdorff Land grant

The Stockton Independent newspaper perhaps put it best, with an article about the Leidesdorff land grant titled "The Grant Curse."[7] A sizeable portion of Spanish and Mexican land grants in California seemed to be cursed with endless rounds of litigation to determine their authenticity and boundaries. The Leidesdorff Mexican land grant, Rancho Rio de los Americanos, was no different.

In March of 1848, William Alexander Leidesdorff proclaimed, "…there's no law here but club law…"[8] Leidesdorff was explaining to the Alcalde of San Francisco why he carried a pistol and was prepared to use it on anyone who insulted him. Since the Mexican government had been defeated by the United States, and no official provisional government had been established, California was operating almost in a state of government limbo at the time.

Leidesdorff, of mixed Danish and Caribbean descent, arrived in California in 1841 at the age of 31. His primary business was shipping at Yerba Buena. He became a Mexican citizen in 1844 and received a land grant from Mexican Governor Micheltorena of 35,509 acres south of the American River, next to John Sutter's grant. Under the terms of the land grant, Leidesdorff had to build a residence on his Rancho Rio de los Americanos land. He built the abode, but his primary focus was on the emerging community of San Francisco.

On May 18, 1848, Leidesdorff died in San Francisco. He died not from any gun fight, but from a virus or bacterial infection. On May 20, a notice ran in the local newspaper that Charles Meyer had been appointed by the presiding U.S. military governor, Colonel Mason, to settle Leidesdorff's estate. All inquiries regarding the estate were to be received by Captain Joseph Libby Folsom, Assistant Quarter Master.[9]

Another army officer who had come to California before 1850 was Henry Halleck. General Bennet Riley, the next military governor after Mason, appointed Halleck Secretary of State. Halleck was college-educated and liked to research and write on historical topics. He was instrumental—some would say influential—as he assisted California's first elected delegates to draft a state constitution in 1849. It was proposed during California's first legislature to employ Halleck to translate all of the Spanish and Mexican land grants, since they rested with General Riley and were under Halleck's control. The lack of funds, as the newly declared state had no taxing authority and was not recognized by the federal government, precluded any serious analysis of the land grants.[10]

Amos P. Catlin

After gold was discovered in 1848, California was flooded with miners in 1849. Property boundaries were pretty much ignored. Sensing an opportunity, Captain Folsom took a leave of absence from the army, tracked down William Leidesdorff's mother, Anna Sparks, in the Caribbean, and got her power of attorney to handle William's estate. In February 1850, represented by the new law firm formed by Henry Halleck, Joseph L. Folsom was awarded the administration of the Leidesdorff estate.[11] By April 1850, Folsom was running notices in the local newspapers that boundaries of the Rancho Rio de los Americanos must be respected, no trespassing without permission, and no cutting of timber. The main road from Sacramento up to the mining regions on the South Fork of the American River ran through the Leidesdorff land grant. Folsom let the existing hotel keepers stay, but rental terms would be negotiated in the future.[12]

In what turns out to be early California fashion, everyone proceeded on their own courses, ignoring, as best they could, protestations of other parties. All of this confusion and uncertainty was generated by Congress, and California, who failed to act by setting up a territorial government, a comprehensive survey and maps of land grants, and a proper process for adjudicating the claims of land grant owners. This failure would plague California for decades, even ensnarling the legitimacy of the Sutter land grant.

By 1853, California had finally gotten around to setting up a land commission to parse out the titles and maps. Governor Bigler encouraged the Board of California Land Commissioners to seize the Leidesdorff property.[13] In April 1854, the land commissioners took up the investigation and examination of the Leidesdorff estate.[14] With a decision imminent in summer of 1855 and high anxiety over land titles, a group of settlers and miners in Prairie City, just inside the Leidesdorff grant, met and urged the State of California to take over the Leidesdorff estate.[15]

A few days after the settlers and miners meeting in June 1855, the land commissioners issued their opinion confirming the claim of Folsom to eight square leagues of land in Sacramento County known as the Leidesdorff land grant. Eight leagues converted to 35,509 acres.[16] All that was left to do was create a map of Rancho Rio de los Americanos. Unfortunately, Joseph L. Folsom would die the next month, on July 19, 1855.[17] Halleck, Peachy & Van Winkle became the executors of the Folsom estate,[18] and A. H. Jones, U.S. Deputy Surveyor, began mapping the land grant in Sacramento County.[19] The final map would be known as the Hays survey, as John Coffee Hays was the appointed U.S. Surveyor-General in California.

At a meeting of miners who had staked claims along the American River, the miners declared they were not in the boundaries of the Leidesdorff land grant. They resolved to fight any map that included their claims in the land grant.[20] The

Amos P. Catlin

position was that the miners would rather file a preemption claim with the federal government than deal with the executors of the Folsom Estate for property and mineral rights.

There was considerable consternation over the future of the Leidesdorff land grant boundaries, as Amos had written in a letter home years earlier, "...uncertainty governs everything." In February of 1856, as the railroad was roaring into Folsom, Amos and attorney Calhoun Benham appeared in District Court during one of the hearings revolving around the adjudication of the land grant boundaries. Amos was in court on behalf of the current occupants of the land grant, if for no other reason than to impress upon the judge that men had investments in the land in question.[21]

In the Spring of 1857, the U.S. Attorney General stated there would be no further appeals over the boundaries of the land grant. U.S. District Court Judge Ogden Hoffman affirmed the decree of the Land Commission of the Leidesdorff land grant.[22] In May 1857, the official map of the Rancho Rio de los Americanos was released. In the same year the map was approved, the California Legislature passed an act authorizing the executors of the Folsom Estate to sell additional Folsom town lots, subject to Probate Court approval.[23] It was at this time that Amos bought more of the Folsom lots and acquired the 9,643 acres from Nystrom.

While the original land grant came with a crude map, included in the documentation were the actual measurements of the land grant. (One league is approximately 2.6 miles.)

"Beginning at an oak tree on the bank of the American River, marked as a boundary to the lands granted to John A. Sutter, and running thence south with the line of said Sutter two leagues, thence easterly, by lines parallel with the general direction of the said American River, and at the distance, as near as may be, of two leagues therefrom, four leagues, or so far as may be necessary to include in the tract the quantity of eight square leagues, thence northerly, by a line parallel to the one above-described, to the American River; thence along the southern bank of said river, and bending thereon to the point of beginning."

The old oak tree, then residing near A. D. Patterson's barnyard, and marking the eastern end of the Sutter land grant, was the only specific marker other than the river. As for an eastern reference for the boundary, the land grant cited the *lomeria*. In Spanish, *lomeria* translates into low hills. What came to be disputed was where the *lomeria* started. On the 1844 map was a small line indicating a creek. This was taken by the opponents of the new Rancho Rio de los Americanos survey as Alder Creek and the beginning of the *lomeria*.

Amos P. Catlin

If Alder Creek was the beginning of the *lomeria*, or the eastern boundary of the land grant, it would shorten the width by two miles. The shortened width would have excluded the town of Folsom. Because the northern boundary was set by the American River, in order to achieve the full eight leagues of land mass, the southern boundary would have to be extended. A southern boundary expansion did not please those settlers who were certain they were not in the land grant.

Amos P. Catlin

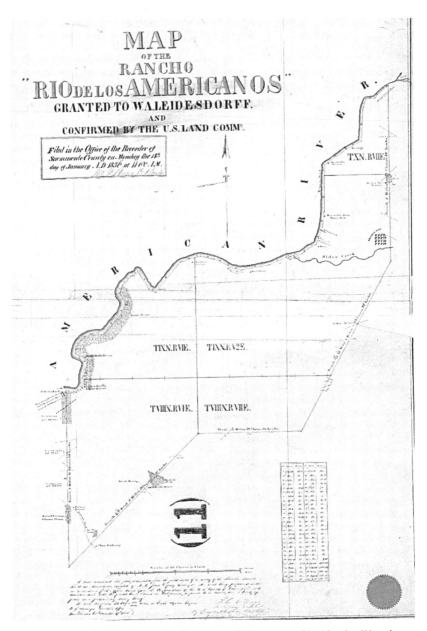

25. Original U.S. Surveyor-General's Office map of Leidesdorff land grant, 1855. John C. Hays, U.S. Surveyor-General.

Amos P. Catlin

Before the Leidesdorff land grant map could become officially recognized, it had to meet the approval of the U.S. government. In September 1858, even though the Commissioner of the Land Office at Washington found the original surveyed map in order for a land patent, Secretary of the Interior Jacob Thompson, under President James Buchanan, disapproved it.[24] Thompson sent the matter back to California to be resurveyed. The reports were that Secretary Thompson thought the boundary ran too far to the east. This is the same conclusion that opponents of the original survey made.

Secretary Thompson ordered a new survey be undertaken with the eastern boundary at Alder Creek, not the low foothills further east that were considered the *lomeria*. The new definition for the boundary directly threatened Amos' investments in the town of Folsom and much of the acreage the Natoma Water and Mining Company had acquired from Nystrom, all of which was east of Thompson's proposed eastern boundary. If such a new interpretation of the Leidesdorff land grant boundaries was allowed to take effect, the litigation surrounding land titles would be massive.

With Thompson's order for a new survey, Amos was now in the thick of the fight to preserve the original Hays' survey. In a brief filed with the District Court, Amos did not suppress his opinion. He wrote, "The opinion rejecting the survey is beneath all criticism, although the main error was effected by assuming that the 'Lomerias' were situated below a ravine known as Alder Creek, and at a distance of only seven miles from the western boundary of the Rancho. None of the persons whose secret and extra judicial affidavits were used 6,000 miles away to produce this error in the Secretary's mind respecting the location of the 'Lomerias,' ever ventured into the District Court of California, where afterwards they had abundant opportunity to affirm their statements and confront the claimants."[25]

Amos was an intervenor in the court arguments. He did not represent the Folsom Estate. He was representing claimants who had a vested interest in the outcome of the dispute. Consequently, he had limited options and influence for curtailing or stopping the second survey. One avenue Amos and the other claimants could take to support the Hays' survey was to produce depositions from men who were familiar with the Leidesdorff land grant. Amos was able to introduce the depositions of John Sutter Sr., John Bidwell, A. D. Patterson, and Willard Buzzle. All the men were in California when Leidesdorff was still alive and had met him. Bidwell even made a map of the Leidesdorff land grant in 1846.[26]

The second survey was undertaken, and the subsequent map was known as the Mandeville survey. The new Mandeville survey held to Thompson's instructions that the *lomeria* were to begin at Alder Creek, some two miles to the west of the original survey. The Mandeville survey was completed in 1859 and then opened

Amos P. Catlin

for examination by interested parties to file exceptions. In the midst of all the new surveys and examination, Congress passed legislation in 1860 that gave new powers to District Courts in California including the authority to order any survey into court and decide on it.

In November 1862, the District Court tossed aside the new Mandeville survey and decreed the original Hays' survey valid.[27] The United States District Attorney then appealed the decision, and it landed on the steps of the U.S. Supreme Court in the form of *United States vs. Halleck, et. al.* As civil war was about to erupt in 1861, California Governor Downey appointed Captain Halleck to be the Major General of the Second Division of the California Militia. Halleck would go on to be general-in-chief of the Union Army under President Lincoln during the Civil War.

With the lead attorney of the Folsom Estate, Henry Halleck, back in uniform defending the Union[28], the honor defending the original map of the Leidesdorff land grant fell to the man who was completely familiar with the history of the case and had a vested interest in a favorable outcome, Amos Catlin. Behind the scenes, Amos was the attorney for the Natoma Water and Mining Company, and by default the town of Folsom, in contesting the revised mapping process.[29] His clients purchased lands from the Folsom Estate outlined in the original 1855 map of the Leidesdorff Rancho. After successful appeals, the final arbiter in the appeals process would be the U.S. Supreme Court.

In early November 1863, Amos and Ruth departed from San Francisco aboard a steamer bound for the East Coast[30] so Amos could argue before the U.S. Supreme Court. He was granted admission to the Supreme Court on a motion from Justice Jeremiah Black. However, it would be several weeks before he was able to argue the case before the Court. When the day came, Amos would take the better part of two days to argue his position for the original map before the Court.[31]

Amos argued before the U.S. Supreme Court in December of 1863. The Court handed down its decision, in Amos' favor, in May 1864. His basic argument revolved around geometry; the western boundary line was two leagues in length. In order to create an area of eight square leagues, the southern boundary line, following a general parallel to the American River, had to have a length beyond Alder Creek, and encompass the town of Folsom. Whereas lawyers will often cite prior legal cases, quote code, and philosophize on the law, Catlin's published comments in the opinion are quite matter-of-fact.[32]

"After first directing the starting-point to be the oak tree, and the first line to run from thence 'south' two leagues, it says, 'thence easterly,' by lines parallel with the general direction of the said American River, and at the distance, as near as may be, of two leagues therefrom."

Amos P. Catlin

"We understand the word easterly in its usual acceptation to mean to the east generally, in contradistinction to west, north, or south, and is correctly applied to any general direction to the east, as opposed to the west, which would not be better indicated by using the terms northerly or southerly. In this decree the term easterly has qualifying words attached to it, showing that it meant the direction of the American River from the oak tree."

In the final opinion, written by Justice Field, the court agreed with Catlin.

"The decree in this case is plain, and admits of only one construction; the object of the appellants is to change the meaning of its language, by showing that the commissioners were ignorant of the true course and direction of the American River, and therefore intended different lines from those they specifically declared, and that they could not have intended the eastern line to run as directed, in disregard of what is asserted to be the true position of the 'lomerias.'"[33]

Amos returned to California in June 1864.[34] The final record and map of the Leidesdorff Patent was confirmed by Judge McKune of the District Court on January 11, 1865.[35] One of Amos' rewards for successfully representing the original Hays survey was being the exclusive land agent for the sale of the remainder of the Rancho Rio de los Americanos under the firm Bowie and Catlin.[36] Three years later, Amos had negotiated the sale of almost all of the land to settlers, miners, and of course, the Natoma Water and Mining Company.[37]

While back east, Amos had time to visit the battlefield at Gettysburg. He picked up some relics and souvenirs

SALE OF THE LEIDESDORFF RANCH.

NOTICE IS HEREBY GIVEN that in pursuance of the order of the Probate Court of the city and county of San Francisco, in the State of California, made on the 17th day of November, 1865, in the matter of the estate of JOSEPH L. FOLSOM, deceased, the undersigned, Executors of said estate, will sell at private sale, upon the terms hereinafter stated, and subject to confirmation by said Probate Court, on

Monday, 18th day of December, 1865,

At 12 o'clock, noon, of that day, at the office of Bowie & Catlin, Attorneys at Law, No. 101 J street, city of Sacramento, all the right, title and interest of the said Joseph L. Folsom, deceased, at the time of his death, and all the right, title and interest that the said estate has, by operation of law or otherwise, other than or in addition to that of said deceased at the time of his death, in and to all the tract or parcel of Land situated in Sacramento county and known as the "LEIDES-DORFF RANCH," and bounded and described as follows : Beginning at a point where an oak tree formerly stood, on the southerly bank of the American river, near the barn-yard of A. D. Patterson, and known as the terminating point of lands claimed by John A. Sutter ; running thence south 421 chains 86 links to a point ; thence north 46 degrees east 452 chains 87 links, to a point ; thence east 252 chains 80 links to a point ; thence north 29 degrees 15 minutes east 337 chains 58 links to a point ; thence west 337 chains 87 links to a point ; thence north 105 chains 67 links to the American river, and thence down and with said river to the place of beginning, containing 25,879 acres of Land, a little more or less.

And the said Executors will receive offers or bids for the entire tract, or any subdivision thereof, at the office of BOWIE & CATLIN, Attorneys at Law, No. 101 J street, city of Sacramento, from this date until and inclusive of the 18th day of December, 1865.

TERMS OF SALE.—At least one-fourth cash upon acceptance of the offer, subject to approval by Probate Court ; the balance within one year from the date of such approval, to be secured by note and mortgage upon the premises purchased, with interest at the rate of ten per cent. per annum until maturity, and thereafter at two per cent. per month until paid. All payments to be made only in gold coin of the United States. Acts of sale to be at expense of purchasers.

Dated November 27, 1865.

HENRY W. HALLECK and ARCHIBALD C. PEACHY, Executors of the last Will and Testament of Joseph L.
n27   Folsom, deceased.   td18

Sacramento Daily Union, November 28, 1865

26. Bowie & Catlin notice of sale of Leidesdorff land grant parcels, 1865.

Amos P. Catlin

from the battlefield that included shot, shells, and a branch that had been perforated with a dozen bullets. He displayed these Civil War relics at meetings of the California pioneer associations in Sacramento and San Francisco.[38]

It was a real boost to Amos' legal career to have successfully argued before the U.S. Supreme Court. There was a time in 1851, after he had vacated Sacramento due to a cholera outbreak, when he was unsure of his future in California. The Leidesdorff land grant litigation was not the most complicated or intellectually challenging case Amos would handle. But if arguing before the Supreme Court and winning set a bar of high expectations for Amos as a lawyer, he would meet and exceed those expectations in the decades to come.

Before Amos traveled back east, in addition to his law practice, he was organizing and investing in some mining ventures.[39] There was also a partnership with two other men, William Lewis and Charles Sawyer, to tunnel underneath Telegraph Hill in San Francisco to extend Montgomery Street.[40] The tunnel was to be 16 feet wide and high enough to allow carriages to pass.[41] Legislation to create the toll road would grant a franchise to collect the tolls for 50 years.[42]

While Amos was back in Washington, D.C., the County of Placer had sold numerous lots he owned in Lincoln, California, at a Constable's Sale for failure to pay property taxes on the lots.[43] However, by 1863, the Central Pacific Railroad was making progress from Sacramento to Auburn and slowly acquiring the freight and passenger traffic that had previously used the Sacramento Valley and California Central railroads. The Central Pacific would go on to acquire both railroads, solidifying a monopoly on railroads in the Sacramento region.

General William Tecumseh Sherman, a figure well known to Californians from his time in the state, was leading his March to the Sea campaign in 1864, and Lincoln was virtually guaranteed to be reelected and the Confederacy defeated. As prayers ran high for the end of the Civil War, Amos' sabbatical from politics was also about to conclude.

---

[1] Sacramento Bee, 1860 October 26

[2] Sacramento Daily Union, Volume 21, Number 3128, 6 April 1861

[3] Sacramento Bee, 1861 June 26

[4] Sacramento Bee, 1862 May 23

[5] Sacramento Bee, 1862 July 5

[6] Sacramento Daily Union, Volume 23, Number 3523, 14 July 1862

[7] Stockton Independent, Volume I, Number 98, 22 November 1861

[8] Californian, Volume 2, Number 43, 8 March 1848

[9] California Star, Volume 2, Number 20, 20 May 1848

[10] *Gold Rush Politics, California's First Legislature*, Mary Jo Ignoffo. California State Senate, State Capitol, Sacramento, 1999

[11] Daily Alta California, Volume 1, Number 48, 24 February 1850

[12] Daily Alta California, Volume 1, Number 95, 19 April 1850

Amos P. Catlin

[13] Placer Herald, Volume 2, Number 10, 19 November 1853
[14] Sacramento Daily Union, Volume 7, Number 945, 4 April 1854
[15] Sacramento Daily Union, Volume 9, Number 1314, 11 June 1855
[16] Sacramento Daily Union, Volume 9, Number 1318, 15 June 1855
[17] Sacramento Daily Union, Volume 9, Number 1351, 25 July 1855
[18] Pamphlets on California Lands, xF862.1 .C18v.3, Bancroft Library
[19] Sacramento Daily Union, Volume 10, Number 1473, 14 December 1855
[20] Georgetown News, Volume 2, Number 12, 17 January 1856
[21] Pamphlets on California Lands, xF862.1 .C18v.3, Bancroft Library
[22] Pamphlets on California Lands, xF862.1 .C18v.3, Bancroft Library
[23] Pamphlets on California Lands, xF862.1 .C18v.3, Bancroft Library
[24] Sacramento Daily Union, Volume 17, Number 2660, 6 October 1859
[25] Pamphlets on California Lands, xF862.1 .C18v.3, Bancroft Library
[26] Pamphlets on California Lands, xF862.1 .C18v.3, Bancroft Library
[27] Sacramento Daily Union, Volume 23, Number 3509, 26 June 1862
[28] Visalia Weekly Delta, Volume 2, Number 28, 29 December 1860
[29] Sacramento Daily Union, Volume 92, Number 60, 20 October 1896
[30] Daily Alta California, Volume 15, Number 4997, 3 November 1863
[31] Sacramento Daily Union, Volume 92, Number 60, 20 October 1896
[32] United States v Halleck et. al., December 1863
[33] United States v Halleck et. al., December 1863
[34] Sacramento Daily Union, Volume 27, Number 4124, 9 June 1864
[35] Sacramento Daily Union, Volume 28, Number 4308, 11 January 1865
[36] Sacramento Daily Union, Volume 35, Number 5372, 15 June 1868
[37] Sacramento Daily Union, Volume 35, Number 5372, 15 June 1868
[38] Sacramento Daily Union, Volume 27, Number 4172, 4 August 1864
[39] Sacramento Daily Union, Volume 25, Number 3832, 3 July 1863
[40] Sacramento Daily Union, Volume 24, Number 3729, 5 March 1863
[41] Stockton Independent, Volume IV, Number 31, 9 March 1863
[42] Stockton Independent, Volume IV, Number 31, 9 March 1863
[43] Placer Herald, Volume 12, Number 27, 5 March 1864

Amos P. Catlin

Chapter Eight: Return to Politics, 1865 - 1867

Even before Amos went back east to argue before the U.S. Supreme Court, he was working to make law his full-time occupation. In January 1862, he sold 265 shares of stock back to the Natoma Water and Mining Co.[1] While Amos was losing interest in the day-to-day management of the Natoma ditch, he still held a fascination with mining. Amos, along with Luther Cutler, invested in the Alpine Horn Gold and Silver Mine in Amador County. Amos was one of the trustees of the mining corporation.[2]

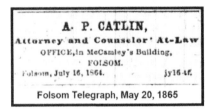

Folsom Telegraph, May 20, 1865

27. Amos Catlin advertisement for his law practice in Folsom, 1865.

Closer to home, Amos invested, with several other men, in the Rhodes Northerly Extension Gold Mining Co. east of Prairie City in the spring of 1863.[3] Also in 1863, Amos purchased 80 acres of mining claims on the American River, one-half mile north of Folsom below the confluence of the North and South Forks.[4] The $100 land investment would eventually be the part of the site of the State Prison at Folsom. Amos was also disposing of the numerous lots he owned in Folsom, selling to old friends and newcomers such as Benjamin Quigley, William Long, Peter Weathers, Henry Waddilove, Harvey Thompson, H.K. Grim, James McClure, James Meredith, Elisha Hoskins, Cyrus Bradley, W.S. Kendall, Joseph Smith, Oliver C. Lewis, Elezer Rulison, William Howard, and Thomas Whitely. Before Amos left for Washington, D.C., he sold Horatio Livermore 32 lots (blocks 86 and 87), bounded by the streets of Bidwell, Persifer, Mill, and Coloma, for $500.

Upon his return from Washington, D.C., after arguing before the U.S. Supreme Court and having confidence that the land titles were secure for the Natoma canals across the Leidesdorff land grant, Amos began to divest of his interest in the Natoma Water and Mining Company. He sold 103 shares of stock to Levi Chandler and another 60 shares to Horatio Livermore in April of 1864.[5] Amos would sell another 746 shares of stock over the next couple of years. Livermore was able to acquire a controlling interest in the Natoma Water and Mining Company by 1868 and moved the corporation to San Francisco in 1870.[6]

As Amos' family life was diversifying, so were his professional engagements. While Amos had occasionally contributed to the pages of the Sacramento Daily Union, he would be named as a political editor of the paper.[7] The Sacramento

Amos P. Catlin

Union, under the leadership of James Anthony, had always endorsed Amos when he ran for elected office. He would write political commentary for the newspaper for several years before his law practice consumed all of his time in the 1860s.

Amos eased back into politics by attending a meeting of the Lincoln and Johnson Club in Folsom as a guest speaker in October 1864.[8] As General George McClellan was gearing up to run against Lincoln, Amos used heavy sarcasm to critique McClellan's conduct of the war and peace plans. His audience, thoroughly disposed for Lincoln, delighted in political rhetoric against McClellan.[9]

1052. The Railroad and Suspension Bridges, Folsom,
Sacramento County.

28. Wire rope suspension bridge next to the California Central Railroad bridge connecting Folsom to Ashland over the American River, 1866. Library of Congress

When news of Lincoln's assassination descended on Sacramento, great crowds started gathering at the Assembly Chambers of the State Capitol.[10] As the numbers swelled, Charles Crocker requested the special meeting of the Sacramento Board of Trustees be moved to the Agricultural Pavilion.[11] A

Amos P. Catlin

committee was proposed to draft resolutions honoring the late President and to make the necessary arrangements for memorial services. Amos was selected to be on the committee, along with George Moore, H.C. Weston, George Oulton, B.B. Redding, and Governor Low.[12]

On April 19th, Amos read the resolutions, in which he was intimately involved in drafting. One resolution articulated the desired hope for the political state to come.

"Resolved. That whether the blow that struck down Abraham Lincoln at the moment when he had achieved for his country and for mankind the greatest blessing for which hero or martyr ever died was the act of an assassin to destroy an individual, or was the consummation of a conspiracy against the national life, as a means for either of those ends, it is as wretchedly impotent as it is infamous, for we feel assured not only that Abraham Lincoln lives, in the hearts of his countrymen, and will survive in the memories of their descendants to the latest posterity, but that the nation itself, instead of being injured by the shock, will receive from the blood of its martyred chief new strength and a sterner resolution to conquer and punish all its enemies, and to make this a land in which the accursed institution of slavery shall be destroyed forever."[13]

The political good will and harmony brought about by the Union victory and martyrdom of Lincoln would not last. Throughout the Civil War, the new Union Party was a home for patriotic voters who tended Republican and for disaffected men like Amos, who identified first as a Whig, then with the American Party. But the singular element that bound the men across a wide range of the political spectrum, the goal of preserving the Union, was now achieved. It was inevitable that men with different visions and philosophies on the function of government would drift apart.

Union Party Civil War

However, no one really anticipated a micro-civil war in the Sacramento County Union Party in 1865. Two factions seemed to come to the convention anticipating a brawl, literally and figuratively. The convention was called to order at 2 p.m. in the Assembly Chamber on July 25th. Over the perfunctory election of a convention Secretary, each side nominated a different man. Following a vote favoring W.H. Barton, opponents of Barton started shouting, "Division," calling for a vote recount.

After more shouting, the chairman called the meeting to order and recognized Barton as elected Secretary. As Barton advanced toward the Secretary's table from the left, delegates from the right side of the room made a rush to prevent him from taking his seat. From this point, the situation went downhill and descended into hand-to-hand combat. As described by the Sacramento Daily Union:

"Then ensued an indescribable and terrible scene, such as was never before witnessed in Sacramento at any political Convention…In a moment the two parties were engaged in hand to hand fight. Solid hickory canes, which appeared to be abundant on both sides, were plied with vigor. Spittoons flew from side to side like bomb-shells on a battle-field. Ink stands took the place of solid shot. Pistols were drawn and used as substituted for clubs. The principal weapon, however, which were used by both sides were the cane-bottom arm-chairs, which were of course within reach of every one. These implements – not very well adapted to purposes of warfare – were swung in the air by the dozens and broken over the heads of the contending parties.

"At the close the anti-Low men, or Long Hairs, who had rallied to the support of Barton, were driven from the field. Several jumped out of windows; others who were badly hurt were assisted out of the building, while the greater portion passed into the ante rooms and the main hall…. The fight was suborn and effective while it lasted on the part of the Long Hairs as well as the Shorts."[14]

The Long Hair faction were known as the anti-Low groups for their opposition to the positions of Governor Low, who was a Union Republican. Following the melee, the Long Hairs retired to the Turn Verein Hall to hold their own convention, while the Short Hairs, those supporting Governor Low, continued their convention in the Assembly Chambers. Amos, whose name was being floated as a candidate for District Attorney, witnessed the brawl. He briefly spoke at the resumption of the Low Union County Convention, making a point on parliamentary procedure and vote counting.[15]

Amos left the Low Union meeting during its break and walked over to Turn Verein Hall, where the anti-Low Long Hairs were meeting. He was called to speak, even though he was not a delegate to the convention. Amos was shocked at the brutality he witnessed over what seemed to be a simple parliamentary ruling error. He added, "But suppose the Chairman did make a mistake in his ruling, it was nothing more than an error in judgment, and should he receive the bludgeon for it?... Gentlemen, it is of no use to talk of union or compromise with such a set of men as those we met with to-day."[16]

Before the anti-Low convention adjourned for the day, Amos was appointed to the Committee on Resolutions along with Israel Luce, Woolson, Barton, and Duncombe. He was also appointed to the Committee for Permanent Organization and Order of Business. With this step toward the anti-Low Long Hairs, Amos was moving away from previous political positions. The Short Hair Low Union Party was the faction that attracted previous Whigs, American Party, Know-Nothings, and Douglas Democrats. But so many of the political lines had been scrambled, it was hard to keep a score card of who was on which team.

Amos P. Catlin

Both conventions developed resolutions that showed little difference between the two Union party factions. The anti-Low Long Hairs became known as the Bolters, for bolting from the established Union convention. The Low Union favored an amendment to the U.S. Constitution to abolish slavery. They counter-balanced that with a resolution arguing against a California constitutional amendment guaranteeing negro suffrage.[17] Amos would echo those sentiments in a campaign speech before the election. His argument was framed in relation to forcing the southern states to comply with reconstruction. As reported in the Sacramento Daily Union, "On the question of negro suffrage, the speaker [Amos] took ground in opposition to the extension of the elective franchise in that direction. He believed the Government to be sufficiently strong to control and regulate the Secessionists of the South without conferring the right of suffrage upon the negro."[18]

The anti-Low Union Party nominated Amos to be its candidate for one of the State Assembly seats in Sacramento County. The Low Union Party nominated Peter J. Hopper,[19] owner of the Folsom Telegraph newspaper and attorney who had collaborated with Amos on numerous court cases. Hopper's newspaper tried to keep the Folsom community, and the relationship between

LOYAL MEN — RALLY! RALLY!

NO AFFILIATION WITH TRAITORS!

Shall the Union Party be Maintained?

A MASS MEETING

OF THE UNION CITIZENS OF SACRAMENTO WILL

BE HELD IN FRONT OF

ODD FELLOWS' BLOCK,

Fourth street, on

SATURDAY EVENING, AUG. 26th.

The following speakers have consented to address the meeting:

REV. M. C. BRIGGS,

HON. C. A. TUTTLE,

A. P. CATLIN, Esq.,

DR. A. B. NIXON.

The speaking will commence at eight o'clock. Seats provided on the balconies for Ladies.

Come One! Come All!

And let us wipe out this secession element that is attempting to destroy the Union party and obstruct the reconstruction of the States.   D. KENDALL,
a26-1t*   Chairman Union Co. Central Committee.

Sacramento Daily Union, August 26, 1865

29. Union Party announcement listing Amos Catlin as one of the rally speakers, 1865.

Amos P. Catlin

Hopper and Amos, cordial by posting an editorial giving some faint praise for Amos.

"...that the immense Union vote given in Sacramento last Fall was measuredly due to those who are in affinity with the ticket which is nicknamed 'Short-hair.' – We do not say it is wholly due to them [Short hairs]...[but they] did more hard and effective work for the success of the Union ticket last Fall, than all the 'Long-hair' candidates put together. With the exception of Nixon, [Amos] Catlin, and McClatchy, who did make a speech or two..."[20]

The race for the Assembly seat between Hopper and Amos Catlin was reviewed and handicapped in a letter to the Stockton Independent newspaper.

"Peter Hopper is proprietor of the Folsom Telegraph, and a great personal friend of your chief editor.... His immediate opponent on the Long Hair side is A. P. Catlin, another Apollo, good fellow enough for anything, and a stiff defender of the Monroe Doctrine. His capillary is muchly elongated and if the standard of comparison was that of gold at the Mint, I should say it was twenty carrots fine; in fact, he is the deepest read lawyer in the courts, and I deem him invincible at the polls."[21]

Amos probably blushed at the gold purity analogy, but reality proved he was not invincible at the polls. Hopper defeated his friend Amos for the Assembly seat.[22] The Union Party factions split the vote at the polls, which helped the Democrats. Popular Sacramento County Sheriff James McClatchy, nominated by the anti-Low Union Party, was running for a second term but was defeated by Democrat James Lansing.[23]

What really tipped the balance against the anti-Low Union Party faction was that the Low Union faction entered into an agreement with the Democrats to create a Fusion Party. At that time, a ticket could be printed by a political party, with the favored slate of candidates, and handed to individuals entering the election polling place. One of the agreed upon Fusion Party tickets was titled, "Democratic White Man's Ticket: The Constitution, Reduce Taxation, Free Mines." The ticket Amos was listed on was titled "The Union Forever: Regular Union Ticket."[24]

Amos was also the target of a political smear campaign. Rumors had been spread that he had accepted a bribe in order to secure his vote, should he be elected to the Assembly, for J.B. Felton for U.S. Senator.[25] Amos categorically denied receiving any money from Felton in consideration for his vote.[26] After a relatively quiet period, free from any political drama and invective, Amos had to wonder why he had stepped back into the political ring. As much as Amos disliked all the political rancor and indecorous behavior, not only would he feel compelled to participate

Amos P. Catlin

in politics, he was often called upon to lead the political parties he as associated with.

Family & Law Practice

On October 30[th][27] 1865, Amos and Ruth Anne had their first child, a baby girl.[28] With the start of his family, Amos also started a formal law partnership with George Washington Bowie. The partners established their offices at the corner of Fourth and J streets in Sacramento.[29] This would mean Amos would be a regular commuter into downtown Sacramento from Folsom. The partnership with Bowie also denoted a change in Amos' law practice. Instead of handling local civil and criminal matters, Amos was branching out into the appellate field. His notoriety gained in arguing before the U.S. Supreme Court opened the door to begin representing appeals before the California Supreme Court.[30] In 1866, Amos would represent no fewer than 17 appeals before the state Supreme Court.

While Amos was building his legal reputation, his family life was a roller coaster of emotions. On July 27, 1866, his daughter Emily, just shy of 9 months old, died. Ruth Anne became pregnant shortly after the tragic death of their first daughter. She gave birth to twins, a boy and a girl, on July 25, 1867.[31] Sadly, the twins did not live to see the next sunrise. Within a year, Amos and Ruth Anne had suffered the horrendous loss of three children.

Union Party Split

Amidst the family turmoil, the Sacramento County Union Party was still in turmoil. The two groups that had split in 1865 still had not reconciled their differences. Specifically, the Sacramento County Union Party Central Committee was developing plans for an election primary that looked outside the rules of California law by allowing Democrats to vote in the Union Primary.[32] Some thirty men met at the law offices of Bowie and Catlin to discuss a response to the Central Committee.[33]

At a subsequent Union Caucus meeting, Amos accused the Central Committee of being the real Bolters from the Union Party as soon as they approved an election primary with rules outside of the Registry law.[34] James McClatchy, who had been defeated as the anti-Low Sheriff candidate, surmised, "The roll of names published indicated the will of the Union party. The Registry law and Primary Election law sprung from the contest and division in this county two years ago. If fraud was designed it would be as easy to put in one hundred illegal votes as a single one. Those who had ignored The Primary law were bound to carry the election, by foul means if necessary."[35]

Amos P. Catlin

McClatchy's conjecture about possible voter fraud would materialize. The names of 61 new voters were collected in a voter registration drive from the Folsom area and forwarded to the Sacramento County Clerk to be recorded on the Great Register in July 1867.[36] The only problem was, no one recognized any of the names of the new voters. Suspicions quickly focused on Grove L. Johnson, an attorney and relatively new resident of Sacramento. Amos was called to testify in the case against Johnson and stated that, although he had resided in the Folsom region since 1849, he could not recognize any of the names on the list.[37]

The names were not added to the Great Register, and Grove L. Johnson resigned his position with Sacramento County. Johnson would continue practicing law in Sacramento, be very active in political circles, and father a young boy who would go on to be Governor of California, Hiram Johnson.

With no reconciliation in sight, the Union Party split into two groups. Each would nominate its own slate of candidates for local and state office. Amos was elected president to the Revised Union Party,[38] not to be confused with the Regular Union Party.[39] Again sounding very judicial, after being elected President, Amos noted, "It is certainly a mark of consideration of which I feel myself unworthy, but with your support, on which I rely as much as on my own personal efforts, I hope to be able to go through the task allotted me firmly and impartially."[40]

Some candidates at the state level were nominated by each party, such as John P. Jones for Lieutenant Governor and Romualdo Pacheco for Treasurer.[41] For the office of Governor, the Revised Union nominated John Bidwell, and the Regular Union nominated George Gorham.[42] Amos was nominated for Sacramento County District Attorney.[43] In his address at being nominated, a familiar tone was sounded, "...I shall perform the duties of the office with firmness and impartiality."[44] Then Amos made some telling remarks, "I have appeared before you so many times today and yesterday that I ought to be able to appear before you without any diffidence whatever, but I find while I can go through with the ordinary public performance, where I am not personally interested, without trepidation, yet when I come before you and ask your votes I feel a certain degree of embarrassment."[45]

Successful politicians cannot suffer from embarrassment or impartiality. Yet, that is what Amos was admitting to in his remarks before the Union Party. These would be personality traits that would continue to surface and that proved to be insurmountable challenges to elected office in the future. On the other hand, the traits of humility and fairness would also assure that Amos would continue to be sought after by men to lead their party or cause.

Another of Amos' personality traits was indefatigable defense of principles. At the Union Party State Convention, the question arose as to whether delegates who formed a fusion with the Democrats in the 1865 election should be seated. A general truce between the two competing Union factions had been achieved before the state convention. Amos spoke for nearly an hour, arguing that certain men had sold out the Union Party in 1865 and should not be seated at the convention.[46] A rebuttal to Amos' protestations was led by Judge John H. McKune,[47] who had been part of the anti-Low Union Party with Amos in 1865. The disputed delegates were eventually seated for the convention.[48]

The real issue with regards to admitting the extra delegates was a careful vote count by the two competing gubernatorial candidates, Bidwell and Gorham. Bidwell supporters feared the extra delegates would lean Gorham over Bidwell. Gorham was finally nominated by the Regular Union Party State Convention.[49] Amos reconstituted the Revised Union caucus and convened a nominating convention in July of 1867. This second Union Party Convention would be alternately called the Bolters' Convention[50] and the Sorehead Convention.[51]

The Sorehead Convention nominated John Bidwell for Governor.[52] In its resolutions, it would make a bold move toward the emerging California Republican Party by favoring impartial suffrage, without distinction of color.[53] Of course, this meant suffrage for men, not for women. John Bidwell would drop out of the race in August, and the Revised Union Party would insert Caleb Fay as gubernatorial candidate.[54]

Amos was conspicuously quiet during this continued turmoil in the Union Party. At a Union Party meeting on August 19th, Amos tried to angle himself out of speaking. Finally, near the end of the meeting, Amos acquiesced and said he would make his comments brief, as the hour was growing late. Nevertheless, Amos launched into a history lesson concerning California and the current state of politics. He said, after considerable deliberation and reflection, he had come to the conclusion that George C. Gorham, gubernatorial nominee of the Regular Union Party, not Caleb Fay, should be elected Governor.[55]

Both the Sacramento Daily Union[56] and the Sacramento Bee[57] endorsed Amos over his Democratic rival, and incumbent, J.C. Goods. Amos would lose to Goods. The Regular Union Party District Attorney candidate, W.R. Cantwell, even though he had withdrawn from the race,[58] garnered 444 votes. Had it been a straight two-person race, and the votes for Cantwell gone to Amos, J.C. Goods would have lost.[59]

End of a Tyrant

Before the election, Amos would leave his part-time position as the political editor at the Sacramento Daily Union.[60] In one of his last columns on July 6th, titled "The End of a Tyrant," Amos defended the execution of Maximilian I by President

Benito Juarez the previous month in Mexico.[61] The opinion piece would be republished throughout the United States and Latin America. As Amos noted, the United States, consumed with its own Civil War, could not come to the aid of President Juarez and support the Monroe doctrine as Maximilian was encouraged and supported by European powers to create a monarchy in Mexico. In an effort to silence opposition to his declared monarchy, Maximilian had thousands of Juarez supporters executed. After being driven from Mexico City, Maximilian himself was executed in June of 1867.

In California, Amos was witnessing what seemed like a similarly confusing set of political events. The Union Party was disintegrating, and President Johnson seemed to be actively sabotaging all efforts at Reconstruction in the South. However, in his assessment of the Maximilian execution, Amos recognized that the political chaos in California's neighbor, Mexico, was different.

"Upon the historic page the career of Maximilian will make a striking episode. No parallel to it will be found in the record of any usurper that ever risked his head to wear a crown... But Maximilian's case stands upon the naked ground of an invader, without the shadow of a justifying or excusable cause. He had not even the robber's plea, that might makes right.[62]

"The enormity of the crime thus expiated will scarcely be comprehended by the present generation of men, either in Europe or America — in the former, because there was too much complicity there in the crime itself; and in the latter, because the public sense has been blunted by a nearer contemplation of other enormities equally repulsive and shocking.[63]

"The wisdom of the act of Juarez in permitting the ax of justice to fall upon the neck of so illustrious a subject has been questioned by some who, we apprehend, do not sufficiently appreciate the importance of always maintaining an erect and resolute front against the pretensions of royalty."[64]

"Juarez has but vindicated the Monroe doctrine, and that is a principle for which the United States can now afford to fight. When that question again comes up for diplomatic discussion, our Government will not have the Southern Confederacy at its throat choking its utterance, but it will be free handed, and willing to defend itself, and its neighbor it needful, against the next effort at Imperial propagandism on this continent."[65]

As with any man enthralled with politics, Amos could bend history to align with his perceptions of the future. From his point of view, the Democrats, whether in California, Southern States, or in the White House, equated to more government dysfunction as a means to appease the former Secessionists. The split of the Union Party was contributing to the dysfunction and chaos by abdicating a united

Amos P. Catlin

opposition. Hence, Amos felt he needed to endorse Gorham for Governor, over the objections of his Revised Union Party compatriots.

The great fear was that if the Democratic Party nominee for Governor, Henry Haight, was elected, California would never ratify the proposed amendments to the Constitution. Haight was elected, and California did not ratify the Constitutional amendments.

---

[1] NWMC Journal, Folsom Historical Society Museum archive

[2] Folsom Historical Society Museum archive

[3] Sacramento County Deed book 18630331, page 117

[4] Sacramento County Deed book 18620425, page 315

[5] Natoma Water and Mining Co. Journal, Folsom Historical Society Museum archive

[6] Natoma Water and Mining Co. Journal, Folsom Historical Society Museum archive

[7] Illustrated History of Sacramento County. By Hon. Winfield J. Davis, Chicago: The Lewis Publishing Company. 1890

[8] Sacramento Daily Union, Volume 28, Number 4246, 31 October 1864

[9] Sacramento Bee, 1864 October 13

[10] Sacramento Daily Union, Volume 29, Number 4390, 17 April 1865

[11] Sacramento Daily Union, Volume 29, Number 4390, 17 April 1865

[12] Sacramento Daily Union, Volume 29, Number 4390, 17 April 1865

[13] Sacramento Daily Union, Volume 29, Number 4393, 20 April 1865

[14] Sacramento Daily Union, Volume 29, Number 4475, 26 July 1865

[15] Sacramento Daily Union, Volume 29, Number 4475, 26 July 1865

[16] Sacramento Daily Union, Volume 29, Number 4475, 26 July 1865

[17] Sacramento Daily Union, Volume 29, Number 4476, 27 July 1865

[18] Sacramento Daily Union, Volume 29, Number 4503, 28 August 1865

[19] Sacramento Daily Union, Volume 29, Number 4476, 27 July 1865

[20] The Folsom Telegraph, 1865 August 5

[21] Stockton Independent, Volume IX, Number 2, 2 August 1865

[22] Sacramento Daily Union, Volume 29, Number 4513, 8 September 1865

[23] Sacramento Daily Union, Volume 29, Number 4513, 8 September 1865

[24] Sacramento Daily Union, Volume 29, Number 4512, 7 September 1865

[25] Sacramento Daily Union, Volume 29, Number 4501, 25 August 1865

[26] Sacramento Daily Union, Volume 29, Number 4501, 25 August 1865

[27] There are conflicting sources as to the date of birth. Some sources report the birth as September 30, 1865

[28] Sacramento Daily Union, Volume 30, Number 4536, 5 October 1865

[29] Sacramento Daily Union, Volume 30, Number 4540, 10 October 1865

[30] Sacramento Daily Union, Volume 30, Number 4575, 20 November 1865

[31] Sacramento Daily Union, Volume 33, Number 5095, 27 July 1867

[32] Sacramento Daily Union, Volume 33, Number 5056, 11 June 1867

[33] Sacramento Daily Union, Volume 33, Number 5034, 16 May 1867

[34] Sacramento Daily Union, Volume 33, Number 5039, 22 May 1867

[35] Sacramento Daily Union, Volume 33, Number 5039, 22 May 1867

[36] Sacramento Daily Union, Volume 33, Number 5089, 20 July 1867

[37] Sacramento Daily Union, Volume 33, Number 6001, 3 August 1867

[38] Sacramento Daily Union, Volume 33, Number 5095, 27 July 1867

[39] Sacramento Daily Union, Volume 33, Number 5051, 5 June 1867

[40] Sacramento Daily Union, Volume 33, Number 5051, 5 June 1867

Amos P. Catlin

[41] Sacramento Daily Union, Volume 33, Number 5095, 27 July 1867
[42] Sacramento Daily Union, Volume 33, Number 5051, 5 June 1867
[43] Sacramento Daily Union, Volume 33, Number 5052, 6 June 1867
[44] Sacramento Daily Union, Volume 33, Number 5052, 6 June 1867
[45] Sacramento Daily Union, Volume 33, Number 5052, 6 June 1867
[46] Daily Alta California, Volume 19, Number 6299, 13 June 1867
[47] Sacramento Daily Union, Volume 33, Number 5058, 13 June 1867
[48] Sacramento Daily Union, Volume 33, Number 5058, 13 June 1867
[49] Stockton Independent, Volume XII, Number 114, 14 June 1867
[50] Daily Alta California, Volume 19, Number 6333, 18 July 1867
[51] Marin Journal, Volume 7, Number 19, 20 July 1867
[52] Marin Journal, Volume 7, Number 19, 20 July 1867
[53] Marin Journal, Volume 7, Number 19, 20 July 1867
[54] Daily Alta California, Volume 19, Number 6353, 7 August 1867
[55] Sacramento Daily Union, Volume 33, Number 5114, 19 August 1867
[56] Sacramento Daily Union, Volume 33, Number 5125, 31 August 1867
[57] Sacramento Bee, September 3, 1867
[58] Sacramento Daily Union, Volume 33, Number 5128, 4 September 1867
[59] Sacramento Daily Union, Volume 33, Number 5131, 7 September 1867
[60] Red Bluff Independent, Volume VIII, Number 9, 28 August 1867
[61] Sacramento Daily Union, Volume 33, Number 5077, 6 July 1867
[62] Sacramento Daily Union, Volume 33, Number 5077, 6 July 1867
[63] Sacramento Daily Union, Volume 33, Number 5077, 6 July 1867
[64] Sacramento Daily Union, Volume 33, Number 5077, 6 July 1867
[65] Sacramento Daily Union, Volume 33, Number 5077, 6 July 1867

Amos P. Catlin

Chapter Nine: Republican to Independent, Railroads, BOE, 1868 – 1873

Life in Folsom for Amos and Ruth was pleasant in 1868, if, unfortunately, childless. Ruth got involved with the public library and became one of trustees for the new Folsom Library Association.[1] They were close to Ruth's father, Dr. Donaldson, while living in Folsom. However, Dr. Donaldson was preparing to move to Sacramento.[2] As most of Amos' law practice centered on Sacramento courtrooms, he was also entertaining thoughts of moving to Sacramento. Of course, Folsom held a strong attraction for Amos, and the local residents held him in high esteem

Amos was the Orator of the Day for the Folsom Fourth of July celebration in 1868.[3] The parade Marshal of the Day was Benjamin Bugbey, whose Natoma Vineyard had attracted much acclaim for the variety of wines, brandy and sparkling wine it was producing. Even though Amos still owned numerous lots in the town of Folsom, he was disposing of those investments as opportunities arose, and he was winding down his ownership and management positions in the Natoma Water and Mining Company. His main attachment to the area was handling the sales of the Leidesdorff land grant for the Folsom Estate. By June of 1868, all of the property in the land grant had been sold.[4]

Republican Party Affiliation

As Ulysses S. Grant began his run for the U.S. presidency to capture the legacy of Abraham Lincoln, the Union Party dissipated. Men like Amos had to decide between the Republican or Democratic parties. Under the banner of the diminishing Union Party, Amos spoke to an assembly of the Grant and Colfax Club.[5] As George Gorham, former gubernatorial Union candidate, identified as Republican, so did Amos.

Because of his fair and impartial leadership, Amos was selected as the Republican moderator for a large political discussion in Sacramento.[6] Also represented were Democrats and the Union Party. It was a trilateral discussion of the positions of the different parties on the issues facing California and the nation. Amos would follow up on this appearance with another speaking engagement in Georgetown for Union Republicans.[7]

Amos P. Catlin

Judgeship

While Amos was taking the Republican Party for a test buggy ride to see if it was to his liking, Ruth Anne became pregnant. She gave birth to their son, Alexander Donaldson Catlin, in Sacramento on January 2, 1869. Amos diversified his law practice by handling more criminal defense matters and civil matters in Sacramento. His judicial temperament, and deep-seated political ambition, was to be a judge. To that end, Amos declared his candidacy for the Sixth District Court Judge position, subject to the approval of the Union Republican Judicial Convention in 1869.[8]

DISTRICT JUDGE.

A. P. CATLIN WILL BE A CANDI-
date for District Judge, of the Sixth Judicial
District, subject to the nomination of the Union Convention.   je9-1m3p*

Sacramento Daily Union, June 21, 1869

30. Announcement that Amos Catlin will be a candidate for District Court Judge, 1869.

Judge McKune was angling for the Union Republican nomination as well. Another contender was Robert Robinson, who was preferred by the Central Pacific Railroad.[9] Robinson was a former law partner with McKune and Edwin B. Crocker. The bitter, derogatory statements of Robinson and McKune, aimed at one another, displayed the personal animus between them.[10]

The Sixth District Court comprised Sacramento and Yolo counties. The judicial conventions were usually separate from the county nominating conventions because district courts typically comprised more than one county. Judge McKune did not have high approval ratings outside of the City of Sacramento. Robinson, who represented the Central Pacific Railroad in many different legal actions, was viewed as suspect by settlers in the region.[11] Amos stayed out of the political gutter fight and was favored by both the Sacramento Bee and Sacramento Union newspapers.[12]

As the Judicial Convention convened, the Yolo County delegation was not present. There were rumors that Robinson supporters had urged the Yolo delegation not to attend, in order to give the delegate edge to Robinson.[13] Amos withdrew his name from consideration, as he thought the convention, less the Yolo delegates, was not an honest nominating contest.[14] The convention was rescheduled for a time when the Yolo delegation could attend.

Amos P. Catlin

The general consensus of the newspapers in Sacramento and the Bay Area was that if Amos was not nominated, the judgeship would go to the Democratic candidate.[15] When the Judicial Convention reconvened, Amos came in third on the balloting.[16] Robinson was nominated and lost to the Democratic candidate Louis Ramage in the general election. Amos came close to being elected District Judge. What he lacked was the energy to play hardball politics to get the nomination.

Railroad Litigation

From Amos' perspective, railroads were good for Sacramento and California. He had been involved with the Sacramento Valley Railroad and the California Central Railroad. But he was displeased with the Central Pacific Railroad's (CPRR) management practices. The CPRR was generally regarded as a bully, bullying landowners over property it wanted for its own operations, implementing monopolistic rates, and quick to litigate to stop competition.

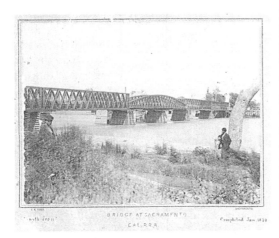

31. California Pacific Railroad bridge over the Sacramento River, completed 1870.

In 1869, the California Pacific Railroad was building a rail line between Vallejo and Sacramento. This would be a shorter route to the Bay Area than the one operated by the CPRR under the name of the Western Pacific Railroad (WPRR.) The WPRR went through Stockton, then over the Altamont Pass and through Niles Canyon, where it proceeded north to Oakland. A vital juncture of the California Pacific RR crossed the CPRR tracks in Sacramento.

The CPRR had tried to stop the California Pacific Railroad from crossing its tracks in Sacramento, but the action was denied in the Sixth District Court. The CPRR then appealed the decision until it reached the California Supreme Court in January of 1870. Robert Robinson and S.W. Sanderson represented the CPRR, and Amos appeared on behalf of the California Pacific Railroad.

Robert Robinson for the CPRR pushed for a decision from the bench on the day of oral arguments. Amos requested 15 days to file briefs, as he had only acquired the case two days previous. The Supreme Court did grant until January 28th to file briefs in the case. Tacked onto the order was an addendum further ordering the California Pacific Railroad to cease and desist any construction related to crossing the CPRR's tracks.[17]

The unusual cease and desist order was not communicated to the California Pacific Railroad employees, who were at that time installing the railroad 90 degree at-grade crossing to allow their trains to enter into Sacramento. Robinson heard that the California Pacific Railroad work was still underway at First Street and visited the site, informing the workers of the order to cease operations. The California Pacific Railroad employees said they needed an order from the engineer Shortt to stop work.[18]

Robinson then ordered his men to go fetch several Henry repeating rifles, in an act of intimidation to halt the work. A conference quickly ensued, and the California Pacific employees stopped their construction and left the site.[19] Amos was stunned by the judicial overreach of the Supreme Court. He was a stickler for the rules and precedence, and he found the California Supreme Court had overstepped its role as an appellate jurisdiction.

When the January date arrived for the Supreme Court to hear the petitions in the original case, bowing to the controversy, they limited the arguments to the issue of whether the Court, being one of appellate power only, could issue injunctions.[20] Amos argued that no appellate court had the power to issue injunctions. The California Supreme Court had done it once previously and quickly acknowledged it did not have the power of injunctions.[21]

Later that evening, the Supreme Court issued an order reversing the injunction: "After a careful consideration of the able oral arguments made on the hearing of this motion, we entertain a grave doubt whether the cross complaint of the Central Pacific Railroad Company presents sufficient grounds for an injunction, though we do not intend to express any opinion in advance of the final hearing on the important question arising on the record. But entertaining these doubts, we do not deem it proper to interpose the extraordinary remedy by injunction, except there be danger that great or irreparable damage will ensue to the Central Pacific Company pending the action, unless the California Pacific Company be restrained by a temporary injunction from crossing the railroad tracks of the former."[22]

The California Pacific Railroad line into Sacramento was eventually completed. Competition and financial difficulties forced the California Pacific Railroad to sell its lines to the CPRR in the 1870s. The practice of the CPRR subsuming other railroads was familiar. The CPRR had squeezed both the Sacramento Valley and

Amos P. Catlin

California Central railroads by 1865 with a more favorable road that attracted more freight and passengers. The CPRR also had government subsidies to assist its operations.

Another victim of the CPRR was the Sacramento, Placer & Nevada Railroad (SPNRR), which had a depot just north of Folsom. The SPNRR ceased operations in 1864, as it was clear that the CPRR could service Auburn from Sacramento more economically. While Amos never invested in the SPNRR, the loss of that railroad, along with his investments in the SVRR and CCRR, dampened the potential economic growth of Folsom. Then, after struggling for several years, the Folsom Literary Institute closed its doors in 1869. Amos' aspiration for Folsom to grow into a vibrant and diverse economic center, similar to towns on the East Coast, was evaporating like water spilled onto the street on a hot August afternoon.

Folsom was full of good people, many of whom were supporters and friends of Amos. However, Amos was at a crossroads in his life and career in 1869. At age 46, he was spending most of his time in Sacramento, either arguing cases before the Supreme Court or attending political events. Amos made the decision to relocate to Sacramento.

In 1870, after several years of a fruitful partnership, Bowie and Catlin was dissolved. Amos set up his solo practice in the office of the Sacramento Savings Bank, on the corner of Fifth and J streets.[23] Amos entered a new partnership with Thomas B. McFarland in December 1870 and set up their law offices at the corner of Second and K streets.[24] In the new law practice, Amos would be listed first, Catlin and McFarland. McFarland was a fellow pioneer who came to California in 1849. Like Amos, McFarland had been a member of the Whig and American parties. McFarland was also a former District Court Judge and, like Amos, had a passion for the law.

Board of Equalization

Newton Booth, former Union Party member with Amos, was elected Governor in 1871. It was during this time that Amos' name kept coming up as a potential candidate for California Supreme Court Justice, either by election[25] or appointment by Governor Booth to fill a vacancy.[26] Appreciative of the acknowledgement of his achievements in his law career, Amos declined invitations to be considered for a Supreme Court seat.[27] He had a full calendar of law cases, his son John was born in March of 1871,[28] and, at the age of 48, he was in his prime earning years.

It was no secret that the salary of any judge or Supreme Court Justice paled compared to the earnings of a private practice. A better opportunity came along in March 1872, one that would allow Amos to serve in state government and also keep his law practice. Governor Booth appointed Amos to the State Board of Equalization to fill the vacancy of Morris M. Estee.[29] The Sacramento Bee proclaimed of the appointment, "...Mr. Catlin is one of the most industrious, clear-headed and deserving of our citizens, and an excellent lawyer."[30]

The State Board of Equalization was the product of deficit state budgets. It was first proposed by Creed Haymond, when he, John McKune, and John Burch were working within the California Code Commission from 1870 to 1872. The concept sounded so good, this Board of Equalization, that it was passed by the State Legislature and signed into law by Gov. Booth.[31] At its core, the mission of the Board of Equalization was to raise additional tax revenue to offset any deficit in the state budget created by overspending by the Legislature.

Each county had a Board of Equalization. The role of the county boards was to assess taxes on property at a rate set by the Legislature for state taxes. The State Board of Equalization had the power to set rules governing how county assessments were determined. If the State Board of Equalization thought a county was undervaluing property, it could reject the assessments and set its own valuations.[32] The goal of the State Board was to equalize the tax revenue collected from the counties so the revenue matched the State budget.

Amos and his fellow Board of Equalization members got right down to work and in early April of 1872 announced several new rules for assessing property, along with an explanatory preamble. From the time the Board was established, there were questions about its constitutionality. A letter from the Board to county assessors was strongly influenced by Amos and was meant, in part, to establish the authority of the State Board. The power of the State Board of Equalization, as outlined in the letter, was derived from the State Constitution and Political Code.

"The assessment and collection of the public revenue of this State under the Political Code is based upon the Constitution of the State, and there are few, if any, questions as to the meaning of that instrument in its relation to this subject which have not been settled by decisions of the Supreme Court."[33]

The rationale behind the creation of the Board was the belief, and most likely factual data, that some counties were undervaluing property in order to reduce the taxes of their residents.

"In a State where for more than twenty years inequality and want of uniformity in the assessment of property for taxation has been the rule rather than the exception (to the great injury of a majority of the citizens and the general detriment of the State), the enforcement of a constitutional system which subjects all property to equal and uniform taxation in proportion to its full value will, doubtless, at first

Amos P. Catlin

encounter some opposition from those who, by long exemption from just and equal burdens have come to regard the sudden change from wrong to right as an act of injustice to them, in the nature of an encroachment upon privileges almost vested by reason of long enjoyment."[34]

The logic was that if all property was equally and fairly assessed, and the owners of the property paid their taxes, the state budget would get balanced, ending the years of deficits. To achieve uniform taxation, the Board issued new rules to county assessors governing the valuation of growing crops, railroads, swamplands, consigned goods and animals.[35] The Board even proposed taxing dogs at their full cash value, if a county so chose to levy such a tax.[36]

San Francisco was seen as a county that had manipulated assessments in previous years. San Francisco was a major port of entry for material, had a large population, and had become the center of banking and finance for the state. It did not take long for San Francisco merchants to balk at the new rules. A month after the edicts and rules governing valuation were sent out by the State Board, San Francisco importing merchants requested that "…solvent debts due to importers for sales of imported goods in original unbroken packages to be deducted from the total amount of their solvent debts" for the purposes of taxation.[37]

The merchants referenced that a tax on solvent debts relative to imported goods interfered with the power of Congress to regulate commerce with foreign nations. In addition, the U.S. Supreme Court reaffirmed such a position.[38] The State Board of Equalization replied to the merchants on May 25th with a firm negative response. They would not entertain easing the rules. The reply, while long and explanatory, also came off as arrogant, self-righteous, and unyielding.[39] Of the three board members, Amos was the only lawyer.[40]

Not only was Amos a Board member, he was also the Board's legal counsel. Based on the State Board of Equalization rules, the Sacramento County Assessor had levied an assessment on Samuel Cross' personal money and his deposits in the Sacramento Savings Bank. It was left up to Amos, who was appearing on behalf of the county Assessor as well as the Board, to explain the apparent double-taxation situation. Amos even questioned Samuel Cross under oath in an effort to discredit his arguments.[41] The Sacramento County Board of Equalization found Amos' arguments convincing and refused to grant an exception to the assessment.[42]

The work of educating county assessors and explaining the rules was not limited to Sacramento. Amos would travel throughout California, as did the other Board members, defending the new assessment rules.[43] The ability for Amos to question petitioners for lower assessments would expose how some corporations were undervaluing their assets. The Central Pacific Railroad petitioned for a reduction of their assessment. Under questioning from Amos, the railroad representatives admitted they had no idea of the original construction costs of the rail line, and they excluded the cost of the bridges from their valuation.[44]

The State Board of Equalization was a radical idea with a noble mission: Ensure that all counties were paying their fair share of taxes to the state. San Francisco, which contributed an estimated 40 percent of total state tax revenue, was not happy with State Board rules or edicts. After the San Francisco Board of Supervisors had reduced some tax assessments, the State Board of Equalization ordered the city auditor to ignore the changes and prepare an assessment roll exactly as it had been created by the San Francisco County Assessor.[45]

There was little doubt in the minds of San Francisco politicians that it was Amos who was driving the hardline legal opinions of the State Board. California was still a relatively young state in 1872. Matters concerning property valuations and taxation were routinely brought to the judicial system for adjudication. Marin County brought an action in the Fifteenth District Court claiming the State Board was making illegal changes to the valuation of its property assessments.[46]

Amos was called to testify on how the State Board made tax rate decisions. He testified that, after much discussion, the Board decided to fix the tax rate at $0.50 per $100 of assessed property value. While some Board members wanted a tax rate of $0.56 per $100, the 50 cents rate would raise $2.3 million for the State. The State Board, in the process of equalization, would add value to some counties and reduce the assessed valuation of other counties. Amos conceded that projected collected tax revenue would still create a state budget deficit of between $600,000 and $800,000.[47]

San Francisco Tax Thieves

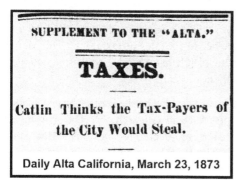

SUPPLEMENT TO THE "ALTA."

TAXES.

Catlin Thinks the Tax-Payers of the City Would Steal.

Daily Alta California, March 23, 1873

32. Amos Catlin is accused of saying San Francisco would cheat on their taxes, 1873.

Creed Haymond, who originally conceived of the State Board of Equalization, was leading the defense of the State Board in court. Amos, during the court proceedings, would normally sit next to Haymond for consultation. At one legal proceeding, County Supervisor Story was being questioned by prosecuting attorney Felton and was asked if he thought the Chairman of the State Board assumed the taxpayers, by

Amos P. Catlin

undervaluing their property, were trying to steal? In a comment to Haymond, Amos remarked, "He was right if he did."[48]

The Daily Alta newspaper headline proclaimed, "Catlin Thinks the Tax-Payers of the City Would Steal."[49] Amos tried to repair the damage to his and the State Board's reputation, but without an apology. He wrote to the Daily Alta, "My remark at the moment was made sotto voce to Mr. Haymond, by whose side I was seated, and for his ear alone, and was made altogether in a jocose spirit and manner, without intending the imputation charged even against the Board of Supervisors. With respect to my real and serious utterances I will resort either to repentance or vindication. In regard to this matter there is no occasion for either."[50]

Amos' explanation of his jocular remark to Haymond did nothing to repair the perception of the State Board who were being characterized as "greedy and pompous State officials."[51] Fortunately for Amos and the Board, their fate did not rest on public opinion. Their mission, methods and operation would eventually be reviewed by the California Supreme Court. Opponents of the State Board of Equalization received a partial victory from the Supreme Court in May 1873. The Court held that a tax on solvent debt for money loaned, whether secured by mortgage or otherwise, represents a case of double taxation. The Court stopped the Board from assessing taxes on certain deposits and loans, but let the agency continue in its mission of equalization.[52]

The California Supreme Court would change. Elisha McKinstry was endorsed by Amos' Peoples Independent Party as a candidate for Supreme Court Justice.[53] McKinstry won and sat on the bench as *Houghton v Austin*, contesting the powers of the State Board of Equalization, was argued before the Court. The Supreme Court ruled that the power to raise or reduce valuations that have been fixed by a county Assessor for the purposes of taxation cannot be conferred to individuals who have not been elected. In other words, the Legislature could not delegate to the State Board of Equalization the power to fix rates of taxation.[54] The March 1874 Supreme Court decision, with which McKinstry mostly concurred, stopped the Board from its mission of equalization.

The California Supreme Court decision was heralded by the Daily Alta newspaper in San Francisco with the headline of "A Dead Oligarchy."[55] The newspaper exaggerated the effects of the decision by declaring the State Board of Equalization an unconstitutional body. The Board was not dead, but its powers were drastically curtailed. In a Sacramento Daily Union editorial, attributed to Amos, the paper stated, "The Supreme Court has shorn the Board of the power to equalize valuation as between counties; but this power is never necessary when the Assessors fairly and justly perform their duties and there is reason for

Amos P. Catlin

believing that under the rules and instructions of the Board, the power to prescribe which remains unimpaired, the Assessors' returns will be such that the loss of the power to equalize will not be seriously felt by the Board."[56]

Fair and impartial - those were guiding principles for Amos. He and many other citizens recognized that the taxation function was too closely aligned with political interests. There were big corporations and well-connected residents who received tax breaks by being allowed to undervalue their property. The equalization goal of fair and impartial assessments was noble, but its method and operation by the Board was determined unconstitutional by the Supreme Court. Amos accepted the ruling and moved on. At 50 years old, Amos had more than enough demands on his time from family, politics, and his law practice.

People's Independent Taxpayers Party

In 1873, Amos was the representing attorney in at least 17 appellate cases before the California Supreme Court. He also continued to represent plaintiffs and defendants in the local District Court. In addition, he had a caseload involving probate and representing clients before city and county elected bodies. Similar to his work at the State Board, Amos's legal work was helping to define the young State of California. Acknowledging rules and proper procedures was a central tenet for Amos. This adherence to a tight ethical lane regularly led to conflict with other men who still leaned heavily on a pioneer perspective of how to operate in politics.

Benjamin Bugbey, chairman of the Sacramento County Republican Central Committee, introduced Amos as one of the vice presidents at a mass meeting in September 1872. Amos was a reluctant Republican. He was one of a group of principled men who felt election rules should be followed, even if there was room to operate at the margins of ethical conduct. The Sacramento County Republican Party was tinkering with the election of delegates to the County Convention to favor current Governor Newton Booth.[57]

Even though Amos was a friend and political ally of Gov. Booth, he had little tolerance for the manipulation of election rules. In June of 1873, he found himself the chairman of a meeting of independent primary voters.[58] If the Republican Central Committee was not going to hold a fair election, the men of the independent movement would. They resolved to hold a primary election that would elect, in their minds, a balanced delegation for a nominating convention. There would be 132 delegates, 69 from the city of Sacramento and 63 from other parts of the county.[59]

This movement of disaffected Republican men would call themselves the Independent Taxpayer's Party,[60] also to be known as the People's Party at the state level. However, the Independent Taxpayer's was not exclusively made up of Republicans. Many Democrats, disappointed by political corruption, also would be represented. At the Independent Taxpayer's Convention in June of 1873, party leaders would receive a letter from the Sacramento Democratic Party offering to cooperate with them.[61]

Amos was wonderfully idealistic at the prospect of communing with men from the opposing party. He wanted to welcome all men who were for fair elections and good governance. As to the communication from the Democratic Party, he said, "These men want to come in as it were in the eleventh hour, and we should treat them as the Savior recommended in Scripture that men repenting in the last hour should be treated. We must combine with every honest element of every party if we would win the fight. Success is our main purpose, and we should see if this proposition will add to our chances if we accept it. If it does not, we can reject it."[62]

In the summer of 1873, the nascent Independent Taxpayer's Party was focused on local issues and elections. Amos was good friends with many Democrats in Sacramento. In the practice of law, it did not matter the party affiliation of any lawyer; Amos worked with them all. As its name implied, the party membership was most interested in low tax rates and judicious public expenditures. The Independent Taxpayer's Party passed resolutions favoring immigration, but not from Asian countries. They wanted Folsom Prison built in order to utilize convict labor. Railroads were good, but the railroad owners had too much power and should be driven out of politics.[63]

There was a sentiment in Sacramento that the Republican Party had fallen under the influence of the Central Pacific Railroad.[64] Critics claimed the railroads received too many subsidies in the form of land, only to return the favor with monopolistic rates on passenger fares and freight.[65] On the second day of the Independent Taxpayer's Convention, Amos nominated Republican Henry Edgerton for State Senator and Democrat Creed Haymond for Assembly. Haymond declined the nomination.[66] When the convention finished, a number of Republicans, as well as Democrats, had been endorsed for local office.[67]

An advertisement for the Independent Taxpayer's meeting left no misunderstanding regarding the Party's position on the railroad. The meeting notice read, "Shall we have a government of the people, for the people, by the people, or by the railroads?"[68] Amos would chair the meeting, better described as a political rally, introducing Henry Edgerton, candidate for State Senate, who was regarded as one of best political orators of the day.[69]

The Independent Taxpayer's movement was gaining recognition and a favorable response from the public. There was interest in having the emerging political party expand beyond Sacramento County. In September of 1873, Amos called a meeting of the local party members to discuss the expansion and nominate candidates to statewide office. Judge McKune wanted to move quickly with organizing a State Convention, while Amos wanted a more cautious approach. Regardless of their differences, and in deference to Amos, who was the guiding hand for the movement, Amos was nominated to begin a statewide campaign.[70]

This independent movement had difficulty selecting a name. Most of the men at the organizing level were attorneys, and not necessarily political operatives with a background in marketing. This lack of name played into the hands of newspapers, who filled the brand vacuum and named the movement the Dolly Vardens. Dolly Varden was a character from a series of popular short stories by Charles Dickens. Dolly was always fashionably dressed, very attractive, spoiled, and naïve. A painting by William Frith depicting Dolly Varden appearing gay and carefree helped inspire a similar look in women's fashion in the 1870s.

The newspapers were dismissive of the Dolly Varden Party. The Sacramento Bee reported, "The Taxpayers, Dolly Vardens, Independents, or call them whatever other name they may assume – for they are now known by all these – met in small numbers in this city yesterday and called a State Convention to meet in Sacramento on Thursday next....The meeting was run by the Governor's appointees Swift, Catlin, McKune, and Hart."[71]

For the statewide campaign, the Independent Taxpayer's Party became the People's Independent Party. The People's Independent State Convention was held on short notice, requiring many counties who wanted to participate to delegate their proxies to men who could attend the meeting. Amos was faulted for holding the proxies of Ventura and Tulare counties and a quarter of Sonoma county's delegates.[72]

If the portrait of Dolly Varden was inspiring women's fashion, the People's Independent Party was hoping to inspire government reform. The grievances expressed in the Party platform were some of the same issues Amos was tackling as a member of the State Board of Equalization. In short, large corporations had too much influence in government and politics. The opening resolution of their platform described the Party members as, "...the opponents of incorporated greed and organized corruption do form themselves into a political body to be known as The People's Independent Party."[73]

The Party platform was also a primer for voters to understand what was motivating men like Amos to toss aside the more established Democrat and Republican parties. The People's Independent Party felt the current political parties demanded too much fealty, manipulated the primary election process, and had become beholden to large corporations. Specifically, they called for an investigation into the Credit Mobilier and Contract and Finance companies associated with the Union Pacific Railroad in the building of the Transcontinental Railroad.[74]

More broadly, the Party was opposed to granting any subsidies for the construction of railroads unless approved by local voters. They also wanted government to get involved with regulating railroad freight and passenger rates and in regulating land acquisition by the railroads. They were absolutely opposed to a system that granted large corporations or railroads vast tracts of land at the expense of displacing current families.[75]

Because political patronage had become so closely associated with corruption, the People's Independent Party called for a thorough reform of the civil service in government. They called on the state to control the rivers and streams for irrigation and prevent large companies from controlling California's water resources. Public schools were to be supported, but immigration from Asian countries needed to be stopped.[76]

Some of the targets for reform were areas in which Amos had been involved. His Natoma Water and Mining Company had created a dam and canal system to distribute water and

INDEPENDENT
TAXPAYER'S TICKET.

FOR SUPERINTENDENT OF SCHOOLS,
A. H. McDONALD.

FOR DIRECTORS,
First Ward.....................JOHN SUVERKRUP.
Second Ward...... ....D. W. WELTY.
Third Ward....................ALBERT LEONARD.
Fourth Ward................. ....DANIEL FLINT.
By order of Central Committee.
A. P. CATLIN, Chairman.
ALBERT HART, Secretary.   n24-td3p*

TICKET

PLEDGED to SEPARATE SCHOOLS
FOR WHITES AND NEGROES.

FOR CITY SUPERINTENDENT,

A. C. HINKSON.

FOR DIRECTORS,
First Ward..................... .....J. F. MONTGOMERY.
Second Ward ....GEO. S. WAIT.
Third Ward........... ....WM. F. KNOX.
Fourth Ward....................H. B. NIELSON.
By order Democratic City Central Committee.
WM. SHATTUCK, Chairman.
JNO. K. ALEXANDER, Secretary.   n21-9t*3p

Sacramento Daily Union, November 26, 1873

33. Amos Catlin's Independent Taxpayer's Ticket vs. Sacramento Democratic party candidates, 1873.

had grown quite powerful in the local region. The company had appropriated water and land with no government oversight, and its water rates were not regulated. Amos had also sat on the boards of directors for the Sacramento Valley and California Central railroads.

The People's Independent State Convention, in addition to drafting platform resolutions, met for the purposes of nominating a candidate to an open seat on the bench of the California Supreme Court. Elisha McKinstry got their nod of approval. After the convention, many of the participants, along with a brass band, marched down the street to Gov. Newton Booth's residence in Sacramento and saluted him.[77]

McKinstry would win the election for Supreme Court Justice. Amos would hold local People's Party meetings at his office in Sacramento.[78] The next election was for school board members and superintendent. They put up a slate of candidates under the heading of Independent Taxpayer's Ticket, A.P. Catlin, Chairman.[79] The competing Democratic Party slate had A. C. Hinkson for City Superintendent, under the heading "Pledged to Separate Schools for Whites and Negroes."[80]

By the early 1870s, Amos was in the canal of local and state politics. The water flow was swift, and he was riding the current to a destination that was uncertain.

---

[1] The Folsom Telegraph, March 28, 1868

[2] The Folsom Telegraph, July 18, 1868

[3] Sacramento Bee, July 7, 1868

[4] The Folsom Telegraph, June 13, 1868

[5] Sacramento Daily Union, Volume 35, Number 5454, 18 September 1868

[6] Sacramento Daily Union, Volume 36, Number 5459, 24 September 1868

[7] Sacramento Daily Union, Volume 36, Number 5486, 26 October 1868

[8] Sacramento Daily Union, Volume 37, Number 5679, 9 June 1869

[9] Sacramento Daily Union, Volume 37, Number 5701, 5 July 1869

[10] Sacramento Bee, July 23, 1869

[11] Sacramento Daily Union, Volume 37, Number 5717, 24 July 1869

[12] Sacramento Bee, July 23, 1869, Sacramento Daily Union, Volume 37, Number 5717, 24 July 1869

[13] Sacramento Daily Union, Volume 37, Number 5716, 23 July 1869

[14] Sacramento Daily Union, Volume 37, Number 5716, 23 July 1869

[15] San Francisco Chronicle, July 28, 1869

[16] Sacramento Daily Union, Volume 37, Number 5720, 28 July 1869

[17] Sacramento Daily Union, Volume 38, Number 5874, 24 January 1870

[18] Sacramento Daily Union, Volume 38, Number 5874, 24 January 1870

[19] Sacramento Daily Union, Volume 38, Number 5874, 24 January 1870

[20] Sacramento Daily Union, Volume 38, Number 5879, 29 January 1870

[21] Sacramento Daily Union, Volume 38, Number 5879, 29 January 1870

[22] Sacramento Daily Union, Volume 38, Number 5879, 29 January 1870

[23] Sacramento Bee, May 19, 1870

[24] Sacramento Daily Union, Volume 40, Number 7041, 7 December 1870

[25] Sacramento Daily Union, Volume 41, Number 7211, 23 June 1871

[26] Stockton Independent, Volume XXII, Number 25, 29 February 1872

[27] Sacramento Daily Union, Volume 41, Number 7211, 23 June 1871

[28] Sacramento Daily Union, Volume 40, Number 7125, 15 March 1871

Amos P. Catlin

[29] Sacramento Daily Union, Volume 43, Number 7443, 22 March 1872
[30] Sacramento Bee, March 22, 1872
[31] Daily Alta California, Volume 26, Number 8756, 22 March 1874
[32] Daily Alta California, Volume 26, Number 8756, 22 March 1874
[33] Sacramento Daily Union, Volume 43, Number 7460, 11 April 1872
[34] Sacramento Daily Union, Volume 43, Number 7460, 11 April 1872
[35] Sacramento Daily Union, Volume 43, Number 7460, 11 April 1872
[36] Sacramento Daily Union, Volume 43, Number 7460, 11 April 1872
[37] Sacramento Daily Union, Volume 43, Number 6603, 31 May 1872
[38] Sacramento Daily Union, Volume 43, Number 6603, 31 May 1872
[39] Sacramento Daily Union, Volume 43, Number 6603, 31 May 1872
[40] Daily Alta California, Volume 24, Number 8213, 21 September 1872
[41] Sacramento Daily Union, Volume 43, Number 6636, 10 July 1872
[42] Sacramento Bee, July 10, 1872
[43] Sonoma Democrat, Volume XV, Number 44, 10 August 1872
[44] Sacramento Daily Union, Volume 43, Number 6639, 13 July 1872
[45] Daily Alta California, Volume 24, Number 8213, 21 September 1872
[46] Daily Alta California, Volume 25, Number 8395, 23 March 1873
[47] Daily Alta California, Volume 25, Number 8395, 23 March 1873
[48] Daily Alta California, Volume 25, Number 8395, 23 March 1873
[49] Daily Alta California, Volume 25, Number 8395, 23 March 1873
[50] Daily Alta California, Volume 25, Number 8396, 24 March 1873
[51] Daily Alta California, Volume 25, Number 8395, 23 March 1873
[52] Sacramento Daily Union, Volume 45, Number 6895, 9 May 1873
[53] Sacramento Daily Union, Volume 46, Number 7020, 3 October 1873
[54] Sacramento Daily Union, Volume 47, Number 7165, 23 March 1874
[55] Daily Alta California, Volume 26, Number 8756, 22 March 1874
[56] San Francisco Chronicle, April 8, 1874
[57] Sacramento Daily Union, Volume 45, Number 6915, 2 June 1873
[58] Sacramento Daily Union, Volume 45, Number 6916, 3 June 1873
[59] Sacramento Daily Union, Volume 45, Number 6916, 3 June 1873
[60] Sacramento Daily Union, Volume 45, Number 6933, 23 June 1873
[61] Sacramento Daily Union, Volume 45, Number 6935, 25 June 1873
[62] Sacramento Daily Union, Volume 45, Number 6935, 25 June 1873
[63] Sacramento Daily Union, Volume 45, Number 6935, 25 June 1873
[64] Sacramento Bee, June 25, 1873
[65] Sacramento Daily Union, Volume 45, Number 6936, 26 June 1873
[66] Sacramento Daily Union, Volume 45, Number 6936, 26 June 1873
[67] Sacramento Daily Union, Volume 45, Number 6936, 26 June 1873
[68] Sacramento Daily Union, Volume 45, Number 6969, 5 August 1873
[69] Sacramento Bee, August 18, 1873
[70] Sacramento Daily Union, Volume 45, Number 7008, 19 September 1873
[71] Sacramento Bee, September 19, 1873
[72] Daily Alta California, Volume 25, Number 8581, 26 September 1873
[73] Sacramento Daily Union, Volume 46, Number 7014, 26 September 1873
[74] Sacramento Daily Union, Volume 46, Number 7014, 26 September 1873
[75] Sacramento Daily Union, Volume 46, Number 7014, 26 September 1873
[76] Sacramento Daily Union, Volume 46, Number 7014, 26 September 1873
[77] Russian River Flag, Volume V, Number 47, 2 October 1873
[78] Sacramento Daily Union, Volume 46, Number 7046, 3 November 1873
[79] Sacramento Daily Union, Volume 46, Number 7066, 26 November 1873
[80] Sacramento Daily Union, Volume 46, Number 7066, 26 November 1873

Amos P. Catlin

Chapter Ten: Libel & Life Changes, 1874 - 1878

Amos would continue at the helm of the Independent Taxpayers Party in Sacramento, organizing a City Convention to nominate candidates for local offices.[1] March 1874 would be a very challenging month for Amos and his family. His father-in-law, Dr. Donaldson, retired Sacramento County Physician, would collapse downtown. Dr. Donaldson was taken to Amos' house at Eighth and I streets, where he would later die.[2]

Later in March, the California Supreme Court would release its decision neutering the State Board of Equalization, determining that the methods Amos had championed to equalize property tax rates were unconstitutional. Justice McKinstry, nominated and endorsed by Amos' People's Independent Party for government reform, concurred with many of the findings of the Supreme Court.

A. P. CATLIN.   T. B. M'FARLAND.

CATLIN & McFARLAND.

ATTORNEYS AT LAW,

Office south-east corner K and Second streets, Sacramento, Cal.

Sept. 16, 1872.   1-tf

Placer Argus, September 20, 1872

34. Advertisement for Catlin & McFarland, Attorneys at Law, 1872.

Amos and his law partner, T. B. McFarland, would dissolve their practice. Amos would retain the office at Second and K streets, while McFarland relocated to the corner of Fifth and K.[3] For all the change and turmoil in Amos' private life, his family still found time to take vacations down in the Bay Area. Amos could have relocated to San Francisco and maintained his successful law practice and involvement with politics. But Sacramento was his home, and he was very much a part of the community.

In early September of 1874, Mr. Ficken, an employee of the Central Pacific Railroad, came to Amos' law office seeking advice and guidance. Ficken admitted to pilfering some tools and a small piece of mahogany wood from the Central Pacific roundhouse, where he worked in maintenance. A cloud of depression and anxiety had settled over Ficken, and he sought Amos' help in rectifying the situation. Amos met with the General Master Mechanic for the Central Pacific, Mr. Stevens, and explained the situation. Stevens agreed to ignore the whole situation if Ficken returned the pilfered items.[4]

Several weeks later, Ficken committed suicide in his room at the St. George building. An examination of his estate revealed he did not need to steal anything, as he had $5,000 in savings in various banks.[5] Amos had not known about Ficken's wealth, but it hadn't mattered: It was Amos' nature to help a person to

Amos P. Catlin

the extent that he was able to. One of the reasons Amos was so well respected in Sacramento was because he was a humble man. He had been of limited means while he was mining in 1849, and he found the means to help other miners.

Sacramento Union Libel Case

Amos had eschewed the big political parties because, as he saw it, they had abandoned the regular working man in favor of large corporations and railroad interests. His interest in organizing the Independent Taxpayers Party was motivated by the improper influence of the Central Pacific Railroad in a Republican Party primary for Sacramento City Board of Trustee election. In March 1873, Horace Adams and James McCleery were vying for the Republican nomination for City Trustee. McCleery was declared to have been nominated by the election board. The Republican Party Central Committee commenced a recount and found that Adams had the majority of the votes.[6]

Edward Robinson, an attorney for the Central Pacific Railroad and member of the Sacramento County Republican Central Committee, took offense to the Sacramento Daily Union's characterization of the recount effort as "A Naked Fraud" and "A Farce and a Failure." Robinson, who was in charge of the initial and recount efforts, sued the Sacramento Daily Union for libel and requested $10,000 in damages to his reputation. Amos and Henry Edgerton represented James Anthony & Co., publishers of the Union, in the court action.[7] As Amos knew, and as came out later in testimony, McFarland, Amos' former law partner, had drafted Robinson's original libel complaint against the Union.

The trial got underway in November 1874. Several of the Republican Central Committee members testified as to the process and procedure for the recount, including Albert Gallatin, who worked for Huntington and Hopkins Hardware. Proprietors Huntington and Hopkins were directors on the Central Pacific Railroad Board. Robinson testified that Leland Stanford and Mark Hopkins, both of the Central Pacific RR, spoke to the Central Pacific employees, encouraging them to vote for Adams over McCleery.[8]

Through cross-examinations by Amos and Edgerton, it was made clear that the Republican Central Committee wanted Adams over McCleery as a city trustee. City trustees who favored the railroad would make it easier for the Central Pacific Railroad to get approval for a whole host of business interests that required Sacramento City Board of Trustees approval. It also became apparent in testimony that the process of securing the ballot boxes and the counting process itself were flawed and sloppy. The verdict of the jury was that the Union had not libeled Robinson.[9]

Amos P. Catlin

Amos and James Anthony, publisher of the Sacramento Union, were close friends. Anthony and his newspaper routinely supported and endorsed Amos' political endeavors. It came as no surprise that, when news broke that Anthony was interested in selling the Sacramento Daily Union, Amos was involved in the negotiations. Speculation centered on Amos attempting to gain control of the Union.[10] Amos denied the rumors.[11]

The smaller Sacramento Record eventually purchased the Union, and it became the Sacramento Record-Union in 1875.[12] Amos and other men organized a banquet honoring the former owners of the Union, Anthony, Paul Morrill, H.W. Larkin, and Samuel Seabough, at the Golden Eagle Hotel.[13] In addition to a change in his close relationship with the Union, Amos was experiencing other shifts in his personal and professional life in 1875.

Thomas McFarland, Amos' former law partner, left their association in 1874 and set up an office down the street. McFarland became a register with the U.S. Land Office and stepped back from case work involving the Supreme Court. The California Supreme Court also shifted its operations. The Court would split its time hearing oral arguments between Sacramento and San Francisco, two months in each location. These changes would reduce Amos' appellant case work before the Supreme Court.

Independent Party Governor Race

Ruth Anne and Amos celebrated the birth of their son Harry on April 11, 1875. While Amos may have been a loving father to his growing family at home, his political reform crusade was being infused with more pugilistic rhetoric. In a call for a meeting of the Independent Taxpayer's Party, the notice read, "To all friends of the cause we say, be not dismayed or deceived by any movement of the enemy, but put on your armor and prepare for another battle and another victory. A. P. CATLIN, Chairman."[14] Of course, the reference to armor echoed St. Paul's letter to the Ephesians, urging them to put on their full armor of God to fight for Christ.

Some people did equate the political reform movement to fighting against the evil forces of Satan, as incarnate in entrenched political parties and corporations. Amos never branded his political adversaries as evil or satanic, even if they may have exhibited some of those traits from time to time. As de facto leader or figurehead of the independent reform movement, Amos' name began to be floated as a potential candidate for Governor.[15] The office of Governor was not within Amos' political ambitions. What he wanted was to be elected as a judge in the Sixth District Court. Unfortunately, his co-conspirator in organizing the independent reform movement was John McKune, who had held the judgeship previously and desperately wanted it back.

Amos P. Catlin

The Sacramento Bee opined that, of all the potential Dolly Varden gubernatorial candidates, Amos was the most able and honest man of the lot. The Bee even prophesied that if Amos did not accept a gubernatorial nomination, and instead ran for District Judge, he would lose both, as McKune was more popular locally and would take the judgeship. McKune was the politician that Amos was not, skilled in retail politics. The Bee noted, "[McKune]…knows all the people, hunts upon their farms, talks alfalfa, leaves the ducks and snipes, brought down by his skill, for the family board, and socially keeps old friends while he is making new ones."[16]

Based on the strength of People's Independent Party contenders in the last election, the Republican Party offered to fuse with the Independents, much as the Democrats had previously. But Amos and the other Independents could not come to any agreement and continued to forge their own path in May of 1875.[17] Newton Booth had ascended to become California's U.S. Senator, so he was out as the nominee for Governor. James Anthony had many supporters urging him to run, and John Bidwell also had strong support within the Independent community.[18]

At the Sacramento County People's Independent Party Convention, organized by Amos, Creed Haymond, a Democrat, opened the meeting by throwing his support to the Independents.[19] Amos' name continued to swirl around as a potential gubernatorial nominee, but his earlier work at the State Board of Equalization had handicapped his popularity. At the People's Independent State Convention in June, James Anthony refused to be nominated for Governor and urged friends to support Amos.[20]

Amos was eventually nominated at the convention, and the governor's race became a three-way run between him, Bidwell, and Estee of San Francisco. The speeches by Bidwell and Amos did not spark any passion for either candidate. Bidwell focused on his passion for the Temperance Movement to stomp out alcohol abuse and spoke of how he had removed all of his own wine grapes, replacing the varietals for raisins. He was convinced that most of society's debauchery, crime, and poverty was a result of intemperance.[21]

Amos gave an equally uninspiring speech. He focused on the important, yet obscure, taxation of debts secured by a mortgage and how the State Board of Equalization rules regarding those assessments had been found unconstitutional by the Supreme Court. His address was a lecture more than a political speech to rally and inspire the men in the room.[22] In the first two rounds of balloting, Amos trailed Bidwell. On the third ballot, Estee from San Francisco dropped out of the race. San Francisco delegates, with a less than favorable view of Amos due to his attempts to raise their taxes through the State Board of Equalization, moved into the Bidwell column to put him over the top.[23]

Amos P. Catlin

District Court Judge

The divisions and acrimony that forced Amos to leave the Republican Party had followed him to the People's Independent Party. The State Convention that nominated Bidwell for Governor had been less than harmonious, with lots of back-room deals attempting to secure convention delegates for one of the nominees. At the Sacramento Independent Party Judicial Convention, a meeting that was expected to eagerly nominate Amos for the position of Judge of the Sixth District Court, the Yolo County delegates decided not to show up. The disruption caused by the absent Yolo delegation was widely attributed to the efforts of "chronic candidate for the office" John McKune.[24]

In addition to fairness and impartiality, Amos believed that when men embraced a higher purpose than their own self-interests, they could work collectively for the good of society. This collective harmony and unity of purpose prevailed during the 1873 Independent Party organizing efforts on behalf of a few offices up for election. In 1875, when all of the state executive offices and many judicial seats were up for election, politically ambitious men put their interests above that of the party.

The Independent Judicial Convention did stumble through the nomination process after many protests and delays. They nominated Amos for the Sixth District Court Judgeship by acclamation.[25] Meanwhile, Bidwell was foundering in his campaign for Governor. The People's Independent Party was strongly against any monopolies, especially over public resources. Bidwell stammered over questions about his own alleged monopolistic practices on Butte Creek above his rancho. The acquisition of his huge ranch in Chico was also called into question.[26] Then there was the issue of the pledge Bidwell had made to the Orphans' Home at Vallejo, on which it seems he never really followed through with the promised monetary donations.[27]

The Republican Party nominated Samuel Denson for the Sixth District Court Judgeship. The incumbent and Democrat, Judge Ramage, was running for reelection. Amos was the third candidate. Judge Ramage was popular in the district, which comprised Yolo and Sacramento counties. There was a high probability voters would split between Denson and Amos, reelecting Judge Ramage who was not in good health, creating mounting pressure for either Denson or Amos to withdraw, in order to secure a victory over the Democrat Ramage.

Efforts to cull one of the candidates from the field began with an offer from Denson to Amos for arbitration. The proposal was to have each man select 12 supporters, then have the 24 men together decide who should drop out of the race.[28] The parlor room deal-making was facilitated by John Rider for Denson and Benjamin Bugbey for Amos. When the deal was brokered, and the 24 men assembled, neither side would capitulate.[29] Amos stayed in the race, but, to the surprise of many, Denson won.[30]

The speculation by the Sacramento Bee that Amos would lose the judgeship if he refused the gubernatorial nomination was partly correct. He did lose the one elected position he most wanted. The odds of him prevailing as candidate for Governor were very slim. The assessments of Amos were that he was honest, intelligent, and organized, but he did not have the charisma to get elected. In something of a political salve, but a duty requiring humility and graciousness, Amos was requested to attend the installation of Judge Denson to the bench. He first escorted Judge Ramage from the bench, then led Judge Denson to his new seat. Amos introduced Judge Denson and said he was satisfied with the choice of the people and that he knew Denson would discharge his duties with ability and dignity.[31]

Eulogist

On June 24, 1875, Edwin B. Crocker died. As an attorney, Crocker had worked with Amos on several cases and had served on the California Supreme Court in the early 1860s. Upon the news of Crocker's death in Sacramento, Amos and several other members of the Sacramento Bar were appointed to write a memorial for Judge Edwin B. Crocker. Over the next 20 years, Amos would routinely be asked to write memorials for fellow attorneys and judges who had died. This was partly because Amos was a gifted writer and also because he had known most of the men from the inception of California. He first met Edwin Crocker in 1853 as an opposing attorney in court. He respected Crocker's character and admired the prodigious opinions he wrote as a Supreme Court Justice.[32]

Amos Finds His Voice

With Bidwell's loss for Governor and Amos' loss for District Court Judge during the 1875 election cycle, the state and local independent reform movements lost their steam. Freedom from politics also seemed to liberate Amos' voice. Without the constraints of managing a political party, attempting to be diplomatic and consensus building, Amos became a little more sarcastic and argumentative in his public comments. In short, he became more entertaining, and the demand for his appearance at political events increased.

In January 1875, the State Board of Education awarded a textbook order to A. L. Bancroft & Co. over an East Coast publisher, McGuffey. John Dreman of Sacramento sought to stop the award and found a Tehama County Judge to issue a restraining order against the State Board of Education. Attorneys for Dreman were H.H. Haight and Creed Haymond.[33] Earlier, Amos had been asked to consult with the State Board of Education on some of the issues in awarding the bid because of recently passed legislation.

The day after the injunction was issued, Amos addressed the State Board of Education stating, "I would disregard such a proceeding on the part of this County Judge – pay no more attention to it than I would if any hoodlum on the street were to notify me, as I was proceeding to my duties..."[34] Amos then educated the Board about the powers of a county judge, which did not include restraining orders, "...I would be willing to enter into a contest with any County Judge upon the question of contempt for disobeying such an order."[35]

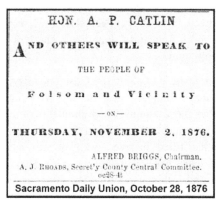

35. *Amos Catlin featured speaker at Folsom political forum, 1876.*

Seemingly, Amos had transferred his fighting spirit for government reform into verbal confrontations with legal counterparts. At a subsequent State Board of Education meeting to review another injunction, this time from a District Court Judge in Placer County, attorney for the petitioner Creed Haymond demanded to address the Board. Amos strongly objected, on the basis that the meeting was not a court of law and Haymond had no standing. Fierce words erupted between Haymond and Amos at this point, but Amos would not back down.[36]

Amos's next confrontation came with California Governor Irwin. Amos was part of a group petitioning the Board of State Prison Directors to finish the uncompleted Folsom Prison. Before Amos could finish his statements to the Board, Governor Irwin interrupted him and informed the attendees that the Board had no power to do anything, and it was useless to discuss it. Amos asked Gov. Irwin how he had arrived at such a conclusion. The Governor replied that the Constitution prohibited contracting a debt to run longer than two years.[37]

Of course, it was a mistake to argue the law or California's constitution with Amos. In reply to the Governor, Amos recited the history of the appropriation for the construction of Folsom Prison and described the nature of the special fund the Legislature established to avoid the two-year debt clause. Amos then offered a hypothetical situation mirroring the current Folsom Prison construction and rhetorically asked what the Governor would do. Gov. Irwin replied that he would

Amos P. Catlin

stop the work immediately until the Legislature passed a new law. Amos' only reply was, "How absurd." Then with a wry and sardonic smile, Amos grasped his hat and bid the meeting farewell.[38]

River Hydraulic Mining

In August of 1872, there was so little water in the Sacramento River that the riverboats were having problems navigating the shallow waters. The steamer Yosemite had left Sacramento at 11 o'clock in the morning for San Francisco and was soon grounded on Heacock Shoals above Freeport.[39] Water flow into the Sacramento from rivers such as the American, Yuba, and Feather was always a trickle in the summer, yet the Sacramento River in front of Sacramento, even with very little water flow, had traditionally been 15 to 20 feet deep. The 1872 water depth issues, which had been occurring more frequently since 1862, had less to do with water and more with sand, silt, and mud.

In March 1875, George Atkinson, who owned land along the Cosumnes River, sued the Amador and Sacramento Canal Company because the river kept overflowing onto his land. It wasn't that the Cosumnes had suddenly started carrying more water; it was the fact that mud, sand, and silt from the canal company's hydraulic mining operations had filled the river. Atkinson was suing for $15,000 in damages for the water and debris washed onto his property. He was represented by Amos, Henry Edgerton, and Tubbs and Cole. The Amador and Sacramento Canal Company hired Creed Haymond and four other attorneys to defend itself against the lawsuit.[40]

The *Atkinson vs. Amador and Sacramento Canal Co.* lawsuit was just one of the many court actions characterized as "farmers versus miners." The practice of hydraulic mining, enabled by the construction of large water canals to deliver to gold mining regions, was depositing millions of cubic yards of debris into creeks and rivers. Where the rivers reached the Central Valley, the debris would overflow the riverbanks and be deposited onto farm and ranchland, causing significant damage to crops and pastureland. Of course, Amos was intimately familiar with the operation of the water canals from his days operating the Natoma and North Fork Ditch canals. In this action, he was representing the farmer against the hydraulic mining industry.

As an indication of how quickly the demographics in California were changing in 1877, when the Atkinson debris trial commenced, the Sacramento Daily Record characterized most of the men involved in the case as "old timers."[41] From the judge, attorneys, landowners and miners, to the jurors, most of the men had arrived in California in the early 1850s. Several of the men, like Amos, had immigrated to California in 1849.

Amos P. Catlin

At the trial, George Atkinson testified that his farmland had been covered in up to 5 feet of mining debris in some places along Arkansas Creek in Sacramento County. This forced him to put in new fencing, as the mining debris covered the original fence, and to cease farming on many acres spoiled by the sand and slickens.[42] Each side brought in numerous witnesses to testify to the condition of the land before hydraulic mining and to counter testimony that the mining debris was harmful to farming. The jury took a break from courtroom testimony and traveled out to Atkinson's farm in southeast Sacramento County to inspect the debris field.[43]

After nine days at trial, the jury heard closing arguments from Amos for Atkinson and from Creed Haymond for the Amador and Sacramento Canal Co. The essence of the defense, which would be echoed in other debris trials, was that mining pre-dated farming. Hydraulic mining, the defendants argued, was a natural extension of the first methods of panning for gold. It had always been customary for miners to discharge their tailings and debris into flowing streams. Finally, the argument went, if a mining company were prevented from using hydraulic means for mining purposes, its claims would have no value.[44]

The debris cases posed an existential question about California: Which industry was more important to the state - farming or mining? California burst forth as a state mostly because of gold mining. Mines sprouted up along rivers and in the mountains in 1849 without any regard for land ownership. But as California matured, gold mining decreased, and agricultural pursuits and property ownership increased. The debris trials that pitted farmer against miner were a struggle over the identity and the future of California's Central Valley.

On January 25, 1877, the jury reached its verdict, awarding Atkinson $4,000 in damages.[45] The award reflected the recognition that discreet portions of his property no longer held value as farmland as a result of the mining debris. Atkinson's complaint never asked for the cessation of mining or the discharge of mining debris that migrated to his property. He only asked for damages for property lost to the debris. All of the adverse decisions against the hydraulic mining companies were appealed in court. California would not get a definitive answer to the propriety of hydraulic mining until the 1880s. Before that decision was handed down, Amos would be involved in an even larger debris trial.

Republican Party Politics

With the demise of the reform political movement, Amos returned to the Republican Party. The Republican Party could no more ostracize Amos than he could stay away from it. He had the ear of too many important politicians to be dismissed. When U.S. Senator Newton Booth arrived in Rocklin by train, who was there to greet him? Amos.[46] When Senator Booth was introduced at a meeting of Republicans, who gave the introduction? Amos.[47] At the 1877 Republican County Convention, Amos found himself in a role in which he was most comfortable when it came to politics, drafting the party platform and resolutions. The final products bore striking similarities to his defunct Independent Taxpayer's Party resolutions: reduce government salaries, reform civil service, repeal taxation of growing crops, negotiate with China to reduce immigration.[48]

After the county convention, Senator Booth and Amos went on an extended speaking tour, stumping for Republican candidates and policies.[49] Even though Amos had found greater license to be more entertaining, sarcastic, and argumentative, his base oratory foundation was professorial in tone. Amos was not content to make a political statement to incite the crowd; he insisted on laying out the factual and historical precedents for his beliefs, just as if he were trying a court case.

Although Amos did not express personal or racial enmity toward the Chinese who had migrated to California during the Gold Rush and who became crucial labor for railroad construction, he was not above capitalizing on anti-Chinese sentiment. In 1877, with the country gripped by recession, deploying anti-Chinese rhetoric was an easy political strategy to cultivate voting men suffering from unemployment or underemployment. Amos obliged the bigotry in a long speech in Sacramento, where he declared, "... the Chinese question, as it is undoubtedly one of the deepest interests to us...has become one of the greatest evils under which the people of this country has suffered, especially the people of the Pacific coast."[50]

While Amos never said the Chinese themselves were evil, he characterized their immigration to the U.S. as a "great evil." The only criticism of the Chinese he expressed was in regard to their propensity to work for lower wages than white men. At the time, there were calls to boycott merchants who employed Chinese labor. Amos never demonized the men who employed Chinese workers, instead stating, "I hold it to be the bounden duty of every man... in this crisis and in view of this great evil, to employ white labor and not to employ Chinamen."[51] The bulk of Amos' lecture traced the failure of treaties with China that were negotiated under Democratic administrations. The Burlingame Treaty of 1868, while nothing special, did not provide the Chinese immigrant with a pathway to naturalization.[52]

With the end of the political season, Amos was consumed with his law practice. He defended the former state Surveyor General against accusations that he pocketed fees on the sale of state lands.[53] He served on a murder defense team[54] and continued representing a few clients in appeals before the Supreme Court in 1877.[55] Senator Booth and Representative Pacheco had begun promoting Amos to be the next Superintendent of the U.S. Mint in San Francisco, a position he did not seek.[56]

The life of the Amos Catlin family would be horribly unsettled with the untimely death of Ruth, mother to Amos' four children.[57] Ruth died on February 17, 1878, while giving birth to another child. She was only 38 years old. Amos now had to reorder his life to care for his children. Politics would take a back seat while he and his family grieved.

---

[1] Sacramento Daily Union, Volume 46, Number 7137, 18 February 1874
[2] Sacramento Bee, March 21, 1874
[3] Sacramento Daily Union, Volume 47, Number 7202, 5 May 1874
[4] Sacramento Daily Union, Volume 47, Number 7314, 12 September 1874
[5] Sacramento Daily Union, Volume 47, Number 7314, 12 September 1874
[6] Sacramento Bee, November 2, 1874
[7] Sacramento Daily Union, Volume 48, Number 7358, 3 November 1874
[8] Sacramento Daily Union, Volume 48, Number 7358, 3 November 1874
[9] Sacramento Daily Union, Volume 48, Number 7361, 6 November 1874
[10] San Jose Mercury-news, Volume VI, Number 71, 3 December 1874
[11] Daily Alta California, Volume 26, Number 9016, 8 December 1874
[12] Sacramento Daily Union, Volume 1, Number 1, 22 February 1875
[13] Sacramento Daily Union, Volume 1, Number 69, 13 May 1875
[14] Sacramento Daily Union, Volume 1, Number 72, 17 May 1875
[15] Sacramento Bee, May 18, 1875
[16] Sacramento Bee, May 18, 1875
[17] Morning Union, Volume 16, Number 2614, 28 May 1875
[18] Morning Union, Volume 16, Number 2614, 28 May 1875
[19] Sacramento Daily Union, Volume 1, Number 98, 16 June 1875
[20] San Francisco Chronicle, June 22, 1875
[21] Sacramento Daily Union, Volume 1, Number 105, 24 June 1875
[22] Sacramento Daily Union, Volume 1, Number 105, 24 June 1875
[23] Sacramento Daily Union, Volume 1, Number 105, 24 June 1875
[24] Sacramento Daily Union, Volume 1, Number 129, 23 July 1875
[25] Sacramento Daily Union, Volume 1, Number 129, 23 July 1875
[26] Daily Alta California, Volume 27, Number 9280, 31 August 1875
[27] Mariposa Gazette, Volume 21, Number 5, 24 July 1875
[28] Sacramento Bee, October 11, 1875
[29] Sacramento, October 18th, 1875
[30] Sacramento Daily Union, Volume 1, Number 215, 23 October 1875
[31] Sacramento Daily Union, Volume 1, Number 276, 4 January 1876
[32] Sacramento Daily Union, Volume 1, Number 108, 28 June 1875
[33] Sacramento Daily Union, Volume 1, Number 249, 3 December 1875
[34] Sacramento Daily Union, Volume 1, Number 250, 4 December 1875
[35] Sacramento Daily Union, Volume 1, Number 250, 4 December 1875
[36] Sacramento Daily Union, Volume 1, Number 251, 6 December 1875
[37] Sacramento Bee, August 9, 1876
[38] Sacramento Bee, August 9, 1876
[39] Daily Alta California, Volume 24, Number 8176, 15 August 1872
[40] Sacramento Bee, January 3, 1877
[41] Sacramento Daily Union, Volume 2, Number 286, 24 January 1877

Amos P. Catlin

[42] Sacramento Daily Union, Volume 2, Number 272, 6 January 1877
[43] Sacramento Daily Union, Volume 2, Number 278, 13 January 1877
[44] Sacramento Daily Union, Volume 2, Number 286, 24 January 1877
[45] Sacramento Daily Union, Volume 2, Number 288, 26 January 1877
[46] Sacramento Daily Union, Volume 2, Number 202, 16 October 1876
[47] Sacramento Daily Union, Volume 2, Number 214, 30 October 1876
[48] Sacramento Daily Union, Volume 3, Number 129, 27 July 1877
[49] Sacramento Daily Union, Volume 3, Number 154, 25 August 1877
[50] Sacramento Daily Union, Volume 3, Number 155, 27 August 1877
[51] Sacramento Daily Union, Volume 3, Number 155, 27 August 1877
[52] Sacramento Daily Union, Volume 3, Number 155, 27 August 1877
[53] Sacramento Daily Union, Volume 3, Number 219, 30 October 1877
[54] Sacramento Daily Union, Volume 3, Number 225, 6 November 1877
[55] Sacramento Daily Union, Volume 3, Number 261, 18 December 1877
[56] Sacramento Daily Union, Volume 3, Number 235, 17 November 1877
[57] Sacramento Daily Union, Volume 3, Number 308, 18 February 1878

Amos P. Catlin

Chapter Eleven: Associate Justice & Criminal Defense, 1879 - 1881

Ruth Anne's funeral was held at Grace Episcopal Church at I and Eighth streets in Sacramento. A large number of people were in attendance to mourn with Amos and his children. Ruth Anne was temporarily laid to rest at the New Helvetia Cemetery in February, until the winter water had receded from the City Cemetery, where she would be reinterred.[1]

Just as Amos' family had undergone radical change with the loss of Ruth Anne, California was also experiencing demonstrable changes. The original state constitution of 1849 just was not efficient at addressing the myriad of issues coming before the legislature and courts. Creed Haymond's work to consolidate the statutes into code sections helped run government run more smoothly, but more was needed. California needed a new constitution.

Constitutional Convention

A constitutional convention was in order and, with it, delegates who could fashion a governing document for 1878 and beyond. The first two names listed as potential candidates to a constitutional convention were that of Amos and T. B. McFarland.[2] Almost as his name was being spoken as a delegate, Amos let it be known that he did not have the time for such an undertaking.[3]

The drafting of a constitution from scratch was what Amos was made for. He loved the law, and he was disgusted at how politics and big corporations were able to manipulate government to their own benefit. Amos had argued before the U.S. Supreme Court and frequently represented cases before the California Supreme Court. He was preparing for an epic courtroom battle, but most of his reluctance to be nominated as a delegate to a constitutional convention probably came from the death of his wife. A new household dynamic was needed both to take care of his young children and also allow him space to continue his law practice.

Regardless of Amos' strong disinterest in being a delegate to the constitutional convention, his name was offered up for nomination in Sacramento. Some of those nominating him hoped that a decisive nominee election would convince Amos to allow his name to be placed on the ballot. When word reached Amos that he had been selected as a nominee, he left his home and traveled the short distance to Turner Hall, where the citizens' convention was meeting. There, he addressed the assembled men, saying he deeply regretted that he must decline the

Amos P. Catlin

nomination. As he was scheduled to be out of the state, it would be folly to accept a seat that he could not fill. Thomas McFarland, Amos' former law partner, was then nominated in Amos' place.[4]

Water Works Accounting Experience

Because of his experience managing a water canal company and his background with the State Board of Equalization, Amos's legal services were frequently sought for cases involving complex financial accounting issues. The Sacramento City Board of Trustees bypassed its own legal staff and retained Amos in a review of the former clerk of the city water works division.[5] Amos was to review the books of the clerk for apparent embezzlement of funds.[6]

George Royster was the City of Sacramento's clerk for collecting fees for water delivered to residents and businesses. For some reason, the forecast for the receipts of the muddy water being distributed to city residents was not matching with the actual amounts deposited. However, Royster had a receipt book that showed the sum of moneys collected that equaled the total of money turned over to the Treasurer. If Royster was not criminally liable for embezzlement, perhaps the City of Sacramento could go after sureties of Royster's bond to recover the missing water receipts.

Upon review of the water sales cash receipt books and the accounting ledgers of the Treasurer, Amos conceded that the cash collected by ex-Clerk Royster matched money deposited with the city. However, something was amiss, he reported to the City Trustees:

"The cash book appears to me to be conclusive evidence that all the money collected which is not entered therein was retained by the Collector and not paid over. It is said that the Collector attempts to explain by saying that the moneys collected, which do not appear to be entered in the cash book are actually entered therein to the credit of fictitious names, and to names of persons who did not actually take or pay for water. In regard to this explanation it may first be confidently said upon the authority of the cash book itself and of the individuals from whom the moneys were collected, that it is impossible for it to be true; and, next it may be asserted with equal confidence, that the attempt to conceal one fraud by the perpetration of another equally flagitious, though a good deal more stupid, aside from its incredibility, would not be accepted in a Court of justice, where reason is supposed to be regarded with some degree of favor."[7]

Amos, himself, was a subscriber of city water. He was as irked as the next Sacramento resident that George Royster, somehow, perhaps with others in the city, had found a way to skim money from the water collections. Based on Amos' analysis, the City Trustees contracted with Amos to bring a civil action against

Amos P. Catlin

Royster.[8] Unfortunately, the accounting deception, so obvious to Amos, was not so for a jury. Neither Royster nor his sureties, it was determined, were liable for any moneys thought not to have been deposited with the City Treasurer.[9]

Cannon History

Amos understood the historic nature of his life, and those of other pioneers, in California. In his own way, when he could, he sought to preserve history. At a meeting of the Sacramento Pioneer Association, he gave the history of the cannon that stood on the south side of the doorway at Pioneer Hall. The cannon came to California via the Russians and was placed at Fort Ross. It was subsequently acquired by John Sutter for his fort in New Helvetia. In 1851, Dalles A. Kneass, hotel keeper and merchant, purchased the cannon and moved it to Mormon Island to be used in 4th of July celebrations. Amos bought the cannon and then sold it to John Nye of Mormon Island for safekeeping. John Nye bequeathed it to the Pioneer Association upon his death. It was then moved from Mormon Island to Sacramento for display.[10]

Enlisted for another act of preservation, Amos, along with John McKune and George Cadwalader was appointed to write resolutions of memorial upon the death of John Sutter.[11] In reflecting upon Sutter's death, the fellow pioneers also took notice of "…their ever-thinning ranks." They noted how, as of 1880, Sutter's Fort had not altogether succumbed to entropy and crumbled away into dust. It would be refurbished in the future. The trio of men called for a marble statue of John Sutter to be sculpted and then placed in the rotunda of the State Capitol.[12]

Supreme Court Justice Nomination

With the ratification of a new state constitution in March of 1879, the California Supreme Court was expanded to accommodate more justices. That meant there would be open seats on the Court. Once again, Amos' name drifted to the top of contenders for a judgeship.[13] Another strong contender for the Republican Party nominee for Associate Justice was Creed Haymond.[14] At the convention, Thomas McFarland nominated Amos.[15] Haymond was also nominated but deferred to Amos, whom he thought had a better claim to the seat, and, and believing that he, as a younger man, would have future opportunities to serve.[16]

Amos received the most votes at the State Republican Judicial Convention, and the top six nominees were forwarded to the slate of candidates for Associate Justice.[17] Many newspapers gave Amos an endorsement with only a scant biography. As the San Jose Mercury News described Amos, "A.P. Catlin, candidate for Associate Justice of the Supreme Court, is a New Yorker by birth, but came to this State many years ago. His present residence is at Sacramento, where his eminent legal ability has secured him a very lucrative practice."[18] Some newspapers tied Amos to Newton Booth and Bidwell: "He was formerly an Independent Republican, having been the Booth candidate for Governor in 1875, and being beaten in Convention by Bidwell."[19] The Santa Cruz Weekly Sentinel characterized Amos as, "...calm, judicial, given to study and reflection, retiring and modest."[20]

Republican State Ticket.

For Governor—
GEO. C. PERKINS, of San Francisco.

For Lieut-Governor—
JOHN MANSFIELD, of Los Angeles.

For Secretary of State—
D. M. BURNS, of Yolo.

For State Controller—
DAN M. KENFIELD, of Tuolumne.

For State Treasurer—
JOHN WEIL, of Sierra.

For Attorney General—
A. L. HART, of Colusa.

For Surveyor General—
J. W. SHANKLIN, of Alameda.

For Clerk of Supreme Court—
FRANK W. GROSS, of San Francisco.

For Supt. of Public Instruction—
F. M. CAMPBELL, of Alameda.

For Justice of Supreme Court—
A. L. RHODES, of Santa Clara.

For Associate Justices of the Supreme Court—
A. P. CATLIN, of Sacramento.
I. S. BELCHER, of Yuba.
JARRET T. RICHARDS, of Santa Barbara
J. E. HALE, of Placer.
M. H. MYRICK, of San Francisco.
E. D. WHEELER, of San Francisco.

For Member of Congress—Third District—
JOSEPH MCKENNA, of Solano.

For Railroad Commissioner—First District—
SEPH H. CONE, of Tehama.

Napa Valley Register, July 8, 1879

36. Amos Catlin, candidate for Associate Justice of the California Supreme Court, 1879.

For history's sake, and his own reference, Amos was given to clipping newspaper articles and placing them in scrapbooks. He clipped the pen portrait of himself from the San Francisco Post. The short biography and word-sketch of Amos the man on the ballot for Supreme Court Associate Justice was probably the most accurate newspaper story Amos ever read.

A. P. Catlin Pen Portrait of an Able Lawyer.

Few men are so quietly conspicuous among their fellows as A. P. Catlin, one of the Republican nominees for Associate Justice of the Supreme Bench. Mr. Catlin is about five feet ten inches in height, stands erect, moves with quiet, nervous vigor, has light sandy hair, full beard of the same color, light gray eyes, and is a trifle over fifty years of age.

In person is slim and wiry; in habit scrupulously neat. A practiced observer would at once say that he is a close and careful student. Like other men of marked individuality, he impresses his characteristics upon all who come in contact with him with very great distinctness, and no one is ever in doubt as to what the man is.

As he is not an emotional, or at all remarkable for his personal magnetism, he impresses himself solely through his mentality. He is highly esteemed as a man for his purity of character and domestic

Amos P. Catlin

habits; but he fails to draw many men towards him by the usual hilarious methods adopted by public men.

At the same time, holds his friends firmly and continuously by the essential and constant fidelity of his nature. He is not distinguished as a jury advocate, though he is implicitly trusted by his clients as a counselor and faithful attorney. Few lawyers equal Mr. Catlin in his comprehensive view of a case and in his close attention to details. And while he lacks the fierceness of the ordinary advocate, he much more than compensates for the deficiency by his absolute thoroughness and precision.

In his mental make-up, Mr. Catlin is singularly free from prejudice and personal influences. In preparing his cases he first acts as a judge and then as an attorney. And as his mind is dominated by ideas more than personal considerations he grasps the ultimate issue of a case long before he is pushed to that point by the rulings of the court.

In short, he is wholly judicial in his mental temperament. With such a man on the Supreme bench there would be little "judge made law." The fundamental principle of our legal system as formulated in the constitution and statutory enactments would dominate his mind as mathematical principles control and command the mathematician.

Under no circumstance could he inject his own personal idiosyncrasies, if he had any, into his decisions. Neither can he be influenced by mere eloquence nor by personal considerations. Against all errors of this class he is thoroughly protected by his inflexible devotion to ideas and principles, and by his controlling mental habits. These natural attitudes of Mr. Catlin have enabled him to acquire a thorough mastery of law as a science, and he now stands an acknowledged peer among those who lead the legal profession of California.

An extensive practice has familiarized him with the entire judicial history of the past, and there is no detail of legislative enactment that has escaped his attention. Besides he has grown up with the State and is thoroughly acquainted with all the various interests of California. As a matter of course, to one possessed of Mr. Catlin's temperament and industry, he is of necessity thoroughly furnished for the work of a Supreme Judge.

To those who know him best, the very fitness of things seems to require the elevation of A. P. Catlin to the Supreme Bench. And just at this time the services of such men are imperatively demanded. We shall hail the election of A. P. Catlin as an omen of good for the future of California. – S. F. Post[21]

Curiously, Amos did not campaign for the Supreme Court Associate Justice seat to which he had been nominated. He let Haymond, McFarland, and other men

Amos P. Catlin

lead the speaking tours touting his experience, wisdom, and judicial philosophy.[22] Amos did not even run any newspaper advertisements. It was as if he wasn't in the race. His embarrassment about asking for votes coupled with a perspective that judges should be elected on merit, not campaign promises, figured into his low-profile candidacy. The reflective, retiring, and modest Amos Catlin lost his bid to be elected to the Supreme Court.[23]

Lost, but not forgotten, Amos was requested to form a committee of attorneys, Haymond, Armstrong, McKune, and Jones, to prepare and submit rules for the new Sacramento Superior Court.[24] The new constitution threw out the District Court model, where several counties could be combined to create one court jurisdiction, in favor of each county establishing its own Superior Court. Amos would get to take the new Superior Court rules for a test drive as the defense attorney in a murder case.

Lamblet Murder

"Muertre, muertre," he shouted as he stumbled down the Folsom street with blood dripping from his wounds, mixing with his sweat and dust from the road. When Francois Lamblet became excited, he always reverted to his native French language. Now he had something to be really excited over: his wife Rosalie had been stabbed, and he had also been sliced on his side. On the hot August night in the town of Folsom, 1879, Francois was running to get help for his wife while shouting "murder, murder" to awaken the sleepy little town at one o'clock in the morning.[25]

As Francois approached the foot bridge at Riley and Figueroa streets, wearing only his night shirt, streaked with blood and sweat, his grandson, who had been staying with him and Rosalie, caught up to him. Frank Mette was 12 years old, asleep, when he heard someone jumping through the window of the room his grandparents shared. Then he heard his grandfather yelling "murder" as he ran away from the house.[26]

As Frank crept towards his grandparent's bedroom he could hear his grandmother call to her little poodle dog, "Here Ruby….sick 'em." Sheepishly, Frank asked, "What is the matter, grandma?" In a weakened voice Rosalie replied, "I am dying, jump out of the window and save yourself." Rosalie, bleeding heavily, lost consciousness and fell against the wall by the window. Without asking any further questions, Frank ran to the little room by the kitchen where he had been sleeping and jumped out the window.[27]

The young boy, having no sense of what was happening, could hear his grandfather yelling as he headed toward town. Frank caught up to his grandfather at the footbridge and proceeded to follow him onto Sutter Street. Francois' shouts

Amos P. Catlin

of murder attracted a small gathering of men in front of the water trough at the Central Hotel. Alexander Milroy joined Mr. Brophy and Charles Sheehan in an excited conversation with Francois Lamblet.[28]

In the chaos and confusion of the moment, Frank did not hear or understand the conversation, beyond hearing the gentlemen asking Francois about the violent knife attack. The young boy saw Francois lift his night shirt to reveal a wound and point to the scratches on his leg. Frank was instructed to head down to the fruit drying warehouse where Mr. Brophy worked and wait there. Francois implored the men to accompanying him home, as his wife had been murdered.[29]

On this dark and moonless early morning in August, Milroy acquired a lantern, and the men, led by Francois, started up the hill to his house. All of the doors to the little house at the corner of Scott and Mormon streets were locked. From one of the side windows, the men could hear a woman moaning. Francois exclaimed, "She is not dead yet, I can hear her." Brophy helped boost Francois through the window, not knowing if the assailant was still present or not. Francois went to the front door, unlocked it, and let the men inside. They found Rosalie, not murdered, but dying from the knife wounds.[30]

Rosalie lay bleeding to death, a thick pool of blood surrounding her body from all of the cuts she had suffered earlier. Francois asked the men present to pick her up and place her on the lounge. Shortly thereafter, Dr. Rhodes, who had been sent for earlier, arrived to dress the wounds. But the loss of blood was too great. Rosalie Remi Lamblet died on August 16, 1879.[31]

As with most immigrants, Rosalie and Francois came to the United States in the early 1850s, seeking a better life. They brought with them their first daughter, Eugenia, who was born in 1848 in Alsace, France. The family made its way to Wisconsin, where they had a son, Camille, born in 1853, and another daughter, Marie Clara, born in 1855.

The family eventually made it to California and settled in Folsom, where Francois could ply his trade as a barber. On September 1, 1865, Francois Lamblet became a naturalized citizen of the United States. One of his sponsors was Peter J. Hopper, a local attorney and publisher of the Folsom Telegraph. Business was good for Francois Lamblet, and he earned enough money to purchase a lot in Folsom, up the hill from the business district on Sutter Street.

Lot 16, in block 51, was at the corner of Scott and Mormon streets. The Lamblets kept a cow and chickens that Rosalie would sometimes sell to the local Chinese immigrants. In 1866, the Lamblets' daughter Eugenia married Henry Mette. Mette had a vineyard and winery on the South Fork of the American River not too far from Folsom. The Mette vineyard was next to Benjamin Bugbey's Natoma

Amos P. Catlin

Vineyard, although not as famous. Both vineyards were delivered water by Amos' Natoma ditch.

Death visited the Lamblet family in February 1873, when Camille, their son, died at 19 years of age. Some people speculated that the death of Camille gave Francois an excuse to consume more alcohol, of which there was no shortage in Folsom. He was frequently seen around town drunk, in between haircuts, shaves, or heading home.

The impression of Francois Lamblet around Folsom was evenly mixed. Some people found Francois to be a nice guy, and others found him rather gruff and distasteful. Of the people who found Francois less than gentlemanly, most were women. The conflicting opinions of Francois mirrored the contradictory statements he gave on the night of the attack and in the days afterward. It did not help that the crime scene was thoroughly trampled upon by neighbors and newspaper reporters, rummaging through the house as the sun rose over Folsom to start another hot August day.

Folsom, in the oppressive heat of mid-August 1879, could be a very sleepy little town. The mining boom had long passed; the Sacramento Valley Railroad, of which Folsom was the terminus, was in decline. On the bright side, construction had just started on Folsom State Prison, which some townsfolk hoped would be Francois' next home. The Natoma Water and Mining Company had extended its network of water canals in and around Folsom. Agriculture, vine and tree fruits, were a big part of the regional economy. Hence, the fruit-drying facilities that Frank Mette retreated to after following his grandfather down to Sutter Street after the attack.

The first law enforcement officer on the scene was Deputy Sheriff Benjamin Bugbey. Francois explained that his wife was in bed when he fled; he ran to the back gate, opened it, and fled down the street. Francois conceded that the motive for the attack must not have been theft, as $25 was still in the cigar box, and both his silver and gold pocket watches were still in his bedroom.

The presence of Deputy Sheriff Benjamin Bugbey became problematic for the prosecution of the case. Bugbey was the first law enforcement officer on the scene because he only lived a couple blocks away from the Lamblets in Folsom. Bugbey had lived in Folsom since 1856 and was the Constable of Granite Township from 1856 to 1860, when he was elected Sheriff of Sacramento County. Bugbey lost the nomination for Sheriff to James McClatchy in 1863. He then spent most of his energies building his winery, producing wines, brandies, and sparkling wines from his Natoma Vineyard on the South Fork of the American River in El Dorado County.[32]

Amos P. Catlin

Bugbey's Natoma Vineyard and winery imploded financially in the early 1870s. The property was subsequently sold at auction, but he was able to retain ownership of his Folsom lots and residence with the help of his wife, Martinette. Unfortunately, the stress of losing his small winery empire, along with impending bankruptcy, drove Bugbey to heavily consume the products he used to produce. It had been only a couple of years earlier that Bugbey, in a drunken stupor, tore up his Folsom house, smashing furniture, and spawning rumors that he was physically and verbally abusive to his wife, Martinette, in 1877.[33] Amos was acquainted with Martinette and Benjamin Bugbey from living in Folsom and from politics. He had handled the probate of Martinette's father, Peter McGlashan, in 1872.[34]

Bugbey's reputation was not enhanced by the rumor that he started the Folsom fire in 1871, destroying not only his own building and the insured winery contents, but also that of the Jolly hardware store.[35] Two short years later, after attempting to shoot a constable, Bugbey was appointed as a Deputy Sheriff by his good friend, Sacramento County Sheriff Moses Drew.[36] But, because of his proximity to the Lamblet residence, Bugbey was in charge of the murder investigation. Bugbey would exacerbate the perception of his own incompetence by failing to secure the crime scene, allowing evidence to be taken away and displayed in town, and failing to prevent Francois from attempting suicide while under his watch.

At the scene, Bugbey was forced to place Francois under arrest pending a formal inquiry. But, instead of transferring him to the county jail in Sacramento, Bugbey put Francois under house arrest and under the supervision of guards. The Lamblets' daughters, Clara and Eugenia, came to visit Francois after the horrific event. As his daughters were outside preparing to leave, Francois took a razor and cut his own throat. He called out to the man who had been guarding him, saying, "Mr. Slater, I have cut my throat."[37]

It would take several weeks for Francois to recover from his wounds and settle his composure. In mid-September, an examination of the facts was initiated before Justice Sheldon of Granite Township in Folsom. Former District Attorney George Blanchard was appointed to represent Sacramento County, and Francois retained Henry Edgerton for his defense. The examination was held behind closed doors and lasted for an unprecedented three weeks. One revelation that did leak out was that Deputy Sheriff Bugbey was under suspicion of being an accessory through his actions to shield Francois Lamblet from being indicted for murder.

The speculation and rumor were so intense that Bugbey must be involved in some sort of coverup on Francois' behalf that District Attorney Blanchard was forced to release a statement to the newspapers. Blanchard first refuted the rumors that Bugbey had insulted a witness and an inaccurate report that the District Attorney had requested that Bugbey be relieved of his duties surrounding the Lamblet case. Neither, Blanchard contended, were true.

District Attorney Blanchard brought the case against Francois before the Sacramento County Grand Jury on October 6, 1879. A large number of witnesses were subpoenaed to testify before the Grand Jury in the murder accusation against Francois Lamblet. Three weeks later, on October 28th, the Grand Jury found a true bill presented by the District Attorney for an indictment of murder against Francois. Now, Francois Lamblet's fate would be in the hands of a jury of his peers.

Francois assembled an impressive team of attorneys for his defense at the murder trial scheduled for early March 1880. First was Amos; then there was Henry Edgerton, a former District Attorney from Napa County, who also served in the California Legislature. Next, William Crossett was also a Republican and had run for Assembly on the same ticket as Peter Hopper for Assembly and Moses Drew for Sacramento County Sheriff in 1875. Crossett owned numerous lots in Folsom very near the Lamblet residence.

The trial commenced on March 6th, 1880, drawing intense interest from Folsom and Sacramento residents. Testimony at the trial would provide additional details that had not made their way into public knowledge during the previous five months since the murder. Amos cross-examined William Fulcher, who found the bloody clothing, and learned that the items were taken into town and shown at Josh Smith's store. Tom Long also showed the bloody clothes to people around town. The dagger was given to Constable Kimble.

On March 12th, Catlin and Edgerton, attorneys for Francois, concluded their review of the evidence and closing arguments. George Blanchard then followed with his closing arguments for the people. Judge Clark then gave instructions to the jury, and it retired into deliberations in the afternoon. The jury returned three hours later with a verdict of "not guilty."[38] With Amos' defense strategy, Francois Lamblet escaped death or a life sentence at Folsom Prison.

In 1881, Amos would form a new law partnership with D. A. Hamburger that would last a couple of years. The law practice would span from consulting work with the city and county of Sacramento, Board of Equalization, Reclamation Districts in the Delta, ever-complicated bank and bond litigation, to representing clients before the state Supreme Court. Amos was also selected as chairman for the formation of a new Sacramento Bar Association in 1883.[39]

The City of Sacramento was still laboring under debt from bonds issued for a variety of public infrastructure improvements. The City Trustees were proposing an increase in taxes in order to cover bond payments. Bond holders were applying pressure to the city to meet bond obligations. The city turned to Amos for his counsel. After researching the topic and the laws, Amos reported that the city had three options; they could comply with the law and increase the tax levy, make a compromise with the bond holders, or enter into dangerous litigation.[40]

The problem for the city was a law that dated back to 1858 under which, for a brief period of time, the city and county were one governing body. The Board of Supervisors could levy a tax of $1 per $100 dollars of personal property value to pay for interest and bond redemption. When the unified city and county experiment was dissolved, various politicians applied different approaches for dealing with the debt.[41] Time had run out to cobble together a solution, as many of the bonds matured in 1877.[42] The only sound solution was a most distasteful tax increase, as the bond holders were not interested in negotiating down repayment.

The Republican and Democratic parties had nominated slates of candidates for mayor and trustee seats. Amos and many other men were tired of the political parties controlling the administration of the City of Sacramento. They proposed a Citizen's Ticket. Amos was not running for any seat, but he was advocating for change. As part of the Executive Committee for the Citizen's Ticket, Amos endorsed the argument that, "It has rarely occurred during an eventful history that Sacramento was ever more in need of wise, disinterested and non-partisan counsel than at the present time."[43]

At the Citizen's Convention, Amos was elected chair of the proceedings. He rebuked both the Democrats and Republicans for meddling in primary elections to usurp the will of the people for party politics. He urged his fellow compatriots to nominate intelligent and skillful men for city government, irrespective of party affiliation.[44] Amos had realized that political parties were incapable of reforming themselves. All he could do was to work with fellow like-minded men to push for a system of non-partisan local offices.

[1] Sacramento Daily Union, Volume 3, Number 310, 20 February 1878
[2] Sacramento Daily Union, Volume 7, Number 64, 4 May 1878
[3] Sacramento Bee, May 18, 1878
[4] Sacramento Daily Union, Volume 7, Number 82, 24 May 1878
[5] Sacramento Daily Union, Volume 7, Number 202, 15 October 1878
[6] Sacramento Daily Union, Volume 7, Number 202, 15 October 1878
[7] Sacramento Daily Union, Volume 7, Number 219, 5 November 1878
[8] Sacramento Daily Union, Volume 7, Number 219, 5 November 1878
[9] Sacramento Daily Union, Volume 8, Number 99, 2 July 1879
[10] Sacramento Daily Union, Volume 7, Number 313, 3 March 1879
[11] Sacramento Daily Union, Volume 11, Number 142, 2 August 1880
[12] Sacramento Daily Union, Volume 11, Number 142, 2 August 1880
[13] Sacramento Bee, June 16, 1879

Amos P. Catlin

[14] Sacramento Daily Union, Volume 8, Number 86, 17 June 1879
[15] Sacramento Daily Union, Volume 8, Number 89, 20 June 1879
[16] Sacramento Daily Union, Volume 8, Number 89, 20 June 1879
[17] Daily Alta California, Volume 31, Number 10660, 20 June 1879
[18] San Jose Mercury-news, Volume XV, Number 86, 21 June 1879
[19] Morning Press, Volume VII, Number 291, 30 June 1879
[20] Santa Cruz Weekly Sentinel, Volume 25, Number 5, 5 July 1879
[21] Amos Catlin Scrap Book. California State Library, Catlin Collection Box 500
[22] Sacramento Daily Union, Volume 8, Number 110, 16 July 1879
[23] Stockton Independent, Volume XXXVII, Number 51, 29 September 1879
[24] Sacramento Daily Union, Volume 8, Number 180, 7 October 1879
[25] Sacramento Daily Union, Volume 11, Number 14, 9 March 1880
[26] Sacramento Daily Union, Volume 11, Number 14, 9 March 1880
[27] Sacramento Daily Union, Volume 11, Number 14, 9 March 1880
[28] Sacramento Daily Union, Volume 11, Number 14, 9 March 1880
[29] Sacramento Daily Union, Volume 11, Number 14, 9 March 1880
[30] Sacramento Daily Union, Volume 11, Number 14, 9 March 1880
[31] Sacramento Daily Union, Volume 11, Number 14, 9 March 1880
[32] "Benjamin Norton Bugbey, Sacramento's Champagne King", Knauss
[33] "Benjamin Norton Bugbey, Sacramento's Champagne King", Knauss
[34] Sacramento Daily Union, Volume 43, Number 6686, 6 September 1872
[35] Letter, Nathaniel Knight to Ambrose Knight, July 2, 1871. Bancroft Library, BANC MSS 98/22 C
[36] "Benjamin Norton Bugbey, Sacramento's Champagne King", Knauss
[37] Sacramento Daily Union, Volume 8, Number 139, 20 August 1879
[38] Sacramento Daily Union, Volume 11, Number 17, 12 March 1880
[39] Sacramento Daily Union, Volume 17, Number 29, 27 March 1883
[40] Sacramento Daily Union, Volume 13, Number 1, 22 February 1881
[41] Sacramento Daily Union, Volume 13, Number 1, 22 February 1881
[42] Sacramento Daily Union, Volume 13, Number 12, 7 March 1881
[43] Sacramento Daily Union, Volume 13, Number 12, 7 March 1881
[44] Sacramento Daily Union, Volume 13, Number 12, 7 March 1881

Amos P. Catlin

Chapter Twelve: Hydraulic Debris Trial & Sacramento Sewers, 1881

Of all the perils the young City of Sacramento faced, flooding was perhaps the most pernicious challenge to mitigate. Heavy rains descended upon Northern California in the winter of 1861. The rain continued into 1862, and high flows in the American River breached a levee on Sacramento's eastern edge. Then another levee failed, and Sacramento was swamped with water for weeks.

The flooding was so persistent that Gov. Leland Stanford traveled to his inauguration in Sacrament via a rowboat. The unified city and county government split apart, as population centers outside of Sacramento balked at paying for the city's flood protection costs. The City of Sacramento embarked on a massive program to not only raise the levees, but also to raise the city by a full story of building height and redirect the flow of the American River further north of the city.

37. Chart of the Sacramento River From Suisun City to the American River, California, 1850.

There was no question that Northern California had seen a deluge of precipitation. The rainfall was unprecedented in the extremely short recorded history of the area. As the water receded from the damaging floods of 1861-1862, a clue emerged as to what potentially had exacerbated the flooding: hydraulic mining debris. Landowners who had experienced an inundation of flood waters across their properties along the American and Sacramento rivers were

Amos P. Catlin

reporting that sand, silt, and slickens had been deposited across fields. The debris covered hundreds of acres and was up to 5 feet deep in some places.

The deposits of sand and silt were also changing the course of parts of the rivers, creating new sand bars and filling sloughs. All the debris was also creating new navigation hazards in both rivers. With each new winter season of heavy rains, the rivers would become clogged with more deposits of sand and silt. Flooding events would become more common after 1862. The finger of culpability pointed directly upstream, at the industry that had given birth to the state of California, the mining industry. Specifically, the debris was the result of the emerging and growing operation of hydraulic mining for gold.

Whereas farmers had been suing the hydraulic mining operators over the damage for several years, now an urban center also was considering legal action. Several people took note of Amos' successful court action for damages in the Amador and Sacramento Canal Company mining case. Sacramento was not interested in collecting damages; the city wanted a cessation to the practice of depositing mining debris in creeks that ultimately led to the American River and settled around Sacramento. The City of Sacramento settled on targeting one hydraulic mining company, the Gold Run Ditch and Mining Company, for legal action and solicited help from State Attorney General Hart to lead the prosecution.

38. Map of City of Sacramento with American River redirected from its original channel, 1873.

After many months of pre-trial hearings, the case of *People vs. The Gold Run Ditch and Mining Company* finally commenced on November 15, 1881,[1] in a Sacramento Superior Courtroom. But Amos was not sitting next to Attorney General Hart. Amos was representing the Gold Run Ditch company in a trial that would last for three and a half months, include 58 days of testimony, and examine

Amos P. Catlin

more than 80 witnesses. This was the longest and most involved trial in which Amos had ever participated.

Amos was part of a team of attorneys defending the Gold Run Ditch Company. His fellow lawyers were Samuel Wilson, W.T. Wallace, J.K. Byrne, A.B. Dibble, and W. Belcher.[2] Each attorney was responsible for different aspects of the defense. Amos undertook a significant portion of the cross-examination of witnesses. Amos and the defense demurred over the complaint that the Gold Run Ditch company was disposing of debris into a creek that ultimately emptied into the North Fork of the American River. It was contended that all hydraulic mining companies, as a function of their operations, diverted mining spoils into waterways.

The team defending the Gold Run Ditch Company pursued several avenues of defense, such as the People's inability to trace the mining debris around Sacramento as having come from the Gold Run Ditch mine above Colfax, over 70 miles of river away from the city. While some estimates of the volume of debris directed into the North Fork of the American River were presented, the trial relied heavily on eye-witness testimony. Most of the men who testified had come to California in 1849 or 1850 and could describe how the rivers had changed in the past 30 years.

Perhaps not lost on Amos was the richly detailed oral history of what Sacramento topography was like before hydraulic mining began in earnest. One of the pioneers whom Amos cross-examined was Benjamin Bugbey.[3] Bugbey, for the prosecution, testified about mining in the American River in 1849 and 1850. He noted how, since the beginning of hydraulic mining, the composition of the river gravel had gone from gray stones to voluminous amounts of white sand and pebbles, indicative of the debris from the Gold Run Ditch company.

Amos probed Bugbey about his memory, since his mining days at Negro Bar were 30 years old. Since Bugbey was a paid expert witness, Amos took the opportunity to allude to Bugbey's financial problems, which were well known, and his current occupation as a salesman of pottery. Bugbey got in his own subtle rub at Amos, reminding everyone that it was Amos who originated the Natoma Water and Mining Company, profiting by supplying water to miners who were sluicing away whole hills into the river.

The City of Sacramento, in addition to the flooding and navigation issues brought about by the mining debris, also contended that their water and sewer systems were impeded from working properly. The sand, silt, mud, and slickens, the city said, prevented the collection and distribution of clean water; raised the water table, making septic systems inoperable for part of the year; and clogged the open sewer canal from delivering untreated effluent back to the Sacramento River

Amos P. Catlin

downstream of the city. The mining debris was jeopardizing the public health of Sacramento, sickening its citizens from the smell of sewage, horrible water, and diseases such as cholera.

Amos, the man who had organized several independent political movements to strip the reins of local government from men beholden to political parties and corporate interests, led the counter-attack against the city's claims. The problem, as Amos saw it, was not so much the mining debris, but the elected officials who had failed to properly address and invest in the public infrastructure.

PLAN OF THE SEWERAGE SYSTEM

— OF —

SACRAMENTO.

39. Map of Sacramento's limited sewer system, 1880.

W.F. Knox, Sacramento Street Commissioner from 1874 to 1880, described the open sewer canal that ran south of the city beginning at R street. A planned canal extension was to dump the effluent into Snodgrass Slough, which connected with the Mokelumne River, but the project was never finished.[4] Professor Thomas

Amos P. Catlin

Price testified about his inspection of the city's sewer system. He noted that some of the pipes were wooden, and collection boxes were of unmortised brick.

Professor Price followed the sewage canal down to Beach's Lake, south of the city, and noted that the one foot of fall per mile was inadequate to carry away waste material. When asked if the drainage system constituted a sewer system, Price replied, "It cannot be regarded in any other light than a very poor apology for one." Price also testified that many homes' cesspools were not connected to any sewer pipe. He calculated the total amount of fecal matter produced in the city to be 25 tons per 1,000 people per year and 91,000 gallons of urine per 1,000 people per year.[5]

The trial, and its outcome relative to the mining interests and City of Sacramento, was followed carefully. The closing arguments of many of the attorneys were printed in the Sacramento Daily Union. With regard to the public health of Sacramento, Amos continued to lay the blame at the feet of the city. He cited a State Board of Health review that compared Sacramento to other cities in the Central Valley.

"They have considered the subject of sewerage of this city. They have criticised its sewerage, as well they might. They have criticised its cesspool system, as well they might. They have called attention to everything they knew upon the subject, yet neither they nor anybody else ever dreamed before that mining, and the mining, especially of this defendant, was responsible for any supposed difference in the health in this city, as compared with former days."

Amos went on to describe the state of the sewer system in Sacramento.

"They complain that the sewerage of this city has been destroyed. Some of the witnesses who spoke upon that subject did not understand what our 'sewerage system,' so-called, was; but they assumed that we had a system of sewerage. I do not think it is necessary to recur to that portion of the testimony in detail.[6]

"There are only six sewers – and we will call them sewers now for the purpose of the argument – running through this city from north to south. That large portion of the city east of Thirteenth street has no sewerage at all, and a very large portion of the inhabitants of this city reside above that street. We are standing on Eleventh street now, and there is no sewer through this street. There is no other sewer until we reach Ninth street, and then there are sewers running through Seventh, Fifth, and Third, and in the alley between Front and Second streets, making six in all which run to R street. Those above Sixth street turn at a right angle on R street and run west to Sixth, and those below Sixth street turn on a like angle at R street and run east to Sixth. They unite at Sixth and R streets, and there pass into the drainage canal......[7]

Amos P. Catlin

"There are also the lateral sewers between these odd number streets which connect with this main sewer, and they are generally made of wood. Some of the main sewers are also of wood and some are of brick, but they are constructed generally with open work on the bottom and sides.[8]

"Instead of the sewers of this city being constructed as sewers are constructed in every city we have ever heard of – constructed for the purpose of confining and carrying away the foul waters to some proper receptacle – these sewers are made expressly to distribute their foul contents in the soil of the city as widely as possible. Perhaps that was a necessity, although it does not seem to me to be so, because no solid or fecal matter is discharged into these sewers, or these drains which we call sewers. The city authorities have strictly adhered to the policy, if it is a policy, of having all the matter sink into the soil upon which the city is built, to saturate it, permeate it, and fester there and breed disease. And a city having a system of sewers like that comes into Court here in the name of the People of the State and complains that we have destroyed its sewerage system. Well, such a sewerage system as that ought to be destroyed. It never ought to be allowed to exist."[9]

In his summation, Amos returned to the poor state of the Sacramento sewer issue.

"Sacramento is gradually saturating her soil with annual accumulations of fecal matter. No means for removing or arresting it have ever been devised or even suggested. The only agent directly operating upon it is the soil water, which is not effective in dry years. Means must soon be taken to arrest the further progress of this evil, more dangerous than any other that can possibly threaten the health of the city."[10]

The portrait of Sacramento that Amos painted was not pretty. The nonfeasance of elected officials in addressing the poor conditions of the water and sewer system was inexcusable as Amos saw it. The state of the city was personal for Amos, as he and his family lived in Sacramento, and he had no intentions of moving.

It would be three months before visiting Superior Court Judge Jackson Temple would issue a ruling. Both sides had approached the trial with the understanding that the verdict would be appealed to the Supreme Court. In June of 1882, Judge Temple ruled against the Gold Run Ditch Company, finding that its operations injured navigable waterways and the sanitary condition of Sacramento City.[11] Later in 1882, Amos' name would again be floated as a gubernatorial candidate, but many speculated that his representation of the hydraulic miners would make him unelectable.[12]

Amos had raised such a stink over the sorry state of sewage disposal in Sacramento that he was asked to review proposals for improving sanitary

Amos P. Catlin

conditions and draft an ordinance for consideration.[13] His proposed ordinance called for all cesspools and vaults that collected human waste to be constructed of water-tight brick and mortar. For homes and businesses that could connect to one of the few underground sewer drains, there were specifications for water-tight pipes and necessary pipe slope to deliver the waste into the sewer. Cesspools and vaults not connected to the city sewer system had to be cleaned out on a regular basis. All waste systems had to have proper ventilation, so no waste gasses could enter buildings.[14]

Finally, where there was no connection to the city sewer, the cesspool vault had to be excavated to a depth of 12 feet, or one foot below the subterranean water level in the month of September. Even though many homes had backyard water wells, there was not much thought given to the introduction of liquid waste into someone's drinking water well.[15]

Bond Tax Increase Issues

40. City of Sacramento water bond, 1866. California State Library

While the debris trial was underway, Amos attended a scheduled meeting of the Taxpayer's Association. The object of the association was to create a permanent

Amos P. Catlin

organization of taxpayers in the City of Sacramento to review the city finances, indebtedness, and, most importantly, taxes to fund the city's budget. Notable men of the city, such as James McClatchy, Newton Booth, and Israel Luce, were appointed to the committee.[16]

The real source of the taxpayer revolt was the fact that the city was proposing a 2 percent tax on property, even though the city charter called for a cap of 1 percent. The extra tax, it was argued, was needed to meet the city bond's interest and repayment for items such as improving sewer drainage and raising and maintaining the levee system around the city. There were many questions as to the legality of increasing the tax rate over what was written in the city charter.

At a subsequent meeting of the Taxpayer's Association, attended by many local attorneys, Amos was called upon to discuss the state of the city's indebtedness. Amos was viewed as being extremely knowledgeable regarding financial issues, given his work at the State Board of Equalization and lectures about the early financial history of California.[17] Unlike a courtroom or lecture hall, where decorum was universally accepted and practiced, Amos was addressing men who did not want to hear the legal foundations of the city's tax increase.[18]

After only a short period of reviewing the history and laws governing city indebtedness, Amos was told to sit down. The assembled crowd did not want to hear how they were hemmed in by laws and legal precedence. But Amos was persistent. The taxpayers, among which he was included, might not like the law, but the law cannot be ignored. The opposition erupted, lobbing strong words against Amos and his position. The Sacramento Daily Union characterized the verbal battle: "...and all hands antagonized Mr. Catlin, who gave battle valiantly, and the air for a time was warm with the wordy combat that even descended to personal allusions and cutting sarcasm."[19]

The prevailing sentiment of the crowd was that the city should just stop paying on the bonds and force the bond holders to negotiate. The only way to get out from underneath the bond obligations was to dissolve the city. The city of Auburn had dissolved their incorporation in order to avoid paying on the railroad bonds they issued.[20] Former Judge John McKune outlined his approach to resisting the tax increase in order to force a test of its legality. Some of the taxpayers alleged that city Trustees were in cahoots with the bond holders, and that, in view of Amos' defense that the bonds were legal contracts that could not be ignored, he also must be aligned with the bond holders.

The next month, the Sacramento Board of Trustee hired Amos to help them defend them against a lawsuit demanding interest on an old coupon from a bond sale.[21] Amos, with his new law partner Hamburger, were also retained by the city to assist in the prosecution of delinquent tax lawsuits.[22] The delinquent tax case

Amos P. Catlin

was essentially an extension of the argument between McKune and Amos over the legality of the increased city taxes. Both sides met in court before Judge Denson in October of 1882, where the taxpayers argued that the City Charter only allowed for a 1 percent tax rate, and nothing more could be authorized. The charter was passed under the old State Constitution, and it had never been repealed and updated.[23]

Amos and the city requested Judge Denson find for the defendants so that the judgment could be appealed to the Supreme Court.[24] Judge Denson, who had won the Superior Court Judgeship over Amos several years earlier, announced his resignation on November 27, 1882.[25] Denson was honest about the reasons for his resignation: He could make more money in private practice. Amos' name was circulated as a replacement, but the appointment went to his old law partner Thomas McFarland.[26]

The Sacramento bond litigation requiring the city to levy a tax to support repayment and interest on the debt finally made its way up to the Supreme Court in 1883. In an adverse, but not unexpected, decision, the California Supreme Court ruled that there was a solemn compact between the city and the bond holders, despite the fact the Legislature had repealed the act that allowed the bonds to be issued. The bonds issued by the City of Sacramento were issued under the conditions that the city levy a tax of $1 per $100 of assessed property value. The city had only levied $0.50 on $100 of assessed value, which underfunded the bond fund for repayment.[27]

Back in 1881, Amos had counseled the Board of Trustees to levy the additional tax to comply with the bond provisions. The Supreme Court decision vindicated Amos' position on debt financing, to which the Taxpayer's Association objected vociferously. There was just no way of wiggling out of the bond debt and necessary tax increases on Sacramento property owners.

From an economic perspective, Sacramento was situated better than most California cities. The Sacramento region received currency into its economy from agriculture, state government wages, and railroad employment. The mining industry still generated local revenue with manufacturing and importing material, but the big growth of hydraulic mining was being pinched off with lawsuits disputing the mining debris in the rivers. Relative to other cities, Sacramento had more indebtedness to finance infrastructure such as levees, potable water supplies, and drainage.

California, once largely self-contained with its own distinct economy, now had closer ties with the rest of the nation. The effects of the panic of 1872 and recession of 1873 were still lingering across most of the United States in 1883. A large factor in the great recession of 1873 was the demonization of silver. While

Amos P. Catlin

California was still primarily a gold-based economy, and most contracts demanded the debt be paid in gold coin, California exporters had to recognize and accept federally issued greenback paper money from the East Coast. Greenbacks were discounted relative to gold coin.

With the industrial and mechanization revolution, especially in the railroads, employers got larger, and employees started to organize for better wages. In 1878, there were faint rumors that delegates to the Workingmen's Party Convention wanted to draft Amos onto their state ticket.[28] Circulation of Amos' name for the Workingmen's Party derived from his political rhetoric against the monopolistic practices of the railroads and his anti-Chinese stance.

In 1883, Amos turned 60 years old. He had spent the past 34 years of his life in California. He had a lucrative law practice and owned property throughout the Central Valley. His children were now into their teenage years, which made it easier for him to travel more frequently to San Francisco and argue before the state Supreme Court and the federal district court.

---

[1] Sacramento Daily Union, Volume 14, Number 75, 16 November 1881
[2] Sacramento Daily Union, Volume 14, Number 75, 16 November 1881
[3] Sacramento Daily Union, Volume 14, Number 95, 9 December 1881
[4] Sacramento Daily Union, Volume 14, Number 123, 12 January 1882
[5] Sacramento Daily Union, Volume 14, Number 125, 14 January 1882
[6] Sacramento Daily Union, Volume 15, Number 46, 15 April 1882
[7] Sacramento Daily Union, Volume 15, Number 46, 15 April 1882
[8] Sacramento Daily Union, Volume 15, Number 46, 15 April 1882
[9] Sacramento Daily Union, Volume 15, Number 46, 15 April 1882
[10] Sacramento Daily Union, Volume 15, Number 46, 15 April 1882
[11] Sacramento Daily Union, Volume 15, Number 96, 13 June 1882
[12] The Pacific Bee, July 29, 1882
[13] Sacramento Daily Union, Volume 18, Number 7, 30 August 1883
[14] Sacramento Daily Union, Volume 18, Number 10, 3 September 1883
[15] Sacramento Daily Union, Volume 18, Number 10, 3 September 1883
[16] Sacramento Daily Union, Volume 15, Number 25, 22 March 1882
[17] Sacramento Daily Union, Volume 1, Number 166, 6 September 1875
[18] Sacramento Daily Union, Volume 15, Number 52, 22 April 1882
[19] Sacramento Daily Union, Volume 15, Number 52, 22 April 1882
[20] Sacramento Daily Union, Volume 35, Number 5305, 30 March 1868
[21] Sacramento Daily Union, Volume 15, Number 73, 17 May 1882
[22] Sacramento Daily Union, Volume 15, Number 144, 8 August 1882
[23] Sacramento Daily Union, Volume 16, Number 52, 20 October 1882
[24] Sacramento Daily Union, Volume 16, Number 56, 25 October 1882
[25] Sacramento Daily Union, Volume 16, Number 86, 28 November 1882
[26] Sacramento Daily Union, Volume 16, Number 102, 18 December 1882
[27] Sacramento Daily Union, Volume 18, Number 33, 1 October 1883
[28] Sacramento Bee, May 4, 1878

Amos P. Catlin

Chapter Thirteen: Light, Divorce, Anti-Chinese Ordinance, 1883 - 1886

The 1880s was probably the most diverse period of Amos' business and professional life. He got involved in some local businesses and represented a variety of clients from individuals to corporations and government. In late 1883, he represented the entire Board of Sacramento County, whose members were being threatened with jail time for failing to approve an injury settlement.[1] The issue stemmed from the Board's failure to approve a $51,000 settlement awarded to a woman injured because of a poorly maintained county road.[2]

Electric Light, Banks, Water, Crocker

Ten years before the City of Sacramento began receiving power from the Folsom hydro-electric plant, electricity was being generated locally. Amos was in on the ground floor of the new Electric Light Company and sat on its Board of Directors. The practice of generating electricity to power streetlights had already occurred in San Francisco, to which Amos had been commuting on a regular basis.[3] The Sacramento Electric Light Company's generating plant was slated to be built at Sixth and H streets, on property known as the Saulsbury Woodyard. The board met at Amos' office in Sacramento and had raised $27,000 in stock purchases toward the completion of the project in February 1884.[4]

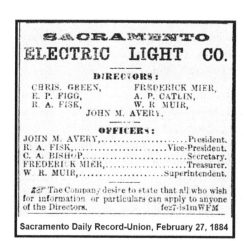

41. Amos Catlin, one of the directors of the Sacramento Electric Light Co., 1884.

While the Sacramento Electric Light Company was raising cash directly from the public, if it needed a loan, the light company may have turned to one of Amos' other associates, the Mechanics' Building and Loan Association. Formed in the summer of 1884, the Mechanics' Building and Loan Association sought to enter the banking landscape at a time when so many similar institutions had failed because of the previous recession. Amos was not a director, but was listed as the association's attorney.[5] Normally,

Amos P. Catlin

a corporate attorney is not listed in any advertisement or press release. However, having Amos identified as the organization's attorney signaled to potential customers that the new banking institution would not fail, as had happened to so many savings banks.

Electricity was not the only utility with which Amos was connected. Sacramento had notoriously disagreeable drinking water pumped out of the Sacramento River. Amos represented a proposal from the California Water and Mining Company to deliver water from Pilot Hill, in El Dorado County, to Sacramento via a pipeline. The pipe would cross the South Fork of the American River at Mormon Island, then follow the Sacramento Valley Railroad right-of-way into Sacramento.[6]

Samuel Denson was also pitching a water proposal from the Amador Water and Mining Company to the City of Sacramento.[7] Even though the scandal involving William Ralston and the Spring Valley Water Company in San Francisco was more than 10 years old, Sacramento, with its deep bond debt, was skeptical Sierra mountain water could be piped into the city by a private contractor. All of the proposals would be rejected, and Sacramento would continue to develop and attempt to treat Sacramento River water for its residents' use.

When it came time for Mrs. E.B. Crocker to donate the vast collection of art that she and her late husband had collected, Amos was instrumental in the city's proposal for the gift. Amos, working with a designated citizens committee and the local museum association, in 1885 drafted the proposition that Mrs. Crocker deed the Crocker Art Gallery to the City of Sacramento, in return for the city's pledge to maintain the property, and free occupancy for the California Museum Association to manage the collection.[8] Amos' son, Harry, took classes at the Sacramento School of Design, which were held at the E.B. Crocker Art Gallery.[9] Of course, Amos' family was thoroughly familiar with the famous Native American paintings by distant relative George Catlin.

At age 62, Amos was one of the busiest attorneys in Sacramento. In addition to his work on numerous bond cases involving the City of Sacramento, he would represent six different cases before the California Supreme Court in 1885. His age did not seem to slow him, and he could be quite animated on occasion. While arguing a case in Superior Court with passion and deliberate steps, his shoe sparked a parlor match that had been tossed on the floor. The ignition of the match startled Amos, as he bounded in the air, earning a general laugh from the judge, jury, and opposing counsel. Amos exclaimed, "Gentlemen of the jury, if I have no fire in my head, I at least have some in my feet."[10]

Amos P. Catlin

Valensin Divorce Case

In general, Amos had cordial and decorous courtroom exchanges with his fellow Sacramento lawyers. It was not uncommon for Amos to partner with an attorney on one case, only for the two to be opposing counsels the following month on a different case. One divorce case, of unusual length, seemed to test Amos' patience for suspect legal maneuvers by the opposing counsel. Alice Valensin had sued her husband, Count Giulio Valensin, for divorce, custody of their son, and control of their Arno Farm. Amos was representing Giulio Valensin in the proceedings before Judge McFarland.[11]

Alice Valensin's mother, Caroline McCauley, was called to testify about Giulio's broken promises and poor treatment of her daughter. On cross-examination, Amos introduced a letter from Caroline to Alice that was uncomplimentary toward Giulio. Attorney for Alice, Henry O. Beatty, objected to the introduction of the private correspondence as evidence, and Judge McFarland sustained the objection. Beatty then instructed Caroline McCauley that she could keep the letter. Caroline then tucked the letter into her dress pocket.

From Amos' perspective, he had just witnessed the theft of his defendant's evidence. Amos jumped to his feet, needing no lit match to energize himself this time, and objected to Judge McFarland that the letter, introduced as evidence, was now in the possession of the defendant and should be returned to the defendant, regardless of its admissibility. Judge McFarland agreed, and the letter was returned to Amos.

In a bit of theatrics to convey his pique over the opposing counsel's sly attempt to gain control over the letter, Amos held the letter aloft and said, "I have been a practicing attorney for upwards of twenty-five years, and this is the first time that I ever saw an attorney in a case attempt to steal a document in open Court."[12] Indignant that anyone would call him a thief, Beatty, a former judge, called Amos a liar. Amos' co-counsel, Grove Johnson, a master of courtroom theatrics himself, saw the imminent physical collision between Amos and Beatty and deftly stepped between the two men.[13]

What was never disclosed was how Giulio came into possession of the letter from Caroline McCauley to her daughter, Alice Valensin. What would become an issue in the divorce case was a meeting between Alice and Amos before Alice filed for divorce. Alice came to Amos hoping he could affect some sort of compromise with her husband to divide the property and custody of their son Pio without the need for a protracted divorce proceeding. Amos drafted an offer that would have Giulio keep 950 acres of the Arno Ranch, pay $12,000 of the $30,000 mortgage, and give complete custody of Pio to Alice. The remaining 1,700 acres of the ranch would rest with Alice. Amos delivered the offer to the attorney representing Giulio at the time, Samuel Denson.[14]

The whole offer and compromise were known to Alice's legal counsel, because Samuel Denson and Henry Beatty were representing her. The legal counsels had completely switched their representation, and Amos was now defending Giulio. In court, Amos was forced to take the witness stand to explain his actions and why his client, Giulio, had never heard of any such offer being made. Alice's attorney, Henry Beatty, had dropped the information on Giulio in cross-examination. Beatty must have taken some delight in seeing Amos in an uncomfortable position of explaining himself on the witness stand.

Beatty then got to question Amos about the course of events and why he withheld the compromise proposal from his client. Amos explained, "I never mentioned the matter to Mr. Valensin, and he knew no more of it than a stranger. I expected Mrs. Valensin to conclude her testimony without referring to the interview with me, but she saw fit [not to], and that, with the introduction of this paper, made it necessary for me to make this statement."[15]

In early June of 1885, Judge McFarland wanted to immediately start closing arguments. Amos protested first on the grounds that he and Grove Johnson had not been furnished with all of the transcripts from the court reporters. When that failed to delay the proceedings, Amos said he was in poor health and would not be compelled to argue the case when he was not physically able to do so.[16] Amos might have been sick of the trial and not physically ill. The following day he was traveling to San Francisco and staying at his favorite hotel, the Lick House.[17]

Grove Johnson proceeded with the closing arguments in Giulio Valensin's case in Amos' absence. Judge McFarland issued his decision in early July of 1885. He denied Alice Valensin's application for divorce, on the grounds that she had not suffered extreme cruelty at the hands of Giulio. The Judge could not address any division of the property, but since the couple was living apart, he awarded custody of Pio to Alice.[18] In spite of Amos' theatrics and ethical issues of withholding information from Giulio, the desired outcome was achieved for Giulio.

Anti-Chinese Ordinance

Grove Johnson would be in opposition to Amos, but it would not be in a courtroom. Johnson was the chairman of the Anti-Chinese Association of Sacramento, at a time when the anti-Chinese movement was gaining members and momentum. At a December 1885 meeting of anti-Chinese men, there was a call for a statewide convention for March 1886, with delegates appointed by each of California's County Board of Supervisors.[19] Grove Johnson, with the help of several other men, drafted an anti-Chinese ordinance for the City of Sacramento Board of Trustees to consider.

The ordinance, if passed, would make it a misdemeanor for any Chinese person to reside within the limits of the City of Sacramento. All Chinese would be expelled by March 1, 1886, or face fines and imprisonment for failure to vacate the city. The wholesale expulsion of a group of individuals was allowed, in Grove Johnson's eminent legal opinion, because the Chinese were not eligible for citizenship, based on the Burlingame Treaty with China. In addition, the California Constitution gave municipalities the power to remove the Chinese, authority that also was fortified by legislative statutes enacted in 1880.[20]

But the near-forced removal of Chinese from their homes seemed a bit extreme to some Sacramentans. While Grove Johnson was a respected attorney in Sacramento, nonetheless, the Sacramento Board of Trustees turned to Amos for his opinion on the Chinese expulsion ordinance. The opinion of Amos to the Board of Trustees, published in the newspapers,[21] took aim at the dubious legal arguments and rationale for such an extreme measure.

"To the Honorable Board of the Trustees of the City of Sacramento: In response to your request for my opinion as to the constitutional validity and binding force of the anti-Chinese ordinance proposed on the 11th instant, for your consideration by a committee of an anti-Chinese association, I have to say:

"That said ordinance is a self-manifest and palpable violation of the Federal Constitution, in that it is aimed to exclude from the city of Sacramento all persons of a certain nationality; that is to say, all Chinese, without regard to age, sex, occupation, or other condition. To some minds this does not perhaps appear so apparent. But to the same minds, if an ordinance were framed, with a whereas even more verbose and extended than this in recitation of supposed evils, followed by a section making it a misdemeanor, punishable by fine and imprisonment for any Italian, Mexican, or Portuguese to reside in or remain within the limits of the city after a specific time, it would at once become perfectly clear that the Federal Constitution (State Constitution and laws to the contrary notwithstanding) does not tolerate, but forbids such class legislation."[22]

Amos then went on to cite the terms of the U.S. treaty with China that allowed for each nation's citizens to travel and reside freely in the other's country. He pointed out Chinese people were guaranteed the same rights of other aliens residing in the United States. Additionally, the Fourteenth Amendment to the Constitution, supported by Section 1977 of the U.S. Revised Statutes, provided that all persons (not all citizens) receive full and equal benefit of all laws that are enjoyed by white citizens. And in case some attorneys may have forgotten, the U.S. Constitution was the supreme law of the land superseding any state or local law.[23]

Amos P. Catlin

To further bolster his legal opinion, Amos cited several federal court cases in which similar attempts to enact unconstitutional ordinances had been struck down. He highlighted the ordinance's flaw of discriminating against a particular class of people, specifically the Chinese. He noted the state's earlier attempts at imposing special taxes on Chinese miners and special bonds on ships transporting Chinese migrants had been "promptly stripped of their thin disguises and consigned by the Federal Courts to deep and early graves."[24]

CITIZENS' MEETING

TO BE HELD TO-NIGHT TO CON- SIDER THE CHINESE PROBLEM.

A Very Able Opinion of Hon. A. P. Catlin Relative to the China- town-Removal Ordinance.

Sacramento Daily Record-Union, January 18, 1886

42. Anti-Chinese Citizens' Meeting featuring Amos Catlin speaking against the Chinese eviction ordinance, 1886.

Amos summed up his argument against the ordinance by chastising its authors: "It is not possible for anyone to be so blind, however much he may affect a mental obliquity, as not to see that, under the paramount law of the land, municipal legislation requiring Chinamen to abandon their leasehold estates in this city, and remove their goods and chattels outside the city limits, would be inoperative, null and void."[25]

Lest a reader of Amos' opinion be misled as to his loyalties and sympathies, he made it clear he was no supporter of the Chinese residents of Sacramento. "Relief from the Chinese evil can be had only through the agency of the General Government. The remedies, so far as legislation is concerned, are exclusively within the domain of Federal power. Any attempted usurpation of its jurisdiction by State, county or municipal interference, especially that kind of interference which proposed to inflict personal injury and wrong upon Chinese residents, will retard, not advance, the efforts that are being made in Congress to obtain such relief. A. P. Catlin."[26]

Grove Johnson was surprised at the weight that Amos' opinion carried, after the hearing on the ordinance was postponed and ultimately defeated. At a later anti-Chinese meeting, Johnson said of Amos "Now, Mr. Catlin has written an opinion; the Sacramento editor has pronounced the ordinance unconstitutional, and I suppose that settles it. Now, Mr. Catlin is an able lawyer and an excellent citizen, but I do not see why – simply because he is asked to write an opinion, and presumably for a fee – he should be set up as a standard and unimpeachable authority on constitutional law. You have all doubtless read patent medicine

Amos P. Catlin

advertisements that say that none is genuine without so and so is blown in the bottle, and I suppose that hereafter all constitutional law will be labeled: This is constitutional law, W.A. Anderson, City Attorney, Correct: Sacramento Editor. Approved A.P. Catlin."[27]

Even though the eviction ordinance was defeated, the attempt and continued racist propaganda against the Chinese further inflamed the activities of the anti-Chinese associations. In February 1886, a group of white men from the Anti-Chinese Club in Nicolaus drove numerous Chinese men, who were working in the hop fields, from the area.[28] Benjamin Bugbey, then a U.S. Commissioner, had the white men arrested under federal laws and brought to Sacramento for a preliminary hearing.[29] Grove Johnson would be one of the attorneys to represent the white men, who were charged with depriving the Chinese laborers of equal protection under the law and violation of the Burlingame Treaty.[30] Bugbey's valiant efforts to make white men accountable for their assaults upon the Chinese fizzled at the federal level.

The question of protecting the Chinese on issues raised by Commissioner Bugbey ultimately rose to the U.S. Supreme Court. The Court, while acknowledging the protection granted within the Burlingame Treaty for the Chinese residents, found that no federal statute was applicable for protecting the Chinese with federal resources.[31] In other words, Congress had not passed a law to prosecute individuals who would deprive the Chinese of equal protection under the law. The remedy lay with state and local governments. Of course, Sacramento public opinion was on the opposite end of the spectrum with regard to protecting the Chinese. The anti-Chinese movement wanted to evict them from the city limits. It was only Amos' begrudgingly accepted legal opinion that eviction was unconstitutional that prevented even darker stains of racism and discrimination from permeating Sacramento history.

---

[1] Sacramento Daily Union, Volume 18, Number 83, 27 November 1883
[2] Sacramento Daily Union, Volume 18, Number 48, 17 October 1883
[3] Sacramento Daily Union, Volume 18, Number 150, 16 February 1884
[4] Sacramento Daily Union, Volume 18, Number 152, 19 February 1884
[5] Sacramento Daily Union, Volume 51, Number 132, 24 July 1884
[6] Sacramento Daily Union, Volume 54, Number 134, 26 January 1886
[7] Sacramento Daily Union, Volume 54, Number 134, 26 January 1886
[8] Daily Alta California, Volume 38, Number 12776, 6 April 1885
[9] Sacramento Daily Union, Volume 58, Number 90, 3 December 1887
[10] Sacramento Bee, May 15, 1885
[11] Sacramento Daily Union, Volume 53, Number 77, 22 May 1885
[12] Sacramento Daily Union, Volume 53, Number 80, 26 May 1885
[13] Sacramento Daily Union, Volume 53, Number 80, 26 May 1885
[14] Sacramento Bee, June 5, 1885
[15] Sacramento Bee, June 6, 1885

Amos P. Catlin

[16] Sacramento Daily Union, Volume 53, Number 93, 10 June 1885
[17] Daily Alta California, Volume 38, Number 12842, 11 June 1885
[18] Sacramento Daily Union, Volume 53, Number 114, 4 July 1885
[19] Sacramento Daily Union, Volume 54, Number 126, 18 January 1886
[20] Sacramento Daily Union, Volume 54, Number 122, 12 January 1886
[21] Sacramento Daily Union, Volume 54, Number 126, 18 January 1886
[22] Sacramento Daily Union, Volume 54, Number 126, 18 January 1886
[23] Sacramento Daily Union, Volume 54, Number 126, 18 January 1886
[24] Sacramento Daily Union, Volume 54, Number 126, 18 January 1886
[25] Sacramento Daily Union, Volume 54, Number 126, 18 January 1886
[26] Sacramento Daily Union, Volume 54, Number 126, 18 January 1886
[27] Sacramento Bee, January 19, 1886
[28] Sacramento Daily Union, Volume 54, Number 155, 19 February 1886
[29] Sacramento Daily Union, Volume 55, Number 18, 13 March 1886
[30] Sacramento Daily Union, Volume 55, Number 20, 16 March 1886
[31] The Chinese Struggle for Civil Rights in 19th-Century America: The Unusual Case of Baldwin v. Franks, 3 Law & Hist. Rev. 349 (1985)

Amos P. Catlin

Chapter Fourteen: Saving Auburn, Bonds, Judah, 1887 - 1889

The money to fund many of Sacramento's public works projects came from bonds issued by the city and bought by investors. The process of repaying the interest and principal on bond debt is usually straightforward. Unfortunately for the City of Sacramento, some of its bond debt had specific stipulations relative to taxing property owners, and many of the bonds were authorized by specific state

1056. Railroad and Suspension Bridges at Folsom, Sacramento County.

43. California Central Railroad bridge over the American River that would connect with the Sacramento, Placer & Nevada Railroad at Ashland, 1866. Library Congress

legislation and under the original California Constitution. Additional complications revolved around bondholders who did not present their coupons until well after the maturity date and property owners who balked at increased taxes to retire the bond debt.

Between the years of 1880 and 1885, 21 different lawsuits were filed against the City of Sacramento over the bonded indebtedness. Most of the lawsuits sought to

Amos P. Catlin

collect interest and principal on the bonds, while others aimed to restrict the City Treasurer from expending funds, keeping them available for future interest and principal payments. Of the 21 different actions, Amos was retained by the city to represent it in four of the lawsuits.

Amos' job was to tease out the specific details and conditions under which some bond principal and interest could be paid out after the maturity dates. In many instances, it was the State Legislature that had passed a bill authorizing the city to incur bond indebtedness for specific projects. Of course, complicating matters further, the State had a new Constitution, plus Sacramento City and County had been one entity for a number of years during which various laws and ordinances governing bond indebtedness were passed. Attorneys for the city had to contend with all of this changing legal landscape, along with Supreme Court decisions relating to municipal bond repayment. Amos loved these sort of arcane government questions. He plowed into the cases, and soon became a noted authority on the topic of municipal bond debt.

Sacramento, Placer & Nevada Railroad Auburn Railroad Bonds

Sacramento was not the only city that struggled with bond debt, but at least it was attempting to address the situation. Another city just walked away from honoring the bonds it had issued. In order to avoid repaying close to $50,000 in railroad bonds issued in 1860, the City of Auburn requested that the State Legislature pass a bill disincorporating the municipality. Auburn would remain unincorporated until Amos offered the community a path back to cityhood. In July of 1886, Amos filed a lawsuit against the defunct City of Auburn over bonds it had issued 26 years earlier.[1] Because the City of Auburn was no longer incorporated, Amos listed prominent residents in the community, many of whom were attorneys, as the defendants.

Before Auburn became associated with the Transcontinental Railroad built, in part, by the Central Pacific Railroad, it was a different rail line that had captivated the town's residents. After the Sacramento Valley Railroad was completed to Folsom in 1856, foothill mining communities such as Auburn, Grass Valley, and Nevada City began advocating for a railroad into their communities.[2] The California Central Railroad was constructing a bridge over the American River in 1858, but the line was planned to head northwest toward Marysville, not toward Auburn. Amos was involved with the California Central Railroad and lived in Folsom at the time. With the completion of the bridge over the American River, a large impediment to, and cost of, a rail line up to the foothills was removed.

Amos P. Catlin

The Sacramento, Placer & Nevada Railroad Company (SPNRR) was formed in 1859, hiring Sherman Day to engineer a railroad from Folsom up to Auburn. Day's report was published in the Placer Herald newspaper on March 31, 1860, and the push was on to raise the capital needed for the rail line.[3] Auburn residents were enthusiastic about the railroad and had their State legislative representatives introduce a bill to incorporate Auburn into a city and allow them to issue bonds to fund the construction of the SPNRR.[4]

June 4th, 1860, was the date set for the special election in Auburn to approve issuing $50,000 in bonds for the SPNRR. The measure passed without a single vote counted in opposition.[5] Construction of the SPNRR began at Ashland very near where the California Central RR landed on the north side of the American River. By September 1862, the SPNRR had 12 miles of track completed, six miles shy of its final destination. The City of Auburn[6] would be the end of the line for the SPNRR.

Meanwhile, the Central Pacific Railroad was rapidly progressing on its path from Sacramento up to Auburn for the Transcontinental Railroad. The SPNRR was not generating enough revenue from either freight or passenger traffic to break even. The prospect of the Central Pacific Railroad, with its more efficient and economical route from Sacramento to Auburn, stifled investment in the SPNRR. SPNRR investor Lester Robinson, who was focused on building his own rail route over the Sierras to compete with the Central Pacific Railroad, moved to foreclose on the SPNRR.[7] The directors of the SPNRR, more aligned with Robinson than Auburn, did not fight the foreclosure. In 1864, the SPNRR was purchased by John Robinson of the Sacramento Valley Railroad.

It was widely known that Lester Robinson wanted the SPNRR's rails for use on the Placerville and Sacramento Railroad. If the rails were removed, even though the SPNRR was essentially dead, the City of Auburn still would be making 8 percent interest payments on almost $50,000 worth of bonds, for an investment that had vanished. What ensued was a minor railroad war. Auburn citizens, led by the Placer County Sheriff Deputies, rode down to the site where the rails were being removed and engaged the hired men.

Shots were fired on both sides in a July 4th skirmish. The dismantling crew was able to capture one of the sheriff deputies, who later escaped.[8] There was a prolonged standoff between the two groups. Granite quarry owner Griffith Griffith, who was using the SPNRR to ship granite down to Sacramento, filed a lawsuit seeking an injunction for the dismantling of the rail line.[9] An expedited judicial hearing process elevated the injunctive relief up to the California Supreme Court, which ruled against the injunction.[10]

Amos P. Catlin

Upon reading the Supreme Court's ruling, the Placer County Sheriff halted any official interference with dismantling the SPNRR. As the SPNRR failed to produce any revenue, the City of Auburn was forced to trigger a special assessment of $2.10 per one hundred dollars of assessed property value.[11] On top of that tax increase, Placer County had voted to assess all property owners to help pay for the Central Pacific Railroad's line through the county.[12] By 1868, Auburn buckled under the pressure of all the taxes and requested that the State Legislature pass a bill disincorporating the municipality, which it did.[13]

Eighteen years after Auburn had abandoned its bond obligations, Amos presented the community with a proposal, which started in the form of the lawsuit. The lawsuit was filed on behalf of Thomas Bell of San Francisco for the recovery of the Auburn bond's interest and principal, but the complaint was something of a ruse. The real plaintiff was Lester Robinson. However, mentioning Robinson in a court action against the former city of Auburn might have stopped any discussions, as Robinson was viewed as the villain in the original dismantling of the SPNRR.[14]

The filing date of the lawsuit was also strategic, as the original bonds were coming up on maturity and, if court action was not taken, any leverage or opportunity to recover bond money would have lapsed.[15] All of these issues were very familiar to Amos, who had been steeped in bond litigation for the last several years in Sacramento. In reality, there was little prospect of recovering any bond money from Auburn, a defunct town. However, Auburn residents were eager to regain their municipal status, which could have been achieved once the statute of limitations had passed on the bond obligation. Amos' lawsuit squashed the chance for a quick return to cityhood.

If the community of Auburn wanted to reincorporate, it would have to negotiate with Amos. In early October 1887, Amos wrote to E.L. Craig of Auburn, offering to negotiate a reasonable offer for the outstanding bonds in exchange for the community's ability to reincorporate.

"The plan for raising the money is a thing I have not thought of, it being a matter naturally to be devised by you and your friends. While cash is very desirable in all cases, my idea has been in this that time was necessary and of course must be conceded. I should think an incorporation of the town, or rather a town most necessary and beneficial. The obligations of the new town or city, in the form of bonds or promises having a reasonably long or short time to run, with interest say at six percent would be all we could ask. The $44,750 of bonds with coupons attached in my hands to be surrendered on receipt of the new bonds."[16]

It would take until February 1888 to come to an agreement. Craig outlined the settlement to Auburn residents at a meeting. Amos was to deposit the bonds into

Amos P. Catlin

the Placer Bank, where they would be held for six months while the residents of Auburn petitioned Placer County to be reincorporated. Then, once a city administration had been established, the City of Auburn would issue new bonds with a face value of $9,350 at six percent interest.[17]

By April, the Placer County Board of Supervisor approved of the Auburn incorporation. On April 24th, an election was held to establish the boundaries of Auburn and elect Trustees. Another election was held in July to approve the new bond swap with Amos. The final result was 167 "yes" votes and 62 "no" votes.[18] With the approval of the new bonds, Amos dropped the lawsuit against the community of Auburn and secured a partial repayment of the bonds to investors.

The 1880s were a pleasant period in Amos' life. His law practice was healthy, he was an esteemed and respected attorney in Sacramento, and he got to spend time with his children on vacations to Monterey.[19] Amos entered into an association with local attorney Clinton White in 1886. That association only lasted a couple years before Amos formed a new partnership with George Blanchard in 1888.[20] Blanchard, a fellow Republican, had been Sacramento County's District Attorney and also worked as the Assistant Attorney-General for California. He was appointed to fill a vacancy for Superior Court Judge in Colusa County. In January 1888, he returned to Sacramento County and formed a law partnership with Amos.[21]

Republican Politics Election Board Opinion

Despite Amos' best intentions to create independent party associations of ethical men, Sacramento party politics still tilted toward the corrupt side of the spectrum. Both the Democratic and Republican parties were controlled by a small group of influential men, also known as political bosses. The Daily Alta California compared the Sacramento political scene to a train wreck. "The local campaign against the bosses is almost the only subject thought of, and the usual commercial business of the city takes the place of secondary consideration. The determination to clean out the entire disreputable gang that has ruled the local politics and governed all the municipal offices and affairs is deeply rooted and the respectable elements of both Republicans and Democrats seem to know no party line nor feeling, but are counseling and working shoulder to shoulder to the one common end."[22]

Particular attention was paid to the Fourth Ward, where ballot stuffing and intimidation by Republican bosses were reported in the primary election of March 1888.[23] The Fourth Ward just happened to be Amos' district, where he also was on the ballot as a delegate to the city Republican convention. Amos, along with several other men, was elected to the convention amidst the protests of other men,

Amos P. Catlin

who challenged the legitimacy of the election. After the tainted election, there was a push to have the Sacramento City Board of Trustees remove the election officers.

One of the leading proponents to remove the existing election officials was Grove Johnson, who, ironically, had back in the 1860s attempted to tamper with the election process. Johnson argued that there was no political code that prevented the Board of Trustees from removing the current election officials, who had ignored the abuses by political bosses in the previous primary.[24] Once again, the Board of Trustees turned to Amos for his legal counsel on the matter of replacing members of the Board of Elections.

Sacramento Mayor Gregory read the opinion of Amos before the assembled audience. In short, Amos concluded that once the Board of Trustees appointed the election officers and called for an election, the Board then became powerless to change the members of the election board.[25] Grove Johnson, while unhappy about the opinion, deferred to Amos' conclusion. Clinton White challenged Amos and the foundation of the legal basis of the opinion.[26]

White accused Amos of already having his mind made up before he wrote his opinion. The two lawyers sparred over differing interpretations of the law. The accusation of bias irritated Amos, who replied that he never wrote an opinion without careful research.[27] The crowd in attendance at the Board of Trustees meeting was decidedly against Amos' opinion. Trustee A. Leonard, who wanted the Election Board members replaced, quipped that he did not think he could find another man who entertained the same opinion as Amos. This so infuriated Amos that he refused to answer any more questions.[28] Regardless, Amos' opinion stood, and no action was taken against the Board of Elections.

Reflections on Past Pioneers

In addition to recognition of his legal acumen, Amos was highly respected as one of the pioneers of Sacramento and of the region. Of course, it helped that Amos was still living as other pioneers were succumbing to old age or had moved out of California years earlier. In 1889, Amos was elected a life-member of the California Pioneers Society in San Francisco.[29] His lifetime of knowledge and experience made him the first source of historical recollections for newspapers whenever a historically prominent person died.

When Henry Caulfield died in July of 1888, Amos was keen to fill in the blank spots of Caulfield's life. Amos knew of Caulfield in 1844, before either of them came to California. Caulfield, as a member of the Emmet Guards, helped squash a movement of anti-rent activists known as Down-renters. In this action, Amos noted, Caulfield was on the side of law and order. In 1850, Caulfield was among the settlers who participated in the squatters' riots. Amos had visited Caulfield following what appeared to be a fatal stab wound, from which he ultimately recovered.[30] Caulfield sold property north of the confluence of the Sacramento and American Rivers to Patrick Bannon. His lasting legacy in Sacramento was that he was known as a street fighter and should have died on several occasions.

William Higgins, who died in August 1889, came to California and settled at Mormon Island. Amos had employed a young Higgins to negotiate, and partly intimidate, some other miners who had jumped one of Amos' mining claims. Higgins became active in politics and was close to James McClatchy and B.B. Redding. He left the Sacramento region in 1856 for San Francisco, where he became leader or boss of the independent Republican movement that resulted in Amos' close friend, Newton Booth, being elected Governor.[31]

Amos was frequently noted in the historical section of newspapers in accounts of what had happened in Sacramento 20- or 30-years prior. Among the mentions from the "Thirty Years Ago" column in 1889 was Amos' selection as an alternate to the meeting encouraging a Transcontinental Railroad,[32] his election as President of the Natoma Water and Mining Company,[33] his role as one of the first buyers of lots in the town of Lincoln,[34] and his role in the grand inauguration festivities of 1860.[35]

Amos wasn't only a part of history; he collected it as well. He collected newspapers connected to significant events in history. In 1888, he displayed his June 1840 edition of the *Log Cabin,* published by Horace Greeley & Co., which supported the presidential candidacy of William Henry Harrison. The paper included the lyrics for the campaign song, "The Tippecanoe Fathering," along with accounts of raising log cabins.[36] Amos also spoke at the Sacramento Harrison Veteran Division, composed of Republicans who voted for William Henry Harrison in 1840.[37] All of this nostalgia was meant to generate support for Benjamin Harrison, grandson of William Henry, who was running for President in 1888.

Amos had not been old enough to vote in the 1840 election, but he told the assembled veterans that he worked hard to get voters to the polls for Harrison.[38] However, until the 1860s, Amos identified more as a Douglas Democrat than a Republican. Whether his comments supporting William Henry Harrison were an embellishment meant to lend support for the current Harrison candidate is anyone's guess. But it would not have been the first time in political speech that Amos would blur some of his past political associations.

When Charles Crocker died in August of 1888, Amos was one of the many men interviewed for his recollections about one of the associates of the Central Pacific Railroad. Amos recalled Crocker's capacity for work: "I knew Mr. Crocker in the

Amos P. Catlin

early days. He was noted for his great exuberance of spirits. He seemed always to look on the bright side of things and was ready to undertake and carry out almost any enterprise. In fact, you could not pick out a man that was more fitted to take hold of any enterprise than Charles Crocker. If he undertook an enterprise he would carry it through to completion."[39]

Of course, Amos had to slip in a reference to Charles' brother, Edwin Crocker, who he said had the same spirit, but whose accomplishments were in the field of law, not railroads. Amos wanted to address some of the criticisms attributed to the Central Pacific Railroad upon the passing of Charles Crocker. Amos recollected, "Charles Crocker would do more work than two ordinary men. Messrs. Huntington, Stanford and Hopkins were conservative, but Mr. Crocker was all push and vim and energy. He possessed just the qualities necessary to complete the great combination. These men have been criticized because they let contracts to themselves. The fact is, the road could not have been built any other way. They advertised in the old Sacramento Union and other papers to let contracts for different sections of the work, but no one would undertake it, and Charles Crocker took hold himself and pushed it through."[40]

Defending Theodore Judah

With the death of Charles Crocker, there were numerous historical accounts of the development of the Transcontinental Railroad and the Central Pacific Railroad. Many of these newspaper articles were plagued with errors, especially about Theodore Judah and his role in the grand project. Since Amos had remained in contact with Anna Judah, Theodore's widow, he wrote to her requesting the history of Theodore and her recollections.

Amos received his reply from Anna in December 1889. She recounts his early childhood, education, and finally Theodore Judah's career path of railroad civil engineer. The letter, written almost 30 years after Theodore's death, imparts the great love she had for her husband and the companionship she lost. She was a pioneer woman and wife. She writes to Amos:

"Sometimes, dear friend, when I am oppressed with the burden of it all, all these long years of waiting, I have felt, oh! oh!, that could I climb to the summit of the Sierras, where I stood with him, those long years ago, looking west and east, over the mighty summits stretching out and on before us, and could shout to the world my story, it would be a revelation indeed..."[41]

Anna recounts how Theodore's first attempt to enlist men in San Francisco to invest in his vision of a Pacific Railroad failed. Theodore and Anna then ventured up to Sacramento to find backers for the Pacific Railroad. Anna summarized the difficulties Theodore had with some of the men who had invested in the Pacific

Railroad. She wrote, they were short-sighted and did not understand, from Theodore's point of view, the fabulous opportunity. The Sacramento investors saw only the wagon road to be constructed and put little faith in a railroad being built over. "He used to say, when he came from the director's meetings, 'I cannot make these men, some of them, appreciate the "Elephant" they have on their shoulders...'"[42]

Theodore Judah then arranged to have other investors come in and take the place of the Sacramento men who were overly cautious about building the Pacific Railroad. He and Anna were on their way to New York to make the arrangements when, as Anna writes, "...it was all laid out but, God willed it otherwise and called him Home!" Then false stories about Theodore abandoning the project were reported and, as Anna writes, they were "cruel as death!"[43]

The Central Pacific Railroad went on to complete the project and get most of the credit and glory. Anna reveals that May 10th, 1867, the day the golden spike was placed in the tie at Promontory, Utah, connecting the Central Pacific and Union Pacific Railroads, was her and Theodore's wedding anniversary. With a hint of bitterness, Anna writes, "It seemed as though the spirit of my brave husband descended upon me, and together we were there unseen, unheard of man."[44]

What triggered Amos to contact Anna about Theodore Judah was an inquiry from the Hubert H. Bancroft's The History Company about Amos' own pioneer biography in 1888.[45] Bancroft then asked Amos if he could obtain historical documents from Anna so he could fashion an accurate history of the Central Pacific Railroad. In 1889, Amos wrote to Anna:

"My Dear Mrs. Judah, a subject which has often been upon my mind, and upon which I have often intended to write to you has quite recently been renewed itself with more than usual force. History is now being made for California and much of it false. You know with what studious zeal efforts have been in a certain quarter to bury the memory of Theo. D. Judah out of sight to the future reader of the history of California. You know also how some of his friends have endeavored at times to preserve that memory.

"The historian Hubert Howe Bancroft is now engaged upon that part of his great work which covers the period of Mr. Judah's work in California, and he is particularly anxious to get reliable data in regard to Mr. Judah's connection with the beginning of the overland RR enterprise. Mr. Bancroft has not failed to discover in a general way the real motive power which lay at the foundation of that enterprise. He wants to do justice to Mr. Judah and has applied to me for information but especially for material."[46]

Amos P. Catlin

Anna Judah would write several letters to Amos venting her anguish over the historical events that separated Theodore Judah from the men in Sacramento and their subsequent fame and fortune upon the railroad's completion. In a letter written by Anna to Amos in 1865, she thanked him for defending Theodore Judah after his death in a newspaper story she had erroneously attributed to Lauren Upson of the Sacramento Daily Union.[47] Anna also sent Amos several packages containing Theodore Judah's documents, notes, and letters relating to the survey of the Transcontinental Railroad, to be forwarded to Bancroft. Through their efforts, the legacy of Theodore Judah's role in developing the historic railroad across the country was strengthened.

At a time when Sacramento was plagued by either flood or fire, it is surprising that many historical documents would survive. Amos would present a map of the Sacramento Valley drawn by John Bidwell and a map of the Rancho Del Paso land grant drawn by John Sinclair to the Sacramento Society of Pioneers for presentation and safe-keeping. Both of the maps were created in 1844[48] and in Spanish.[49] Amos never said how he came by the maps, but he was also the man who bought an old Sutter's Fort cannon in order to preserve its legacy in Sacramento history.

Amos did recount how he came to own one of his prized historic newspaper editions, an edition of the Boston Post from 1761. While Amos was visiting the cabin of a miner in the hills 40 years earlier, the miner had received a package from Boston. The package was wrapped in old newspapers. Amos immediately recognized the old paper, then over 90 years old, as a significant piece of history. As the miner did not care about the wrappings, he let Amos take the newspaper as a memento of his visit. In 1894, a reporter for the Sacramento Daily Union spied the newspaper in Judge Amos' chambers. Amos was happy to recount the story of how he happened across the newspaper relic.[50]

Alaska

For the most part, California provided Amos with all the travel experience he desired. He was a frequent visitor to San Francisco and the Lick Hotel. He vacationed with his family in the Bay Area and Monterey. Occasionally, he took trips to property he owned in Lassen and Fresno counties. The East Coast, Europe or Asia did not tug at his imagination as places necessary to visit. However, for some reason, he was captivated by Alaska and finally made a trip to that northwest outpost in 1889. He gave a lengthy interview to the Sacramento Daily Union about his trip. Amos was amazed at the size of the mining operations but even more impressed with the glaciers. "We visited two or three of the larger glaciers in that vicinity, and it can truthfully be said that no one who has not seen a glacier can form any idea of its grandeur. All that one may read on the subject will not give him a correct comprehension of one of these moving, flowing, tumbling mountains of ice."[51]

As far as the perception that Alaska was perpetually snowbound, Amos commented, "I made the great mistake of taking too much clothing with me. Dr. Cluness, who was up there a few years ago, told me to take few outer garments, but not to forget an umbrella and rubber shoes. He said I would require no heavier clothing than in Sacramento. And I wished I had followed his advice before I had been long on shore. It was very pleasant, indeed, with the exception of the rain."[52] An odd aspect of the visit for Amos was the length of the daylight: "The strangest experience of the tourist in that locality is the shortness of the nights. The sun sets say at 9 or half-past 9 o'clock P.M., but the twilight continues for hours afterward—quite up to midnight, in fact. And then, about 2 o'clock in the morning— before one can scarcely realize that there had been a night at all—the sun shows up again for another long day. While we were there it hardly got dark enough for one to see the stars in a cloudless sky."[53]

Without actually verbalizing it, Amos was reminiscing about the similar wonder and awe men had experienced when they first traveled into California in 1849. California was such a different environment from anything on the East Coast, with large mountain ranges, towering trees, and massive amounts of potential. Amos remarked that Alaska "...will be the great center of attraction for summer tourists in the coming years. Americans are just finding out that there are on these continent localities the wildness and grandeur of which are not surpassed, if equaled, anywhere on the globe, and every summer henceforth will find great throngs of people fleeing from the intense heat of our inland cities to enjoy the mild climate and grand sights to be met with in our northern Pacific possessions."[54]

---

[1] Auburn Journal, Volume 2, Number 41, 7 July 1886

[2] Placer Herald, Volume 8, Number 18, 7 January 1860

[3] Placer Herald, Volume 8, Number 30, 31 March 1860

[4] Placer Herald, Volume 8, Number 31, 7 April 1860

[5] Placer Herald, Volume 8, Number 40, 9 June 1860

[6] Placer Herald, Volume 11, Number 3, 20 September 1862

[7] Placer Herald, Volume 12, Number 28, 12 March 1864

[8] Sacramento Daily Union, Volume 27, Number 4149, 9 July 1864

[9] Sacramento Daily Union, Volume 27, Number 4150, 11 July 1864

[10] Sacramento Daily Union, Volume 27, Number 4154, 14 July 1864

[11] Placer Herald, Volume 11, Number 29, 21 March 1863

[12] Placer Herald, Volume 12, Number 33, 16 April 1864

[13] Sacramento Daily Union, Volume 35, Number 5305, 30 March 1868

[14] Auburn Journal, Volume 4, Number 1, 28 September 1887

[15] Placer Herald, Volume 36, Number 3, 1 October 1887

[16] Auburn Journal, Volume 4, Number 3, 12 October 1887

Amos P. Catlin

[17] Placer Herald, Volume 36, Number 24, 25 February 1888

[18] Placer Herald, Volume 36, Number 33, 28 April 1888

[19] Sacramento Daily Union, Volume 51, Number 139, 1 August 1884

[20] Sacramento Daily Union, Volume 58, Number 139, 31 January 1888

[21] An Illustrated History of Sacramento County, California, Containing a History of Sacramento County from the Earliest Period of Its Occupancy to the Present Time, Together with Glimpses of Its Prospective Future ... Portraits of Some of Its Most Eminent Men, and Biographical Mention of Many of Its Pioneers and Also Prominent Citizens of Today – Winfield J. Davis, 1890

[22] Daily Alta California, Volume 42, Number 14074, 13 March 1888

[23] Sacramento Daily Union, Volume 59, Number 11, 5 March 1888

[24] Sacramento Daily Union, Volume 59, Number 18, 13 March 1888

[25] Sacramento Daily Union, Volume 59, Number 18, 13 March 1888

[26] Sacramento Daily Union, Volume 59, Number 18, 13 March 1888

[27] Sacramento Bee, March 12, 1888

[28] Sacramento Daily Union, Volume 59, Number 18, 13 March 1888

[29] San Francisco Examiner, October 15, 1889

[30] Sacramento Bee, July 3, 1888

[31] Sacramento Daily Union, Volume 62, Number 1, 22 August 1889

[32] Sacramento Daily Union, Volume 1, Number 16, 1 September 1889

[33] Sacramento Daily Union, Volume 1, Number 23, 20 October 1889

[34] Sacramento Daily Union, Volume 1, Number 28, 24 November 1889

[35] Sacramento Daily Union, Volume 1, Number 31, 15 December 1889

[36] Napa Register (Weekly), Volume 25, Number 49, 20 July 1888

[37] Sacramento Daily Union, Volume 59, Number 127, 20 July 1888

[38] Sacramento Daily Union, Volume 59, Number 127, 20 July 1888

[39] Sacramento Daily Union, Volume 59, Number 154, 21 August 1888

[40] Sacramento Daily Union, Volume 59, Number 154, 21 August 1888

[41] Anna Ferona Pierce Judah correspondence concerning her husband, Theodore D. Judah, [1889]. Bancroft MSS C-D 800

[42] Anna Ferona Pierce Judah correspondence concerning her husband, Theodore D. Judah, [1889]. Bancroft MSS C-D 800

[43] Anna Ferona Pierce Judah correspondence concerning her husband, Theodore D. Judah, [1889]. Bancroft MSS C-D 800

[44] Anna Ferona Pierce Judah correspondence concerning her husband, Theodore D. Judah, [1889]. Bancroft MSS C-D 800

[45] A. P. Catlin biography, April 29, 1888. Bancroft Library MSS C – D 810 Box 1

[46] Amos Catlin Collection, Box 500, Folder 11, California State Library

[47] Amos Catlin Collection, Box 500, Folder 8, California State Library

[48] Sacramento Daily Union, Volume 80, Number 118, 7 January 1891

[49] Sacramento Bee, January 6, 1891

[50] Sacramento Daily Union, Volume 87, Number 17, 13 March 1894

[51] Sacramento Daily Union, Volume 1, Number 10, 21 July 1889

[52] Sacramento Daily Union, Volume 1, Number 10, 21 July 1889

[53] Sacramento Daily Union, Volume 1, Number 10, 21 July 1889

[54] Sacramento Daily Union, Volume 1, Number 10, 21 July 1889

Amos P. Catlin

Chapter Fifteen: Campaign for Superior Court Judge, 1889 - 1890

In between Amos' jaunts to Alaska and providing reminiscences on the passing of Sacramento pioneers, he had a full case load for a 66-year-old man. He was actively representing several cases before California's Supreme Court. Sacramento County hired Amos for legal work regarding Swamp Land District No. 407, for which he was reimbursed $1,102.00.[1] He was on the Sacramento City committee reviewing bonded debt and taxation, along with Newton Booth, Platt, Bohl, Birdsall, Weinstock, and Steffens.[2] He was handling numerous estate cases before the Superior Court as well as private civil litigation.

Amos' legal services were not inexpensive. Lawyers who were highly sought after for their skills would sometimes accept an interest in the property in dispute as collateral or payment for services rendered. It was such an arrangement that resulted in Amos's ownership of 483 acres in southeast Sacramento County.[3] In 1881, Mr. Brison originally owned the property in Sacramento County. He deeded the land to his wife while he went to Arizona to work and earn enough money to pay off the mortgage on the property.

When Mr. Brison returned to Sacramento County several years later, Mrs. Brison refused to deed the ranch back to him. To complicate matters, Mrs. Brison had leased the land out, and the gentleman to whom she had leased had sub-leased the property to another individual. Margaret Crocker, who had loaned money to the Brisons to purchase the property, also had an interest. In short, it was a messy legal affair, and Amos was retained to sort out the land titles and rents. The end result was that Amos became owner of the 483 acres. Lawyers such as Amos typically did not set out to acquire land as payment for their legal services. Such arrangements were just among the ways of bartering that led to some attorneys of the time amassing large landholdings.

W.W. Brison originally deeded the land to Amos in 1888. After lengthy litigation in the courts, Amos was granted full title in 1892.[4] In 1895, Amos filed a declaration with the County Recorder on the disposition of the Brison Ranch. Upon the sale of the property, Margaret Crocker or her heirs would be paid the $15,615 outstanding mortgage loan plus interest of $2,093.05. The next payees in line would be Amos and attorney W. Armstrong for legal services. Finally, if any funds were left, the remainder would go to W.W. Brison.[5] Amos hired attorney H.G. Soule to petition the court to allow for the sale of the property to repay the Crocker debt. The court agreed to the sale, relieving Amos of the property management in 1896.[6]

Amos P. Catlin

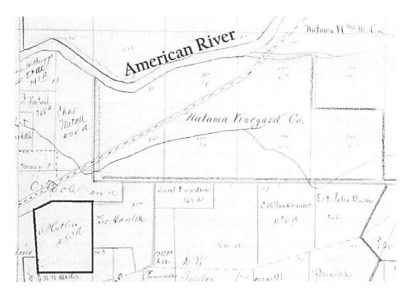

44. Formerly the W.W. Brison Ranch, Amos Catlin granted title to the 483 acres in the early 1890s. Sacramento County Assessors map

A similar land title transfer occurred in 1871. A.J. Rhodes would sell block 333 in San Francisco to Amos for $200. The block was north of Potrero and bounded by Nevada, Yolo, and Indiana streets. Within this transaction for legal services rendered, Amos also acquired the Rhodes farm on the Cosumnes River in Sacramento County.[7]

1888 Superior Court Judge Nomination

If there was anything missing in Amos' career that he would have liked to have achieved, it would have been election to a judgeship. He did not pursue this aspiration to any great lengths later in life, as the income from private practice was far superior to any salary paid to an elected judge. He saw many of his contemporaries either appointed or elected to judgeships. Amos' former law partner, Thomas McFarland, had been elected as an Associate Justice on the California Supreme Court in 1886. John Currey, Amos' law partner from 1850, had himself served on the California Supreme Court in the 1860s.

At the 1888 Republican County Convention, Amos was nominated for the Superior Court Judgeship with a great deal of enthusiasm. The contest was between Amos and his much younger contemporary, Charles N. Post, born in El Dorado County and then serving as Sacramento's Justice of the Peace.[8] Amos was seen as being part of the old guard of the Republican Party and aligned with the

Amos P. Catlin

political bosses. Clinton White, who had disagreed vehemently with Amos' opinion regarding the Board of Trustees power to change Board of Election members after apparent fraud in the last election, said of Amos, "A.P. Catlin knew more law before the other candidates were born than they do now. For any other office in the world, I would support Mr. Post, but for this office I cannot."[9]

Hiram Johnson endorsed Charles Post on the basis of his youth and readiness to take on political corruption, should it arise in his courtroom. On his own behalf, Post alluded to his youth, remarking, "I probably am not as old or distinguished as the other gentleman who has been named here, but when reference is made to the candidate of the bosses, I ask the people of Sacramento, which is the boss candidate?" Post continued that Amos had confided to a group of men that he did not think men of his age should be elected to such positions, nor did he want the judgeship.[10]

Amos was fairly unflappable to political criticism of age or association. He calmly replied to Post in his comments for the nomination, "I think my friend, Judge Post, has been misinformed about my remarks about young men. I said young men with legal minds who go on the bench at early life generally ripen into our best Judges. I say so now and Judge Post can take all the comfort out of that he can." It was a subtle critique that must have left a wry smile on the faces of many of Amos' supporters. Alas, it was not Amos' time, as Post received 120 votes to win the nomination to his 84.[11]

Sacramento City Charter

In 1890, the City of Sacramento was contemplating a new city charter. At the top of the list of men proposed to lead an overhaul of the charter, intended to give the city more flexibility to meet its obligations, was Amos.[12] One of the big questions at issue was whether a new city charter would obviate the Funded Debt Commission, whose role was to manage the bond debt, repayment, and issuing of new bonds for public works projects. The Funded Debt Commission was at times a constraint on the city's ambitions. The fiscal hawk managing the Funded Debt Commission was attorney Henry Beatty, and he was very much concerned that a new charter would allow the city to wiggle out from under the fiscal management imposed by the commission.[13]

The Sacramento Bee requested Amos' opinion regarding the Funded Debt Commission and whether it would survive under a new charter. From Amos' perspective, the Funded Debt Commission was organized under special legislation in 1872. The Supreme Court had ruled that the 1872 act authorizing the commission did not violate the State's Constitution. Therefore, the Funded Debt Commission could remain in place.[14]

Amos P. Catlin

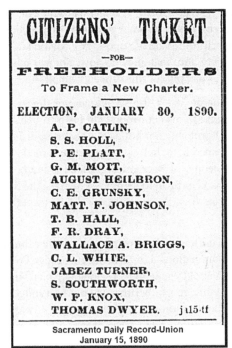

CITIZENS' TICKET

—FOR—

FREEHOLDERS

To Frame a New Charter.

ELECTION, JANUARY 30, 1890.

A. P. CATLIN,
S. S. HOLL,
P. E. PLATT,
G. M. MOTT,
AUGUST HEILBRON,
C. E. GRUNSKY,
MATT. F. JOHNSON,
T. B. HALL,
F. R. DRAY,
WALLACE A. BRIGGS,
C. L. WHITE,
JABEZ TURNER,
S. SOUTHWORTH,
W. F. KNOX,
THOMAS DWYER.   j 15 tf

Sacramento Daily Record-Union
January 15, 1890

45. Amos Catlin nominated as candidate for a freeholders' committee to draft a new charter for the City of Sacramento, 1890.

In general, Amos favored a new charter for Sacramento for a variety of reasons. The city had unique challenges that other cities did not face, such as the necessity of maintaining a levee system, a sewer system below the elevation of the Sacramento River, increased judicial demands created by disputes within the State Capitol, and the need to manage the growing number of convicted criminals continually being released from Folsom Prison. The need to adapt the new charter to accommodate state laws, including those specific to Sacramento as state capital, complicated the effort.

In late January of 1890, a citizens meeting was called to discuss some of the challenges the drafting of a new charter might create for Sacramento. Amos was selected to chair the meeting. At the beginning of the meeting, Amos announced that he had reconsidered his earlier position on the need for a new charter. After further study and consultation, he now recommended postponing any action toward drafting a new charter. His change-of-mind was cemented with the introduction of a proposed amendment to the state's Constitution, which, if approved, would remove any objections regarding the new charter and Sacramento's bond debt. Amos' opinion, unanimously endorsed by those in attendance, persuaded the Board of Trustees to postpone any action on a new city charter.[15]

Further bolstering Amos' reputation as someone who had Sacramento's best interests in his heart, the California Supreme Court sided with Amos and W.A. Anderson in a case involving Sacramento City bonds. The Supreme Court ruled, as argued by Amos and Anderson, that bond coupons do not draw interest after maturity. This was heralded as a great victory, as it saved the City of Sacramento from having to pay more than $400,000 in interest on bonds past their maturity date.[16]

Amos P. Catlin

Residence of James Scadler, O street, between Eighth and Ninth.
From a photograph by THE BEE's Camera.

Sacramento Bee, May 23, 1891

46. Identified by The Sacramento Bee as Amos Catlin's former house at 819 O street.

Even though Amos had not lived in Folsom for two decades, he still maintained ties to the community, along with the Natoma Water and Mining Company. Foreshadowing the eventual electrification of Sacramento, Amos represented Folsom in its request to the County Board of Supervisors to permanently close several streets and alleys in the town. The purpose of the closure was to allow the Folsom Water Power Company to build a water canal from the dam next to Folsom Prison down to a new powerhouse at the foot of Scott Street on the American River.[17] The petition was granted, and five years later, in 1895, Sacramento would receive electricity from the new Folsom powerhouse.

In May of 1890, Amos would have celebrated 30 years of marriage to Ruth.[18] Since the death of his wife in 1878, Amos had made a comfortable life for himself and his children at 819 O Street.[19] By 1890, most of the children were fairly independent and either starting careers or in high school. Alexander Catlin, Amos' oldest son, became a Notary Public and was working at Amos' law office.[20] Truly cementing Amos' place and stature in Sacramento, his portrait was included in the 1890 publication "An Illustrated History of Sacramento County."[21]

An Illustrated History of Sacramento County, California, Wm. J. Davis, 1890

Superior Court Judge Nomination

47. Portrait of Amos Catlin in "An Illustrated History of Sacramento County, California," Wm. J. Davis, 1890.

To have one's portrait in a history book generally signifies either that you are dead or that your big accomplishments in life have already taken place. While Amos was not slowing down in terms of his law practice or withdrawing from providing sage advice to the city and county, he was no longer climbing political hills. At the 1890 Republican County Convention,

Amos P. Catlin

with little rancor and a good dose of harmony, Amos was selected to be the party's nominee for Sacramento Superior Court Judge.[22] Amos made no grand speech and only commented that it had been the custom of his friends to call him "Judge," and he saw a fair prospect of honorably acquiring that title.[23]

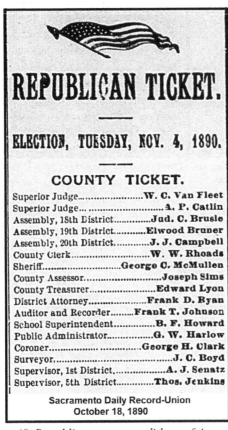

The Sacramento Daily Union stated, "In the selection of Hon. A.P. Catlin for the other Judgeship of the Superior Court, the Convention did itself honor and recognized the high legal attainments and eminent services of one of the foremost citizens of the State. His nomination is a tower of strength to the ticket, and but a small reward to one of the first of pioneer Republicans and a citizen who has done so much for his State."[24] The Sacramento Bee endorsed Amos with the headline, "The Reputation of Judge Catlin Stands Unchallenged."[25]

At the Democratic County Convention, the delegates endorsed Amos for Superior Court Judge along with the Republican incumbent W. C. Van Fleet.[26] An independent citizen's ticket, meant to nominate men who were free from political control, also endorsed Amos and Van Fleet.[27] Typical of Amos, he did not campaign, but it was only he and Van Fleet on the ballot. On

48. Republican party candidacy of Amos Catlin for Sacramento County Superior Court Judge, 1890.

November 4, 1890, Amos was elected a Sacramento Superior Court Judge. Van Fleet garnered 8,346 votes, and Amos tallied 8,345 ballots cast in his favor.[28]

In December, Amos' old friend, Charles Lincoln Wilson, died. Wilson had only recently visited Amos to congratulate him on his election win.[29] Amos knew Wilson from the early days, when Wilson started the Sacramento Valley Railroad endeavor. Wilson introduced Amos to Theodore Judah, and Amos stayed in contact with Judah's widow, Anna, after Judah's death. Amos and Wilson also

Amos P. Catlin

owned property together in Tehama County. As many of Amos' old acquaintances were passing away, he was starting a very exciting and demanding chapter of his life as a judge.

Before Amos was sworn in as a Sacramento Superior Court Judge, he had to wrap up most of his law practice business. The Sacramento Trustees were staggered to receive a bill from Amos for $5,000 to cover his legal services. The invoice covered 31 different actions, most of them related to lawsuits brought by bondholders.[30] While the invoice was a surprise to the city, it had been Amos' legal work and guidance that had saved Sacramento 10 times that amount claimed by bondholders seeking interest on bonds that were several years past their maturity dates.

[1] Sacramento Daily Union, Volume 60, Number 24, 18 September 1888
[2] Sacramento Daily Union, Volume 59, Number 142, 7 August 1888
[3] Sacramento Union, December 6, 1888
[4] Sacramento County Deed book 18921202, pages 155 and 156, November 26, 1892
[5] Sacramento County Deed book 18950610, page 484, February 21, 1895
[6] Sacramento Daily Union, Volume 91, Number 145, 21 July 1896
[7] Sacramento County Deed book 18810317, page 359, October 13, 1871
[8] Placer Herald, Volume 36, Number 47, 4 August 1888
[9] Sacramento Daily Union, Volume 59, Number 133, 27 July 1888
[10] Sacramento Daily Union, Volume 59, Number 133, 27 July 1888
[11] Sacramento Daily Union, Volume 59, Number 133, 27 July 1888
[12] Sacramento Daily Union, Volume 1, Number 35, 12 January 1890
[13] Sacramento Daily Union, Volume 62, Number 145, 7 February 1890
[14] Sacramento Bee, January 20, 1890
[15] Sacramento Daily Union, Volume 62, Number 133, 24 January 1890
[16] Sacramento Daily Union, Volume 62, Number 133, 24 January 1890
[17] Sacramento Daily Union, Volume 79, Number 12, 7 March 1890
[18] Sacramento Daily Union, Volume 1, Number 51, 4 May 1890
[19] Sacramento Daily Union, Volume 58, Number 78, 19 November 1887
[20] Sacramento Daily Union, Volume 79, Number 47, 18 April 1890
[21] Sacramento Daily Union, Volume 79, Number 49, 19 April 1890
[22] Daily Alta California, Volume 83, Number 25, 25 July 1890
[23] Sacramento Daily Union, Volume 79, Number 130, 25 July 1890
[24] Sacramento Daily Union, Volume 79, Number 131, 26 July 1890
[25] Sacramento Bee, June 14, 1890
[26] Daily Alta California, Volume 83, Number 88, 26 September 1890
[27] Sacramento Daily Union, Volume 80, Number 44, 11 October 1890
[28] Sacramento Daily Union, Volume 80, Number 80, 22 November 1890
[29] Sacramento Bee, December 11, 1890
[30] Sacramento Bee, December 29, 1890

Amos P. Catlin

Chapter Sixteen: Judge Amos, Libel, McClatchy Contempt, 1891 - 1896

It was the most demanding job he had ever had. It was the most time-consuming job he had ever had. The duties of Superior Court Judge in Sacramento County would demonstrate to Amos why youth was an important attribute for performing the job. The judgeship would take a toll on his health. His temper would flare, and his patience would wear thin. There were also young adult children, aging relatives, and estate litigation vying for Judge Amos' attention. It all made for one of the busiest periods of Amos' life. However, despite all the challenges of the job and family, Amos was perhaps never happier than when swimming in the lake of law all day long.

49. Sacramento Superior Court Judge Amos Catlin, ca 1891. California State Library

Judge Amos' court would be Department One, and Judge Van Fleet's Department Two. The significant difference between the two departments was that Van Fleet agreed to handle all of the murder trials, although Amos did have to sit for one murder trial and sentencing. Plus, because Amos had represented Sacramento City in numerous bond lawsuits, Van Fleet handled certain litigation brought against the city. Otherwise, over the six years that Amos sat on the bench, he adjudicated a wide variety of civil and criminal actions.

Some of the court actions that filled Judge Amos' court calendar for six days of the week were:

• Appeals to regional Justice of the Peace and city court decisions, including numerous habeas corpus rulings;

Amos P. Catlin

- Divorce cases, with the top reasons to dissolve the marriage being desertion, cruelty, failure to support financially, and habitual intemperance;

- Civil lawsuits involving contracts, government disputes and libel;

- Criminal complaints for arson, assault, burglary, grand larceny, theft, and one murder trial;

- Grand Jury supervision and impaneling of Grand Jurors;

- Insolvency cases in which individuals could no longer meet their financial obligations. Similar to bankruptcy cases, the judge would order certain items of the petitioner sold for debt repayment and issue a protective order to prevent other assets, such as a home, from being seized;

- Issuing orders, such as a writ of mandamus, to a Sheriff for action;

- Juvenile crimes and delinquency cases, in which Amos sentenced several minors to the Whittier Industrial School;

- Naturalization of foreign-born individuals (from countries including Australia, Austria, Azores Islands, Canada, Denmark, England, France, Germany, Italy, Mexico, Norway, Portugal, and Switzerland) to become U.S. citizens; and

- Probate cases involving authorization of an individual to dispose of the assets of the deceased.

Layered on top of his Sacramento County duties, Amos would also occasionally fill the seat for a Judge in Yolo or Placer counties who may have been taken ill or had a conflict of interest in the case presented. There were also times when judges from those neighboring counties sat in place of Amos when he was not able to oversee a case.

The first couple of weeks for Judge Amos were routine and sedate on the bench. There was the constant stream of divorce suits, an election case involving disputed ballots, insolvent debtors, and a runaway teenager.

Then Judge Amos traveled to Auburn to substitute for Placer County Superior Court Judge Prewett. There, Amos was greeted by 15 different lawyers representing different clients in an action against the owners of the Eclipse Mine in Ophir, down the road from Auburn. It would take all afternoon to hear the pleadings of each of the attorneys outlining the mountains of documents they were filing. The Auburn Journal noted, "...and before night Judge Catlin wished he was dead or in jail."[1] Amos packed up all of the court filings in the Eclipse Mine case and headed back to Sacramento; he had other cases to attend to while he did his research.

Family Court

Before there was a Family Court department, there were Superior Court Judges making decisions about the welfare of minor children. One case was of the runaway teenager whose brother wanted his sister back home at Robber's Hill near Folsom.[2] Seventeen-year-old Mary, a native of Portugal, had not run away from her brother, but was living with another family in the Robber's Hill area. When asked why she left her home, her response was that her brother did not approve of her boyfriend, so she had decided to live with another family, where she would be allowed to see her beau.[3]

Judge Amos' decisions involving the young lady's residence were not of any legal consequence, as he just followed the law and precedence. The discussion between Judge Amos and the lawyers provides a glimpse of Amos' attitudes toward young women and how, in 1891, perceptions regarding a woman's independence were shifting. Attorney Estabrook, arguing on Mary's behalf, stated, "She has a right to keep company with whom she pleases… and there is no law to stop her."[4]

Somewhat surprised at the attorney's argument about a young woman's freedom of choice, Judge Amos replied to attorney Estabrook, "You think so, do you? Well, I can inform you differently. This young lady is a minor and cannot do as she pleases. She is not her own mistress until she is of age. She cannot keep company with whom she pleases, with the view of getting married."[5] Estabrook continued to protest that Mary was old enough to make her own decisions regarding living arrangements and potential marriage. Amos held firm. "I am not satisfied… to allow this young lady to remain with a person who, knowing her to be a minor, had encouraged her to marry, when it was in violation of the law, besides knowing that her intended husband was a worthless character who could not support her after he married her. She is alone in the world, and in a strange country. Her brother is her only relative in America, and I think his motive in trying to save her is very praise worthy."[6]

Heavily influencing Judge Amos' decision to award custody of Mary to her brother, an employed and stable adult, was his own experience as a father. His daughter, Ruth, was also 17 in 1891. Ruth was fortunate that, even though she lost her mother when she was five, Amos had provided a secure and comfortable home for her and her brothers. Amos did not need to sit in judgment of numerous divorce cases thus far in his short career on the bench to have gained an understanding of the trainwrecks people can make of their lives with ill-conceived decisions based on love. In making his ruling, he truly believed he was helping a young woman avoid making a mistake that would affect the rest of her life.

Superior Court judges in 1891 also had to rely on their own experiences with humanity to determine the sanity of individuals accused of crimes. Judge Amos visited Thomas English, incarcerated at the county jail and accused of shooting his stepfather, Joseph Morrow, in Elk Grove. English declared that he was King of the United States, and Morrow had worked to depose him of his position.[7] With little dispute from doctors or attorneys, Amos ordered English committed to the Stockton asylum for the insane.[8]

Carpenter Impeachment

Another young man whose sanity might have been called into question was Stockton attorney Amos Carpenter. Judge Amos, in an almost routine case, found attorney Carpenter, along with his client D.M. Vance, in contempt of court for violating an injunction related to property Vance claimed to own, and the dispute was in the courts. Judge Amos sentenced both Carpenter and Vance either to pay a fine of $200 or spend 100 days in jail.[9]

Carpenter was so incensed with the sentence that he drew up articles of impeachment against Judge Amos and mailed them to the Speaker of the California Assembly. As foundation for the impeachment action, Carpenter wrote that Judge Amos "...willfully, maliciously, corruptly and fraudulently found Carpenter and D.M. Vance guilty of contempt...."[10] The problem for Carpenter was that Judge Amos was in possession of letters from Carpenter instructing Vance to violate the court injunction by renting the property in question to another individual.[11]

Members of the Assembly and Amos were surprised by the impeachment request. Judge Amos said, "I thought of making the punishment heavier, but finally determined to make the amount of the fine $200, since there were two of them involved in the affair."[12] Judge Amos then went through how he listened to testimony in the case for an entire day and then rendered a written opinion. To show how lenient he had been with Carpenter and Vance, Judge Amos said, "When I sentenced the men last Saturday, at Carpenter's request, I withheld the commitment [to pay the fine] until next Saturday. I don't know what will be done by the Legislature, but I can say that both of these men will have to pay their fines Saturday, or I'll send them to jail."[13]

The following Saturday, in a defiant tone, Carpenter told Judge Amos he would not pay the fine. Carpenter and Vance were then escorted to the Sacramento Jail.[14] The Assembly Judiciary Committee convened and dismissed all impeachment articles against Judge Amos.[15] Carpenter and Vance appealed their sentences to

Amos P. Catlin

the California Supreme Court, which declined to intervene in their sentence.[16] Carpenter stated that he would rot in jail before paying the fine.[17] However, in less than a week, Carpenter decided to pay the fine of $182, reduced by $2 for each day spent in confinement. Carpenter's client, Vance, decided he liked the jail food and elected to remain in custody.[18]

Grove Johnson Law School

Judge Amos was not above learning new aspects of the law, even from the attorneys representing their clients in court. In one particular case, Grove Johnson was defending a gentleman accused of being part of an illegal gambling operation. Because a witness was absent, the court agreed to have previous testimony of the absent witness read by the stenographers. The testimony was very damaging to Johnson's client.

Even though Johnson had initially objected to the reading of the testimony, his mood lightened, and he asked for more of the testimony to be read aloud. The additional testimony read included Johnson's client testifying about another man on trial for the same crime. Both District Attorney Ryan and Judge Amos were surprised by Johnson's encouragement that all the damning testimony be read to the jury. At the conclusion of the recital, Johnson asked for the jury to be excused so he could make a motion for consideration by the court.

When the jury had recessed, Johnson asked Judge Amos to acquit his client of the gaming charges. His argument was based on Section 334 of the Penal Code, which stated that a person who testifies in a gaming trial cannot be prosecuted for any offense concerning which he previously testified. In a sense, the law had been written to provide immunity to witnesses who would testify against other individuals charged with a crime of gaming.

District Attorney Ryan protested vehemently. Judge Amos cleaned his glasses and proceeded to read, and then re-read, the code. He then looked up at District Attorney Ryan and said that Grove Johnson was correct. The jury was called back into the room, and Judge Amos informed them the defendant was entitled to an acquittal.[19] It had been a big gamble for Grove Johnson to employ the witness immunity strategy. But Johnson knew that, even though he and Judge Amos had engaged in bitter political and legal fights in the past, as a judge, Amos was true to his word to be impartial in all matters brought before him.

Words mattered, and Judge Amos could be a literalist. His decision in the gambling case hinged on the words "trick," "fraud," "witness," and "testimony" in order to determine that Grove Johnson's client should be acquitted. Amos had argued enough cases before the Supreme Court to understand that it was the words and their definitions, not necessarily assumed legislative intent, that determined the reach of a law. Of course, the men executing those laws, such as police, sheriff, and district attorneys, would assign their own liberal interpretations of the laws' meaning.

Ah Jim Peanuts

In the spring of 1891, Ah Jim, a man of Chinese descent, was found guilty of selling peanuts without a license on the streets of Sacramento. Ah Jim appealed the decision of Police Court Judge Cravens to Superior Court Judge Amos. The foundation of the appeal was that the city ordinance specified that a license was needed to peddle fruits, nuts, and candy from a hand basket. Ah Jim was selling his peanuts out of a sack.[20]

From the perspective of Judge Amos, Ah Jim was not guilty because he was using a sack, not a hand basket. In reversing the decision of Judge Cravens, Judge Amos stated, "The ordinance is not against peddling peanuts, but is against peddling them in a hand-basket. I can readily understand that there might be no objections to the peddling of peanuts, while the mode of peddling them might be objectionable. As a matter of construction, I am limited to the words used and cannot speculate upon the intention of the authors of the ordinance. I can find no way of construing a 'sack' to mean a 'hand-basket'. If the ordinance had been directed against peddling from a 'sack' I would find it difficult to construe the word 'sack' to mean a 'hand-basket.'"[21]

Chinese Habeas Corpus

General public sentiment in Sacramento at that time was anti-Chinese. This fact led some law enforcement officers to interpret or enforce certain laws in a more discriminatory fashion against Chinese individuals. Oddly, there were sometimes conspiracy scenarios between law enforcement personnel and some Chinese people, when the outcome was beneficial to both parties. Judge Amos had already expressed his opinion that, even though he was not a supporter of Chinese residency in California, nonetheless, Chinese residents must receive equal treatment under the law.

Amos was not naïve to either the discrimination or the conspiracies that were part of the relationship between law enforcement and the Chinese, and he was not going to tolerate it in his courtroom. But as a judge, Amos was forced to participate in complicated drama and dealings that were not unique in 1890s Sacramento.

Gum Ho, a Chinese woman who had been living in Colusa, was arrested by Sacramento Police based on a letter from the Marshall of Colusa stating she was the victim of a kidnapping. In fact, the Chinese men with her appeared to be aiding her transport to San Francisco. Shortly after Gum Ho's arrest, Mrs. Kepperson of the San Francisco Chinese Mission arrived and informed Police Chief Moses Drew that Gum Ho's intent was to reach San Francisco, in order to escape the life of prostitution into which she had been forced in Colusa. Chief Drew told Kepperson he was following the regulations and holding Gum Ho for Marshal Scroggins of Colusa, to be returned to her husband.[22]

Kepperson then engaged attorney Charles Jones to represent Gum Ho, and he filed a habeas corpus petition for her release. All of the confusion and obfuscation surrounding the case landed in the courtroom of Judge Amos. The next day, at the appointed hour, Judge Amos' courtroom was filled with Chinese men from San Francisco and Colusa, along with law enforcement officials from Colusa. Judge Amos found no legal grounds for detaining Gum Ho and ordered her released, but not until the 10:40 AM train to Colusa had left the station. In fact, Amos had stalled Gum Ho's release, to prevent Colusa law enforcement from seizing Gum Ho on some other charge and transporting her back to the house of prostitution.[23]

As speculated, once the order to release Gum Ho was finalized, a Sheriff Deputy from Colusa arrested her and led her from the courtroom. Summoning the loudest voice he could muster, the 68-year-old Judge Amos demanded Gum Ho be brought back into his courtroom. With a dead-straight gaze, Judge Amos inquired who the arresting officer was, directly pointing at the man with outstretched arm and index finger. The man replied that his name was Scroggins, Marshal of Colusa City.[24]

"Well, Mr. Scroggins," lectured Judge Amos, "don't attempt to arrest that woman in this courtroom. I won't allow any such proceeding here!" Scroggins apologized and promptly arrested Gum Ho outside of the courtroom, on embezzlement and theft charges. Since the train to Colusa had already left town, Scroggins and Gum Ho were forced to linger in the city. This gave attorney Jones enough time to draft a new writ of habeas corpus, which Judge Amos promptly signed.[25]

Marshall Scroggins engaged George Blanchard, Amos' former law partner, to represent his case before Judge Amos at the habeas corpus hearing. Attorney Jones argued that the complaint was filed by the husband of Gum Ho. Blanchard argued that the relationship between the complainant and Gum Ho was not known and not relevant. However, the Chinese gentleman, hoping to get Gum Ho back to Colusa, had brought with him the certificate of marriage between him and Gum Ho.[26]

The marriage certificate, intended to be used to affirm the gentleman's right to take Gum Ho back to Colusa, instead proved to be his undoing. Judge Amos opined that the law was clear that a husband cannot testify against his wife on a charge of embezzlement. Were it true that the husband was the complainant, under

Amos P. Catlin

the law, he must release Gum Ho. By this point, the purported husband had disappeared from the courtroom.[27] Judge Amos had no choice but to have Gum Ho remanded into the custody of the Sacramento County Jail.[28]

The charade of Colusa law enforcement's effort to arrest Gum Ho would continue into Judge Van Fleet's courtroom. In between habeas corpus hearings and the filing of new arrest warrants, lawyer Jones was able to secure the release of Gum Ho from jail, as she technically was not being held on any charges. Jones escorted Gum Ho to a waiting carriage, which it was suspected would take her to San Francisco.[29]

Gum Ho's absent husband, Hong Lung Chung, was arrested in Sacramento in the Chinese quarter on I street on attempted kidnapping charges and was found to be concealing numerous weapons, including a knife and pistol.[30] Sam Wo, a Sacramento Chinese man attempting to help Gum Ho escape to San Francisco, reported to the police that he had been warned that he was marked for death by a Chinese gang who wanted the young woman returned to Colusa.[31]

Disconcerting to all involved was the appearance that Colusa law enforcement was in cahoots with Chinese criminal activity. Amos was angered that elected and deputized men, sworn to uphold the law, would use the justice system, and his courtroom, to sustain seemingly unlawful activities. Shortly after the courtroom incidents involving Gum Ho, Amos' home was burglarized.[32]

Ah Wing Whiskey

Like any good judge, Judge Amos suppressed his own personal opinions regarding some laws passed by the legislature. Some laws clearly were discriminatory, especially to the Chinese and Native Americans, and ultimately might not withstand the scrutiny of the Supreme Court if challenged. Ah Wing, a Chinese gentleman, pleaded guilty to selling liquor to Native Americans working on a hop farm. The Native American men gave money to Ah Wing to buy whiskey for them. Ah Wing did not know it was illegal to buy alcohol for Native Americans. Upon review of the facts of the case, Judge Amos imposed a light sentence. The lenient sentence was Judge Amos' small judicial commentary on the absurdity of a law under which the Legislature had, as he noted in court, recently made buying Native Americans alcohol a felony.[33]

H Street Burglary

Judge Amos had moved from his home on O Street[34] to H Street, making for a shorter commute to the Sacramento County Courthouse. In the first burglary of Amos' home, his son, Alex, scared the intruders away.[35] The third burglary was the most daring, as the intruder forced the live-in housekeeper, Kate Rogers, to

Amos P. Catlin

ingest laudanum. This gave the burglar more time to rifle through the house looking for items to steal.[36] Amos was finally awakened by the young woman's groans for help. The thief was gone, all the doors to the house left open. Amos grabbed his shotgun and searched the vicinity, with no sighting of the villain.[37]

Sacramento County Superior Court was one of the busier courthouses because Sacramento was the State Capital. Disputes arising from state operations often landed first in the Sacramento Courthouse. Since Amos had been in the Legislature, had a lifetime of court experience, and was thoroughly knowledgeable about the state's Constitution, few men were in a better position to adjudicate disputes within the executive branch of government.

Ramie Murray Decision

In June of 1891, the State's Controller was refusing to pay the salary of the newly appointed superintendent for the promotion of ramie culture, on the basis that the law creating the position was unconstitutional. The Legislature passed "An Act to encourage the cultivation of ramie in the State of California, to provide a bounty for ramie fiber and to make an appropriation therefor; to appoint a State Superintendent of Ramie Culture and make an appropriation for his salary."[38] Judge Amos ruled in Controller Colgan's favor in determining the Act was unconstitutional.

Specifically, Judge Amos ruled, the Act was contrary to the thirty-fourth section of article 4 of the Constitution, which stated that no law shall contain more than one appropriation of money except the State Budget. The Act contained two appropriations, one to pay farmers for planting the ramie crop and another to pay the salary of Superintendent of Ramie Culture W. H. Murray. Judge Amos noted in his decision, "It would be difficult to frame an Act more clearly in violation of the section of the Constitution above quoted. It needs no reasoning nor argument to make it apparent. The mere reading of the Act and the Constitution is sufficient. It is imperative upon the court to disregard the Act, and to hold it null and void."[39]

Bailiffs

While Judge Amos normally ran a relaxed courtroom, patiently listening to the arguments of attorneys and not rushing the proceedings, there were operational aspects beyond his control. A constant irritant for Judge Amos was the shortage of bailiffs. The sheriff deputies assigned to be courtroom bailiffs would routinely be pulled away to serve subpoenas, round up jurors, or locate witnesses. The shortage of bailiffs boiled over in the summer of 1891. When no bailiff was present for Judge Amos during a case, he instructed his clerk to summon Sheriff Stanley to explain the lack of deputies assigned as bailiffs to his courtroom.[40]

Amos P. Catlin

In Sheriff Stanley's stead, Under Sheriff Benjamin Bugbey arrived in the courtroom to plead the case that the Sheriff's department was understaffed. Judge Amos examined Bugbey: "Why is it, sir, that my court is not attended by a Sheriff?"[41]

Bugbey replied, "Well, your honor, we have been caught in another pinch and have not men enough to do the work. Our deputies are all out on court business, though—serving subpoenas for you. The trouble is, we have not enough deputies." In an irritated tone, Judge Amos quipped, "Go and hire some more." Bugbey replied, "Well, if we do that, we will have to pay them ourselves —the Supervisors won't."[42]

It was no surprise to Judge Amos that Sacramento County ran a lean operation in light of the demands of the court. He replied to Bugbey, and to the courtroom in general, "It strikes me that it is rather poor economy on the part of the county, to allow such an important office as this to go unequipped. I will insist upon having a bailiff here constantly during the session of the court. I will look into this matter."[43]

On another occasion, needing the assistance of a court bailiff, Judge Amos deputized a court janitor to carry on some court business. In yet another pique, Judge Amos had decided to command Sheriff Stanley to hire more deputies, and he would compel the County Supervisors to pay them. Sheriff Stanley was not averse to this judicial strategy of increasing his staff of deputies.[44]

Divorce Court

Judge Amos had represented many different individuals in divorce suits as an attorney. He understood that private lives can be messy and chaotic, as opposed to his own sedate private life. As a judge, Amos quickly grew weary of some of the drama and spitefulness that accompanied private disputes. On more than one occasion, he revealed his opinions about some of the frivolous and vengeful actions toward the parties in the divorce cases.

After five years of attempting to gain a divorce from her husband, Mrs. Wagner finally succeeded in 1891. Mr. Wagner had always contested the divorce proceedings, but a divorce was finally granted on the grounds of desertion; Mr. Wagner was no longer living with his wife. A few weeks after the divorce was granted, Mrs. Wagner married a Mr. Wohlfrom from Yolo County. At the beginning of October 1891, the newly married Mrs. Wohlfrom commenced action to order her ex-husband to pay her court costs and legal fees associated with the divorce Mr. Wagner never wanted.[45]

Amos P. Catlin

Before Judge Amos, attorneys Hiram and Albert Johnson, representing Mr. Wagner, read a long affidavit sworn out by Mr. Wagner. He contended that, along with never wanting a divorce, he was only earning $50 to $60 per month as a mechanic. His income had been reduced on account of an injury that had left him without the use of one hand. His savings were depleted on account of the constant legal costs associated with fighting the divorce from his ex-wife. Finally, his ex-wife's new husband, Mr. Wolhfrom, had property in Yolo County assessed at $55,000, indicating he was in a better position to cover her court costs and legal fees for the divorce she wanted.[46]

Former Judge McKune, the esteemed and venerable pioneer lawyer of Sacramento, objected to Judge Amos' musing that Mr. Wohlfrom should pay his new wife's legal fees. McKune quipped, "Does your honor propose to decide this case without hearing our side?" Judge Amos replied, "Oh, I know all about the case. I remember when the testimony was being taken and am familiar with it. This man is a cripple, really, and not a sound workingman. She has married a man who is more than able to pay all of her litigation expenses."[47]

McKune argued that Judge Amos was proposing that an outside party pay for the legal expenses of someone else. That certainly was not normal procedure under any circumstances. Judge Amos concurred with McKune. However, McKune persisted to argue that the new husband should not be liable for his new wife's divorce court costs. To which Amos replied, "What's the use of her having a husband?"[48]

The spectators in the courtroom, understanding the sarcasm of the exchange, burst into laughter. Judge Amos let McKune continue his arguments as to why Mr. Wagner, and not Mr. Wohlfrom, should pay the legal fees. Hiram Johnson rose to rebut McKune's arguments, but Judge Amos waved him off. Judge Amos then rendered his opinion quickly from the bench, "I think that this new husband should help his wife as far as helping her pay her court costs, anyhow. The defendant Wagner is only getting a small salary, and is not able to make any great outlay, I will deny the motion to have him pay the costs and counsel fees."[49]

Not all divorce cases had an acrimonious ending. The Rodgerdts had filed for divorce, and the case was being heard by Judge Amos. Attorney Grove Johnson, representing one of the parties, announced before the beginning of one of the court hearings that the couple had decided to drop all further proceedings and resume their former marital bliss. Judge Amos, in a note of resignation and irritation at having the court's time wasted, remarked, "It seems to have required the labor of several attorneys and sixteen days labor of this court to convince these parties that they ought to live together."[50]

Amos P. Catlin

Workload, Illness

By all accounts, Amos aggressively tackled his new job as a Superior Court Judge in his first year. While his demeanor on the bench was slow and deliberate, it was noted that he quickly rendered decisions and did not tolerate foolishness on the part of the attorneys. By the end of the year, clearly exhausted, Amos was taken ill. His doctor advised him to rest at home for several days.[51] Attention to his absence was muted by the fact his courtroom was being renovated to match that of Judge Van Fleets.[52] An update on his health condition in the local papers reported that Judge Amos hoped to be back in the office in the first week of January 1892.[53]

FILLING UP FOLSOM.

———

Judge Catlin's Contribution This Afternoon.

———

HE DISPOSES OF CRIMINALS IN SHORT ORDER.

Sacramento Bee, December 4, 1891

50. Judge Catlin noted for quick verdicts and sentencing, filling up Folsom State Prison, 1891.

In the spring of 1892, Amos would become ill once again, requiring a lengthy stay at home. His illness may have been related to his son, who had the mumps a few weeks earlier. Judge Prewett of Placer County came down from Auburn and filled in for Amos until he recovered.[54] It would take several weeks for Amos, the California pioneer, to recover and resume normal courtroom duties.[55]

One issue that slowed down the court system was poor administration. Judges Van Fleet and Amos demanded that the county send them the names of 400 trial jurors and 100 grand jurors. Both judges had immense problems with lists sent over from the county with misspelled names or containing individuals not subject to jury duty.[56] The county's poor management of juror selection continued. In a group of 60 men called to be jurors in March 1893, only nine met the requirement of being on the property assessment roll, as required by law. Frustrated at the waste of time, Judge Amos said the Board of Supervisors ought to be indicted for misconduct, as many men were summoned and put to the trouble of traveling to court unnecessarily.[57]

Court Banter

Judge Amos took liberties with some of the old guard lawyers in Sacramento, such as John McKune and Grove Johnson. Many of the attorneys practicing in Sacramento since the 1850s knew each other, were old friends, and over the years had been co-counsel in cases as well as opponents in the courtroom and in the political arena. Since stepping into the role of judge, Amos could be more relaxed in his discourse with attorneys representing clients before him.

Judge Amos enjoyed needling his old lawyer friends presenting their cases. It was during an arson case that Judge Amos already knew the strategy the defense lawyer, Grove Johnson, was going to play. Johnson was reading select sections of a witness testimony in defending his client related to the arson fire at the Galt Arcade Stables. District Attorney Ryan objected to the selected passages as being out of context with the testimony.[58]

Grove Johnson was instructed by Judge Amos to read the whole testimony. Johnson objected to having the court dictate the presentation of his case. Judge Amos replied, "Then Mr. Ryan may read it." Angered to have the prosecuting attorney presenting his defense case, Johnson began a lengthy objection. Judge Amos stopped Johnson and remarked, "Now, don't interject a long speech into an objection."[59]

As Attorney Johnson continued to pursue his objection, Judge Amos relented: "Well, how much of a speech do you want to make?" he asked, prompting muffled courtroom laughter. Johnson said, "I got through when you interrupted me." Judge Amos, feeling a little spry and having some fun, continued, "No, you're not through yet, you're still talking. Read the testimony, Mr. Ryan." After District Attorney Ryan finished reading the transcript, Judge Amos overruled District Attorney Ryan's objection, and the evidence introduced went as lawyer Johnson had wanted the whole time.[60]

There were other times when Judge Amos spoke to no one in particular from the bench. During the murder trial of two Chinese men, the proceedings were disrupted by the long, loud whistle that signaled noontime at the railroad shops. Interrupting the examination of a witness, Judge Amos said, "I don't know which makes more noise, the Chinese, the lawyers, or the whistles. We'll take recess until 1:30 to ascertain, and in the meantime, we can have our lunch."

Legal Opinions and Rulings

Superior Court is usually the first judicial branch to issue rulings on whether a practice or action established under local and state laws is consistent with California's Constitution. Often, these rulings and orders would eventually be appealed to the California Supreme Court. Judge Amos issued his fair share of rulings defining practices, which then became the rule if or until they were overturned by the state Supreme Court.

In lieu of a federal bankruptcy petition, local individuals would apply to the Superior Court to be declared insolvent debtors when their debts were greater than

---

SUPERIOR COURT.

Department One—Catlin, Judge.

FRIDAY, July 29, 1892.

Mary J. Warren vs. Frank Warren—Demurrer withdrawn, ten days to answer.

M. Denzer vs. Fred Cox, et al.—Continued one week

Alexander Scroggs vs. P. G. Wermuth, et al. —Set for September 24th.

W. H. Devine vs. Frank Swift—Continued one week.

In re P. B. Bradford, an insolvent debtor— Petition to set aside homestead granted.

T. M. Lindley & Co. vs. John Skelton—Judgment for plaintiff.

Honsage vs. Keefer—Continued one week.

In re J. S. O'Callaghan—An insolvent debtor.

Trial Calendar, Department One—A. P. Catlin, Judge.

COURT CASES.

City of Sacramento vs. J. M. Gattman—September 19th.

Kirk, Geary & Co. vs Burn et al.—September 19th.

R. Wood vs. Washburne–September 20th. Davis vs. Parker—September 5th.

Fisher vs. Martin—September 22d.

Burr vs. Comstock—September 22d.

Churchman vs. Todd—September 24th.

Scroggs vs. Wermuth—September 24th.

Warren vs. Connor—September 26th.

Stuber vs. McIntire—September 26th.

Warren vs. Brissell—September 28th.

Peters vs. Garzia et al.—September 5th.

Burris vs. Clark—October 31st.

American Hosiery Company vs. Fred Mason—September 21st.

JURY CASES.

People vs. Hickey & Brown—October 3d.

People vs. Eben Bent—October 3d.

People vs. J. J. Sullivan—October 4th.

People vs. Ah Jim—October 4th.

People vs. John O'Brien—October 5th.

People vs. Louis Myers—October 5th.

People vs. William Johnson and James Wilson—October 6th.

People vs. Minnie Tobin—October 6th.

People vs. Jack Taylor—October 10th.

People vs. Fong Ah Foon—October 17th.

Wilder vs. Kaerth—October 24th.

Startsman vs. Brissell—October 25th.

Denzer vs. Cox—October 26th.

Warburton vs. Graham—October 27th.

In re W. J. O'Brien—October 27th.

Shannon vs. Wittpen—October 25th.

**Sacramento Daily Record-Union
July 30, 1892**

51. Judge Catlin's court calendar for July 1892.

their assets, hiring a lawyer to facilitate the insolvent debtor petition. In one such case in 1892, attorney Isaac Joseph filed his fee for the insolvent debtor application of Gus Elkus as a preferred claim upon the estate to be liquidated. The law partnership of Johnson, Johnson, and Johnson, representing Elkus' creditors, objected to Joseph's fee being paid out of the liquidated proceeds. They argued that Gus Elkus, not the estate, should be responsible for paying the attorney's fee.[61]

Under the headline "Judge Catlin Decides a New Point in Insolvency Law," the Sacramento Daily Union reported on Judge Amos' ruling for Isaac Joseph:

"These services were apparently beneficial to the estate and to the general creditors, I cannot find that the question has ever been directly determined in this State. It does not follow as a matter of right that in all cases the attorney for the insolvent, is entitled to be paid for his services as a preferred claim, for his services may not in all cases be beneficial to the estate. But where such services are in the ordinary course, and are beneficial to the whole estate, it seems to me that a reasonable compensation should be made out of the estate."[62]

Amos P. Catlin

Insolvent debtor petitions were a routine part of Judge Amos' court calendar, and justices had some latitude approving the insolvency, liquidation of assets, and repayment terms. One of the petitioners for insolvency who came before Judge Amos was Benjamin Bugbey, former Under Sheriff and Republican Party acquaintance. Bugbey in 1893 had debts from a Shasta County gold mine, a home mortgage, and an ailing wife. Judge Amos granted insolvency status to protect Bugbey's home on N street from foreclosure.[63]

Judge Amos, like many judges, paid close attention to the circumstances that led petitioners to insolvency. Dry goods store owner Mr. Orth was swindled out of money by another individual, which led to financial problems. Orth owed $1,000 to the Bank of D.O. Mills & Co. Lawyers for Orth's creditors requested an order stipulating Orth turn over $1,100 in sales over to his creditors. Judge Amos refused the order declaring, "You can't make a man pay in money which he hasn't got. I do not see any reason why any order should be made of the kind asked."[64]

Another of Judge Amos's rulings that went against law enforcement strategy occurred when he ruled a defendant's confession could not be admitted as evidence because it was coerced. Mr. Dobson had been arrested in the arson of a Galt livery stable. The District Attorney, Chief of Police, and Sheriff all visited Dobson in jail and intimated they knew all about the conspiracy to burn down the livery stable. Dobson confessed to his involvement in the crime.[65]

Dobson's defense attorney, Grove Johnson, brought up the argument that a recent Supreme Court ruling stated that a confession elicited based on inducements or immunity could not be admitted as evidence.[66] In listening to the testimony of the law enforcement officers and Dobson, Judge Amos deduced that there was a reasonable supposition the confession was based on perceived leniency from the District Attorney.

Judge Amos ruled that the confession was not voluntary, and the jury should find the defendant not guilty.[67] The ruling shocked law enforcement and prosecutors. As the Sacramento Bee put it, "A decision which is probably good law, but which cripples the peace and good order of society."[68] This ruling did not score any points with the general public and bolstered Judge Amos' image as being too lenient in his sentencing of convicted criminals.[69] In one instance, Judge Amos allowed a man to reduce a plea of not guilty of assault to commit murder to simple assault. Pedro Rodriguez was arrested for stabbing another man in the back. Upon his admission of guilt on assault charges, Judge Amos sentenced Rodriguez to just 15 days in the county jail.[70]

Even though the mining boom had faded from the region decades earlier, the quest for gold still continued in some parts of Sacramento County. Specifically, John

Amos P. Catlin

Cardwell had excavated tunnels under the town of Folsom to glean gold dust. Jacob Hyman sued Cardwell to stop mining under the streets of Folsom. An action to dissolve the injunction was brought before Judge Amos, a former resident and property owner in Folsom.[71] He refused to dissolve the injunction, preventing Cardwell from creating more tunnels under Leidesdorff Street.[72]

Controversial Rulings, Libel and Contempt

As early as 1892, District Attorney Ryan was lobbying for the State Legislature to authorize a third Superior Court Judge for Sacramento County. The two existing Judges were overwhelmed with civil matters, pushing the DA's criminal trials out several weeks.[73] Judge Van Fleet announced his retirement from the bench in the summer of 1892, citing low pay and the heavy workload.[74] In addition to an explosion of insolvency cases resulting from a sluggish economy, the number of libel lawsuits was also increasing.

In February 1894, while Judge Amos was trying to establish his trial calendar, he was deluged with attorneys representing libel cases. The cases could either be decided by a jury trial or by the court. If the plaintiff wanted the court to rule on the action, that meant Judge Amos would be required to carefully research the precedents and court cases, then render a detailed opinion. Consequently, Judge Amos, overwhelmed with civil and criminal cases, preferred jury trials for libel cases.

As Judge Amos went through the cases, he called out, "Royster vs. V.S. and C.K. McClatchy for libel." Before any of the attorneys in the case could voice their preference, Judge Amos said, "Jury." One of the attorneys tried to plead for a court case. Judge Amos cut him off, saying, "That case goes before a jury." Next up was People vs. McClatchy, and Judge Amos, in exhaustion and exasperation, said "Let these go over for the term, I've had enough."[75]

Libel is simply false statements that are published that are damaging to a person's reputation. Libel law, however, is anything but straightforward. The laws governing libel in California changed frequently. Not only must a judge apply the most recent iteration of the libel law, the actual content and intention of the publisher had to be determined and considered.

Thus, libel cases could be very time consuming. Because Judge Amos liked to thoroughly research every decision he made, libel cases in which he had to rule required an extra amount of work. Consequently, he much preferred libel cases be decided by jury trial, letting men of Sacramento decide if printed statements were libelous and how badly injured the complainant was by the newspaper reporting. Unfortunately, aware of the complicated nature of libel cases, attorneys bringing libel suits preferred that Judge Amos make the decision.

Amos P. Catlin

Gillman v Bee Libel Suit

GILMAN GOES A-FISHING.

WHAT HE EXPECTS TO CATCH.

SOUP

WHERE HE WILL MOST LIKELY LAND.

Sacramento Bee, October 11, 1892

52. The Sacramento Bee editorial cartoon on the merits of the Gilman libel lawsuit, 1892.

There was one case Judge Amos could not toss to a jury: Libel by the Sacramento Bee in the attempted rape case against Charles Gillman. During pre-trial hearings, it became clear that the lawyers for the Sacramento Bee planned to revisit the entire set of assault and rape allegations, with numerous witnesses, in defense of the newspaper. The presentation of evidence made it entirely plausible that a jury would be confused whether their job was to decide Gillman's guilt or innocence or whether they were to determine he had been libeled by the Bee. In addition, testimony about Gillman's behavior would be likely to prejudice the jury against him. In this case, Judge Amos would have to rule.

Stella Truitt had found work as a housekeeper for the Charles H. Gilman family in August of 1892. The Gilman's lived on G Street near 19th, and Gilman was the owner of the long-established dry goods store, Red House, on J Street. Shortly after Truitt was employed by the Gilman's, where she had a room in the house, Mrs. Gilman left for a vacation. After his wife departed, Gilman, as reported in the Sacramento Bee, assaulted Truitt on two separate occasions. As he was naked at the time of the assaults, it was surmised that he wanted to rape her.[76]

After the first assault, because Truitt was desperate for work, she continued working at the house, rationalizing that it was Gilman's drunken state that had led to the assault. The second incident was more violent. Truitt succeeded in pushing Gilman off of her, but Gilman hit her and dislocated her jaw. Truitt decided to leave the residence and the employment. She then swore out a complaint of assault and rape with the Sacramento Police.[77]

Gilman was subsequently arrested and posted bond for his release. He declared that Truitt was released from his employment for neglect of her duties as a house servant. He further stated that Truitt's complaint was an attempt to blackmail him for money. When the criminal matter finally wound its way up to Superior Court in late September, Judge Van Fleet dismissed the accusations as fanciful and improbable. Judge Van Fleet further stated that Gilman never should have been held to answer to the charges with so little evidence.[78]

In early October, Charles Gilman filed a libel lawsuit against the publishers of the Sacramento Bee. Gilman did not sue the competing paper, the Sacramento Union, for libel, as its story was shorter, gave fewer lurid details, and cast doubt on Truitt's story. The Union article led with "A woman named Mrs. Stella Truitt, who says she is a widow, has caused the arrest of C. H. Gilman on a charge of criminal assault."[79] In contrast, the Sacramento Bee's opening paragraph began, "Mrs. Stella Truitt, a widow of twenty-one years, whose husband was killed by falling from a building in Portland, Oregon, told a severe story to Chief Rodgers at noon today. Mrs. Truitt has every appearance of an honest woman, and as she told her story, tears rolled down her cheeks."[80]

Both the Bee and the Union noted that Truitt's jaw was broken or dislocated in a struggle with Gilman, and that she later patronized Gilman's store to buy a hat. The August 20th Bee went further in describing the assaults, reporting that Gilman, in the first attack was, "…partly drunk, and entirely devoid of clothing. According to Mrs. Truitt he engaged in beastly conduct that cannot be described in print." In the second attack, the Bee reported, "He came into her room after she had got into bed, threw himself in a nude state upon the bed, and conducted himself in a most scandalous and indescribable manner."[81]

Gilman hired Grove Johnson as his attorney to sue the Sacramento Bee publishers for libel, demanding $50,000 in damages. The Bee, whose leadership had become accustomed to the parade of libel suits against it, published a cartoon about Gilman. The cartoon depicted Gilman fishing for a $50,000 fish, only to fall into a bowl of his own soup.[82]

The attorneys for the Sacramento Bee, Charles T. Jones and Alvin J. Bruner, waived their right to a jury trial, putting assessment of libel in the hands of Judge Amos. The trial began in late January 1894. The Gilman-Bee libel case would be an 11-day affair. As expected, most of the testimony entered into the record was not about libel. Because the charges of assault and rape against Gilman had been

Amos P. Catlin

dismissed, the Bee attorneys attempted to show Gilman was guilty of the accusations, thereby making the Bee's reporting of the incident factual.

The monotony of the cross examination took a toll on all the participants. Gilman had a hard time recalling certain conversations he had with different people, including Pat Barry, another employee. Gilman was getting and became confused by the questions attorney Jones asked him about Pat. Judge Amos stepped in, directly asking Gilman, "Did you deny it to Pat?" Gilman replied, "I do not know that I did deny it to Pat, as it looked so unreasonable." Then Judge Amos offered, "Then you stood pat on the statement you had made?" A loud groan of "Oh, Judge!" was exclaimed by attorney Grove Johnson. Amos worked hard to suppress a grin, and then the rest of the courtroom caught on to the pun.[83]

Grove Johnson was a rather expressive and emotional lawyer and politician. He never held back, and his closing arguments in the libel case were no different. Johnson directed some of his comments toward his fellow attorneys representing the Bee, Jones and Bruner.

"If the time ever comes, and it may come to you, Mr. Jones, and to you, Mr. Bruner, proud as you may be of your record and your life, you will realize that to be arrested is a very serious matter even in the city of Sacramento. Wait until the shoe pinches your foot, if you both don't cry worse than Gilman did, I misjudge you both."[84]

Grove Johnson had been arrested and put in prison on the charge of voter fraud in the 1860s. He knew how cruel the newspapers could be when it came to unproven accusations. Johnson continued, "No newspaper proprietor yet was ever bold enough to make the charges on the street face to face with the man he libeled in his newspaper. They put in the newspapers things they dare not say on the street. There breathes no newspaper man that dares to repeat to a man on the streets the libels that he published in his paper in the most dastardly and cowardly manner." When Johnson concluded his emotional closing arguments, Judge Amos took the matter under advisement.[85]

On March 27, in the case of C.H. Gilman vs. C.K. McClatchy, et. al, Judge Amos rendered his verdict in favor of Gilman. Judge Amos concluded that $500 was proper compensation for the injury caused to Gilman by the Sacramento Bee's libelous reporting. Judge Amos' rationale for finding that the Sacramento Bee had committed libel was based on his assessment that Stella Truitt's complaint was not supported by the evidence.

"The facts do not produce a belief beyond a reasonable doubt, nor even a belief based upon a preponderating weight of evidence, that there was an attempt made

Amos P. Catlin

to commit the offense. Much less does the evidence support a belief that the crime, charged by the defendants as having been attempted, was actually committed."[86]

Because the Bee did not publish the story with malice toward Gilman and included Gilman's statement that he thought blackmail was afoot, Judge Amos ruled there should be no vindictive damages assessed.[87] The decision against the Bee set off a cacophony of criticism about Judge Amos across the spectrum of different newspapers. The Sacramento Union was one of the few to support Judge Amos's decision. The opinion of the Sacramento Union was that Judge Amos was just applying the law as set down by California.

The Sacramento Bee remained defiant, declaring in print, "If that be the law of the State, then no newspaper will hereafter feel safe in recording the facts connected with any man's arrest until after he has been convicted." They concluded, "If Mr. C.H. Gilman is banking on getting $500, or any other sum, from this paper, he had better postpone his hilarity until he hears from the Supreme Court, for certainly The Bee does not propose to permit this matter to rest here. The fight has only commenced."[88]

The Bee did appeal the libel decision to the California Supreme Court. In March of 1896, the Supreme Court upheld Judge Amos' decision.

"No newspaper has any right to trifle with the reputation of any citizen, or by carelessness or recklessness to injure his good name and fame or business. And the reporter of a newspaper has no more right to collect the stories on the street, or even to gather information from policemen or magistrates, out of court, about a citizen, and to his detriment, and publish such stories and information and facts in a newspaper, than has a person not connected with a newspaper to whisper from ear to ear the gossip and scandal of the street. If true, such publication or such speaking may be privileged, but if false the newspaper, as well as the citizen, must be responsible to anyone who is wronged and damaged thereby."[89] – California Supreme Court, 1896.

McClatchy Contempt Ruling

The quarrels between the Bee and Judge Amos did not end with the libel suit. The court's numerous divorce cases, with their sensational details of the private lives of Sacramento residents, made good copy for the evening Bee newspaper. One divorce case that caught the public's attention was that of a 71-year-old Delta farmer and his very young wife.

At age 71, Charles Talmadge entered into a hasty marriage with Martha Myers in September 1893. Talmadge owned 148 acres outside of Courtland along the Sacramento River. His wife had died in 1891, and he had taken to visiting

Sacramento houses of prostitution, at one of which he met Martha. At the time of their marriage, Martha was 20 years old.[90]

Several weeks after the marriage, Martha was finally able to move into the Talmadge ranch house where Charles' daughter, Mary Jane, also lived. The arrangement did not go well. Both Charles and Mary Jane were abusive to Martha. Mary Jane resented Martha's presence. Charles was frequently drunk and regretted the marriage. Shortly after the marriage in mid-September, Charles Talmadge deeded most of his property to Mary Jane and his other children, excising Martha out of any future death benefit.[91]

JUDGE CATLIN, OF DEPARTMENT NO. TWO.

From a sketch by "The Bee's" artist.

Sacramento Bee, April 21, 1893

53. Sacramento Bee illustration of Judge Catlin presiding in his courtroom, 1893.

After living with Charles for two years, Martha left and filed for divorce. The divorce suit came before Judge Amos in March 1896. The Judge had the discretion to close the proceedings to the public and press, but Judge Amos opted to leave the courtroom doors open. Two of the attorneys from the Gilman-Bee libel suit were present, but now working on opposing sides. Charles Jones was representing Martha Talmadge, and Alvin Bruner was attorney for Charles Talmadge.[92]

The divorce trial was proceeding normally, with all the anticipated accusations of drunkenness, abuse, and treachery, until Charles Talmadge was put on the witness stand at the end of the third day. Even though Charles was so deaf he needed an ear trumpet to hear questions from his lawyer, his ability to hold a grudge was sound.[93] Charles Talmadge blamed the whole marriage affair on attorney Charles Jones, who was representing Martha Talmadge.[94]

Charles Talmadge testified that he had hired Charles Jones to recover some letters from another woman he had met in a house of prostitution on L Street. Talmadge claimed the woman was going to use them to extort money out of him. After Jones took care of the extortion attempt by

Amos P. Catlin

recovering the letters, Talmadge said Jones invited him to a different house of prostitution on 2nd Street in Sacramento.

At the second house of ill-repute, Jones allegedly encouraged Talmadge to pursue one of the women employed there. That woman turned out to be Martha (Minnie) Myers, whom Charles Talmadge would later marry.

After the startling testimony that a prominent Sacramento attorney, very active in local politics, had patronized a house of prostitution, Jones stopped by the Sacramento Bee office to set the record straight. He denied ever coaxing Talmadge to visit the establishment where he met Martha. However, the part of the reported testimony that most irked Jones and his associate, J.B. Devine, was the implication that Jones had gouged Talmadge for $10,000 to recover the letters in the attempted extortion scheme.[95]

The Sacramento Bee reported the courtroom testimony.

"The most dramatic scene was when Talmadge attacked Charles T. Jones, attorney for Mrs. Talmadge. He declared that at one time Jones had 'gouged' him out of $10,000 and at another time he had paid him and I. J. Simmons $1,700 for nothing. The story of the alleged latter transaction was brought out on cross-examination. Talmadge said that he had at one time visited a crib on lower L Street, and the woman in the crib [house of ill-repute] afterwards claimed to have obtained some letters from him which she intended using to make trouble for him. He told his troubles to attorney Jones, who agreed to help him out."[96]

Attorney Devine appealed to Judge Amos to declare the reporting false and a fabrication. Judge Amos agreed, "I have no hesitation in saying that the statement to which counsel has just referred is a grossly false statement – a gross fabrication. There was not the slightest ground in the testimony of Mr. Talmadge upon which such a statement could be based, and it is a reflection upon Mr. Talmadge, as much, perhaps, as it is on Mr. Jones. Mr. Talmadge never made the statement that, as this article states, he had visited a crib on L street, etc. etc. I do not know that, as at present advised, the court has any power to prevent such conduct on the part of newspaper reporter, or to punish them for such gross outrages." The one power Judge Amos did have was to close the doors to the trial to public and press, and he did.[97]

On May 29th, after the doors to the trial had been closed to reporters, Charles K. McClatchy, editor and one of the publishers of the Sacramento Bee, wrote an editorial excoriating attorneys Jones and Devine and Judge Amos. McClatchy asserted that the reporting of the Talmadge testimony was accurate and intimated that Judge Amos was in cahoots with the attorneys.

Amos P. Catlin

"The Bee of yesterday was the statement he [Talmadge] made upon the stand at Wednesday afternoon's session. The Bee will go farther than that. It will declare that both the attorney before the bar and the Judge on the bench knew that the statement made in The Bee was essentially correct epitome of the testimony given by Mr. Talmadge, at the very moment when they unhesitatingly, shamelessly, and brazenly declared it to be a 'gross fabrication.'

"There is no paper anywhere that has a higher regard for fair and impartial Courts than has The Bee; but there is no paper anywhere that has a supremer contempt than has The Bee for a Judge who will approve the unmitigated falsehood of an attorney, as Judge Catlin today approved the brazen misstatement of Judge J.B. Devine."[98]

Attorney Jones decided to convert McClatchy's contempt into reality. Jones swore out a statement in a deposition on June 1st that the editorial by Charles McClatchy amounted to contempt of court. Jones alleged that the editorial "...[was] contemptuous toward the said Court and Judge, and tend to and were intended to degrade the said Court and excite public prejudice and odium against it, and were unlawful interferences with the proceedings of said Court in the trial of said action."[99]

McClatchy was arrested and brought before Judge Amos on contempt charges. McClatchy was represented by attorney Pat Reddy. As noted by Reddy, his whole defense of McClatchy rested upon the Barry Act passed in 1891, which curbed the powers of the courts with respect to contempt proceedings. In what would be a rare divergence for Judge Amos, he disagreed with Reddy, not on case law or Supreme Court decisions, but in his own assessment that the Barry Act was unconstitutional.

"As I said before, I had fully considered all of the objections which have been raised by this demurrer, although the point that you presented that under the new Constitution the Legislature was authorized to place limitations upon the power of the courts in addition to those already existing, had never been presented before me, but the very point attracted my attention in considering this matter, and I have come to the conclusion that it was not the intention of the Constitution to deprive the courts of those necessary powers as one the three equal branches of Government. That it was necessary, in order that it should maintain itself, and enable it to freely administer justice as between individuals. The great duty of a court is to freely and independently try and decide all matters of controversy involving the rights of property between individuals or involving their rights of personal liberty. And I hold that any obstruction or interference with the freedom on the part of the courts is an unlawful interference. The matter upon which this proceeding arises was a matter of evidence in the case, a matter of evidence

Amos P. Catlin

material to the controversy, and more or less material in the judgment of the court, and claimed by both parties to be material. Upon the mere statement by the court as to what was or was not the evidence this defendant interferes through his newspaper directly in the matter by charging in language which was coarse, violent, insolent and insulting that the court's comments on a matter of evidence before it was false, and brazenly and unmitigatedly false, etc. You have seen the language. I do not like to repeat it. If that is not an interference with the just rights and powers of the court it would seem to me to be almost impossible to find one that would be. But as this matter comes up on demurrer, and there may be something more in the answer, I do not care to further comment upon it at this time, and I merely wish to say just what is sufficient to overrule the demurrer. I will direct that the demurrer be overruled."[100]

54. The Sacramento Bee declares Judge Catlin to be a czar after finding C.K. McClatchy guilty of contempt of court, 1896.

Judge Amos fined Charles McClatchy, editor of the Sacramento Bee, $500 for contempt of court. McClatchy refused to pay the fine and was able to secure his release from jail on $1,000 bail. McClatchy also announced his intention to file a writ of certiorari with the Supreme Court for an immediate review of the contempt decision and fine.[101]

The Bee wasted no time in castigating Judge Amos for his decision. "The Czar Hath Spoken" was the headline in the next evening's newspaper.[102]

As the contempt citation spread across the country, there was near universal condemnation of Judge Amos in newspapers. Tyrant was another term applied to Judge Amos, for what many newspapers considered an assault on a free press. In reaction to what many journalists considered an effort to suppress free speech, calls were made to reorganize the Free Press Defense Association and push for a constitutional amendment to protect newspaper editors from the whims of judges.[103]

Reelection Campaign Trail

If the Sacramento Bee had a stinger, Judge Amos was the bullseye. The newspaper reprinted every negative editorial from any newspaper published about Judge Amos. Since 1896 was an election year, the Sacramento Bee's sights were set on defeating Judge Amos. The contempt fine was not the only point of contention. The Sacramento Bee cited Judge Amos' age, 73, the slow pace at which he was conducting the court, his purported leniency with criminals, and potential conflicts of interests involving Judge Amos's son, John Catlin,[104] now a practicing attorney.[105]

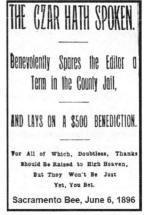

THE CZAR HATH SPOKEN.

Benevolently Spares the Editor a Term in the County Jail,

AND LAYS ON A $500 BENEDICTION.

For All of Which, Doubtless, Thanks
Should Be Raised to High Heaven,
But They Won't Be Just
Yet, You Bet.

Sacramento Bee, June 6, 1896

55. The Sacramento Bee targets Judge Catlin as a czar, vows to appeal contempt ruling, 1896.

For the first time in many years, Judge Amos was forced to go on the campaign trail in his bid to retain his judgeship. He made speeches at different Republican rallies throughout the county. He saw that the Sacramento Bee's crusade against him was having the desired effect of shifting public opinion away from him. For years, when running for an elected judgeship, he had avoided talking politics, lest it seem he would be biased as a judge. In light of the current circumstances, Judge Amos now proclaimed in a speech that he saw no reason why a man who held a judicial position should not express a political opinion.[106]

Judge Amos endorsed Republican presidential nominee William McKinley over William Jennings Bryan. Judge Amos stated that, in terms of trade, Henry Clay had been his guide, and, like Clay, he favored protectionist policies. A big populist issue of the time was the return to a monetization of silver, or "free silver," as the U.S. had demonetized the metal in the early 1870s. Judge Amos had studied the issue and saw the merits of silver monetization, especially during the current economic downturn, but he towed the party line and spoke against silver coinage.[107] The Silver Republican party was active in Sacramento at the time, and many people, especially farmers, believed that a lack of silver coinage had hurt their businesses.

In addition to the criticisms leveled at Judge Amos regarding his age and slowness on the bench, his past affiliation with the Know Nothing Party was brought into the conversation. Judge Amos flatly denied ever being a Know Nothing.[108]

Amos P. Catlin

Technically, he may have been telling the truth, but in 1856 and 1857 he was involved in the American Party, the official party organ of the xenophobic anti-Catholic movement. Winfield J. Davis, a historian of the day and present as a stenographer at many political conventions, disputed Judge Amos' claims that he was not involved with the Know Nothings; "While it might be well argued that the truth or error of these assertions cuts no figure in the question of Judge [Amos] Catlin's present fitness or incapacity, still the students of political history of this State should learn it straight and correctly, and not have it crowded with errors."[109]

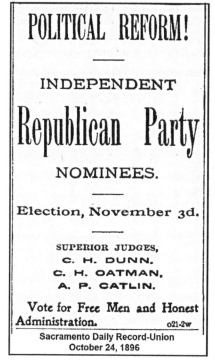

POLITICAL REFORM!

——

INDEPENDENT

Republican Party

NOMINEES.

——

Election, November 3d.

——

SUPERIOR JUDGES,
C. H. DUNN.
C. H. OATMAN.
A. P. CATLIN.

Vote for Free Men and Honest Administration.   o21-2w

Sacramento Daily Record-Union
October 24, 1896

56. To counter Sacramento Bee criticisms, Judge Catlin runs for reelection as a political reformer, 1896.

The Sacramento Daily Union did everything it could to support and promote Judge Amos' election. The newspaper printed numerous editorials describing him as fair and honest. The Union labeled the Bee's attacks on Amos as shameful, malicious, and malignant.[110] The fear was that Amos was so popular, and so many men would assume he would be reelected, that they would not bother to vote. Consequently, there was a large emphasis on reminding men to cast a ballot in Amos' favor.[111]

The other concerning issue was that there were numerous younger men in Sacramento who were not acquainted with this septuagenarian running for judge. The Union published lengthy articles intended to educate the voting populace on the historical Amos and his record. They recounted Judge Amos' important work to defend the original boundaries of the Leidesdorff land grant before the U.S. Supreme Court. Most importantly, it was Judge Amos who put Sacramento on the map, by introducing legislation to move the state's Capital to Sacramento.[112]

But the county voters decided Judge Amos was not their first choice for Superior Court Judge. Judge Amos came in fourth in the vote tally, resoundingly defeated by a Democrat.[113] The Sacramento Bee was gleeful at Judge Amos' defeat and its own prominence at influencing local elections.[114] It would take another year, but

Amos P. Catlin

the Supreme Court also ruled against Judge Amos in the McClatchy contempt case. The Court did not address the contempt, but overruled Judge Amos on the grounds that McClatchy was denied his constitutional right to be heard in his defense.[115]

On January 4, 1897, Judge Amos made a few remarks on his retirement from the bench and passing the gavel on to his successor. "This day terminates six years of unremitting labor devoted to the service of the people in the administration of the important duties of this office. I feel that I can truthfully say—I know that I can conscientiously say—that I have at all times acted upon the single motive and endeavor to do exact justice within fixed and adjudicated rules of law and equity as far as my knowledge of such rules has enabled me to do, aided and assisted as it has largely been by a bar of marked ability and intelligence."[116] Several members of the Sacramento Bar also made remarks honoring Judge Amos' integrity and knowledge of the law.[117]

[1] Auburn Journal, Volume 7, Number 18, 28 January 1891

[2] Sacramento Daily Union, Volume 80, Number 133, 24 January 1891

[3] Sacramento Daily Union, Volume 80, Number 138, 30 January 1891

[4] Sacramento Daily Union, Volume 80, Number 138, 30 January 1891

[5] Sacramento Daily Union, Volume 80, Number 138, 30 January 1891

[6] Sacramento Daily Union, Volume 80, Number 138, 30 January 1891

[7] Sacramento Daily Union, Volume 80, Number 162, 27 February 1891

[8] Sacramento Daily Union, Volume 80, Number 163, 28 February 1891

[9] Sacramento Daily Union, Volume 2, Number 41, 1 March 1891

[10] Sacramento Daily Union, Volume 81, Number 10, 5 March 1891

[11] Sacramento Daily Union, Volume 81, Number 10, 5 March 1891

[12] Sacramento Daily Union, Volume 81, Number 10, 5 March 1891

[13] Sacramento Daily Union, Volume 81, Number 10, 5 March 1891

[14] Sacramento Daily Union, Volume 81, Number 12, 7 March 1891

[15] Sacramento Daily Union, Volume 2, Number 42, 8 March 1891

[16] Sacramento Daily Union, Volume 81, Number 14, 10 March 1891

[17] Sacramento Daily Union, Volume 81, Number 15, 11 March 1891

[18] Sacramento Daily Union, Volume 2, Number 43, 15 March 1891

[19] Sacramento Daily Union, Volume 81, Number 36, 4 April 1891

[20] Sacramento Bee, April 20, 1891

[21] Sacramento Bee, April 20, 1891

[22] Sacramento Daily Union, Volume 82, Number 10, 2 September 1891

[23] Sacramento Daily Union, Volume 82, Number 10, 2 September 1891

[24] Sacramento Daily Union, Volume 82, Number 10, 2 September 1891

[25] Sacramento Daily Union, Volume 82, Number 10, 2 September 1891

[26] Sacramento Daily Union, Volume 82, Number 10, 2 September 1891

[27] Sacramento Daily Union, Volume 82, Number 12, 4 September 1891

[28] Sacramento Daily Union, Volume 82, Number 10, 2 September 1891

[29] Sacramento Daily Union, Volume 82, Number 14, 7 September 1891

[30] Sacramento Daily Union, Volume 82, Number 12, 4 September 1891

[31] Sacramento Daily Union, Volume 82, Number 12, 4 September 1891

[32] Sacramento Daily Union, Volume 82, Number 18, 11 September 1891

Amos P. Catlin

[33] Sacramento Bee, October 19, 1893
[34] Sacramento Bee, May 23, 1891
[35] Sacramento Daily Union, Volume 82, Number 18, 11 September 1891
[36] San Francisco Call, Volume 70, Number 115, 24 September 1891
[37] Sacramento Daily Union, Volume 82, Number 29, 24 September 1891
[38] Pacific Rural Press, Volume 41, Number 25, 20 June 1891
[39] Sacramento Daily Union, Volume 81, Number 97, 15 June 1891
[40] Sacramento Daily Union, Volume 81, Number 137, 31 July 1891
[41] Sacramento Daily Union, Volume 81, Number 137, 31 July 1891
[42] Sacramento Daily Union, Volume 81, Number 137, 31 July 1891
[43] Sacramento Daily Union, Volume 81, Number 137, 31 July 1891
[44] Sacramento Daily Union, Volume 81, Number 137, 31 July 1891
[45] Sacramento Daily Union, Volume 82, Number 37, 3 October 1891
[46] Sacramento Daily Union, Volume 82, Number 37, 3 October 1891
[47] Sacramento Daily Union, Volume 82, Number 37, 3 October 1891
[48] Sacramento Daily Union, Volume 82, Number 37, 3 October 1891
[49] Sacramento Daily Union, Volume 82, Number 37, 3 October 1891
[50] Sacramento Daily Union, Volume 83, Number 36, 2 April 1892
[51] Sacramento Daily Union, Volume 82, Number 111, 29 December 1891
[52] Sacramento Daily Union, Volume 82, Number 112, 30 December 1891
[53] Sacramento Daily Union, Volume 82, Number 114, 2 January 1892
[54] Placer Herald, Volume 40, Number 27, 28 May 1892
[55] Sacramento Daily Union, Volume 83, Number 98, 14 June 1892
[56] Sacramento Bee, January 20, 1892
[57] Sacramento Bee, March 15, 1893
[58] Sacramento Daily Union, Volume 83, Number 71, 13 May 1892
[59] Sacramento Daily Union, Volume 83, Number 71, 13 May 1892
[60] Sacramento Daily Union, Volume 83, Number 71, 13 May 1892
[61] Sacramento Daily Union, Volume 83, Number 126, 16 July 1892
[62] Sacramento Daily Union, Volume 83, Number 126, 16 July 1892
[63] Sacramento Bee, August 30, 1893
[64] Sacramento Bee, March 7, 1893
[65] Sacramento Bee, January 4, 1893
[66] Sacramento Union, January 4, 1893
[67] Sacramento Bee, January 4, 1893
[68] Sacramento Bee, January 4, 1893
[69] Sacramento Daily Union, Volume 84, Number 56, 25 October 1892
[70] Sacramento Daily Union, Volume 85, Number 4, 25 February 1893
[71] Sacramento Daily Union, Volume 86, Number 130, 20 January 1894
[72] Folsom Telegraph, January 27. 1894
[73] Sacramento Bee, December 15, 1892
[74] Sacramento Daily Union, Volume 84, Number 4, 25 August 1892
[75] Sacramento Daily Union, Volume 86, Number 142, 3 February 1894
[76] Sacramento Bee, August 20, 1892
[77] Sacramento Bee, August 20, 1892
[78] Sacramento Daily Union, Volume 84, Number 30, 24 September 1892
[79] Sacramento Daily Union, 22 August 1892
[80] Sacramento Bee, August 20, 1892
[81] Sacramento Bee, August 20, 1892
[82] Sacramento Bee, October 11, 1892
[83] Sacramento Daily Union, Volume 86, Number 139, 31 January 1894
[84] Sacramento Bee, February 7, 1894

Amos P. Catlin

[85] Sacramento Bee, February 7, 1894

[86] Sacramento Bee, March 27, 1894

[87] Sacramento Bee, March 27, 1894

[88] Sacramento Bee, March 28, 1894

[89] Sacramento Daily Union, Volume 91, Number 26, 24 March 1896

[90] Sacramento Bee, May 25, 1896

[91] Charles Talmadge Last Will and Testament, Sacramento County, December 1899, filed March 1914

[92] Sacramento Bee, May 25, 1896

[93] Sacramento Bee, May 26, 1896

[94] Sacramento Bee, May 28, 1896

[95] Sacramento Bee, May 28, 1896

[96] Sacramento Bee, May 28, 1896

[97] Sacramento Bee, May 30, 1896

[98] Sacramento Bee, May 29, 1896

[99] Sacramento Bee, June 2, 1896

[100] Sacramento Daily Union, Volume 91, Number 99, 5 June 1896

[101] Morning Union, 6 June 1896

[102] Sacramento Bee, June 6, 1896

[103] San Francisco Call, Volume 80, Number 13, 13 June 1896

[104] Sacramento Bee, October 31, 1896

[105] Sacramento Bee, October 22, 1896

[106] Sacramento Daily Union, Volume 92, Number 65, 25 October 1896

[107] Sacramento Daily Union, Volume 92, Number 65, 25 October 1896

[108] Sacramento Daily Union, Volume 92, Number 68, 28 October 1896

[109] Sacramento Bee, October 28, 1896

[110] Sacramento Daily Union, Volume 92, Number 59, 19 October 1896

[111] Sacramento Daily Union, Volume 92, Number 61, 21 October 1896

[112] Sacramento Daily Union, Volume 92, Number 60, 20 October 1896

[113] Sacramento Daily Union, Volume 92, Number 76, 5 November 1896

[114] Sacramento Bee, November 4, 1896

[115] Sacramento Bee, December 28, 1897

[116] Sacramento Daily Union, Volume 92, Number 136, 5 January 1897

[117] Sacramento Daily Union, Volume 92, Number 136, 5 January 1897

Amos P. Catlin

Chapter Seventeen: Administrator, Reminiscing, Legacy: 1891 - 1900

When Amos became a Superior Court judge, he was able to step away from his law practice, but not from his personal life and the demands therein. There were events he was requested to attend because of his stature as a '49er pioneer attorney, and there were family matters that demanded his attention. He also still had young adult children living at home. While Judge Amos was able to escape for short vacations, there would be no grand retirement trip reminiscent of his earlier Alaska adventure.

Wilson Estate

With the death of Charles Lincoln Wilson, Amos and N.D. Rideout were named as executors of the Wilson estate.[1] Not only were Wilson and Judge Amos long-time friends, they also owned property together. In June of 1891, the last will and testament of Charles Wilson was admitted to probate, and appraisers were appointed to evaluate the estate. Probate of the Wilson estate would not be an easy process, and Charles Wilson's son decided to contest the will.

As Charles Wilson Jr. was contesting his father's will in court, he was being foreclosed upon by the Pacific Mutual Life Insurance Company. The foreclosure was on property in Butte County on which Wilson Jr. had obtained a $40,000 mortgage.[2] Wilson Jr. then sued Judge Amos and attorney Rideout, executors of the Wilson estate, for one half of the Butte-Tehama property known as Bosquejo, or Lassen Rancho. The property was estimated to contain 4,500 acres.[3]

Judge Amos, in his younger years, was a frequent visitor to the Lassen Rancho, where his sons would go on hunting trips. Two of his sons, Alexander and John, were born in Lassen. Amos had secured a Land Patent to 160 acres in Tehama County (Township 25 North, Range 2 East, Section 26, Northeast ¼) near Pine Creek and Kiefer's Sawmill.[4] The property was not too far from Campbellville and the Cohasset Stage Road.

The litigation over the Wilson estate forced Judge Amos to travel to Oroville, the seat of Butte County. He requested that the case be transferred to Sacramento County so he would not have to spend so much time on the road.[5] A compromise was struck, and the lawsuit was transferred to Yuba County. Judge Amos now only had to travel to Marysville, the county seat, to attend court hearings.[6]

No sooner had Judge Amos struck a compromise with Charles Wilson Jr. for $30,000,[7] than the Methodist Episcopal Church in Lincoln commenced a lawsuit against the Wilson estate. Before Charles Wilson died, he had promised the church $1,000 for its building fund. The church now wanted what was promised.[8] Judge Prewett of Placer County found that the estate had to make good on the promise Wilson made to the church before he died.[9] Then, the Bank of Chico also filed suit, claiming the Wilson estate owed it $1,380 in interest on a loan.[10]

Finally, in September 1894, in an effort to settle the Wilson estate, Judge Amos bought 8,106 acres from the Central Pacific Railroad Company and Metropolitan Trust Co. of New York for $9,322.80. The property was in Tehama County and part of the Lassen Ranch, where Judge Amos had secured the 160-acre Land Patent a couple of years earlier. Judge Amos then transferred the property to Charles Wilson Jr. for $10.

Collis Huntington

Judge Amos was one of the featured speakers at a celebration of Collis Huntington's contributions to Sacramento City. The grand fete was held at the Sutter Club in April of 1892. The topic upon which Judge Amos spoke was pioneer law in California. Amos noted how Huntington was just a youth back in the Gold Rush. The state had been organized by boys, and it had been rare to see a gray head in the Sacramento of those days, as opposed to the room now so full of men with gray hair.[11] Pioneer law was akin to mob law, which, while violent, was effective in quickly dispensing a rough form of justice.

Pioneer law, Judge Amos surmised, was better than the legal system of the 1890s. Pioneer law was not slow and burdened with technicalities. Pioneer law, Judge Amos asserted, was closer to mob law, and in many instances that was preferred for executing justice. He could not recall an instance where injustice has been done to anyone.[12] Of course, Judge Amos was talking about criminal matters before California had a fully functioning judiciary. Plus, the comments were meant to evoke the nostalgia of early California as they toasted Huntington.

For Judge Amos and many of the other men in the room, an era governed by a system of law, driven by the people and producing quick results, was an exciting and novel period, never to be replicated. Forty-three years later, Judge Amos and his fellow pioneers could reflect on the enthusiasm and novelty that was the California Gold Rush. Those gathered in the ornate Sutter Club to toast C. P. Huntington could revel in the notion that they were a part of history in a very tangible way.[13]

Newton Booth

It was the pleasure of Judge Amos to marry his old friend and former U.S. Senator Newton Booth in February 1892.[14] Booth married the widow of his former law partner. After the private nuptials, the couple hopped on a train for New York.[15] In less than six months, in July 1892, Booth, who was ill when he married, died.[16]

Luther Cutler

Luther Cutler, Judge Amos' close mining and sawmill partner, died in 1882. Cutler, who had finally found enough soap and water to get clean, married and made his home in El Dorado County. Even though he left a will, his numerous mining claims and property made untangling his estate a challenge. Judge Amos was appointed an executor and administrator of Cutler's estate. Along with co-executor John Blair, Judge Amos would wrap up distributing Cutler's property to his heirs and creditors in 1890.[17]

Arthur Jee

Judge Amos was a loyal man. Arthur Jee, a distant cousin of Judge Amos by marriage, was in failing mental health. Jee's wife, Lucy Eliza Jee, who had been her husband's primary caretaker, died in January 1892. Over the next several years, Judge Amos would have to make frequent trips to the Bay Area to attend to Jee's property and fight in court with people who wanted to control Jee's sizable assets.

Arthur Jee had accumulated his wealth while working as Secretary for the Union Pacific Salt Company, which operated in Alameda County, but was headquartered in San Francisco.[18] Jee's confused mental state and reported assets of $100,000 led to a competency hearing in San Francisco that Judge Amos attended. Also in attendance was Clara Morrison, who purported to be Jee's grandniece and was advocating to become Jee's guardian.

At the hearing, Judge Amos was declared Jee's guardian, and Miss Morrison vowed to contest the appointment.[19] While Morrison tried to claim that Judge Amos was not fit to be Jee's guardian, Judge Amos had John Beach, an old friend of Jee's, employed as Jee's caretaker at his Oakland home. Unfortunately, Beach's own mental state began to deteriorate. Judge Amos' daughter, Ruth, would occasionally visit the men to see how they were doing. Finally, Beach was declared incompetent and moved to an institution in 1895.[20]

Rumors flew that Judge Amos orchestrated Beach's commitment to a mental institution. When Judge Amos was shown the newspaper stories of Beach's account of being railroaded into a mental institution, Judge Amos set the record straight. Judge Amos had been paying Beach $50 per month to take care of Jee. Beach was never Jee's guardian. Amos' daughter, Ruth, was only an occasional visitor and never served as the men's housekeeper. Upon reviewing the San

Francisco newspaper, Judge Amos sighed and said, "I have never seen so many untruths crowded in the same space."[21]

Capitol Threatened Move

It was a different newspaper that would irritate Judge Amos in 1893. The Sacramento Bee had published some scathing stories on the State Legislature. One story, titled "Senators Do Not Take Kindly to Morning Hour," implied the members were lazy for not arriving on time for the morning meeting. Another story, based solely on rumors, alleged that a legislator had been scammed out of $4,000 while attempting to have an extra-marital affair.[22]

The members of the Legislature did not like the Bee's negative coverage and editorial comments. In March 1893, a Concurrent Joint Resolution was introduced to move California's Capitol out of Sacramento. The serious threat to move the capital from Sacramento set off alarm bells in the city, and Mayor Comstock called a special meeting to address the issue. Judge Amos was appointed to a Sacramento citizen's Resolutions Committee. The resolutions offered repudiated the coverage of the Sacramento Bee as being libelous.[23]

Of course, the threat of moving California's Capitol struck at the core of Judge Amos' legacy in Sacramento. If any man had a reason to be outraged at the suggestion of moving the capital, it was Amos. However, his public comments reflected his modesty and pragmaticism.

"The matter before us is one of a serious moment. The Capital was brought here in 1854 by a simple Act of the Legislature. It would be an easy thing to remove it, even now, although a vote of two-thirds of each house of the Legislature is required to start the ball. The latter has already been done. I said in the committee tonight, and I say now, that if I had been a member of the Legislature, I would have voted as they did. I would have held the people of Sacramento responsible for the libels in last evening's Bee. On cooler deliberation I would have changed my vote, and that is what we are now asking the members of the Legislature to do. If the matter goes before the people, I believe that, as between this city and San Jose, we will have a hard fight of it."[24]

When the Sacramento Bee tried to interview Amos regarding the Legislature's intent to move the state's Capitol, he replied, "You can't interview me. Newspaper men never report a man correctly." Grove Johnson, who was on the citizen's committee to save the State Capitol also declined a Bee interview. The Bee reported when its reporter approached Grove Johnson at his office, Johnson replied, "I decline to answer any questions for the Bee that are proposed. Hiram, isn't that right?" Hiram Johnson responded, "What is it, questions, for the Bee. To hell with the Bee."[25]

Amos P. Catlin

Some legislators had offered a compromise, requesting that if Board of Trade, a chamber of commerce organization, would refrain from advertising in the Bee, the lawmakers would reconsider the resolution to move the Capitol. The Bee wanted to know if Amos was involved in the backroom conspiracy to deprive the newspaper of advertising dollars. In a letter to the Bee, Amos finally gave them a reply.

"March 19, 1893, Publisher of 'The Bee:' Your communication of date yesterday, received. I know nothing personally of the subject referred to, and nothing upon hearsay, except what I have read in newspapers, in one of which I saw it stated that a member of the Legislature had expressed his opinion to the effect that the resolutions of Sunday evening did not go far enough in condemnation of The Bee, and that if they had not been deficient in that respect, the removal would have been reconsidered. I am unable to recall to mind the name of the paper or of the member. Yours, etc. A.P. Catlin"[26]

Amos refused to give the Bee any satisfaction. He was too smart to get sucked into the news story and have his opinion twisted to fit the perspective of the Bee. Amos was appointed chair of an executive committee to save the Capitol, along with H. Weinstock and Grove Johnson.[27] A lawsuit to stop the Legislature's attempt to remove the Capitol from Sacramento finally reached the state Supreme Court, which ruled the Concurrent Resolution was unconstitutional.[28]

Lawyer Family

There were several Sacramento attorneys whose children followed them down the career path of law. Grove Johnson and his sons, Albert and Hiram, all practiced law together as a family and represented actions before Judge Amos. Laura Tilden, daughter of former Sacramento City Attorney Marcellus Tilden, followed him into the practice of law, becoming the first woman to practice law in Sacramento. In 1894, she represented a young boy before Judge Amos. The judge agreed with Tilden that the young man had not broken into his father's house but was only returning home to find something to eat.[29]

After attending school in Berkeley,[30] John Catlin, Judge Amos' second child, was admitted to the California Bar and started practicing law in 1892.[31] John Catlin had not inherited his father's courtroom calm demeanor and restraint of tongue. While representing a client before Judge Johnson, Catlin made some sharp comments to Assistant District Attorney Jones. A brawl ensued, with both men throwing punches at one another in the courtroom. Both men had to stand for contempt of court charges.[32]

John and Judge Amos took a short vacation to Bartlett Springs following the attorney's courtroom affray. On their way back, their stagecoach dropped off the road, injuring all aboard.[33] After a short period of recuperation, Judge Amos returned to the bench, and John returned to representing clients in court. At the age of 70, Amos had narrowly escaped serious injury and death from a routine stagecoach trip.

While Judge Amos was still going strong, if not a little slower, he was watching his fellow pioneers move into the cemetery on a regular basis. Even men younger than Amos were dying. With each passing, Amos was called upon to write a memorial for the departed. Judge Amos and Creed Haymond had been close political associates from the days when Amos served on the Board of Equalization. At Haymon's passing in January 1893, Judge Amos addressed the Sacramento Bar from the bench.

"I have been acquainted with this bar closely from the year 1849. It has had many prominent, able and very many distinguished men as lawyers, politicians and statesmen, but there was none that I can call to mind that I would be willing to say is more entitled to memory among mankind than Creed Haymond. I noticed particularly that peculiarity of his character that has been alluded to. He seemed never to be capable of entertaining enmity against even the strongest of his adversaries, not only in political contests, but contests at the bar. He seemed to have a soul above that, and undoubtedly to that trait of character is to be attributed a great deal of his personal popularity and a great deal of his personal success."[34]

Shortly after Haymond's death, George Blanchard died. Blanchard had been a judge up in Colusa County. When he moved back to Sacramento, he and Judge Amos formed a law partnership. Of all his law partners over the years, Judge Amos said, it was Blanchard in whom he had complete trust on all matters of law and on whose opinion he relied when approaching important cases.[35]

Coxey's Army

Amid all the deaths of close associates and family drama, Sacramento also was experiencing political and economic turmoil in the streets. A nationwide economic recession, railroad strikes and the rise of the ranks of the unemployed across the country, marching on towns, demanding reform and jobs, all were part of 1894. The first big protest march was organized by Jacob Coxey, who led several thousand men to descend on Washington, D.C. The protesters were dubbed Coxey's Army, and a similar group organized in San Francisco, intending to protest in Sacramento.

Judge Amos was called upon to preside over an emergency citizen's committee, convened by the mayor to strategize on how to handle the mob about to descend on Sacramento. The mayor, chief of police, and county sheriff all spoke of law and order and the possibility of calling out the National Guard. The marchers were not proposing any destruction of property. The biggest problem was expected to be feeding the estimated 1,000 men protesting the present economic state.[36]

When the unemployed men protesting the economic conditions of the country arrived in Sacramento, their ranks were much thinner than had been estimated. Dubbed the Industrial Army, for it resembled a military organization, approximately 225 men settled in at Sutter's Fort.[37] The Industrial Army paraded around Sacramento, but, except for a few arrests for vagrancy, there was no trouble. Local residents launched an effort to raise money for protesters to buy railroad tickets back to their homes in the Bay Area.[38]

Railroad Strike

The railroad strike in the summer of 1894 caused more disruption in Sacramento and nationwide. Known as the Pullman Strike, the work stoppage, boycott, and protests in Sacramento had an enormous impact on both passenger and freight service. In July 1894 Governor Markham called up the National Guard to help quell the striking protests and get the railroads back running again. Three men from Dunsmuir were arrested for commandeering a train that ultimately led to a train wreck.

As the men were having a preliminary hearing before Judge Amos, a U.S. Marshall with 10 soldiers, fully armed, stationed themselves outside the courtroom. The general assumption was that the U.S. Marshall, with the armed soldiers, had arrived to take custody of the men facing charges of grand theft railroad. When informed of the presence of the soldiers in the corridor, Judge Amos leapt to his feet and ordered, "I call upon the Chief of Police, the Sheriff, and all citizens present to resist any such attempt." The doors to the courtroom were quickly secured to thwart entry of the army.[39]

Assistant U.S. District Attorney Samuel Knight for the prosecution explained to Judge Catlin that he had to call the U.S. Marshall and soldiers as witnesses.[40] This did not satisfy Judge Amos, who called the U.S. Marshall into the courtroom to explain why he should not be punished for contempt of court.[41] Upon learning all of the facts that led to the confusion, Judge Amos dismissed the contempt charges against the U.S. Marshal.[42] However, Judge Amos' actions were questioned by the San Francisco Call newspaper, which hypothesized that he was secretly disloyal to the Union and a rebel.[43]

Arguments For Third Judge

Newspaper attacks on Judge Amos, or any other justice, were common when their decisions went against the newspaper editorial bent. The Sacramento Bee printed rumors that some lawyers felt Judge Amos was falling behind on adjudicating

Amos P. Catlin

cases because of this age and health.[44] The members of the Sacramento Bar stepped up to defend Judge Amos with resolutions denouncing allegations that he was physically incapable of attending to the court's business.[45]

The issue was not the physical stamina of Judge Amos, but the amount of business the Sacramento Superior Court had to consider. The county had gained 15,000 residents since 1880, for a population of 50,000 in 1895. The Southern Pacific Railroad was a major employer and drew people from all over the country. When Folsom Prison released a prisoner, he often migrated to Sacramento. Finally, Sacramento Superior Court was often the first legal jurisdiction to take up numerous complaints dealing with California's bureaucracy.

Sacramento County had only two Superior Court judges, but lawsuits and probate cases were up 25 percent for the same time period eight years prior. Criminal cases had tripled across both court departments in the same time span. Not included in a review of court operations was the explosion of divorce and insolvency cases since the beginning of the economic recession in 1893.[46] Sacramento County needed another Superior Court judge to handle the expanded workload, and a bill was introduced into the Legislature to expand Sacramento's bench.

Because the expense of a third judge would fall on the taxpayers of Sacramento County, there was considerable resistance to the added expenses and assumed tax increase. Judge Amos attended a Senate hearing in early February 1895 to testify to the need for a third judge. Former Police Judge Cravens, who had several of his decisions overturned by Judge Amos, testified for the county residents opposed to expanding the bench.[47]

Judge Cravens was opposed to a third judge because of the enormous expense it would create for the county, because he felt a third judge was not needed, and because Sacramento County already carried too much debt. Frank Miller also spoke against the expense of a third judge. He also organized a citizens' petition that gathered 614 names of men who opposed expanding the bench.[48]

Judge Amos was asked to address the Senate after all of the opposition comments. He was underwhelmed with the arguments. First, he estimated the annual expense for the third judge to be $7,000 annually. In response to Judge Cravens' assessment that the two judges were not "worked to death," Judge Amos replied that he routinely worked until 11 or 12 o'clock each evening on court matters. He also noted that there had been much suffering on the part of litigants in the county because their cases had to be postponed while the two judges addressed long criminal trials.

Amos P. Catlin

Then, out of judicial character, Judge Amos turned his attention to the opponents of the bill. Judge Amos said that Frank Miller knew no more about the business of the court than if he had been born yesterday. As far as Judge Cravens was concerned, he knew no more about the caseload and workings of the Superior Court than an Apache Indian. He conjectured that not more than five of the 600 signers of the petition understood what they were signing or opposing. By a unanimous vote, the Senate committee recommended the bill to add a third Sacramento County Superior Court Judge be approved.[49]

Folsom Electricity

Judge Amos was seated next to other dignitaries, including the mayor of Sacramento, Judge Johnson, and the chairman of the Board of Supervisors. All were watching the parade of lights from the grand reviewing stand on Tenth Street, next to the Capitol grounds. The occasion in 1895 was the celebration of the first distribution of electricity from the Folsom Power House down to Sacramento.[50] Looking back, Amos could easily recall the steam engine he had employed at Mormon Island for mining, the building of dams for the Natoma ditch and North Fork Ditch, and his work with the Livermore family to make the Folsom Power House a reality.

Few men alive in Sacramento in 1895 could lay claim to such intimate involvement with the region, from Gold Rush to state Capitol, railroads to electrification. Judge Amos was a witness to history from a unique position. He had seen Sacramento grow from dusty streets and canvas houses to a modern city with electricity, lighting up a bright future. Where Sacramento's future once was lit with the gleam of gold, and now with electric lights, the glow of the city's dominance was beginning to fade.

As the 19th century was beginning to close, Sacramento's influence was waning. The Bay Area and Southern California were growing at rapid clips. Judge Amos was appointed to a committee of Democrats and Republicans to discuss retaining important political conventions in Sacramento.[51] Even though Sacramento was the state capital, the growing urban centers of San Francisco and Los Angeles, with generally cooler summer temperatures, were vying to host the important political conventions.

Return to Private Practice

In 1897, with the help of the Sacramento Bee, Judge Amos, after his reelection loss, retired from the bench and went back to private practice. He would eventually form a law partnership with his son John and A.L. Shinn, to be known as Catlin, Shinn, & Catlin.[52] His son Harry Catlin, being quite familiar with the workings of government, was appointed as clerk of Judge Hart's court.[53] Outside the world of law, Judge Amos found considerable enjoyment in swimming. He was an early subscriber to the construction of a new swimming pool in Sacramento.[54] While he was not known to ride a bicycle, Judge Amos helped organize a men's bicycle race in 1897.[55]

In 1895, Judge Amos' son, John Catlin, married Lucie Routier at St. Paul's Church.[56] The following spring, Judge Amos became a grandfather when John and Lucie gave birth to a daughter.[57] The proud grandfather was also watching as Sacramento fell into a decrepit state. Judge Amos was representing the owner of the old Post Office building in a case in which the city was trying to force the construction of a new sidewalk. While the Street Commission deemed the existing sidewalk safe, the City Surveyor did not.[58]

This part of Sacramento had been raised one story to protect against flooding. Next to some of the buildings, a subterranean walkway was left between the building and raised street. The report noted that the sidewalks had been supported by timbers, which were beginning to rot. Below street level, water would collect to a depth of 2 to 3 feet.[59] Judge Amos argued that building owner James Bailey was amenable to repairing the sidewalk, but not to replacing it. The city condemned the sidewalk and erected barricades to prevent an accident at the rotting sidewalk of 4th and K streets.[60]

Pioneer Lawyers

Unlike many other professions, the legal profession is one in which anyone with a clear mind and voice enough to object in court can engage. Judge Amos, in addition to his regular swims, continued to practice law, not just in consultative fashion, but in the courtroom. It was a reporter for the Sacramento Daily Union who possessed enough knowledge of local history to understand the historical significance of the courtroom battle between former judges Amos and John McKune. Both men were '49er pioneers of California and Sacramento.

Judge McKune was representing Eli Mayo, while Judge Amos was counsel for L.C. Chandler; both litigants had long histories in Sacramento. As the reporter aptly noted, a quick glance into Judge Hart's courtroom might have transported the viewer 40 years into the past, when younger Amos and McKune also were opposing attorneys. As if age had only refined the two elder lawyers, each was smooth and composed while discussing points of law and evidence and criticizing one another's arguments before the judge.[61]

It was a rarity for such esteemed and veteran attorneys to be practicing law at that time. Judge Amos understood the grace that had been extended to him for his time in Sacramento. At a memorial for the death of fellow attorney N. Greene Curtis in July of 1897, both McKune and Amos were overcome by emotion, not only for the passing of Curtis, but at the specter of their own dwindling remaining time on earth.[62]

Age Takes A Toll

Judge Amos' time was nearly concluded when he slipped from an electric streetcar at 10th and J streets, rendering him unconscious and with a deep gash above his eye.[63] He healed enough to be a pallbearer for Mrs. M. E. Gregory, along with Mayor William Land and Charles K. McClatchy.[64] Late in 1898, while representing the executors of the Solomon Runyon estate before Judge Hughes, Judge Amos was taken ill. The color drained from his face, as he complained of pain across his stomach and was unable to continue with his arguments before Judge Hughes.[65]

The issue before Judge Hughes was the $7,500 fee invoiced by Judge Amos for his work on the Runyon Estate. The estate was very large, and Judge Amos had worked for more than a year in collecting mortgages and settling a complicated estate worth $500,000. Those contesting what was considered an exorbitant amount for an attorney's fee, priced Amos' legal work at $4,500. Judge Amos testified that he valued his time at $500 per month. When he considered the time he had spent for the past 18 months on the estate, he figured $5,500 was a reasonable amount. Judge Hughes concurred and allowed Judge Amos to be paid that amount from the estate.[66]

As the 20th century dawned in Sacramento, Judge Amos was still in demand as a speaker and still working as an attorney. Judge Amos spoke to a large audience at the 50-year jubilee celebration of the Congregational Church in Sacramento.[67] The cornerstone of the church, which had been cut from a granite block at Mormon Island, had been donated by Judge Amos in the 1850s.[68]

He represented Swamp Land District No. 551 before the Sacramento County Board of Supervisors.[69] While he had slowed down, he still found time to travel down to Oakland to petition the Alameda Superior Court to allow Arthur Jee to sell 486 shares of the Union Pacific Salt Company.[70] Another part of his legacy to Sacramento was his role as the mentor of Peter J. Shields, who once studied law in Judge Amos' office and was now a candidate for Superior Court judge himself.[71]

History was important to Judge Amos, and he understood the importance of having it documented and remembered. In 1896 Judge Amos applied to The California Society of the Sons of the American Revolution to have his lineage recognized. Judge Amos's connection to the American Revolution was his grandfather, David Catlin, with whom he had once lived with back in Kingston, New York.[72] Judge Amos also filed an application on behalf of his son Alexander, whose connections to the American Revolution were David Catlin and Zebulon Butler on his mother's side of the family.[73]

Legacy Management

While Judge Amos was ensuring his legacy was properly documented, he wanted his memory to be defined by the associations he valued. In 1899 he submitted his biography, along with a check for $15, to the Standard Genealogical Publishing Company.[74] Published after his death, the book celebrating notable citizens of California included the conspicuous paragraph on Judge Amos.

"The Judge never identified with any secret societies, but was an esteemed member of the Sacramento Society of California Pioneers, the California Historical Society, the Bar Association of San Francisco, and the Sons of the American Revolution."[75]

It is true that Judge Amos was never a member of any fraternal order, such as the Masons, that may have been identified as secret. However, Judge Amos also wanted it known that he was never a member of the secret "Know Nothing" political party. It irked him that he was associated with that political party, even though in fact he was a member of the American Party, closely aligned with the principles of the Know Nothings.

Conspicuously absent from the biography was Judge Amos' involvement in the Natoma Water and Mining Company or in the North Fork Ditch. The emphasis of the entry was Judge Amos' ability and successes as a politician, and specifically, an attorney. However, it would be his involvement in those water ditches that would provide his most lasting legacy in the Sacramento region.

The esteemed mentor of many young lawyers and highly respected member of the Sacramento Bar died November 5, 1900, at his home on H street at the age of 77.[76] In his last days, Judge Amos was surrounded by his children Ruth, Harry and John and his wife Lucie, along with their 4-year-old daughter. Also attending to Judge Amos in his last days was his younger cousin, Julia Grannis.[77] Miss Grannis had come to Sacramento early in its history.[78] In the early 1890s, she moved into the Catlin home on H street. Judge Amos' funeral was held at St. Paul's Church, with Grove Johnson and Judge John McKune as two of the pallbearers.[79]

Judge Amos knew that Arthur Jee, for whom he was guardian, would most likely survive him. With his death, he knew there would be attempts by unscrupulous people trying to gain control of Jee's assets under the guise of guardianship. On one of his last trips to the Bay Area, Judge Amos dropped off a letter to his Oakland attorney who handled Jee's legal work. At a hearing after Judge Amos' death, the attorney read the letter aloud that accused one of the guardianship applicants, Percy Coward, of committing fraud when he was Jee's caretaker eight years earlier.[80] The posthumous letter sank forever Percy Coward's attempt to gain control of Jee's assets.

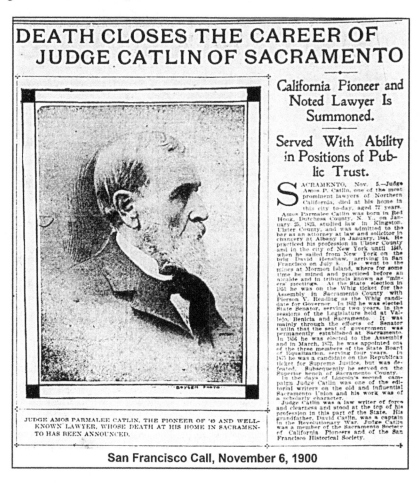

DEATH CLOSES THE CAREER OF JUDGE CATLIN OF SACRAMENTO

California Pioneer and Noted Lawyer Is Summoned.

Served With Ability in Positions of Public Trust.

SACRAMENTO, Nov. 5.—Judge Amos P. Catlin, one of the most prominent lawyers of Northern California, died at his home in this city to-day, aged 77 years.

Amos Parmalee Catlin was born in Red Hook, Dutchess County, N. Y., on January 25, 1823, studied law in Kingston, Ulster County, and was admitted to the bar as an attorney at law and solicitor in chancery at Albany in January, 1844. He practiced his profession in Ulster County and in the city of New York until 1849, when he sailed from New York on the brig David Henshaw, arriving in San Francisco on July 8. He went to the mines at Mormon Island, where for some time he mined and practiced before an alcalde and in tribunals known as "miners' meetings." At the State election in 1851 he was on the Whig ticket for the Assembly in Sacramento County with Pierson V. Reading as the Whig candidate for Governor. In 1852 he was elected State Senator, serving two years, in the sessions of the Legislature held at Vallejo, Benicia and Sacramento. It was mainly through the efforts of Senator Catlin that the seat of government was permanently established at Sacramento. In 1856 he was elected to the Assembly and in March, 1872, he was appointed one of the three members of the State Board of Equalization, serving four years. In 1875 he was a candidate on the Republican ticket for Supreme Justice, but was defeated. Subsequently he served on the Superior bench of Sacramento County. In the days of Lincoln's second campaign Judge Catlin was one of the editorial writers on the old and influential Sacramento Union and his work was of a scholarly character.

Judge Catlin was a law writer of force and clearness and stood at the top of his profession in this part of the State. His grandfather, David Catlin, was a captain in the Revolutionary War. Judge Catlin was a member of the Sacramento Society of California Pioneers and of the San Francisco Historical Society.

JUDGE AMOS PARMALEE CATLIN, THE PIONEER OF '49 AND WELL-KNOWN LAWYER, WHOSE DEATH AT HIS HOME IN SACRAMENTO HAS BEEN ANNOUNCED.

San Francisco Call, November 6, 1900

57. Obituary of Judge Amos P. Catlin, San Francisco Call, 1900.

Judge Amos put pen to paper in May 1890 and wrote out his last will and testament. He appointed sons John and Harry executors of his estate. To his daughter Ruth, he left all of the jewelry that had belonged her mother. To John and Harry, he left his extensive law library and furniture. For Harry specifically, Judge Amos left his coin and gold specimen collection. He left his collection of

Amos P. Catlin

historical ephemera to all his children equally. For Alexander, his oldest son, he left his gold watch and all mining claims and shares in mining companies.[81]

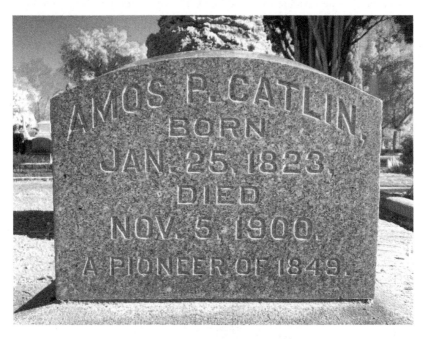

58. Grave marker of Amos P. Catlin at the Sacramento Historic City Cemetery.

Within the will were specific instructions for all the children, "I charge upon all my said children the duty and obligation to support during her life my cousin Miss Julia Grannis." Recently elected Superior Court Judge Peter Shields oversaw the probate proceedings. Entered into the record of expenses to be paid out of the proceeds of the estate were the property taxes. The receipt for the property tax payment was signed by Sacramento County Tax Collector and old acquaintance from Folsom, Benjamin N. Bugbey.[82]

Amos P. Catlin

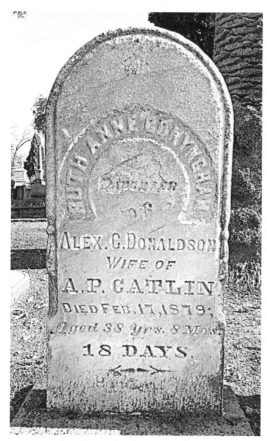

59. Grave marker of Ruth Anne Conyngham (Donaldson) Catlin, next to her husband, Amos, at the Sacramento Historic City Cemetery.

After marrying Paul Wagener, Ruth Catlin would die in August 1904. Alexander, who pursued his interest in mining, died in a Nevada mining camp in 1908. Harry moved to San Francisco, where he worked for the San Francisco Chronicle and was a partner in the Catlin and Catlin law firm with his brother John. Harry died in 1916 in San Francisco. John moved to the site of many Catlin family vacations, Monterey. He died in Monterey in 1951. Julia Grannis, cousin of Amos, died in Sacramento in 1911.[83]

---

[1] The Placer Argus, Volume 19, Number 38, 22 May 1891

[2] Auburn Journal, Volume 8, Number 8, 18 November 1891

[3] Oroville Register, January 7, 1892

[4] Government Land Office Document 9045, May 19, 1892

[5] The Placer Argus, Volume 20, Number 27, 11 March 1892

[6] Placer Herald, Volume 40, Number 37, 30 July 1892

[7] Sacramento Bee, January 6, 1893

[8] Auburn Journal, Volume 10, Number 36, 1 June 1894

[9] Placer Herald, Volume 42, Number 40, 7 July 1894

[10] Red Bluff Daily News, Volume IX, Number 141, 14 June 1894

[11] Sacramento Daily Union, Volume 83, Number 59, 29 April 1892

Amos P. Catlin

[12] Sacramento Daily Union, Volume 83, Number 59, 29 April 1892
[13] Sacramento Daily Union, Volume 83, Number 59, 29 April 1892
[14] San Francisco Call, Volume 71, Number 72, 10 February 1892
[15] Sacramento Daily Union, Volume 82, Number 147, 10 February 1892
[16] Sacramento Daily Union, Volume 83, Number 127, 18 July 1892
[17] County of El Dorado Deed Book B 37, page 609, February 28, 1890
[18] 1874 Directory Oakland, Arthur listed occupation as secretary, Union Pacific Salt, Co. (S. F.)
[19] San Francisco Call, Volume 73, Number 141, 20 April 1893
[20] San Francisco Call, Volume 77, Number 99, 19 March 1895
[21] Sacramento Bee, March 19, 1895
[22] Sacramento Bee March 11, 1893
[23] Sacramento Daily Union, Volume 85, Number 17, 13 March 1893
[24] Sacramento Daily Union, Volume 85, Number 17, 13 March 1893
[25] Sacramento Bee, March 16, 1893
[26] Sacramento Bee, March 20, 1893
[27] Sacramento Bee, March 22, 1893
[28] Sacramento Daily Union, Volume 87, Number 32, 30 March 1894
[29] Sacramento Daily Union, Volume 86, Number 138, 30 January 1894
[30] Sacramento Daily Union, Volume 60, Number 108, 25 December 1888
[31] Sacramento Daily Union, Volume 84, Number 41, 7 October 1892
[32] Sacramento Daily Union, Volume 85, Number 67, 10 May 1893
[33] Sacramento Daily Union, Volume 86, Number 6, 28 August 1893
[34] Sacramento Daily Union, Volume 84, Number 138, 28 January 1893
[35] Sacramento Daily Union, Volume 85, Number 10, 4 March 1893
[36] Sacramento Daily Union, Volume 87, Number 57, 28 April 1894
[37] Sacramento Daily Union, Volume 87, Number 59, 1 May 1894
[38] Sacramento Daily Union, Volume 87, Number 60, 2 May 1894
[39] Sacramento Daily Union, Volume 87, Number 128, 17 July 1894
[40] Sacramento Daily Union, Volume 87, Number 128, 17 July 1894
[41] San Francisco Call, Volume 76, Number 48, 18 July 1894
[42] Sacramento Daily Union, Volume 87, Number 133, 23 July 1894
[43] San Francisco Call, Volume 76, Number 48, 18 July 1894
[44] Sacramento Bee, January 23, 1895
[45] Sacramento Union, January 28, 1895
[46] Sacramento Union, January 28, 1895
[47] Sacramento Daily Union, Volume 88, Number 140, 2 February 1895
[48] Sacramento Daily Union, Volume 88, Number 140, 2 February 1895
[49] Sacramento Daily Union, Volume 88, Number 140, 2 February 1895
[50] Sacramento Daily Union, Volume 90, Number 17, 10 September 1895
[51] Sacramento Bee, February 24, 1896
[52] Sacramento Daily Union, March 11, 1898
[53] Sacramento Daily Union, Volume 92, Number 144, 13 January 1897
[54] Sacramento Bee, July 24, 1890
[55] Sacramento Daily Union, Volume 93, Number 61, 23 April 1897
[56] Sacramento Bee, March 19, 1895
[57] Sacramento Daily Union, Volume 91, Number 48, 16 April 1896
[58] Sacramento Daily Union, Volume 93, Number 148, 20 July 1897
[59] Sacramento Daily Union, Volume 93, Number 148, 20 July 1897
[60] Sacramento Daily Union, Volume 95, Number 131, 2 July 1898
[61] Sacramento Daily Union, Volume 93, Number 155, 27 July 1897
[62] Sacramento Bee, July 21, 1897
[63] Sacramento Daily Union, Volume 95, Number 55, 17 April 1898

Amos P. Catlin

[64] Sacramento Bee, June 1, 1898

[65] Sacramento Bee, November 2, 1898

[66] Sacramento Daily Union, Volume 96, Number 75, 4 November 1898

[67] Sacramento Bee, October 24, 1899

[68] Sacramento Daily Union, Volume 98, Number 63, 23 October 1899

[69] Sacramento Bee, May 9. 1900

[70] Oakland Tribune, July 27, 1900

[71] Sacramento Bee, November 2, 1900

[72] Application National Number 3596, The California Society of the Sons of the American Revolution, June 27, 1896.

[73] Application National Number 3597, The California Society of the Sons of the American Revolution, June 27, 1896.

[74] Amos P. Catlin Probate Documents, Sacramento County

[75] A Volume of Memoirs and Genealogy of Representative Citizens of Northern California, 1901

[76] San Jose Herald, Volume LXIX, Number 112, 5 November 1900

[77] 1900 Census, Amos Catlin, 1021 H street, Sacramento, Ca

[78] San Francisco Call, January 11, 1911

[79] Sacramento Bee, November 8, 1900

[80] San Francisco Call, Volume 87, Number 173, 20 November 1900

[81] Sacramento County Probate Records

[82] Sacramento County Probate Records

[83] San Francisco Call, January 11, 1911

Amos P. Catlin

Thoughts on Amos P. Catlin

Judge Amos P. Catlin has been largely forgotten in Sacramento and in accounts of its early history. There is a park in Folsom named for him, along with a plaque commemorating his involvement in the Natoma Water and Mining Company. However, the biographies Judge Catlin wrote, dictated, or influenced either omit the Natoma ditch or give it only a passing mention.

Water Projects

Judge Amos was cognizant of the nature of his life and accomplishments. Had Judge Amos not initiated the Natoma ditch, some other group of men would have. The demand for the water was evident. It only took a little organization and engineering to make the Natoma water works project a reality. What is understated and often overlooked is how the Natoma ditch and North Fork Ditch water projects influenced the growth of northeast Sacramento County. The water flowing in the water canals was diverted to service the communities of Orangevale, Fair Oaks, Citrus Heights, and Folsom.

Abundant clean water for drinking and irrigation was an indispensable requirement for the thousands of homes and businesses in the suburbs outside of Sacramento City. The water rights established by the Natoma Water and Mining Company continue to be held by the City of Folsom. Similarly, water flow established by the North Fork Ditch now rests with the San Juan Water District in Granite Bay.

With respect to water canals and the eventual widespread utilization of diverted river water for hydraulic mining, some people will find it noxious that Judge Amos defended the Gold Run Mining Company against charges of fouling the American and Sacramento Rivers with so much debris. Of course, he had previously represented a farmer in a complaint about hydraulic mining debris and won a judgment in favor of the farmer. In the Gold Run hydraulic mining case, Judge Amos took the opportunity in his closing arguments to indict the City of Sacramento for its lack of a decent sewer system. From his point of view, the Gold Run debris did not make the Sacramento sewer system inoperable, because Sacramento had failed to provide the city with a working sewer system in the first place. As a resident of Sacramento City, Judge Amos was not pleased with the lack of attention to basic urban infrastructure to remove human waste and prevent associated diseases.

Amos P. Catlin

Leidesdorff Land Grant

Another accomplishment for Judge Amos was the defense of the original Leidesdorff land grant map. Judge Amos was in a unique position in his understanding of the history of the land grant and development of the property – himself a land owner within the grant. This understanding, combined with his skills as an attorney, helped steam his enthusiasm to fight against Washington, D.C., politics. The land grant map that was ordered to be redrawn did not include the town of Folsom that Theodore Judah laid out nor hundreds of acres purchased by the Natoma Water and Mining Company. Had the U.S. Supreme Court not affirmed the original Leidesdorff land grant map, bolstered by Judge Amos' oral arguments, the town of Folsom would have been thrown into chaos. All the sales of the town lots were predicated upon the fact that Captain Joseph Folsom held title to the land.

California State Capitol

While Judge Amos is rightfully credited with sponsoring the legislation to move the State's Capitol to Sacramento, it probably would have happened eventually regardless. Sacramento had hosted the legislature in 1852, before its permanent move in 1854. Most legislators were not necessarily opposed to Sacramento as the center for government. Given the state of the alternatives – Benicia, Vallejo, San Jose – the Capitol would have found its way to Sacramento possibly in 1855 or 1856. However, following the epic floods of 1862, Sacramento would have been scratched off the list of capital contenders. There were even attempts to move the state's Capitol after the flooding of 1862.

Judge Amos most wanted to be remembered for his legal achievements and contributions to clarifying California's Constitution and laws. Unfortunately, California has so radically changed in the 20th century that Judge Amos' contributions are merely interesting footnotes. Judge Amos did inadvertently shape California libel laws: After his decision that the Sacramento Bee was guilty of libel in 1894, the floodgates of condemnation were opened upon the judge.

It cannot be understated how the public, the press, and legislators reacted to the libel award. From everyone's perspective, far more libelous content had been published across a spectrum of newspapers. The end result was that libel laws were amended to protect newspaper reporters and editors from being found guilty of libel within the bounds of their regular reporting of the news. Judge Amos gets no credit for this progressive legislation to protect the press in California, nor would he necessarily want any attribution.

Amos P. Catlin

Land & Property Rights

Almost baffling, although somewhat ameliorated by the context of 1849 California, was Judge Amos' disregard for one area of law that he had been trained in: property rights. California, for all intents and purposes in 1849, was federal property. Given, there were few laws pertaining to unauthorized use of federal land, nonetheless, Judge Amos and thousands of other men almost gleefully pushed Native Americans out of their way and off the land so they could disfigure the rivers in search of gold. Then, when the riverbed placer gold ran out, they focused their attention on the riverbanks.

Judge Amos led a group of men to dam two rivers, dig more than 40 miles of ditches, and then sell the water to whomever would pay for it. Almost all that investment and work occurred on federally owned land, with no permission from any government official. The Natoma ditch cut across not only federal land, but the Leidesdorff land grant. The land grant, whose boundaries were universally recognized by local residents, was owned by a citizen of the United States, Captain Joseph Libby Folsom. The construction of the water ditch across the Leidesdorff land grant was tantamount to trespassing.

Judge Amos would staunchly defend the land the Natoma Water and Mining Company had acquired from the Folsom Estate from men cutting down trees and sought to evict them. He stated that he was driven to purchase the 9,643 acres in order to quiet the threats of a lawsuit from the Folsom Estate over the ditch crossing the land grant. Somehow, Judge Amos rationalized that the benefit of the water ditch was superior to the rights of either the federal government or Mexican land grant ownership. He had to capitulate the argument with the purchase of the land grant property.

Pioneer Law

Judge Amos would never have engaged in such a taking of property had he stayed in New York. Not until 1866 would Congress pass an act recognizing the property rights of water ditches. Judge Amos was all about the Constitution and the laws passed by democratically elected representatives. The '49ers were operating in their own little world, absent any organized and effective local, state, or federal government. Judge Amos rationalized his behavior, and that of others in early California, by extolling pioneer law.

However, Judge Amos' praise for pioneer law was given in the context of celebrating the contributions of Collis Huntington, and by extension, of all the '49ers. It was a speech meant for public consumption and not necessarily an accurate reflection of his own belief system. There was the judicial, logical, and rational Judge Amos, and then there was the public-political Amos Catlin. In his younger days, there was little divergence between the private and political Amos. As with most men, his political perspective would evolve over time.

As a Senator, Judge Amos did vote to extend the Fugitive Slave Law in California. When he was in the Assembly, a proposed bill came up for debate that would have restricted and prevented the immigration of negroes into California. Assemblymember Catlin proposed an amendment that would have excluded extended family members of a black man already in California from the immigration prohibition.[1] A small attempt on his part, perhaps, to blunt the overall cruelty of the proposed law.

Anti-Chinese

As enmity and animus toward Chinese immigrants eclipsed the general dislike of Black Americans in California, Judge Amos walked a political tightrope. In an 1877 speech supporting Republican candidates, Judge Amos was obligated to denounce the presence of Chinese immigrants in California.[2] Unlike other speakers, Judge Amos did not vilify the Chinese based on their dress, culture, religion, or customs. He kept his remarks focused on the issue of labor. Chinese immigration represented an increase in the labor pool, which in turn, depressed wages, as some employers were willing to hire Chinese labor at a cheaper hourly rate than demanded by white labor.

Judge Amos saw it as his contribution to the anti-Chinese conversation to provide a historical background. He did believe that the Chinese immigrants were somehow slaves or coolies imported by several companies. He opined that 90 percent of Chinese immigrants did not voluntarily come to the United States. Whether the errors in Judge Amos' characterization of the Chinese as reluctant slaves immigrating to the United States was intended to cast the Chinese in a more favorable perspective or whether it reflected a deeply held personal belief is unknown.

What is undeniable is that Judge Amos put the onus of the Chinese problem on the federal government. A succession of poorly written treaties, the last of which was the Burlingame Treaty, were the sole source of increased Chinese labor in California. In addition, there was nothing California could do about Chinese immigration at the state level. The treaties had to be renegotiated at the federal level. Amos even equated the Chinese to immigrants from Europe. When asked if Chinese were being naturalized under the current system, Judge Amos responded, "No, sir; not since the Burlingame treaty; but prior to that treaty it was competent for any Chinaman to be naturalized in this country, as much so as any immigrant from England, Ireland or Germany."

Amos P. Catlin

Judge Amos would use the white immigrant analogy in arguing that all men should be extended equal treatment under the law in 1886, when he gave his opinion on a proposed City of Sacramento ordinance to evict all Chinese from the city limits.[3] His basic argument was, substitute the word "Chinese" with "Italian," "Mexican," or "Portuguese," and it would become apparent how ridiculous the city's eviction proposal was. The Constitution of the United States, over which a Civil War was fought 25 years earlier, set the standard for equal treatment of men and women. That federal standard of treatment could not be superseded by a local ordinance.

Regardless of the contradictions highlighted by the review of a man's entire life, actions speak louder than rhetoric. Judge Amos came to California in 1849, settled in the Central Valley, and never called another place home. Judge Amos could have relocated to San Francisco and made even more money than his Sacramento law practice provided. He could have moved back East to New York. But he didn't. For a variety of reasons, Judge Amos fell in love with California and never felt compelled to die anyplace else.

Ethics, Integrity, Honesty, Modesty

Judge Amos is worthy to be remembered for his entrepreneurial, political, and legal accomplishments. His political and legal views can be debated and frowned upon by 21st century standards. What cannot be assailed is his honesty and integrity. It's possible that the values he held high in his life were a significant reason for his avoidance of running for political office later in life. Both the Republican and Democrat parties were corrupt at some level. Once elected to political office, the incumbent had to play the political games that were so odious to Judge Amos and others of a higher moral character.

It was a mixture of integrity and inflexibility that led to Amos' reelection loss as a Superior Court Judge. Judge Amos never should have found Charles McClatchy in contempt of court, in a clear case of constitutionally protected free speech and free press. The Bee did add elements to the story that must have come from a confidential source after the testimony was given. But the offense, and McClatchy's defending of the reporting, did not rise to the level of interference in court proceedings.

Judge Amos was trying to protect the integrity of the court system. He had become inflexible in his reaction to newspaper stories that were not properly deferential to judges and court proceedings. His brittleness at accepting criticism eventually broke his public persona of competent adjudicator on the bench. Of course, by 1896 he was 73 years old, performing the incredibly demanding job of judge in a

Amos P. Catlin

courtroom day after day, with no air conditioning throughout the Sacramento summers.

Amos Catlin had two goals in immigrating to California. The first was to mine for gold and build up some savings. His second goal was to practice law. He accomplished both of his goals and, along the way, became an integral part of the history of the development of Folsom and Sacramento.

---

[1] Sacramento Daily Union, Volume 15, Number 2208, 24 April 1858
[2] Sacramento Daily Union, Volume 3, Number 155, 27 August 1877
[3] Sacramento Daily Union, Volume 54, Number 126, 18 January 1886

Amos P. Catlin

Vital Statistics

Amos Parmalee Catlin

Birth: January 25, 1823, Red Hook, New York
New York departure: January 8, 1849
California arrival: July 8, 1849
California State Senator: 1853 – 1854
California State Assemblymember: 1857
California Board of Equalization: 1872 – 1876
Sacramento Superior Court Judge: 1891 - 1896
Death: November 5, 1900, Sacramento, California

Ruth Anne Conyngham (Donaldson) Catlin

Birth: September 1840, Davenport, Iowa
Marriage to Amos Catlin: May 1, 1860, Sacramento, California
Death: February 17, 1878, Sacramento, California

Children of Ruth Anne and Amos Catlin

Emily Butler Catlin

Birth: September 30, 1865, Vacaville, California
Death: July 27, 1866, Sacramento, California

Catlin Twins, boy and girl

Birth, death: July 25, 1867

Alexander Donaldson Catlin

Birth: January 2, 1869, Lassen, California
Death: January 9, 1908, Searchlight, Nevada

John Conyngham Catlin

Birth: March 12, 1871, Lassen, California
Death: July 9, 1951, Monterey, California

Ruth Butler Catlin

Birth: May 24, 1873, Sacramento, California
Death: August 26, 1904

Harry Crispell Catlin

Birth: April 11, 1875, Sacramento, California

Amos P. Catlin

Death: July 27, 1916, San Francisco, California

Photographs, Maps, Newspaper Images

Amos P. Catlin

Amos P. Catlin

Property Transactions

Property titles recorded with Sacramento, Placer and El Dorado county clerks involving Amos Catlin in the transaction. Some dates, people, and descriptions are missing as a result of poor-quality images of the deed book pages.

Date – Grantor/Seller - Grantee/Buyer – Consideration, Description

1852, June 1: John W. Strass to Amos Catlin, $2,500

      Mormon Island: Exchange Hotel, undivided half interest

1853, March 14: Amos Catlin to Samuel Crofs, $455

      Sacramento: Northside K St, 6 & 7, Rialto Hotel

Amos P. Catlin

1854, July 11: John Shaw to Amos Catlin, $300

    Mormon Island: Southside of the plaza in Mormon Island

1856, January 1: Amos Catlin to John Young, $2,500

    Mormon Island: Exchange Hotel - stable, out buildings

1856, February 26: Folsom Estate to Amos Catlin, $321

    Folsom: Block 38 lot 16
                  Block 58 all 16 lots
                  Block 59 all 16 lots
                  Block 68 lots 5, 6, 7, 8
                  Block 70 all 16 lots
                  Block 71 all 16 lots
                  Block 72 lots 4, 5, 6, 7, 8, 9
                  Block 82 all 16 lots
                  Block 83 all 16 lots
                  Block 86 all 16 lots
                  Block 87 all 16 lots
                  Block 98 all 9 lots

1856, May 1: Charles Keen to Amos Catlin, $50

    Mississippi Township: 30 acres, 1 mile above Folsom on American River

1856, August 15: John S. Bowker to Amos Catlin, $2,000

    Folsom: Block 47, Lots 7, 8, Mansion House, barn, furnishings Hotel

1857, January 12: Amos Catlin to Leverett Bradley, $250

    Folsom: Block 70 all lots
                  Block 71 all lots
                  Block 73 all lots
                  Block 68 all lots
                  Block 98 all lots

1857, August 25: John Semple to Amos Catlin, $5,000

    Rancho de San Juan, undivided fifth interest

1857, September 15: H.G. Livermore to Catlin & Trustees, Donated

Folsom Literary Institute, Trustees: A. Catlin, A. Donaldson, S.V. Blakeslee, Francis Clark, E.D. Hoskins, C.T.H. Palmer, Levi Bradley, A.G. Kinsey

Amos P. Catlin

Folsom: Block 27 lots 9 - 16
              Block 29 lots 1 - 16
              Block 30 lots 1 - 16
              Block 31 lots 1 - 16
              Block 55 lots 1 - 8

1857, November 23: Folsom Estate to Amos Catlin, $1,340

Folsom: Block 4   lots 3, 4, 5, 6, 7, 8
              Block 6   lots 13, 14, 15, 16
              Block 9   lots 1, 2
              Block 10 lots 5, 6
              Block 11 lots 1, 2, 15, 16
              Block 12 lots 1, 2, 3, 4
              Block 13 lots 9, 10, 11, 12, 13, 14, 15, 16
              Block 14 lots 1, 2, 3, 4, 5, 6, 7, 8
              Block 17 lots 13, 14, 15, 16
              Block 18 lots 1, 2, 9, 10, 11, 12
              Block 19 lots 10, 11, 12
              Block 33 lots 9, 10, 15, 16
              Block 35 lot 9
              Block 37 lot 10
              Block 41 all 16 lots
              Block 48 lots 1, 2
              Block 66 all 16 lots
              Block 74 all 16 lots
              Block 90 all 16 lots

1857, December 2: Amos Catlin to D.A. Dryden, $50

Folsom: Block 98, triangular with approx. 6 lots

1857, December 11: Amos Catlin to C.G.W. French, $100

Folsom: Block 38, lot 16

1857, December 21: Frank S. Wood to Amos Catlin, $600

Folsom: Block 49, lots 2 -8

1858, February 1: Amos Catlin to B.C. Quigley, $214

Folsom: Block 49, lots 2, 3, 4, 5, 6, undivided half interest

1858, March 3: Charles W. Nystrom to Amos Catlin, $36,800

Amos P. Catlin

Leidesdorff land grant: 9,643 acres, northeast portion of Leidesdorff land grant, excludes Folsom and SVRR

1858, March: Amos Catlin to Natoma Water & Mining Co., Declaration of Trust

Leidesdorff land grant Purchase, held for the benefit of the stockholders

1858, June 21: James B. Wilson to Amos Catlin, $400

Folsom: Block 48, lots 3, 4, 5, 6, 7, 9, 10, 13, 14, 15

1858, June 25: James B. Wilson to Amos Catlin, $100

Folsom: Block 48, lot 16

1858, June 26: James B. Wilson to Amos Catlin, $100

Folsom: Block 48, lot 8, Quit Claim

1858, July 19: Amos Catlin to William Howard, $412

Folsom: Block 48, lots 3, 4, 5, 6, 7, 8, 9, 10, 13, 14, 15

1858, August 1: William Howard to Amos Catlin, $412

Folsom: Block 48, lots 3, 4, 5, 6,7, 8, 9, 10, 13, 14, 15, Quit Claim

1858, February 16: H.F. Kellum to Amos Catlin, $100

Folsom: Block 37, lot 13

1859: Amos Catlin to Benjamin C. Quigley, $2,050

Folsom: Block 49, lots 3, 4, 5,

1859: Amos Catlin to Thomas Whitely, $125

Folsom: Block 33, lots 9, 10

1859: B. C. Quigley to Amos Catlin and others, $5

Folsom: Block 49, lot 2, Quit Claim

1859, March 7: B. C. Quigley to Amos Catlin, $100

Folsom: Block 49, lot 6

1859, September 15: Amos Catlin to John Currey, $2,000

Rancho de San Juan, undivided fifth interest

Amos P. Catlin

1859, November: Amos Catlin to Benjamin C. Quigley, $250

    Folsom: Block 59, lot 6

1859, November 1: Benjamin Wadleigh to Amos Catlin, $10

    Folsom: Block 19 lots 10, 11, 12
               Block?   lot 16
               Block 37 lot 13
               Block 38 lots 15, 16
               Block 49 lots 3, 4, 5, 6, 7, 8,
               Block?   lot 11

1859, November 24: Charles L. Wilson to Amos P. Catlin, $340

    Lincoln: Block 27 lot 1
              Block 38 lot 1
              Block 38 lot 2
              Block 43 lot 1
              Block 58 lot 2
              Block 59 lots 3, 15
              Block 60 lot 13

1859, December 12: Amos Catlin to Samuel Hannak, $525

    Folsom: Block 48, lot 1

1860: A.C. Donaldson to Amos Catlin, $350

    Sulky Flat, mining claim, 1 1/2 miles south of Folsom, recorded 1865, April 22

1860, January 6: Amos Catlin to William M. Long, $200

    Folsom: Block 58 all lots
              Block 83 all lots

1860, January: Amos Catlin to Peter J. Weathers, $175

    Folsom: Block 48, lot 6

1860, January 31: Amos Catlin to Henry B. Waddilove, $175

    Folsom: Block 49, lots 6, 7

1860, March 2: Amos Catlin to Harvey A. Thompson, $2,000

    Folsom: Block 66 all lots
              Block 49 lot 8

Amos P. Catlin

Block 49, lot 7, part interest
Block 37 lot 13
Block 33 lots 15, 16
Block 19 lots 10, 11, 12
Grounds of Mansion House

1860, March 21: Stephen Addison to Amos Catlin, $182.50

Western side of SVRR, 4 acres, D. H. Taft's (Brayton) House

1860, June 12: Amos Catlin to H.K. Grim, $1,000

Folsom: Block 91, all lots

1860, October: Jules Vaillant to Amos Catlin, $1,500

Vaillant Ranch, 160 acres, south of Folsom

1860, November 19: Amos Catlin to Harvey A. Thompson, $1

Folsom: Block 33, lots 15, 16

1861, January 10: Amos Catlin to James L. McClure, $125

Folsom: Block 9, lots 1, 2

1861, February 5: Charles L. Wilson to Amos Catlin and B.F. Hastings, $10,000

Lincoln: 450 acres, Township 12 N, Range 6 E, section 15, excepting Lincoln town lots

1861, October 1: Amos Catlin to Jane I. Bates, $100

Folsom: Block 35, lot 9

1861, October 11: Amos Catlin to J.H. Working, $50

Folsom: Block 59, lot 10

1861, October 11: Amos Catlin and B.F. Hastings to Harry Rood, $10,000

Lincoln: 450 acres, Township 12 N, Range 6 E, section 15, excepting Lincoln town lots

1861, October 11: Harry W. Rood to Amos Catlin, $2,000

Lincoln: Block 27 lot 8
Block 38 lot 6
Block 43 lot 3

Amos P. Catlin

Block 44 lots 4
Block 58 lots 6, 8
Block 59 lots 2, 14
Block 60 lots 4, 12
Block 9   all lots
Block 15 all lots
Block 24 all lots
Block 26 all lots
Block 31 all lots
Block 46 all lots
Block 63 all lots
Block 68 all lots
Block 78 all lots

1861, December: Oliver C. Lewis to Amos Catlin, $100

Folsom: Block 37 lot 13
Block 40 lots 7, 8
Block 48 lots 3, 4, 5, 13, 14, 15, 16

1861, December 26: Amos Catlin to James S. Meredith, $100

Folsom: Block 6, lots 14, 15, 16

1861, December 30: James S. Meredith to Amos Catlin, $100

Folsom: Block 6, lots 5, 6, 7, 8

1862, February: Elisha D. Hoskins to Amos Catlin, $1,050

Folsom: Block 50 lot 1
Block 62 lots 9, 10
Block 63 lots 1, 2, 3

1862, February 6: Amos Catlin to Harry W. Rood, Gift

Lincoln: Block 63, all lots, Trust for Sarah E. Wilson, wife of Charles L. Wilson.

Block is to be controlled solely by Sarah with no interference by Charles, she may sell or rent for profit.

1862, February 10: Amos Catlin to Elisha D. Hoskins, $100

Folsom: Block 6, lot 19

1862, February 15: Amos Catlin to Cyrus H. Bradley, $500

Amos P. Catlin

Folsom: Block 59, lots 1 - 9, 11 - 16

1862, February 25: Amos Catlin to B. C. Quigley, $1,300

Folsom: Block 6   lots 5, 6, 7, 8, ?
                 Block 56 lot 1
                 Block 62 ?

1862, February 26: Natoma W&M Co. to Amos Catlin, $750

Sulky Flat, 240 acres, section 2, T9N, R7E, South 1/2 North West 1/4 , North 1/2 South West ¼, South West 1/4 North East 1/4., North West 1/4 South East ¼, except water ditches

1862, March 20: Amos Catlin to F.B. Higgins, $150

Lincoln: Block 60, lot 4

1862 April 1: Harry W. Rood to Amos Catlin, $100

Lincoln: Block 69, all lots

1862, April 5: Amos Catlin to W.S. Kendall, $50

Folsom: Block 48, lot 7

1862, April 5: Amos Catlin to E.D. Hoskins, Joseph Smith, James Meredith, $100

1/2 mile above Folsom, approximately 80 acres

1862, April 28   Amos Catlin to   William L. Uhler $1,200

Lincoln: Block 9   all lots
              Block 15 all lots
              Block 24 all lots
              Block 26 all lots
              Block 27 lots 1, 2, 8
              Block 31 all lots
              Block 38 lots 1, 2, 6
              Block 43 lots 1, 3
              Block 44 lot 4
              Block 46 all lots
              Block 58 lots 5, 6, 8
              Block 59 lots 2, 3, 14, 15
              Block 60 lots 12, 13
              Block 63 all lots
              Block 69 all lots

Amos P. Catlin

Block 78 all lots

1862, May 7: H.A. Thompson to Amos Catlin, $2,000

    Folsom: Block 19 lots 10, 11, 12
                   Block 33 lots 15, 16
                   Block 37 lot 13
                   Block 49 lot 8
                   Block 49 lot 7 part interest
                   Block 66 all lots
                   Grounds of Mansion House

1862, May 7: Amos Catlin to Oliver C. Lewis, $200

    Folsom: Block 19, lots 10, 11, 12

1862, May 15: Amos Catlin to Elezer Rulison, $1,200

    Folsom: Block 49 lots 8,
                   Block 49 lot 7 part interest

1862, May 16: Moses Lowell & wife to Catlin, Joseph Smith, James Meredith, E.D. Hoskins, $100

    1/2 mile above Folsom, approximately 80 acres

1863, March 28: Rhodes Northerly Extension Gold Mining Co. to Amos Catlin, Gustave Dussol, J.E. Rine, Theodore LeRoy, A.G. Kinsey

    Prairie City, mining interests

1863, April 5: James Meredith to Catlin, E.D. Hoskins, Joseph W. Smith, $100

    1/2 mile above Folsom, approximately 80 acres

1863, May: Oliver C. Lewis to Amos Catlin, $200

    Folsom: Block 18, lots 13, 14, 15, 16

1863, September 11: Amos Catlin to E. Rulison, $25

    Folsom: Block 49, lot 7 partial

1863, October 19: Amos Catlin to Horatio G. Livermore, $500

    Folsom: Block 86 all lots
                   Block 87 all lots

Amos P. Catlin

1864, August 20: Amos Catlin to Natoma W&M Co., $750

> Vaillant Ranch, approximately 80 acres, 1/2 mile wide x 1/4 mile, land between SVRR and American River

1864, November 8: Amos Catlin to Murray Morrison, $500

> Folsom: Block 74, all lots

1864, November 13: Amos Catlin to Horatio G. Livermore, $200

> Folsom: Block 1   all lots
> Block 4   lots 5, 6, 7, 8,
> Block 82 all lots

1865, January 14: Amos Catlin to Father Neal Gallagher, $650

> Folsom: Block 66, all Lots

1865, February 24: Justus Hovey to Amos Catlin, $400

> Lincoln: Block 9   all lots
> Block 15 all lots
> Block 24 all lots
> Block 26 all lots
> Block 27 lots 1, 2, 8
> Block 31 all lots
> Block 38 lots 1, 2, 6
> Block 43 lots 1, 3
> Block 58 lots 5, 6, 8
> Block 59 lots 2, 3, 14, 15
> Block 60 lots 12, 13
> Block 63 all lots
> Block 69 N 1/2 lot 11, N 1/2 of lot 6 and Lots 4, 5, 12, 13, 14, 15, 16
> Block 78 all lots

1865, April 8: Amos Catlin to Natoma W & M Co., $2,000

Folsom: Block 4, lots 3, 4, land deeded to Catlin by SVRR on eastside of tracks Catlin (Vaillant) Ranch, section 2, T9N, R7E

1865, December 19: Amos Catlin to J.M. Nagle, $10

> Lincoln: Block 69, E 1/2 lot 5, SE 1/4 lot 4, NE 1/4 lot 6

1865, December 22: Amos Catlin to J.T. Hamilton, $108

Amos P. Catlin

Lincoln: Block 9   all lots
          Block 15 all lots
          Block 24 all lots
          Block 26 all lots
          Block 27 lots 1, 2, 8
          Block 31 all lots
          Block 38 lots 1, 2, 6
          Block 43 lots 1, 2
          Block 58 lots 5, 6, 8
          Block 59 lots 2, 3, 14, 15
          Block 60 lots 12, 13
          Block 63 all lots
          Block 69 lots 12, 13, 14, 15, 16, S 1/2 11
          Block 78 all lots

1865, December 23: Amos Catlin to John Bennet, $300

    Folsom: Block 48, lots 15, 16

1866, June 25: Amos Catlin to Horace Kilham, $500

    Folsom: Block 5   lots 9, 10, 11, 12,
             Block 37 lot 1
             Block 38 lots 12

1865, June: Catlin & Rulison to Edward Christy, $50

    Folsom: Block 18, lots 15, 16

1866, September 11: A.C. Donaldson to Ruth A.C. Catlin, $800

    Folsom: Block 34, lots 9, 10,

1868, August: Amos Catlin to Ephraim Plaza, ?

    Indecipherable

1869, January: Amos and Ruth Catlin to B. C. Quigley, 900?

    Folsom: Block 34   lots 9, 10

1870, October: Edward E. Eyro to Amos Catlin, $150

    Sacramento: Block H & I, 6 & 7 street, East ½, 7th street

1871, October 13: A.J. Rhodes to Amos Catlin, $200

    San Francisco: Block 333, bounded by Nevada, Yolo, Indiana, & ? Streets

Amos P. Catlin

Sacramento County: Cosumnes River Farm

1872, April 19: Amos Catlin to Mary O'Niel, $50

Folsom: Block 48, lots 3, 4

1872, April 19: Amos Catlin to Peter J. Hopper, $50

Folsom: Block 48, lots 13, 14

1872, May: Amos Catlin to Michael McManus, $150

Sacramento: Block H & I, 6 & 7 street, East 1/2 7th street

1874, September: Amos Catlin to The Pacific Granite Co., $20

Folsom: Block 13 lots 9 - 16
Block 14 lots 1 – 8

1874, October 20: Amos Catlin to Elisha Haaws, $50

Folsom: Block 10 lots 5, 6
Block 11 lots 1, 2
Block 12 lots 1, 2, 3, 4

1881, November 21: Amos Catlin to John Williams, $100

Folsom: Block 11, lots 15, 16

1881, March 12: Amos Catlin to Wm. W. Wade, $800

Sacramento County: Sheldon Tract Rancho Omachumnes, 1/2 mile wide, 2 miles width, 750 acres, Consumnes River land

1884, September 26: Gallagher Estate to Amos Catlin, $230

Sacramento: Block O & P, Front & 2nd, lot 4, North 25 feet

1888, November 13: W.W. Brison to Amos Catlin, $5

Sacramento County: Brison Ranch, 530 acres

1888, June 27: Amos Catlin to John O. Kane, $100

Sacramento: Block O & P, Front & 2nd, lot 4, North 25 feet

1891, October 29: Franklin B. Smith to Amos Catlin, $1,900

Sacramento: Block G, H, 10th, 11th streets, East 1/4 Lot 7

Amos P. Catlin

1892, April 13: S.C. Denson, Mary Denson, Frank Miller to Amos Catlin, $10

    Sacramento: Block G, H, 10th, 11th streets, lot 6

1892, November 26: A.L. Hart to Amos Catlin, Judgement

    Sacramento County: Brison Ranch, 483 acres

1892, November 26: W.P. Harlow to Amos Catlin, Judgement

    Sacramento County: Brison Ranch, 483 acres

1895, February 21: Amos Catlin to Margaret I. Crocker

    Sacramento County: Brison Ranch

    Held in trust -

    1. Any sale proceeds to Crocker to repay $15,615 mortgage to her

    2. Remainder to Catlin and Jno. W. Armstrong for services and advances

    3. W.W. Brison remaining amounts

1897, May 17: Haggerty, Striening, Elliot to Amos Catlin, $250

    El Dorado County: Twin Sailor Quartz Mine, T10N, R9E, section 17

Amos P. Catlin

Index

Amos P. Catlin

Amos P. Catlin

Amos P. Catlin

Amos P. Catlin

Amos P. Catlin

Made in the USA
Monee, IL
04 March 2022

92147827R00164